D0848858

AN ELUSIVE SCIENCE

AN ELUSIVE SCIENCE

THE TROUBLING HISTORY OF
EDUCATION RESEARCH

Ellen Condliffe Lagemann

THE UNIVERSITY OF CHICAGO PRESS
Chicago and London

Ellen Condliffe Lagemann is professor of history and education, director of the Center for the Study of American Culture and Education, and chair of the Department of Humanities and the Social Sciences in the School of Education at New York University. A past president of the History of Education Society, she is currently president of the National Academy of Education. Lagemann is author or editor of eight previous books, including *The Politics of Knowledge: The Carnegie Corporation, Philanthropy, and Public Policy* and, most recently, *Issues in Education Research* (edited with Lee S. Shulman).

The University of Chicago Press, Chicago 60637
The University of Chicago Press, Ltd., London

© 2000 by The University of Chicago
All rights reserved. Published 2000

Printed in the United States of America

09 08 07 06 05 04 03 02 01 00   1 2 3 4 5

ISBN: 0-226-46772-4 (cloth)

Library of Congress Cataloging-in-Publication Data

Lagemann, Ellen Condliffe
    An elusive science : the troubling history of education research / Ellen Condliffe Lagemann.
        p.   cm.
    Includes bibliographical references and index.
    ISBN 0-226-46772-4 (alk. paper)
    1. Education—Research—United States—History.   2. Education—Research—Social aspects—United States.   I. Title

LB1028.25.U6L33   2000
370'.7'2—dc21
                                                                99-086832

♾ The paper used in this publication meets the minimum requirements of the American National Standard for Information Sciences—Permanence of Paper for Printed Library Materials, ANSI Z39.48-1992.

In Memory of Lawrence Cremin

Scribere est agir

CONTENTS

In January of 1891, when the inaugural number of *Educational Review* appeared, its first article was by Harvard philosopher Josiah Royce. Entitled "Is There a Science of Education?" the essay suggested that teachers should have "a scientific training for their calling," by which Royce meant opportunities to learn to reflect on their craft. According to Royce, however, teachers should not be asked to master any formal pedagogical system, since none was or could be adequate. In Royce's opinion, there was "no universally valid science of pedagogy . . . capable of . . . complete formulation and . . . direct application to individual pupils and teachers." Royce's self-described "unwillingness to apply so pretentious and comforting a name as 'Science' to any exposition of the laborious and problematic art of the educator" has been frequently quoted and commented upon.[1] Whether there is or can be a "science" of education remains controversial to this day. Despite the persistence of the issue, education became a subject of university study at the end of the nineteenth century, and as that happened, a new domain of scholarship began to emerge.

Neither singular in focus nor uniform in methods of investigation, education research grew out of various combinations of philosophy, psychology, and the social sciences, including statistics. The variety that has characterized educational scholarship from the first, combined with the field's failure to develop a strong, self-regulating professional community, has meant that the field has never developed a high degree of internal coherence. For that reason, much that I will treat would not fit within strict conceptions of either science or research, which is why I shall use the terms "educational scholarship" and "educational study" interchangeably with "education research." In education, lines between research about curriculum, as one example, and efforts to develop or evaluate curricula have often been unclear. Especially during the early years when schools and departments of education were first founded, efforts to study education in order to understand it—research—were also often indistinguishable from efforts to acquire professional knowledge and credentials—educational study. What is more, since those early years, questions concerning the appropriate links and overlaps between and among research, design, development, and evaluation have often elicited a wide range of divergent views. In light of all that, what might seem like imprecise terminology in another instance seems, in fact, to suit the case at hand.

In what follows, I will seek to engage questions pertaining to the historical development of the large and diffuse enterprise that comprises education research. My focus will be the hows and whys of the enterprise as it has developed over roughly one hundred years. I will consider a wide variety of efforts to inform and improve—in a sense, to educate—education. How was the historical character of educational scholarship defined, and how has it changed over time? Which traditions, trends, people, events, and institutions were important in establishing as well as disestablishing the most essential features of education research? Why has this domain of scholarly work always been regarded as something of a stepchild, reluctantly tolerated at the margins of academe and rarely trusted by policy makers, practitioners, or members of the public at large? And last, but hardly least important, what does the history of educational scholarship suggest about the current situation of education research? Can history point toward a reconfiguration that might have positive outcomes not only for a better understanding of education, but also for the improvement of educational policy and practice through research?

More than is the case with many historical studies, this book is an argument from history about current problems associated with educational scholarship. It has been intentionally shaped to be more interpretative than comprehensive. Even though I have drawn a wide perimeter, much that has been important in the history of this very broad, amorphous field does not appear in this book. In addition, I have self-consciously sought to make the book both critical and reformist, while also freely admitting that much about the history of education research can be read several different ways and, beyond that, that much about the history remains perplexing. A word about my stance may therefore be in order.

Once it was established within the university, the study of education took a new turn, a turn toward "science." In the chapters that follow, I shall be concerned with exploring how that "science" was defined and how it related to both the practice of education and efforts to mediate the cultural or social significance of education. Gender, professionalization,

and institutional conflict and competition will be important in my exploration, as will the romance with quantification that has so profoundly
influenced the behavioral sciences, including education, during the past
century. The circuslike confusion caused by the decentralized policy-
making apparatus for education that exists in the United States will also
be central. So will the tensions between evangelical expectations for education, on the one hand, and popular disdain for education and educationists, on the other. Those tensions have been a powerful force in all
aspects of educational history since the colonial period.

To someone who embraces, as I do, the highly contextualized, holistic, deeply social and pragmatic conception of science that John Dewey
described in *The Sources of a Science of Education* (1929) and others of
his works, there is much that is troubling about these developments. Indeed, I believe it would not be inaccurate to say that the most powerful
forces to have shaped educational scholarship over the last century have
tended to push the field in unfortunate directions—away from close interactions with policy and practice and toward excessive quantification
and scientism. Clearly, however, educational scholarship has not been
monolithic. Rather, as I have argued elsewhere, it has consisted of
plural worlds.[2] Although it is true, I believe, that Edward L. Thorndike,
the Teachers College psychologist, "won" and the philosopher John
Dewey "lost," Thorndike's triumph was not complete. Thus, even though
the forces favoring a narrowly individualistic, behaviorally oriented, and
professionalized conception of educational study were sufficiently strong
during the first decades of the twentieth century to marginalize those
people who favored broader, less technocratic, more situated and developmentally oriented conceptions of education and educational study,
their victory was not total. Indeed, during the 1920s and 1930s,
many scholars who belonged to the more "progressive" camp spoke out
strongly for their points of views, and for a time, some found a relatively
wide following. During the 1960s, that happened again. Beyond that,
even though the history of educational scholarship has been filled with
contests between and among different groups and individuals, it is always
worth remembering that the story is not one in which the soldiers of dark-
ness have been pitted against the soldiers of light.

In itself, recognizing that educational scholarship has proceeded in
multiple, uneven ways makes the history of educational scholarship complex. This is not a simple tale of declension or opportunities lost. What
is more, the complexity of the story is increased when one takes two additional factors into account. First, the motivations that led most (but not

all) early educationists to develop a sadly narrow problematics for the field were, however unfortunate, both human and, within the context of their era, comprehensible. Eager to elevate school leaders to the place of respect and independence they believed they deserved, early educationists tried to emulate their brethren in the "hard" sciences (or at least the more developed social sciences) and failed to realize that their goals might have been better served by instead pondering what distinctive characteristics might comprise rigor and relevance in this particular domain of scholarship. In addition, the early educationists accepted and perpetuated the myopias common to their world, especially biases concerning race, ethnicity, and gender. The vision of many of the early educationists was mightily flawed, I believe, but I think it would be inaccurate to see the early educationists as more limited than many of their peers.

A second factor that introduces additional complexity into the history of educational scholarship pertains to the multifaceted relationships that have existed between scholars of education, on the one hand, and the society that sustained them, on the other. It is hardly a secret that people who study and practice education are engaged in low-status work. This is a phenomenon I shall explore in more detail in the chapters that follow. In various ways, low status has undermined possibilities for developing a strong professional community and generative scholarly traditions. Lacking public appeal and respect, educational scholarship has rarely won adequate financial support, public or private, or developed the prestige and public deference needed to gain a serious, sustained hearing. It may be a chicken-and-egg situation, in which weak financial support led to weak research, which led to weak public regard, which, in turn, led to weak financial support. However that may be, I believe that low status has been deeply implicated in the troubling developments one can see in the history of education research; put otherwise, I believe that many of the flaws of education research derive from the contradictory and often ill-informed attitudes Americans have held about education generally.

If, as Richard Hofstadter pointed out brilliantly almost forty years ago, anti-intellectualism has been a central theme in American life, the related phenomenon of antieducationism has also been important.[3] Antieducationism is a compound of all the qualities Hofstadter saw in anti-intellectualism—especially a skepticism toward intellect and a preference for instrumental knowledge, know-how, over less purposive reflection, speculation, or pondering. Antieducationism also encompasses assumptions concerning the lack of knowledge, skill, ambition, and competence needed and possessed by educators—to paraphrase George Bernard

Shaw, "he or she who can, does; he or she who cannot, teaches." It encompasses as well assumptions concerning the simplicity, sterility, and, more often than not, irrelevance or pointlessness of the educational process. Antieducationism thus allows one to believe that excellence can be achieved in and through education even when investments in personnel, research, materials, and equipment are limited. As one can see throughout the history of educational scholarship, antieducationism has helped to undermine the effectiveness of all aspects of education. In light of Americans' reliance on education as a central social policy and their professed belief in the importance of education, the pervasiveness of antieducationist sentiments is dismaying.

Can things be changed? As I suggest in the last chapters of this book, I hope they can be, and I believe there are modest grounds for hope in recent developments. Really since the 1950s, but especially since the 1960s, there have been significant improvements in policy research. In addition, insights gleaned from cognitive science and applied to classroom instruction, combined with greater understanding of the ways in which cultural differences influence classroom exchanges, have opened a new potential for effective schooling. Despite these and other causes for optimism, I think it is clear, however, that change will take determined effort. Indeed, this account of the history of education research offers a cautionary tale that describes the major difficulties that have plagued educational scholarship. These will need to be overcome before significant and lasting change is likely to occur. Hopefully, however, as the problems that have heretofore militated against scholarship that could meet the twin tests of rigor and reliability, on the one hand, and enlightenment and usefulness, on the other, become more widely and incisively understood, opportunities for strengthening education research and for supporting promising new developments will increase. In fact, being an optimist and a convinced believer in the importance of education, I have written this book in the hope that it will help us inch toward more scholarship that can foster improvements in our understanding of education as well as our capacity to develop sensible policies and practices that will have wide and perhaps even universal benefit.

From the above, it should be clear that I view the history of educational scholarship not as the isolated history of an intellectual field, but rather as an ongoing story about larger constellations of social values and views that have often found their clearest manifestations in debates about education, including education research. Even though I thus view the problems I shall address broadly, as questions fundamental to American culture and social policy, I have conceived this book as a discipline history and should explain why that is so.

Disciplines are the intellectual maps that demarcate different bodies of subject matter and their related university departments and professional associations. They are socially constructed and change over time; they are made, not given in nature. As historian of science Robert Kohler once put it, discipline history asks "why the world of knowledge is divided up as it is, or how it got that way."[4] By problematizing definitions of academic and professional fields, discipline history seeks to reconstruct the processes by which maps of knowledge are constructed. By emphasizing that currently taken-for-granted intellectual constructs did not necessarily exist in their familiar forms in earlier eras, it calls attention to conflicts and negotiations as well as to patterns of historical choice and chance.[5]

Discipline histories investigate the changing ecology of knowledge and the politics that has been part of that. And since this is just the kind of investigation that I will undertake in seeking to understand the history and current situation of education research, it has been useful to think of this inquiry as a discipline history. I am, of course, aware that many people would insist that education is not itself a discipline. Indeed, because it does not have distinctive methods or a clearly demarcated body of subject matter and is not seen as a tool for the analysis of other subject matters, I would tend to agree. Instead, I see education as a field of study and professional practice that is illuminated by a wide variety of disciplinary and multidisciplinary approaches. That aside, the questions essential to my study—regarding the primary forces shaping the study of education over the last one hundred years; how the enclosure of education in special, distinct schools and departments affected the study of education both inside and outside those preserves; and what the history of educational scholarship can tell us that has value for the present situation of education in the United States—are what discipline history is about.

Studying the history of educational scholarship this way involves complications, but it is worth the challenge, I think, for at least two reasons. First, even though education has long been one of the largest fields of university teaching and research, educational scholarship has been largely ignored in recent writings about the university and its research endeavors.[6] While historians of education have concerned themselves with the history of educational policy, the history of school administration, and, more recently, the history of teachers and teaching, historians interested in the social history of ideas have focused on the social sciences, psychology, and the various professions, especially medicine. Neither group has studied education research. One of my hopes therefore is to begin to address a rather egregious vacuum in the historical literature that has diminished our understanding of education, research, and the university.

The second reason I have chosen to write a discipline history of the scholarship of education derives from my belief that many of the most difficult educational problems that exist in the United States today are related to the ways in which the study of education has been organized and perceived within universities. Problems related to the quality of teaching in many universities are an example. In recent years, there has been wide complaint about poor teaching, and there have been efforts to place teaching on a par with research in assessing professorial achievement. Leaving aside the difficulties involved in accomplishing the latter goal, there is no question that the status of education and the isolation of educationists within universities are not irrelevant to the current situation. The status and affective maps of universities have discouraged interest in pedagogy among noneducationists and encouraged the priority they have placed on research over teaching.

Without multiplying the examples, the point I would make is simply this: to improve education in enduring ways, we will need to strengthen education research, and to do that, we must change the circumstances that have historically constrained the development of educational study. Research universities have been tremendously important sources of knowledge, authority, and social status over the last one hundred years. Whether universities will continue to hold that central place during the next one hundred years remains to be seen. However that may be, in the immediately foreseeable future, the ways in which education is defined, organized, studied, and regarded within universities will help to determine possibilities for education in universities and elsewhere, including in the nation's public schools. Because history can provide a powerful way to think about the present, I very much hope that this book can help to enhance those possibilities, while enriching our understanding of American education and culture during the last century.

Especially because this book has been in the making for a long time, I have many people and institutions to thank. I began chipping away at the research on which this book is based while I was a fellow at the Center for Advanced Study in the Behavioral Sciences in Stanford, California, in 1991–92. The center is a miracle of a place, and I am profoundly grateful to Phil and Jean Converse, Bob Scott, Gardner Lindsey, the staff of the center, and, most of all, my "fellow fellows" for a wonderful year and many helpful conversations. While at the center and since then, my work has been generously—and extremely patiently—supported by the Spencer Foundation, to whom I would express my continuing gratitude. More recently, a gift from the John L. Weinberg Foundation has given me degrees of financial freedom in pursuing my research that are rare and wonderful. I owe John and Sue Ann Weinberg abundant thanks. I was a visiting scholar at the Carnegie Foundation for the Advancement of Teaching in Menlo Park, California, as I finished revising this book. Variously involved in trying to study, improve, and dignify teaching, the Carnegie Foundation is home to a lively group of researchers who asked many thoughtful questions and whose work stimulated my own. I am grateful to Lee Shulman, John Barcroft, and their colleagues for having given me such a comfortable and congenial perch.

Many people at New York University (NYU) and elsewhere have read and commented on various versions of all or parts of the book. At NYU, I would especially thank my colleagues in the new Department of Humanities and the Social Sciences in the School of Education, many of whom were members of an informal discussion group where I presented parts of the book, even before our department was created. Gert Brieger, Joan Cenedella, David Cohen, Larry Cuban, Tom Ehrlich, Howard Gardner, Herbert Ginsberg, Pat Graham, Carl Kaestle, Lee Shulman, David Tyack, Andrea Walton, Joel Westheimer, Jonathan Zimmerman, and, way beyond the call of duty or friendship, Fritz Mosher read drafts of chapters and talked with me about my ideas over many years, and their comments kept me going. Once a year at the American Educational Research Association meeting, John Tryneski of the University of Chicago Press would ask me how I was doing. Far more than I think he realized, that, too, helped ensure that, however belatedly, this book would finally come to be. Even more important, John's comments and support during the last stages of revisions were vital.

I have been lucky in the research assistants I have had. At Teachers College, Andrea Walton and Andrew Mullen not only searched for material, but also asked questions and shared ideas that helped me shape this book. More recently at NYU, John Spencer and Dan Prosterman went patiently off to libraries and archives with endless queries. Many thanks to all of you.

At the end of my prolonged pilgrimage, my uncle, Arthur Rosenthal, provided much-needed help with titles, and Glorieux Dougherty scrutinized proofs with her specially meticulous eye for errors and infelicities.

This book is dedicated to the memory of Lawrence Cremin, my late mentor, colleague, and friend. Larry was still alive when I first began thinking about investigating the history of education research, and it deeply saddens me that he cannot read the book that has resulted. Still, I hope the book conveys some measure of what I learned from him and of the convictions we shared about education, history, and, not least important, John Dewey. Memory can inspire, and remembering years of conversation about many of the people, institutions, ideas, and events that appear in this book often sparked my most fruitful thinking.

Happily, my family has always reminded me that there is more to life than John Dewey—indeed, my son Nick has urged gothic novel writing for many years (easier and more lucrative he promises!). Beyond that, my family has helped me live a life that I love because it is fun. Especially to Kord, thanks can never even begin to suffice.

E.C.L.

A Slow Evolution: Education Becomes a Subject of University Research

Until the 1820s, the term "teacher" could have described any one of a host of different people—an entrepreneur operating a pay school or a dancing class in New York City; a Harvard graduate holding school temporarily in a small New Hampshire town; a mother teaching the letters of the alphabet to her own children and those of her neighbors while working in her kitchen; or a minister tutoring a young man in Greek, Latin, and Hebrew in preparation for advanced study in Europe or one of the early American colleges. Needless to say, too, since teaching had not yet come to be narrowly associated with school keeping, ministers preaching and citizens giving 4th of July orations were also, in the common parlance of the day, "teaching."[1] Soon thereafter, however, the dynamics that would define the study of education after it became established within universities at the end of the nineteenth century began to emerge. Among these, none was more important than the feminization of teaching.

The Feminization of Teaching

Once a predominantly male occupation, school teaching became a predominantly female occupation in the United States in conjunction with the spread of common schooling between roughly 1830 and 1865. Spurred by the fact that women were willing to work for significantly lower salaries than men—in mid-nineteenth-century Massachusetts, women schoolteachers on average were paid 60 percent less than their male counterparts—local and state school authorities hired increasing numbers of women teachers, initially to hold school during the summer when men were needed in the fields and eventually to cover both the winter and the summer sessions of the local common schools.[2] By 1837, 60.2 percent of the teachers in Massachusetts were female, and the proportion grew steadily thereafter, reaching 80 percent by 1857 and 88 percent by

Table 1 Proportion of Female Teachers, 1869–1979

Year	Number of Teachers*	Percentage Female
1869	201,000	61.3
1879	287,000	57.2
1889	364,000	65.5
1899	423,000	70.1
1909	523,000	78.9
1919	680,000	85.9
1929	854,000	83.4
1939	875,000	77.8
1949	914,000	78.7
1959	1,387,000	71.0
1969	2,131,000	67.6
1979	2,300,000	66.0

SOURCE: National Center for Educational Statistics, *120 Years of American Education: A Statistical Portrait* (Washington, D.C.: U.S. Department of Education, 1993), 34–35.
*This category also included librarians and other nonsupervisory instructional staff.

1867. By the end of the Civil War, women were also a majority of the teaching force nationally (see table 1).

Samuel Read Hall, who in 1823 organized the nation's first school for teachers in Concord, Vermont, lamented the shift from male to female in the nation's teaching force.[3] According to Hall, local school committees were unwilling "to make adequate compensation to teachers of approved talents and qualification." As a consequence, "at a time when the merchant is overstocked with clerks, and the professions of law and medicine are thronged with students, there is . . . a lamentable deficiency in the number of those who have the inclination and ability to engage in the business of instruction."[4] Unlike Hall, many advocates of female teachers contributed to the emergence of an ideology that turned economic necessity into claims concerning a "natural" and highly desirable state of things.

During the antebellum years, arguments concerning the special suitability of women for teaching became commonplace. Although many men and women contributed to the development and dissemination of this belief, no one was more important in doing so than domestic reformer Catharine Beecher. A member of a large and prominent family of evangelical ministers and reformers, Beecher devoted her life to the cause of women's education. She founded and helped operate female seminaries in Hartford, Cincinnati, and Milwaukee. She ran institutes for young women preparing to leave Albany and Hartford to become teachers on the frontier. She developed a plan for spreading seminaries all through the West that would provide women teachers with instruction on a par with the colleges for men. And she lectured and wrote frequently about the special value of employing women as teachers.[5]

Beginning in 1835, when she published *An Essay on the Education of Female Teachers*, Beecher argued that women were especially "fitted by disposition and habits and circumstances . . . [to] aid in educating the childhood and youth of this nation."[6] Thanks to their tact and moral power, they were uniquely able to inspire virtue and morality in the young, she believed. If this made it advisable to hire women as teachers, so did the advantages serving as a teacher would offer women themselves. According to Beecher, there was no conflict among teaching, marriage, and motherhood. "Maiden school-teachers will be better prepared to en-ter the marriage state, after the term of three or four years in the office of instructor," she maintained, since they will have avoided "earlier mar-riages [which] are productive of much of the unhappiness of married women."[7]

The arguments supporting feminization that were developed and de-ployed by domestic feminists like Catharine Beecher and other advocates of women teachers resonated with themes central to Protestant evangel-icism. The belief that education was essential for all people and that the education of young children would be most effective if based on an appeal to the heart was part of that, as was the emphasis on moral rather than purely intellectual training. In important ways, then, the feminization of teaching derived from a tension that has been and continues to be central to all aspects of education in the United States, including its study, prac-tice, and public perception. However manifest, in connection with chang-ing religious and political beliefs as well as changing demographic and economic circumstances, this tension has involved an optimistic "evan-gelical" faith in education and, in opposition to that, a pervasive, anti-intellectual tendency to discount the complexity of education. This ten-sion has fueled an impulse to extend education to more and more people and to rely on it for an ever-increasing range and variety of social pur-poses, while also encouraging a reluctance to bear the costs of supporting education at truly adequate levels. Whether this tension has served as a surrogate for even more fundamental conflicts between and among his-toric ideals like equality and individualism, the point here is simply that in the mid-1800s it fostered the perception that teaching was "woman's work."

The Initial Development of Professional Education for Teachers

At roughly the same time that teaching was being feminized, it was also beginning to be professionalized.[8] Starting in the 1820s, teaching became increasingly associated with a specialized form of work, and institutions offering teachers special training began to appear.

From then until the end of the Civil War, there were three distinct but overlapping forms of "professional" education available to teachers throughout the United States except in the South. The first was the teachers' institute, which initially developed in Connecticut in emulation of a "Teachers' Class" organized by Henry Barnard, Connecticut's first state commissioner of education. Teachers' institutes were meetings held usually over several weeks that offered lessons in the basic school subjects and opportunities for observing instructional practices in local schools. As Henry Barnard himself explained, they were also intended to serve as "an educational revival agency" that would "awaken" character and moral commitment.[9] Their worth thus depended on the reputation and charisma of the men and, on occasion, the women who conducted them. When they were led by Thomas H. Gallaudet, the founder of the American Asylum for the Deaf and Dumb in Hartford, or Emma Willard, the founder of Troy Female Seminary, teachers' institutes could provide powerfully inspiring experiences. But their caliber was varied and their availability intermittent.

In addition to teachers' institutes, many men and women interested in teaching attended the local academies that were abundantly sprinkled across the United States during this period. Offering a rather eclectic mix of post–common school studies, academies were private institutions that often received assistance from the state. They were open to all, including women; they were intended to be more practical than grammar schools, the sole purpose of which had traditionally been college preparation; and many of their graduates became teachers—in fact, at the time of the Civil War, well over 50 percent of the teachers in New York State had attended an academy.[10] Although precise numbers are impossible to find, reliable estimates suggest that academies were much more numerous than antebellum colleges, but much less numerous than common schools. According to Henry Barnard, in 1855 there were in the United States 239 colleges, 6,185 academies, and 80,978 common schools. The colleges enrolled 27,821 students; the academies enrolled 263,096.[11]

Beginning in the late 1830s, state-supported normal schools also began to appear. They were kindred to academies, though more focused in purpose, and they were also like teachers' institutes, though being settled institutions, they were more permanent in form. Massachusetts was the first state to sponsor normal schools, with other states in the Northeast and the Midwest quickly following suit and the southern and western states continuing the trend after the Civil War. Between 1839 and 1865, fifteen state normal schools began operation; by 1871, there were twenty-six; and by 1890, the number had increased to ninety-two.[12]

Although there was extreme variation between and among normal schools, two models came to predominate. One, pioneered in Massachusetts, was the more professional model. It involved a curriculum built around the typical common-school subjects as well as the "art of teaching" and "the science of school government."[13] Coursework was usually supplemented by school observation and by opportunities to try one's hand at teaching either the other students (often called "normalites") in one's cohort or children assembled in an affiliated "practice school." The second model, which was more common in the Midwest and West, was a more general, multipurpose one. Because Midwestern normal schools were often the only accessible institutions providing instruction beyond that available in the local district schools, there was considerable pressure on them to become what Jurgen Herbst has described as "a people's university open to young men and women from all walks of life."[14] As late as 1885 when the territory of Arizona decided to establish a state normal school at Tempe, the legislature mandated that it provide instruction "in the art of teaching and in all the various branches that pertain to a good common school education . . . in the mechanical arts and in husbandry and agricultural chemistry, in the fundamental laws of the United States, and in what regards the rights and duties of citizens."[15] Normal schools of the general, multipurpose type were more like twentieth-century community colleges than what we would recognize today as institutions of professional training.

Especially in relation to the contradictory attitudes toward education that encouraged feminization, gender was a powerful, if subtle, force in the development of professional education for teachers. Because women were barred from most colleges until after the Civil War, the increasing employment of women as teachers encouraged the development of new institutions. Even though writing about the history of women's higher education in the United States has tended to focus on the women's colleges opened after the Civil War, it was the normal schools and academies that were really the pioneer institutions.[16]

Less positively, some of the pre–Civil War institutions of teacher education, particularly the normal schools, seem to have been limited in what they were expected to achieve by the intellectual limitations then commonly believed to be inherent in the female sex. It is striking to observe that almost without exception normal school principals and supervising authorities, who tended to be male, found their students, most of whom were female, lacking in academic competence. The Reverend Cyrus Pierce, first principal of the Lexington Normal School (subsequently moved to Framingham) in Massachusetts, spoke for many when he claimed that "the normal students are . . . in the very undesirable position of being familiar with the books without knowing anything they contain."[17] Characterizing their work as "clumsy," Pierce maintained that the young women in his charge lacked "curiosity."[18] Some thirty years later the board of visitors of the Wisconsin State Normal School at Oshkosh reported that the students had "no well defined knowledge, no power of expression, no power of reflection, and no good habits of study."[19] Despite the great differences between these two institutions, the former exemplifying a "professional" model and the latter a general one, the similarity of the complaints about students is striking.

Given such negative comments, which fitted with and very likely reflected common views of female capacity, it seems fair to suggest that gender (and perhaps also matters related to social class) helped limit normal school curricula. However indirectly, the stark contrast between the intellectually thin curricula of most normal schools and the curriculum established by Emma Willard at the Troy Female Seminary may demonstrate the point. At the Troy seminary, but not at most normal schools, students were expected to study math, science, modern languages, Latin, history, philosophy, geography, and literature. Unlike the men responsible for the design and management of normal schools, Willard never doubted the intellectual competence of the female students in her charge.[20]

If views of female intellect set a ceiling on the rigor and richness of normal school curricula, those views also fostered the emergence of a gender-related bureaucracy within education. According to Horace Mann, first secretary of the Massachusetts board of education (1837–48), whose annual reports were circulated, read, and quoted throughout the United States, the female school teacher "holds her commission from nature. In the well developed female character there is always a preponderance of affection over intellect. However powerful and brilliant her reflective faculties may be, they are considered a deformity in her character unless overbalanced and tempered by womanly affections."[21]

Thus described, women's "natural" talents ideally fitted them for elementary instruction, but not for advanced instruction. Despite that, economics encouraged the hiring of women to staff the graded schools that began to emerge in urban areas during the 1840s. There, population was sufficient to justify more complex school arrangements than existed in rural common schools. As schools expanded in this way, increasing numbers of supervisory positions were created. In most instances, these were filled by men, the logic being that male principals and superintendents could assist women teachers with discipline and curriculum problems and deal more effectively with the public constituencies upon which public schools depended for support.[22] If assumptions concerning female competence both created and limited the educational opportunities women could find through programs of professional preparation for teaching, those same assumptions tended also to limit possibilities for female career advancement through the hierarchy of occupational grades just beginning to emerge at mid-century within the public schools.

Conflict and Competition: High Schools, Normal Schools, Colleges, and Universities

Before the Civil War, then, two of the coordinates that would subsequently define the study of education were already in place. The first was gender. Because teachers tended to be female and supervisors tended to be male, attitudes toward gender and relationships defined by gender would have continuing salience. So would questions pertaining to the strength and coherence of education as a profession. Having once been a part-time, temporary, often incidental occupation, by mid-century teaching and school administration were well on the way to becoming distinct occupations for which there was special preparation. Despite that, there continued to be open questions about the status, power, and exclusivity of education as a self-conscious and externally recognized community of peers—education as a profession—and that would also play a role in subsequent developments. In addition, after 1865, owing to several profound changes in the general ecology of educational institutions, a third factor entered the mix. Institutional competition, often intertwined with competition between and among competing ideas and perspectives, now also assumed importance in the dynamics that would shape educational scholarship.

This was evident in the fate of the three types of institutions of professional education for teachers that had developed before the Civil War. Of the three, two failed to thrive after 1865. Teachers' institutes were held less and less frequently, as normal schools, their more settled incarnation,

Table 2 U.S. Schooling, 1890–1990

Year	Enrollment K–8	Enrollment 9–12	Pop. 17 Years Old	High School Grads	Personnel Teachers	Personnel Principals	Personnel Other Staff
1890	14,036	298	1,259	44	364	—	—
1900	16,225	630	1,489	95	423	—	—
1910	18,340	1,032	1,786	156	523	—	—
1920	20,863	2,414	1,855	311	680	13.6	6.6
1930	23,588	4,741	2,296	667	854	30.9	6.9
1940	20,985	7,059	2,403	1,221	875	31.5	4.8
1950	22,095	6,397	2,034	1,200	914	39.3	9.2
1960	32,242	9,520	2,672	1,858	1,355	63.6	13.8
1970	36,610	14,647	3,757	2,889	2,023	90.6	31.5
1980	31,639	14,570	4,262	3,043	2,185	106.0	35.0
1990	33,978	12,472	3,485	2,587	2,357	125.6	—

SOURCE: National Center for Educational Statistics, *120 Years of American Education: A Statistical Portrait* (Washington, D.C.: U.S. Department of Education, 1993), 36–37, 46–48, 55.

NOTE: All numbers in thousands

became well established. And academies, which had been well adapted to the needs of a rural population, did not long survive the widespread establishment of public high schools and the demographic shifts that made cities increasingly important centers of the population after the Civil War. Some academies closed; some were absorbed into public school systems; some became colleges; some assumed a more socially or academically elite character.[23] In their original form, none remained important as centers of professional education for teachers.

While these antebellum institutions withered, two new institutions emerged. The first was the public high school. Although high schools had existed in the United States since 1821 when the "English Classical School" was established in Boston, their growth had been slow and their form extremely varied.[24] By the end of the nineteenth century, however, the high school had become the nation's paradigmatic institution of secondary education. High school enrollment grew steadily from the 1870s forward and doubled every decade between the 1890s and 1930s. Enrollment reached 4,399,000 in that year, 5,725,000 by 1950, and 13,332,000 by 1970 (see table 2).

The development of high schools led not only to the demise of many academies, which by the 1870s were increasingly seen as less democratic institutions than they had, in actuality, been, but also to the transformation of the normal school. Because high schools often offered normal

Table 3 Male and Female High School Enrollment, 1890–1990

Year	Male Enrollment	Female Enrollment
1890	132,985	163,748
1900	271,941	358,107
1910	453,999	578,462
1920	907,189	1,134,119
1930	2,137,719	2,317,002
1940	3,352,749	3,486,650
1950*	3,344,000	3,312,000
1960	5,184,000	5,065,000
1970	7,400,000	7,300,000
1980	7,300,000	7,300,000
1990	6,500,000	6,400,000

SOURCES: U.S. Department of Commerce, *Statistical Abstract of the United States* (Washington, D.C.: U.S. Government Printing Office, 1930, 1940, 1950, 1970, 1995). *Beginning in 1950, the enrollment figures were estimated according to Census population controls.

classes to their majority female student bodies, they competed with normal schools as centers of teacher training. More important, a new job market for teachers and administrators was created by the development of high schools, and this caused other institutions also to become interested in the education of educators (see table 3).

One such institution was the research university, which developed at roughly the same time as the high school. Growing up as a result of new endowments and a new interest in science and empirical research, research universities began to emerge in the 1870s. Johns Hopkins, which is usually described as the nation's "first" research university, was founded in 1876. Some research universities—for example, Stanford and Chicago—were created as new institutions; others—for example, Harvard and Columbia—resulted from the growth and transformation of antebellum colleges; still others—especially the state universities—grew via funds provided under the (federal) Morrill Act of 1862. Many were led by one or another of the extraordinarily ambitious and effective cadre of men Thorstein Veblen so aptly described as "captains of erudition."[25]

With these powerful and deliberate leaders at the helm, universities quickly assumed managerial roles in the development and dissemination of knowledge and in the professionalization of many different fields of service and their associated knowledge domains. It was as part of that, that universities moved increasingly to establish schools and departments of education within their own precincts.[26] These became the spawning grounds for education research.

Initially to create materials to use in training teachers, especially high school teachers, and school administrators, university professors began to study, compare, and describe the workings of different schools and school systems. Over time, service activities of various kinds, especially school surveying, also generated data and were regarded as "research." Last, but hardly least important, within university departments and schools of education, scholars trained in one or another of the disciplines—most likely philosophy, psychology, history, or sociology—began to consider the bearing of those disciplines on educational problems, the result being new hybrid fields of research, educational psychology doubtless most important among them. As was the case in many new domains of professional training circa 1900, including social work, engineering, diplomacy, and public administration, research in education grew up in an ad hoc, essentially opportunistic fashion.

The State University of Iowa created a normal department and the nation's first "Chair of Didactics" in 1873, with California, Indiana, Michigan, Minnesota, Nebraska, North Carolina, and Wisconsin, among others, following suit before the 1890s were out. During the early 1890s, Columbia, Chicago, Clark, Harvard, and Stanford also became involved in the training of educators. According to U.S. Commissioner of Education William Torrey Harris, there were more than two hundred colleges or universities offering teacher preparation by 1894–95, of which twenty-seven had organized actual departments or schools of pedagogy.[27]

To read this growth as unvarnished enthusiasm for sponsoring educational study would be a mistake. It makes more sense to read it as evidence of university aspirations to corner new markets and, even more, to assume a regulatory role that would ensure university leadership of the full panoply of educational institutions within a particular city, state, or region—or even nationwide. These aspirations were usually sufficient to override widespread skepticism concerning the wisdom of trying to develop a science of education or even of offering educators "professional" training; but skepticism persisted, and it would have a highly corrosive effect on the scholarship that emerged.

The establishment of research universities created conflict and competition among institutions interested in providing instruction about education. This would continue well into the twentieth century, and, indeed, it continues to this day. Conflict and competition resulted from the ambition shared by many university leaders to organize the nation's multitude of schools and colleges into a more coherent, pyramid-like hierarchy with universities at the top. More specifically, it arose as university leaders like Charles W. Eliot of Harvard, William Rainey Harper of Chicago, and Nicholas Murray Butler of Columbia became interested in issues of articulation between the high schools and the colleges. They believed, as the National Education Association's Committee of Ten chaired by Charles Eliot announced in 1893, that, even though only a very small fraction of its graduates actually went on to college, college preparation should be the common controlling purpose of the high school.[28] This would help ensure college and university oversight of high school curricula, which was initially exercised through faculty accreditation visits and then increasingly through regional accrediting associations like the North Central Association of Colleges and Secondary Schools founded in 1895 and college entrance services like the College Entrance Examination Board founded in 1900. College and university oversight of the high schools was also fostered by private philanthropies like the Carnegie Foundation for the Advancement of Teaching, which became a primary agent in advancing the organizational ambitions of elite university presidents.

Beginning to be a priority for university leaders before the turn of the century, close articulation between high schools and colleges could be advanced if university departments of education were able to capture the new market for training teachers and administrators. The problem, however, was that normal schools also sought access to this market. Even though the curricula of normal schools tended to lack the disciplinary focus thought essential for teaching beyond "the grades," some normal school leaders argued vociferously that their institutions should be encouraged to raise their standards and expand their curricula to serve the needs of all prospective educators.

As was often the case in matters concerning teacher preparation, issues of gender played a role in the thinking of normal school reformers who were seeking to resist university encroachment. Typically, David Felmley, president of the Illinois State Normal University from 1900 to 1930, insisted that "the normal school must make provision for the adequate training of teachers fitted to direct or to perform the work of every phase of the common school from the primary school to its culmination in the public high school."[29] This would avoid segmentation, Felmley explained, waxing eloquent concerning the equality that should exist between "the professional aristocracy of the high school and the commonality of the grades."[30] As Jurgen Herbst has observed, however, despite the democratic rhetoric, what was really on Felmley's mind was gender. Although most normal school students had always been female, normal schools had been able to sustain some level of coeducation by appealing to men who planned to move into supervisory positions in education. In the Midwest, normal schools had often been the only available state institution of post–common school education and therefore the only free route to advanced schooling. For male students, a normal school education had therefore provided a relatively inexpensive route to career mobility. If the development of university departments of education now served to restrict normal schools to the preparation of elementary school teachers, Felmley feared men would shun them altogether. Were that to happen, normal schools in the Midwest and West would suffer the kind of degradation of status that Felmley associated with normal schools in the East, which had been hurt by their tendency to be single-sex, single-track institutions.[31]

Unfortunately for Felmley and other advocates of an expanded role for normal schools, many university leaders openly dismissed the possibility of normal school development along these lines. They tended to assert, as University of Iowa President Frederick E. Bolton once put it, that normal schools were not and could not be "fitted to train high-school teachers . . . [who needed] above all else a broad outlook upon life, deep and thorough scholarship, and liberality of attitude."[32] This view was easy to justify because many normal school faculty members had not been to college; they were themselves normal school graduates. Because normal schools were implicitly equated with the social characteristics of their students, who tended not only to be female, but also to come from nonelite farming and blue-collar families, normal school graduates were presumed to lack the gentility, cultivation, and learnedness conveyed by terms like "broad outlook" and "liberality of attitude."

Beyond that, some university leaders, especially those from the most elite institutions, championed larger political aims for which support of college and university as opposed to normal school training for high school teachers was instrumental. William Rainey Harper and Nicholas Murray Butler, for example, were actively involved in helping to centralize control of the public schools in their respective cities. They believed that centralization would end the graft and educational inefficiency they associated with local control. Dressing their efforts in a rhetoric of disinterest and public benefit, they were actually seeking to replace neighborhood leaders with well-educated, affluent civic leaders in the governance of their cities' schools. Neighborhood leaders were often immigrant shop-keepers and workingmen; by contrast, the civic leaders favored by Harper and Butler tended to be university donors and trustees and well-known figures on the national scene.

As Marjorie Murphy has shown in her study of teachers' unions, "reshaping the school teacher" was instrumental to the centralization sought by university leaders.[33] So long as teaching required little or no formal training, working-class and immigrant women predominated as public school teachers, while more affluent and better-educated women shunned the field. As educational requirements were increased, however, the situation changed markedly. Higher educational requirements drew a better "class" of women. That it was University of Chicago President William Rainey Harper who led the fight to raise the educational requirements in Chicago was not a coincidence. By raising educational requirements, Harper hoped to diminish the numbers of working-class and immigrant teachers, which could be conducive to centering control of the schools in the hands of the city's upper-class elite. Working-class and immigrant teachers were more likely to unionize than their more affluent and educated sisters, and they were more likely to have close personal and familial ties to the local neighborhood school boards that stood in the way of administrative centralization.[34]

As things turned out in turn-of-the-century Chicago, President Harper's sights proved too high for the political realities of the city, and Harper was unable to win passage for a bill requiring that teachers have a college degree. Nevertheless, he continued to work in other ways to make the University of Chicago, rather than competing institutions, the center for professional education in Chicago. Harper's interest in school centralization was inseparable from his ambitions for the development of educational study at the University of Chicago, and for Harper, as for others in positions like his, this made competition between the universities and normal schools virtually inevitable.

Institutional competition was expressed in many ways, including entreaties to state legislatures, thinly veiled public appeals published as statements of sound educational policy in journals like *Atlantic Monthly* and *Educational Review* and, most telling of all, catalogs and other announcements of institutional mission. Always written in the rhetoric of public service, these publications were careful not to criticize normal schools directly. Instead, they simply asserted their mission as a superior one. Repeatedly, these publications asserted that the university study of education, unlike normal school study, was intended for those planning to teach beyond the elementary grades or otherwise preparing for leadership positions.

Typically, the catalog for the School of Pedagogy founded in 1890 at the University of the City of New York (later renamed New York University), explained that the school's work "begins where the normal school ends." The school's purpose was to "acquaint its students with the scientific investigations already made and . . . to train its students so that they shall be able to take advantage of these investigations and put into actual and successful practice a more scientific pedagogy."[35] Similarly, the University of Buffalo announced that its School of Pedagogy was "in no sense [intended] to duplicate the work of Normal Schools but to continue and complete the work they so ably begin." The students Buffalo sought should be seeking "positions as teachers in secondary schools, as training teachers, principals, and also superintendents of schools."[36]

Though the claim was more abstract, the Department of Pedagogy at the University of Illinois also wanted to enroll "those who have preparation and patient purpose to attain unto the highest phases of pedagogical thinking." In the words of historians Henry C. Johnson Jr. and Erwin V. Johanningmeier, the Illinois Department of Pedagogy was "to be the crown of the state's system of normal schools," a place for "the continued and higher study of pedagogy."[37] The New York College for the Training of Teachers, which subsequently became Teachers College, an independent institution affiliated with Columbia University, claimed to be both "a superior normal school" and "an experiment station" whose "aggressive work" would help elevate public and private schools across the nation as well as agencies educating special populations, "the Indian, negro, [and] poor white."[38]

Institutional competition also forced changes within many institutions. As David Felmley of Illinois State Normal University had advocated should be the case, university claims to superiority, combined with a host of local factors, spurred many normal schools to imitate their competitors. Though most private normal schools closed before 1920, state institutions instead moved to raise the standards of their faculties, students, and curricula. Over time, many evolved into state teachers colleges, then state colleges, and eventually state universities. As part of this evolution, the traditional normal school focus on teacher preparation gave way to broader vocational purposes, which included preparation for many occupations and many educational roles.

Despite normal school efforts to establish themselves on a par with universities, none among them would initially gain premier rank among

Table 4 Graduate Degrees in Education, 1890–1990

Year	Doctoral-Granting Institutions Education	B.A.	M.A.	Ph.D./Ed.D.	Total Doctorates, All Fields
1890	—	—	—	—	149
1900	—	—	—	—	382
1910	—	—	—	—	443
1920	34	—	—	48	562
1930	53	—	—	268	2,075
1940	60	—	—	470	3,277
1950	86	—	—	1,038	6,535
1960	116	89,002	33,433	1,591	9,829
1970	173	164,080	79,293	5,895	29,866
1980	196 (1985)	118,169	103,951	7,941	32,615
1990	199 (1991)	104,715	86,057	6,922	38,238

Sources: National Research Council, *A Century of Doctorates* (Washington, D.C.: National Academy of Sciences, 1978), 12–13, 95; Seymour E. Harris, *A Statistical Portrait of Higher Education* (New York: McGraw-Hill, 1972), 317; National Center for Educational Statistics, *120 Years of American Education: A Statistical Portrait* (Washington, D.C.: U.S. Department of Education, 1993), 85–87; National Center for Educational Statistics, *Digest of Educational Statistics* (Washington, D.C.: National Center for Educational Statistics, 1988 and 1995), 214 (1988), 277 (1995).

institutions offering work in education. This was demonstrated by opinion surveys conducted in the 1930s. As Geraldine Jonçich Clifford and James W. Guthrie observed in *Ed School,* this was because the status and rank of schools of education tended to reflect the status and rank of the universities with which they were affiliated.[39] The schools of education that were ranked as "premier" institutions in the 1930s—Chicago, Harvard, Iowa, Ohio State, Michigan, Minnesota, Stanford, Teachers College, the University of California (Berkeley), and Yale—were all parts of (or, in the case of Teachers College, affiliated with) universities that produced large numbers of undergraduates headed for graduate school and unusually large numbers of doctoral degrees (see table 4).

Within the universities themselves, institutional competition also had important effects. As universities moved to establish departments and schools of education, noneducationists who had once taught education or lectured to teachers found themselves on the sidelines. As professionalization advanced, experience as a teacher could no longer qualify one to teach "the science and art of teaching," as, for example, University of Chicago President Henry Judson had done as a professor of history at the University of Minnesota between 1885 and 1891.[40]

In addition, as the university study of education became professionalized, its association with teaching—"woman's work"—came into play. Especially at the elite eastern universities, the association of education with "woman's work" marginalized the new "ed schools" relative to other faculties. The extreme instance of this was Columbia, whose board of trustees would accept a contractual affiliation with Teachers College, but would not accept the college as a regular faculty of the university. Instead, like Barnard College, the Columbia-affiliated college for women, it remained legally and geographically just outside Columbia's gates.[41]

Even within coeducational universities, the association of teaching with "woman's work" made the study of education vulnerable to long-standing patterns of disdain and discount. Ironically, of course, these were the very same patterns of disdain and discount that had given universities an advantage relative to normal schools in the competition for control of the high school and administrator training market. Though teacher advocates like Ella Flagg Young of Chicago constantly urged university departments and schools of education to offer their students curricula as rich as those offered to other students, the university study of education came to be defined by many of the same stigmas that had helped characterize normal schools as second-rate.[42] In consequence, when professors of education claimed that theirs was a "cultural subject," their arguments fell on deaf ears.[43] Closely related, though students in "ed schools" may not have been described as "clumsy," as their normalite predecessors had been, they were commonly thought of as "dumb," a characteristic that was repeatedly confirmed by standardized tests that measured intelligence, rather than altruism or idealism, which would-be teachers were said to possess in abundance.[44]

Both stimulated and constrained by institutional competition, the study of education spread rapidly from one to another of the nation's ever-increasing colleges and universities. As that happened, newly appointed professors of education began to write textbooks, to formulate laws and theories, and to invent all sorts of ways to investigate education "scientifically." The result by 1920 was a fairly clear consensus concerning the problematics of education research. Something of a false dawn, this consensus would rather quickly fall victim to fragmentation and dispute. That notwithstanding, between roughly 1890 and 1920, education research emerged as an empirical, professional science, built primarily around behaviorist psychology and the techniques and ideology of quantitative measurements. Inevitably, as this approach gained acceptance, other approaches to the study of education—most important, the approach developed by John Dewey at the University of Chicago between

1894 and 1904—were pushed to the margins, though they were never totally eclipsed and would reappear from time to time. From the first, contests tinged with issues of gender and professional status, as well as with a host of more immediate circumstantial factors, were central to the history of education research.

IN QUEST OF SCIENCE: THE EARLY YEARS OF EDUCATION RESEARCH

What the expert in the science of education deems scientific has the greatest probability of being so.

Edward L. Thorndike

The sources of educational science are any portions of ascertained knowledge that enter into the heart, head, and hands of educators, and which, by entering in, render the performance of the educational function more enlightened, more humane, more truly educational than it was before.

John Dewey

In the early 1890s, when Harvard philosopher Josiah Royce published his essay "Is There a Science of Education?" the question he posed was of lively interest to many Americans. In part, this was a result of growing interest in improving the nation's schools and a related increase in debate between and among supporters of different philosophies of education, the Pestalozzians, Froebelians, Hegelians, and Herbartians, among them. At a time when rapid economic, demographic, and social change seemed to be altering everything about small-town American life, finding ways to modernize the public schools was an urgent matter to many citizens.

In part, too, talk of educational science simply represented the extension to education of growing interest in systematic, empirical investigation—science. At the time, this was remaking conceptions of truth and knowledge across the full range of human concerns and causing fundamental changes in the ways colleges and universities organized themselves. Once devoted entirely to teaching, universities were now also hosts to a variety of research activities. Faculty members were expected both to teach and to carry on original investigations.[1] Resulting in increasing specialization, the university's embrace of science eventually fostered a historically radical separation of facts and values. However, as Julie A. Reuben has argued in her recent reinterpretation of the history of higher education, that separation was more an unanticipated outcome of university development than a purposefully pursued goal, and in the 1890s, it was still unimaginable.[2] Scholars who embraced Darwin and scientific ideals could still at the same time believe that reason and morality were inseparable. In 1897, while working to develop a science of education at the University of Chicago, John Dewey even said: "the teacher always is the prophet of the true God and the usherer in of the true kingdom of God."[3] Having, in a sense, gained science, but not yet lost faith in the unity of truth, morality, and beauty, Americans felt an optimism about intellectual and social progress that is now difficult to imagine. More to the point here, no group felt this somewhat strenuous confidence more keenly than the liberal Protestant, white, Anglo-Saxon descendants of rural America who predominated among the mostly male scholars who would become the first university scholars of education.

By the 1920s, the situation had changed markedly. After participating in World War I, the United States seemed to lose what historian Henry F. May once described as its prewar innocence.[4] As part of that, the language of reform lost its earlier moral overtone and began to focus on social control and efficiency.[5] This would have far-reaching consequences for educational scholarship. Indeed, it helped create a way to market the newly defined expertise of educationists, who wanted to provide guidance to the nation's public schools.

By the 1920s, the university study of education was also well established institutionally. As early as 1915, 300 of the 600 colleges in the United States offered courses in education, and for the next fifty years, there was unprecedented growth in educational study, especially at the doctoral level.[6] Inspired with the zeal of missionaries, the first generations of scholars of education had been extraordinarily successful in developing a knowledge base for the school leaders they wished to counsel. In the process, they had invented educational psychology, educational testing, educational administration, the history of education, and what were called general and special (teaching) methods, all of which became central foci for research. In addition, while advising school boards and administrators about their organizational problems, they had founded new professional journals and organizations and had begun to gain entrée into relevant national organizations, government agencies, and philanthropic foundations. As doctors and engineers had done earlier, the pioneer educationists had set out to create order and standards in a previously local and nonstandardized domain of public concern, and they had been quite successful in doing so. Among other things, increasing bureaucracy in the public schools testified to that.

Inevitably, perhaps, the science of education that emerged during the first decades of the twentieth century reflected attitudes prevalent in American society. Despite interest in school reform, widespread skepticism concerning whether education could be a science therefore became important. Even though this did not prevent psychologists from taking advantage of popular interest in education when doing so might advance their careers, skepticism about educational science, combined with an unwillingness to be too closely associated with teachers, did encourage an ambivalence that one could readily observe in the lives of two early giants, G. Stanley Hall and William James.

Beyond that, the biases, values, and social agenda of the early educationists were driving forces in the early definition given to this field. Seeking to be just as scientific as their university peers, while also gaining the status and authoritativeness of established professionals, especially doctors, the pioneer scholars of education placed a great emphasis on quantification as well as on identifying what were taken to be invariable certainties—laws of learning, formulas for administrative efficiency, and the like. Convinced that philosophy led to conflict—to wit the debates among the followers of Pestalozzi, Froebel, Hegel, and Herbart—they believed the findings of science could and would guarantee consensus.[7] Presenting their discoveries in a rhetoric that increasingly featured objectivity and disinterest, they used the ideas and techniques they invented to introduce and sustain hierarchies between and among the different parties involved in operating the public schools and between and among students.

The trends evident in the early history of education research were supported by, and indeed were part of, trends in American culture generally. And yet the patterns established were neither predictable nor inevitable. Indeed, during the 1890s, a rather different approach to educational study than the one that prevailed emerged at the University of Chicago. Growing out of John Dewey's involvement in an experimental school that he and his wife, Alice Chipman Dewey, established there, this approach was based on a psychology that differed in fundamental ways from the behaviorism that became so prevalent in educational circles. But this alternative approach to educational study failed to thrive at Chicago and other major universities because it demanded different ways of organizing educational study than those that became established at most universities.

If Dewey's conception of educational study was difficult to institutionalize within the increasingly professionalized and bureaucratic structures of research universities, those of a number of his contemporaries fit more easily. This was the case with the approach developed and very effectively promoted by Edward L. Thorndike at Teachers College, which resonated well with the approach followed by Charles Hubbard Judd, Dewey's successor at Chicago. Causes aside for the moment, what is best described as Thorndike's triumph and John Dewey's defeat was an important event in the early molding of educational scholarship. Limiting educational scholarship in ways that became more apparent over the years, Thorndike's triumph and Dewey's defeat were essential to the early educationists' quest to define a science that could help them rationalize the nation's public schools.

CHAPTER ONE

Reluctant Allies: Psychologists Turn to Education

During the 1890s, the map of higher learning changed profoundly in the United States. As pressures to organize learning around post-Darwinian conceptions of science mounted with growing acceptance of natural evolution, belief in human agency apart from divine intervention grew apace. This altered preferred modes of "scientific" investigation and explanation. Increasingly, innovation and progress came to be associated with specialization and experimentation, one result being that new disciplines multiplied.

Challenged by these developments, philosophy underwent a thoroughgoing transformation. Once almost exclusively the province of men with ministerial training, it now became a secular academic profession. In addition, having been an expansive, even comprehensive, field in scope, philosophy now became more narrowly focused. Just as natural philosophy had earlier evolved into the various natural sciences, so now moral philosophy evolved into the various social sciences—economics, sociology, political science, and the rest. Those aspects of mental philosophy or psychology that might be studied in a laboratory also gained distinct disciplinary definition. Before the opening of the twentieth century, psychologists had developed their own professional association and journals to facilitate communication and mark the autonomy of their new community.

The separation of psychology from philosophy had important consequences for education, which was just then beginning to gain acceptance as a subject of university study. Because psychology involved the study of mental functions and structures, its relevance to education was clear. What is more, unlike philosophy, a discipline in which one's search for truth was guided by abstract values or theological beliefs, psychology involved empirical research. This lent an aura of "objective science" to psychology that philosophy lacked. Seeming to provide education with a scientific basis, psychology quickly became a popular topic among teachers and reformers interested in education.

This was helpful to psychologists, who were just gaining a toehold in academe, and they exploited the possible synergy between psychology and education. At the same time, however, popular demand for instruction in education was also somewhat dismaying to these new scientists, since addressing questions related to "pedagogics" diminished the time they could give to what they saw as their true profession, which was psychological research. Beyond time, being linked to education would involve activities that were presumed to be women's special concern. Responding to these cross-pressures, members of the first generation of professional psychologists reluctantly became involved in efforts to link psychology to education. One can see this clearly in the careers of G. Stanley Hall and William James. Very different men, with very different ideas about psychology, Hall and James embodied an ambivalence toward education that was not uncommon among scholars in their day—or in our own.

G. Stanley Hall and the Child-Study Movement

In 1896, U.S. Commissioner of Education William Torrey Harris claimed that "the present widespread study in this country of the child in school and in the family is due, more than to anyone else, to the enthusiastic efforts of Dr. G. Stanley Hall."[1] Harris was not a fan of child study. A philosopher and long-time editor of the *Journal of Speculative Philosophy,* the first American journal devoted entirely to philosophy, Harris believed that the study of education should begin not with investigations of child development—"so much mere froth," he said—but with analyses of the different branches of human learning and how those might be organized as curricula for the schools.[2]

Harris's position stemmed from his close association with the St. Louis Hegelians. His preference for rather traditional, subject-matter-centered curricula reflected their belief that the purpose of schooling was to join the individual to society, which necessitated "effort" and formal discipline. That view set Harris and other Hegelians at odds with the Herbartians, a group organized by admirers of the writings of Friedrich Herbart, who now insisted that "interest" should determine what would be taught and in what order. It also separated them from people like Hall, who believed that systematic studies of children could provide a new and improved basis for educational practice.[3] At issue, though unstated, was the primacy of psychology, rather than philosophy, in the study of education. Long a revered statesman in and for education, by the middle 1890s, Harris was forced to concede that his beliefs had lost standing in education reform circles and that this was due in considerable measure to Hall's efforts.

Beginning in the early 1880s, Hall had became a popular lecturer on pedagogical subjects, often addressing groups of teachers or parents, local child-study societies, and even the National Education Association. As he acknowledged in his autobiography, Hall was neither the first person to study the mental and physical growth of children nor the first to see the relevance of child study to teacher training, child study having been part of the curriculum at the Oswego Normal School as early as 1863. Still, he was early in recognizing that "the applications of psychology to education" would offer a "most promising line of work," and he did capture the interest of many of the growing number of reformers and educators who were concerned that "home life had shriveled, city children were left to the street . . . school life and work were mechanical, and mass methods that ignored individuality and even child nature were everywhere prevalent."[4] A man of commanding presence, powerful speech, evangelical rhetoric, and compelling prose, Hall encouraged belief in educational progress through the scientific study of the child.

Hall's standing as a leader among child-study advocates was initially established in 1883, when he published an essay in the *Princeton Review* entitled "The Contents of Children's Minds." The essay reported a survey of Boston schoolchildren that Hall had carried out with support from Pauline Agassiz Shaw, the younger daughter of Louis Agassiz, the Swiss émigré professor of biology at Harvard.[5] Shaw was the wife of one of New England's wealthiest businessmen and a prominent philanthropist in her own right. She was especially interested in child rearing, which she thought was the "[great] problem of the race," and became the sponsor of many educational institutions in Boston, including a system of charity kindergartens.[6] It was with children recruited from these kindergartens that Hall's study was carried out.

The study involved sixty-four teachers asking hundreds of children ordered series of questions that had been composed by Hall.[7] Beginning with queries to determine whether, for example, a child had seen a cow or a sheep, the questionnaires went on to more specific queries designed to test what children knew as a result of their acquaintance with the object in question—for example, that cows are not blue in color, are a source of milk, and can have horns and hoofs. Discarding incomplete questionnaires or ones that were judged invalid, Hall then analyzed the data to determine what percentage of the two hundred remaining children were familiar with cows, or bluebirds, or butterflies; "knew green by name"; knew "where the ankles are"; had "seen [a] hoe"; or possessed the "concept of an island."[8] The data were important, Hall stated in the article, because "all now agree that the mind can learn only what is related to other things learned before, and that we must start from the knowledge the children really have and develop this as germs."[9] Studies of children's minds would support "practical educational conclusions of great scope and importance," he continued; and since the mind developed by a process of unfolding in which all previous stages of human development were implicit—ontogeny recapitulates phylogeny—they would be of "great importance for anthropology and psychology."[10]

In subsequent early writings, Hall repeated and elaborated claims similar to the ones he made in "The Content of Children's Minds." Some of what he had to say pertained to the reform of schools and the training of teachers. Studying children's physical and mental growth should provide a new and improved basis for the "reconstruction of school methods and matter," he insisted.[11] "The teacher must know two things: (1) the subject matter to be taught, and (2) the nature and capacity of the minds in which it is to be rooted," he asserted.[12] Child study would hopefully help prevent "the mutilation which so powerful an engine as the modern school may inflict upon the tender souls and bodies of our children, and thus upon our entire national future."[13] In the process of developing such arguments, Hall presented a new and expansive conception of research, which was based on a broad and synthetic view of education. Maintaining that, in the future, child study would depend on the work and cooperation of many different people, including "teachers, parents, and men of science," Hall projected a time when there would be cooperation between and among all "scientific departments and methods."[14] He thought this was possible because "the one chief and immediate field of application for all this work is its application to education, considered as the science of human nature and the art of developing it to its fullest maturity."[15]

Despite these expansive statements, Hall had become involved in child study and education of necessity rather than choice. For an able and ambitious young man like Hall, the gender-related discount that had already been placed on those subjects made them less than optimally appealing.

Hall's Search for Vocation

Born in 1846, in Ashfield, Massachusetts, Hall had been reared in a modestly comfortable, culturally literate family, whose life revolved around the Congregational Church. After graduating from Williston Seminary and Williams College, he had enrolled for advanced theological studies at Union Theological Seminary in New York City. Like many of his contemporaries, he had interrupted his theological studies with a sojourn in Germany, where the lectures of Berlin philosopher Friedrich Adolf Trendelenburg, combined with a previously unknown sense of personal and social freedom, had shifted his vocational goals from the ministry to philosophy. His mother had not been pleased. "Now Stanley," she had written him, "wherein is the great benefit of being a Ph.D. . . . and wherein would it give you *credit, influence,* or usefulness?"[16] Undeterred by this motherly caution, Hall had set out on what proved to be a prolonged vocational quest.

Having decided to teach psychology rather than to preach, Hall faced very limited occupational prospects. Despite change, instruction in psychology at most colleges was still included under the rubric of philosophy, which remained, as it had throughout the nineteenth century, the province of the college's president. Hall's first post was therefore not academic— he became a tutor in the household of New York banker Jesse Seligman. His second job was as a faculty member at Antioch College in Yellow Springs, Ohio, where, in his own oft-quoted phrase, he occupied a "whole settee," teaching French, German, rhetoric, English literature, Anglo-Saxon, and, during an interim year between presidents, one course in philosophy.[17] When Antioch's financial problems forced him again to search for work, he was again unable to find an academic appointment. In the fall of 1876, he therefore returned to graduate study, this time at Harvard, where William James, then an instructor of physiology, was seeking to gain a foothold for the new scientific psychology.[18]

Introduced to physiological psychology by James, Hall devoted some of his time at Harvard to studies in the Harvard Medical School physiology laboratory, established in 1871 by James's friend Henry P. Bowditch. His doctoral thesis, which was published in 1878 as "The Muscular Perception of Space," offered a new approach to an old question posed by Kant: Does thought originate in experience or in the mind? It presented an argument supporting the possibility that the perception of movement resulted from physical reactions.[19] Although the thesis won him the nation's first Ph.D. in psychology, it did not result in employment.

The frustration Hall felt had already boiled over into print. In September 1876, he had written a letter to the editor of the *Nation,* arguing that college instruction in philosophy was "generally given into the hands of one of the older and 'safer' members of the faculty, under the erroneous belief that it should be the aim of the professors of this department to indoctrinate rather than to instruct—to tell *what* to think, [rather] than to teach *how* to think."[20] Now, having again chosen to study in Germany as an alternative preferable to being unemployed or choosing a new career, he wrote a lengthy article on "Philosophy in the United States" for *Mind,* in which he criticized the dated definition of the field in general and complained in particular that "business conspires with Bethel to bring mental science into general disfavour."[21] According to his autobiography, Hall's discouragement had reached a point where he had "decided that neither psychology nor philosophy would ever make bread" and was therefore now considering a career in medicine.[22]

As things turned out, however, Hall's skill as a lecturer, combined with the information he had gathered during visits to German schools, saved him from yet again having to reorient his career. When he returned to Boston in 1880, he contacted old acquaintances in search of something besides his "unremunerative writing" to help him support himself and his new wife, who was then pregnant with the couple's first child.[23] Soon thereafter Harvard President Charles W. Eliot invited him to give two series of lectures, one on the history of psychology and the other on pedagogy. Although Hall would have preferred the psychology lectures to be the more successful, it was the ones on pedagogy that drew a full house.

In considerable measure, this was because Boston was a city already interested in education reform. Beginning in the 1870s, many prominent citizens wrote and spoke in favor of education reform. One among them, regulatory reformer Charles F. Adams Jr., had become a special champion of pedagogies that were more child centered and less rigid and academic. According to Hall, Adams opposed old, academicized conceptions of the high school, even describing them as a "fetish [that] no more revives antique culture than the soil is fertilized by the smell of the dung-cart driven over it."[24] Through speeches and popular tracts like *New Departures in the Common Schools of Quincy, and Other Papers on Educational Topics* (1879) and *The Public Library and the Common School: Three Papers on Educational Topics* (1879), Adams had helped draw national attention to reforms in the Quincy, Massachusetts, schools instituted by Colonel Francis W. Parker, who later became the famed head of the Cook

County Normal School in Chicago, Illinois. Adams had also lectured the National Education Association (NEA) on the need for well-trained school superintendents who had studied "the operation of the child's mind, the natural processes of growth and assimilation which goes on in it, [and] its inherent methods of development and acquisition."[25]

Adams helped set the stage for Hall's talks, which even Charles Eliot, who was disdainful of the very notion of a scientific approach to pedagogy, had to admit were "remarkably successful."[26] This prompted Eliot to invite Hall to continue lecturing on pedagogy and also to design a university department of pedagogy at Harvard, of which Hall might well have become chair.[27] Despite that, Hall was still determined to teach psychology and continued to hope that when he found a suitable job, "the educational line of study will be speedily subordinated to it."[28]

Eventually, in 1882, Daniel Coit Gilman, president of the newly founded Johns Hopkins University in Baltimore, did offer Hall a post. Initially only a half-time appointment, Hall's position was changed to full-time professor of philosophy and pedagogy in January 1884.[29] Although he now had a job, Hall's title included "pedagogy," which, as he explained in his autobiography, was a designation that was added "against my own wish."[30] A self-conscious professionalizer, who happened also to be something of a misogynist, Hall had finally secured a position as a psychologist at a premier university, but was in the sorry position of having been forced to accept a title that suggested an affiliation with "woman's work."[31] As his biographer Dorothy Ross has observed, his response was telling. Hall's Hopkins years were notable for a lack of attention to child study or education.[32]

Clark University: "The Perfect Non-University of G. Stanley Hall"

Hall's time at Hopkins was brief. Shunning child study and education, he had achieved prominence as a champion of "strictly scientific" psychology.[33] Having arrived in Baltimore in 1882, he left to become president of Clark University in Worcester, Massachusetts, in the spring of 1887. Founded by Jonas Clark, a wealthy hardware merchant who wanted to create "a college where boys of limited means . . . could obtain an education at low cost," thanks to Hall's influence, Clark instead became a university modeled on Johns Hopkins.[34] When the university opened in the fall of 1889, its faculty included many outstanding scholars divided into five departments: mathematics, physics, chemistry, biology, and psychology. As befit a university presided over by the nation's first Ph.D. in the "new" psychology, Clark University thus became home to the nation's first autonomous psychology department, which encompassed neurology, anthropology, philosophy, and education.

In spite of its auspicious founding, there was trouble at Clark from the first, and before the end of the second academic year, two-thirds of the senior faculty and three-quarters of the junior faculty of the university had left, roughly half of them for positions at the newly founded University of Chicago.[35] Contrary to his own account, Hall appears to have deserved a large measure of responsibility for this sorry state of affairs. Even at Hopkins, his professional relationships had been marked by jealousy and personal nastiness. "Dr. Hall has not acted honorably toward me," James McKeen Cattell, the pioneer of mental tests who was then a Hopkins graduate student, had written to his parents in 1884 when his fellowship was not renewed. Although Hall had praised Cattell to his face, he had recommended John Dewey, then also a Hopkins graduate student, for the fellowship, which, in similar fashion, was denied to Dewey the following year.[36] In flight from Hall, Cattell had finished his graduate studies in Leipzig with famed psychologist Wilhelm Wundt, while Dewey had worked primarily with Hegelian philosopher George Sylvester Morris. Subsequently, Dewey would explain that among contemporary psychologists and philosophers, it was a "matter of common repute that Dr. Hall is incapable of either permitting men near him to work freely along their own lines of interest, or to keep from appropriating to himself credit for work which belongs to others."[37]

At Clark, Hall's professional relationships were just as stormy and mean as they had been at Hopkins. He promised faculty members more than he could deliver. He alienated them through his autocratic and mean-spirited approach to administration—characteristically, Hall reduced the stipend of an impoverished graduate student who had remained at home for a few days beyond the end of a vacation period to care for his sick mother. Hall also misled Jonas Clark about his intentions—for example, Hall never believed that the university should have an undergraduate college even though it was this that Clark most wanted. Hardly least important, he even mishandled the university's finances. As William Koelsch has argued in his history of Clark, "in the folklore of American higher education, Jonas Clark has been cast as the villain of the early Clark University melodrama. . . . [However,] Hall's many self-pitying statements aside, primary responsibility for what in other minds than Hall's was the tragedy of Clark University lay with the president, in his relationships with the founder and with his faculty."[38] By 1892, Clark was "a torso of a university," or, in the apt phrasing of Laurence Veysey, "the perfect non-university of G. Stanley Hall."[39]

Within the shell that remained of a university that had begun with an endowment and a faculty comparable to those of Johns Hopkins and Harvard, child study came to assume new importance. Titles aside, while at Johns Hopkins, Hall had been able to concentrate on psychology without really concerning himself with either child study or "pedagogics," but different pressures at Clark forced child study to the fore. The Clark endowment had never been capitalized at the level initially hoped, and there were no undergraduate tuitions to support graduate instruction as was the case at most other institutions, including Hopkins. However noble Hall's conception of a graduate university may have been, it was problematic financially. In consequence, Hall needed to appeal to his Worcester neighbors as potential patrons and could not afford to ignore the more popular applied side of psychology in favor of the more scientifically prestigious theoretical and experimental sides, which he had primarily pursued in Baltimore. Finances thus forced a revival of his interest in the child.

In 1891, Hall founded a journal called the *Pedagogical Seminary*— he had already founded the *American Journal of Psychology* in 1887. This provided an outlet for publishing the studies carried out by his students and colleagues at Clark and by an increasing number of disciples all over the country. Typically, these studies reported data—often voluminous data describing hundreds, even thousands, of children—gathered via questionnaires or through observation and measurement of children. They covered subjects like "Thoughts and Reasoning of Children" and "Imitation in Children."[40]

In July 1892, Hall also inaugurated a two-week summer school at Clark called the Clark Summer School of Higher Pedagogy and Psychology, with Hall himself teaching "the study of children."[41] Hall's courses were aimed at parents, teachers, and normal school principals, although, in other instances, Hall tended to avoid close contact with teachers, especially if they were women.[42] He promised that those who came to the summer session could participate in subsequent efforts to gather data concerning the twelve topics that were central to child study at Clark, including anger, crying and laughing, toys and playthings, fears, the early sense of self, and religious life.[43] In this way, Hall and his associates spawned a large, informal network of mothers' clubs, classes, and associations built around child study. Often organized around "syllabi" sent out from Clark, which offered for discussion all that was known on hundreds of specific topics like "The Language Interest in Children," "Dreams," "Curiosity and Interest," and "The Teaching of Geography," child-study groups were usually short-lived. But a few, for example, the New York City Society for the Study of Child Nature, which eventually became the Child Study Association of America, continued to thrive.[44]

The year after beginning the summer school at Clark, Hall led a three-day meeting on "Experimental Psychology and Education" at the Chicago World Exposition, which was dramatically positioned to compete with meetings on "Rational Psychology and Education," led by William Torrey Harris and his fellow philosopher James McCosh. Hall's meeting drew crowds and notice, while Harris and McCosh's sessions were poorly attended. That, combined with other well-attended sessions at NEA meetings, prompted the NEA to sanction the establishment of a new Child Study Department in 1894, which became still another vehicle for the dissemination of Hall's views.[45] Ever the opportunist, Hall had by then dropped his earlier reluctance and was ready to declare:

> Our program is to gradually center all study of psychology, philosophy, ethics and perhaps other cognate branches by teachers about child study. This is not only in accordance with the evolutionary tendencies increasingly dominant in nearly every other field, but it will save the philosophical side of pedagogy from its present decline, and place education for the first time on a scientific basis, and be the center around which the education of the future will be organized.[46]

William James's Search for Vocation

Hall's personality and evangelicism alienated many of his contemporaries, not least his former teacher William James. Having been prevailed upon by President Eliot to lecture to Cambridge teacher groups in whom Harvard had a keen interest, James had told his audience not to be overly concerned about child study. "I fear that some of the enthusiasts for child-study have thrown a certain burden on you," he remarked, referring without name to Clark University's president. Unlike Hall, James did not believe all teachers should or could contribute to child study. "The best teacher may be the poorest contributor to child-study material, and the best contributor may be the poorest teacher," he said.[47] Very different from Hall in virtually every way, and of much greater and far more lasting intellectual stature, James was nonetheless like him in wanting to pursue "pure" psychology, while needing to accommodate the demands of the world around him.

Four years older than Hall, James was the oldest of the five children (after William, Henry, Wilkerson, Robertson, and Alice) born to Henry and Mary Walsh James. The senior Henry James was independently wealthy, his father having been one of the promoters of the Erie Canal. Never needing to work, though he wrote works of theology and became involved in various reform causes, the elder James devoted abundant time to his children. A close friend of Ralph Waldo Emerson, he preferred educating his children through travel and exposure to varied people, places, and ideas than through sustained enrollment in school. Even though they lived primarily in lower New York City, while William was a youth, the James family traveled almost constantly. In consequence, William was educated in Paris, Geneva, and Newport, Rhode Island, as well as New York. As Jacques Barzun aptly put it, the James youngsters played "hide-and-seek with schoolmasters."[48] After a fairly prolonged flirtation with the study of art, William entered the Lawrence Scientific School at Harvard in 1861. Though made rather quickly, the decision to give up art for science, which was something of a capitulation to the will of his father, was a painful one for James.[49]

While a student at Harvard, James initially studied chemistry with Charles Eliot, who would soon become president of the university. Then he moved on to comparative anatomy and physiology with Jeffries Wyman. In 1864, he entered the Harvard Medical School, in true James style, only to leave again the following spring, when he set off on an extended zoological expedition to the Amazon with Louis Agassiz. A rather frail young man who was painfully self-conscious and reflective, James suffered recurrent health problems on the journey. Nevertheless, he found in it some of the aesthetic pleasures that he had earlier found in art. "The brilliancy of the sky and the clouds," he wrote to his brother Henry, "the effect of the atmosphere, which gives their proportional distance to the diverse planes of the landscape, make you admire the old gal Nature. I almost thought my enjoyment of nature had entirely departed, but here she strikes such massive and stunning blows as to overwhelm the coarsest apprehension."[50]

Despite that pleasure, James was keenly aware that as he collected zoological specimens, his brothers Wilkie and Bob were soldiers in the Union army. "You have no idea how I pine for war news," he wrote his brother Henry in May 1865.[51] Coming of age at a time when newly industrializing America offered young men unprecedented vocational options, James's generation was defined historically both by the frequency with which its members endured a prolonged search for vocation and by the

Civil War. As George Cotkin has argued, those who did not fight suffered not only from guilt and feelings of cowardice, but also from an inability to make decisions about their careers.[52] Even those male members of James's generation who did not fight in the Civil War were scarred by it. Although G. Stanley Hall's prolonged vocational quest was caused primarily by changing occupational structures, William James's continuing uncertainties and vacillations may have indeed derived from his inability, owing to poor health, to participate in the war.

However that may have been, James returned to Cambridge in the spring of 1866. Although he completed an internship at the Massachusetts General Hospital and eventually graduated from the Harvard Medical School in 1869, it had become clear to him that he did not want to be a physician. Deciding instead to pursue experimental physiology, he went to Germany in 1867, only to discover there that he also did not want to be "a teacher of physiology, pathology, or anatomy." As he told his Harvard Medical School friend Henry Bowditch, this was because eye and back trouble made it impossible for him to do extended laboratory work.[53]

This realization put James in something of a quandary. "I can never do laboratory work, and so am obliged to fall back on something else," he wrote to Oliver Wendell Holmes Jr. in the spring of 1868. "I shall continue to study, or rather begin to, in a general psychological direction, hoping that I may get into a particular channel. Perhaps a practical application may present itself sometime—the only thing I can now think of is a professorship of 'moral philosophy' in some western academy, but I have no idea how such things are attainable, nor if they are attainable at all to men of a non-spiritualistic mold."[54] Because positions teaching moral philosophy were still not open to men of his unusual religious background—Henry James Sr. was a Swedenborgian—James recognized his good fortune when asked to teach physiology at Harvard and accepted an appointment as an instructor of physiology beginning in August 1872. "I decide today to stick to biology for a profession in case I am not called to a chair in philosophy," he noted in his diary, while also averring that philosophy was and would remain his true "vocation."[55] As one of his many biographers noted, philosophy appealed to him because it raised "universal questions" of wide, multifaceted significance.[56]

In time, James was able to redefine his responsibilities. In 1875, he began to teach a course entitled "The Relations between Physiology and Psychology" and established a demonstration laboratory. It was at this time that Hall became his student. Although Hall would later claim that he had established the first psychology laboratory in the United States while he was at Hopkins, in fact, that honor fell to William James. Indeed, when Hall published a claim to priority, James reminded him that when studying at Harvard, Hall had worked in that laboratory. That aside, by 1877, James was offering a course on "Physiological Psychology—Herbert Spencer's Principles of Psychology" and then, finally, in 1880 was appointed to an assistant professorship in the Harvard Philosophy Department, which then still included work in psychology.[57]

Psychology and Education at Harvard

Elected president of Harvard in 1869, Charles W. Eliot set out to modernize the institution. Introducing student course selection, he needed to enlarge and diversify the faculty, which, in turn, required that he raise faculty salaries. To keep up with Johns Hopkins and other new universities, which were developing novel provisions like sabbatical leaves for faculty research, Eliot had to find additional funds. He planned to do this primarily through student enrollment growth, which would, of course, bring increased tuition income.

In light of Eliot's plans, the fact that William James was a very engaging and popular teacher was important. Unlike James, who wrote Eliot long and detailed letters explaining the importance of psychology, Eliot was not particularly interested in the subject. However, he was interested in shaking up Harvard's Department of Philosophy, which was led by Francis Bowen, well known as a champion of Harvard's old ties to the Unitarian faith. Contra Bowen, Eliot wanted Harvard to become more secular, scientific, and cosmopolitan. He was also distressed because the Philosophy Department was not drawing students to its courses. Chastising Bowen for teaching "philosophical subjects" with "authority" and failing to introduce the "disputed matters, open questions, and bottomless speculations," Eliot gave in to James's entreaties to allow him to move away from physiology and toward psychology and philosophy in the hope that this might help unseat the orthodoxy of the department.[58]

The year after James began teaching "Physiological Psychology," his life took an important turn. In June 1878, he signed a contract with Henry Holt and Company to write a text on psychology, and then, in July of that year, he married Alice H. Gibbens. As Ralph Barton Perry remarked in his still definitive biography, without Alice, who brought unprecedented composure into James's life, the text would probably never

35

have been completed.[59] As it was, the book took James twelve years to write, and he found writing it extremely arduous. In a letter to his novelist brother, Henry, he stated:

> It must seem amusing to you, who can throw off a *chef d'oeuvre* every three months, to hear of my slowness. But . . . almost every page of this book of mine is against a resistance which you know nothing of in your resistless air of romance, the resistance of *facts,* to begin with, each one of which must be bribed to be on one's side, and the resistance of other philosophers to [contend] with, each one of which must be slain. It is no joke slaying Helmholtzes as well as Spencers. When this book is out I shall say adieu to psychology for a while and study some other things.[60]

Trying to avoid simple, schematic descriptions of the mind, James was laboring to craft a book that would focus on consciousness and the actual functioning of the mind. He thought in this way he might be able to "make the confusion less" in a field in which there were so many "different tendencies—the classic tradition, the associationist analysis, the psychogenetic speculations, the experimental methods, the biological conceptions, and the pathological extensions."[61] Drawing on literature in French, German, and English, the synthesis that resulted was extraordinary in its coverage of prior thought, its originality, and its literary grace.

In *The Principles of Psychology,* James argued that habits were built through the repetition of acts. Habits allowed people to "economize the expense of nervous and muscular energy" and made it possible not to pay attention to everything one was thinking, doing, or experiencing. Over time, they came to define one's social and personal character.[62] Coming together to form consciousness, or "stream of thought," a phrase James originated, habits made it possible to digest all the myriad, diverse stimuli to which one was subject.[63] Positing that the process of conscious thinking and the objects of one's thought were one and the same thing, James linked his presentation of habit and consciousness to a conception of consciousness of self, which, he explained, was nothing more than "the active element in all consciousness."[64] From there, he went on to explain that human will, which provided the basis for voluntary actions, was, in turn, a result of images built up in memory from involuntary random reflexes, which were now implanted in one's consciousness.[65] As portrayed by James, human thought and awareness were grounded in biology, which at once constrained and made possible those qualities that were unique to human beings.

While James was at work on *The Principles of Psychology,* Eliot was becoming more and more involved in educational affairs outside of Harvard. Among the questions that agitated him was the relationship between the Massachusetts high schools, which were growing in number, and the state's system of higher education. Like many of his fellow college and university presidents in other states, Eliot wanted the high schools linked upward so they could be defined as feeders for institutions of higher education. This placed him in conflict with the secretary of the Massachusetts Board of Education, who wanted the high schools to be seen as the capstone of the state's public school system and, as part of that view, wanted the state's normal schools, rather than its colleges, to be responsible for teacher education. Simmering throughout the 1880s, this tug-of-war exemplified the institutional conflict and competition that were so important in shaping educational study. At Harvard, this led to the creation of a set of courses for teachers, which, as chance would have it, were initiated in the same year that *The Principles of Psychology* appeared.[66]

Like most Harvard faculty members, Eliot did not believe there was or should be a science of education. But he agreed to encourage Harvard faculty members to teach teachers about the subjects they professed. Lukewarm even to that idea, the faculty reluctantly acquiesced to a proposal presented to them by Eliot so long as the word "normal" was stricken from the program description and so long as women were denied admission.[67] Beginning in 1890–91, therefore, thirteen short courses were offered to male college or scientific school graduates who wanted to be teachers. James was among the Harvard professors tapped to teach a course, beginning in 1892. Reluctant to say no to Eliot, James was not enthusiastic about the prospect. As he later told another psychologist, he did not think teachers "need *much* psychology." What is more, after a few years of teaching teachers in Cambridge, he concluded that "teachers have less freedom of intellect than any class of people. . . . A teacher wrings his very soul out to understand you, and if he does ever understand anything you say, he lies down on it with his whole weight like a cow on a doorstep so that you can neither get out or in with him. He never forgets it or can reconcile anything else you say with it, and carries it to the grave like a scar."[68]

Primarily to make money, James translated *The Principles of Psychology* into lectures, which he gave at Harvard and other universities. These were subsequently published as *Talks to Teachers on Psychology.* Lacking the dense source material that justified James's argument in the original two-volume work, the lectures were brief, clear, schematic, humorous, and humane. In addition to explaining matters like interest, attention, and will, the lectures offered James's views about the ways in which psychology could inform what he called "the teaching art"—like his Harvard faculty colleagues, he scrupulously avoided using the word "science." [69] Praising teachers for their intense efforts at self-improvement, he warned them not to indulge "fancies that are just a shade exaggerated" about what psychology could do for them. "You make a great, a very great mistake, if you think that psychology, being the science of the mind's laws, is something from which you can deduce definite programmes and schemes and methods of instruction for immediate schoolroom use," James told the teachers. "Psychology is a science, and teaching is an art; and sciences never generate arts directly out of themselves. An intermediary, inventive mind must make the application, by using its originality." [70] Given the views James subsequently expressed about the bovine qualities of most teachers' minds, he was not likely to have been very optimistic about the outcomes of his efforts to introduce teachers to psychology.

Having long wanted to return to philosophy, James took decisive steps in that direction as soon as *The Principles of Psychology* appeared. Personally raising $4,300 for a new laboratory to replace the one he had set up around the time Hall had studied with him, James convinced Eliot to hire Hugo Munsterberg, a German experimentalist. [71] One of the leading students of Wilhelm Wundt, with whom, among others, Hall had once studied, Munsterberg was a difficult person. Combined with the fact that he was Jewish, this made advancement in German academic circles unlikely despite unusual success early in his career. With some reluctance, he therefore accepted James's offer of an initial three-year appointment at Harvard from 1892 until 1895, which was followed (after a two-year return to Germany) by appointment to a regular professorship from 1897 until his untimely death in 1916 at the age of 53. [72]

With a junior colleague now carrying on the work in psychology, James was free after 1892 from having to lecture to the teachers on that subject. Although from time to time he continued to teach teachers in order to earn a summer salary at Berkeley, Stanford, or other institutions with growing departments and schools of education, James had never been eager to involve himself in education. And his successor in psychology felt the same way. Indeed, if James believed psychology had little to offer teachers, Munsterberg believed psychology had nothing whatsoever to offer them. Soon after his arrival in Cambridge, he became a leading member of a faculty group that waged active warfare against vocationalism generally and against involvement in teacher education specifically. While work in psychology continued to grow at Harvard, relationships between psychology and education failed to thrive.

From Child Study to Child Hygiene

William James died in 1910. The previous year G. Stanley Hall had brought Sigmund Freud to the United States. Marking Clark's twentieth anniversary, the visit was a fitting tribute to the relative peace that had settled in at Clark after 1892 and to the more concentrated focus on psychology that had come to prevail within the scaled-back, close-knit community of scholars that came to exist there.

As Lewis M. Terman, who enrolled at Clark in 1903, described the university at the time, it "was a university different in important respects from any other. . . . The informality and freedom from administrative red tape were unequalled. . . . *Lernfreiheit* was utterly unrestricted."[73] Perhaps for these reasons, many Clark graduates imbibed Hall's deep interest in "scientific psychology," his strong belief in genetic determinism, and his ambivalent and even expedient regard for child study and education. Of Hall's students, the one who most prominently continued his interest in child study was Arnold Gesell, who received the doctorate from Clark in 1906. That Gesell subsequently chose to become a medical doctor and to marry his investigations of children more closely to pediatrics than to education suggests the degree to which the continuing low status of education directed not only Hall, but also his students toward other fields. That aside, having never been fully embraced by the first generation of professional psychologists, child study rather quickly migrated to the periphery of the emerging scholarly community in education. When the NEA moved explicitly away from child study, it did so in acknowledgment of this. On the nomination of Leonard P. Ayres of the Russell Sage Foundation, a resolution was passed in 1911, stating: "WHEREAS, In the opinion of the membership of the Department of Child Study of the National Education Association, the work and interests of this department have outgrown the scope and intent of the term 'child study' and have become centered upon problems for the mental and physical hygiene of children; be it *Resolved,* That . . . the name of this department [be changed] . . . to the 'Department of Child Hygiene.'"[74]

Just as the earlier creation of the Department of Child Study had reflected the waning authority of W. T. Harris's generation, now the creation of the Department of Child Hygiene signified the rise to prominence of a new generation, one that included, among others, three of G. Stanley

Hall's most successful students, Henry Goddard, Lewis Terman, and Arnold Gesell, as well as at least one psychologist who had studied with James, Edward L. Thorndike. Beyond that, the name change suggested the degree to which links between psychology and education would be more likely to result in practical applications than in continuing exploration. Markets for educational products, especially tests, were expanding in 1911 and would continue to do so throughout the century. As schooling was opened to more and more people, for greater lengths of time, in relation to multiplying subjects of study, opportunities not only to gain financial profits but also to engage in "service" often short-circuited a continuing quest for basic knowledge about education. Just as Hall and James had responded to the opportunity structures of their world, so would successive generations of psychologists who were—reluctantly or otherwise—associated with education.

CHAPTER TWO

Specialization and Isolation: Education Research Becomes a Profession

Unlike his teacher G. Stanley Hall and his admiring fellow philosopher William James, John Dewey willingly embraced the study of education. Indeed, when Dewey left the University of Michigan in 1894 to become chair of the Department of Philosophy at the newly opened University of Chicago, he requested that the department also become home to the university's work in pedagogy. At the time, few people had given much thought to how the scientific study of education should proceed. Of course, a number of European philosophers, including G. W. F. Hegel, Johann Pestalozzi, Friedrick Froebel, and Johann Friedrich Herbart, had developed systems of ideas about the purposes of education and the practices that should follow from those. In addition, G. Stanley Hall was developing an approach to child study at Clark, and William H. Payne had begun teaching and writing about the "scientific" aspect of education while serving as the professor of the science and art of teaching at the University of Michigan between 1879 and 1887. More and more American universities were beginning to develop offerings in education.

Although it was only for three years, Dewey and Payne overlapped at the University of Michigan, Dewey arriving there fresh from graduate study at Hopkins in 1884 and Payne leaving in 1887 to become chancellor of the University of Nashville (Vanderbilt today) and president of the Peabody Normal School. However briefly, the two men worked closely together, visiting Michigan schools to ensure their suitability as preparatory institutions for the university and collaborating in the founding of the Michigan Schoolmaster's Club. In light of the close acquaintance, it is not surprising that Payne's belief in the importance of linking psychology, philosophy, and education appears to have influenced Dewey's views. Psychology according to Payne "stands in the same relation to teaching that anatomy does to medicine. The teacher's art is addressed to [the] mind, and if this art is to be rational, if it is to be administered in the scientific or professional spirit, for these are usually identical, the teacher should know much of the philosophy of spirit."[1]

Starting with ideas for which he was indebted to Payne, during the ten years he spent at Chicago, Dewey developed an approach to educational study that was unusual and important. Unlike his approach to philosophy, however, Dewey's approach to educational study was quickly eclipsed when, owing to a misunderstanding with President William Rainey Harper, Dewey resigned from the University of Chicago in 1904. Thanks to profound differences in their personalities, social orientations, and thinking, Charles Hubbard Judd quickly got rid of Dewey's approach when, in 1909, he followed Dewey as chair of education at Chicago. What is more, at Teachers College, which was at the time the trendsetting institution, the very different approach developed by Edward L. Thorndike became far more influential than that associated with Dewey. Frequently claimed to have been the father of progressive education and otherwise to have had a profound impact on American education, Dewey may have inspired all sorts of people to do all sorts of things as a result of his ideas, but few among those who claimed him as their inspiration were true disciples, and few examples of "Deweyan education" were truly or accurately Deweyan. To suggest that Dewey has served as something of a cultural icon, alternatively praised and damned by thinkers on both the right and the left, might capture his place in the history of education more accurately than to say he was important as a reformer. Certainly, his ideas about a science of education did not create a template for educational study.

Dewey's thinking about educational science flowered for ten years and then failed to take root partly as a result of the circumstances of his life. In addition, because his departure from the University of Chicago was precipitous, he was never able to evaluate what had been accomplished at the Laboratory School there, which might have provided a continuing research agenda.[2] Beyond the role of coincidence and chance, however, there was a more general matter. As institutions of higher education grew in size and in number, they came to encompass many of the knowledge-generating and -transmitting activities that had once gone on in autonomous scientific, cultural, and professional societies. As this happened, fields of study multiplied in number and narrowed in scope. Psychology separated from philosophy and then proceeded to fragment into further specialties, for example, education psychology, genetic psychology, and industrial psychology. Once conceived as a unified whole, social science evolved into the discrete social sciences. As this occurred, mastery of a special field came to be equated with professional commitment.

Dewey's ideas were not well aligned with the increasing specialization and professionalization so evident in the worlds of learning of the early twentieth century. By contrast, those of Thorndike and Judd fit well within the emerging social structures of knowledge and meshed easily with widely held beliefs and values that Dewey warred against, including what he would have called unreconstructed individualism and competition. For all these reasons, Dewey's conception of a science of education failed to thrive.

John Dewey's Youth and Early Career

Dewey was born on October 20, 1859, in Burlington, Vermont. His father, Archibald Sprague Dewey, was a prosperous grocer and tobacconist of somewhat boisterous humor. He advertised his store with the slogan "Hams and Cigars—Smoked and Unsmoked." Dewey's mother, Lucina Rich Dewey, was twenty years younger than her husband and very different in temperament. Deeply evangelical and strict with John and his two younger brothers, though also affectionate, Lucina often asked John if he was "right with Jesus." When John was eleven and it came time for him to join the local Congregational church, it was his mother who wrote the petition, saying: "I think I love Christ and want to obey him." [3]

Dewey had a rather idyllic childhood in Burlington, roaming the woods with his brothers and friends and attending the local schools. At fifteen, he entered the University of Vermont, an institution with a few hundred students and eight faculty members. His four years there divide into an initial two, which he spent following the classical curriculum of Greek, Latin, ancient history, analytical geometry, and calculus and reading conventionally, and the final two, when an introduction to evolutionary ideas and to philosophy sparked Dewey's thinking and set him to serious reading and study. This continued after his graduation in 1879, which was followed by a year of looking for a teaching job and then two years of employment at the high school in Oil City, Pennsylvania.

During the time Dewey lived in Pennsylvania, he had two formative experiences. The first was a religious epiphany, during which he claimed to have found an answer to the question "whether he really meant business when he prayed." As he later described it to Max Eastman, foreshortening his slow move away from formal religion, "There was no vision . . . just a supremely blissful feeling that his worries were over." He told

Eastman: "I've never had any doubts since then, nor any beliefs."[4] The second experience encouraged his subsequent study of philosophy. In the fall of 1881, after Dewey returned to Vermont to teach in a small academy there, W. T. Harris, Hall's adversary who edited the *Journal of Speculative Philosophy,* accepted an essay Dewey had written entitled "The Metaphysical Assumptions of Materialism." Encouraged by this success and by Harris's acceptance of a second article on "The Pantheism of Spinoza," as well as by long conversations with H. A. P. Torrey, who had been his philosophy teacher at the University of Vermont, Dewey decided to apply to Johns Hopkins for graduate study. Accepted without a fellowship, Dewey borrowed money from an aunt and set off for Baltimore in the fall of 1882.

At Hopkins, Dewey encountered G. Stanley Hall. Although he subsequently told his wife that "Hall threatened harm to our culture with his combination of crude fact & edifying piety," Dewey's initial exposure to psychology was through work with Hall.[5] Owing to Hall's meanness, however, Dewey turned to philosopher George Sylvester Morris, an idealist who encouraged his close reading of Kant and Hegel. He also studied with some of Hopkins's leading social scientists, notably Richard T. Ely and Herbert Baxter Addams. Upon graduation, Dewey followed Morris to Michigan, where the older philosopher had found a home when Hall, rather than Morris, had been awarded the Hopkins professorship in 1884.

Not quite twenty-five when he went to Michigan, Dewey was a stereotypically shy and bookish young professor. Indeed, when President Daniel Coit Gilman had said good-bye to him after his graduation from Hopkins, Dewey's earnestness had been so pronounced that Gilman apparently felt compelled to tell him: "Don't be so bookish; don't live such a secluded life; get out and see people."[6] Heeding Gilman's advice, Dewey had met many people, including Harriet Alice Chipman, a Michigan undergraduate, who was enrolled in one of his philosophy courses. The two got to know one another around the dining table of the rooming house where they both lived. They were married on July 28, 1886. Bright, forceful, and socially committed, Alice was as rooted in the immediate social side of things as John was tangled in intellectual abstractions. In fact, she impressed people as infectiously engaged by life. "She helps me to think of life, real activities, more than the subjectivities of my own communings with self," George Herbert Mead's wife, Helen Castle Mead, wrote in 1893.[7] "She is one of the most refreshing persons I have come in contact with. A mind rich and varied—with wide experience—

and finding the world constantly entertaining and interesting," another acquaintance observed.[8] According to one of the Deweys' daughters, Alice was "largely responsible for the early widening of Dewey's philosophic interests from the commentative and classical to the field of contemporary life."[9] Dewey himself merely said that his wife had put "guts and stuffing" into his thought.[10]

Encouraged by his wife, Dewey began to involve himself in public questions, in the process joining with many others of his generation in transferring the religious aspirations of his evangelical Protestant upbringing to the contemporary social situation in which he lived. His initial efforts to enact his political beliefs resulted in at least one fiasco. Establishing a brief alliance with eccentric journalist Franklin Ford and his brother Corydon, Dewey took part in plans to publish a newspaper, *Thought News,* that was to distinguish itself from other papers by selling "the truth." The scheme was a disaster, and it brought the young philosopher considerable ridicule in the Michigan press. Testifying to his naivete in judging people—according to one biographer, Dewey "had a lifelong weakness for quacks"—the incident also revealed his growing wish to find practical, socially progressive outlets for his professional philosophical skills.[11] While still at Michigan, Dewey wrote: "The philosopher, even he, is a social being, and works out his ideas by expressing them, by trying them on others, by making them influence the actions of others."[12] Having been a graduate student at Hopkins when the possibilities of empirical, hypothesis-testing science were still novel and electrically exciting, when, in Josiah Royce's words, "one longed to be a doer of the word, and not a hearer only, a creator of his own infinitesimal fraction of a product," Dewey was eager for chances to merge thought and action.[13] After the *Thought News* disaster, he increasingly turned to education with that in mind.

In part, too, of course, Dewey's movement toward education was a result of his responsibilities as a University of Michigan faculty member. Because Michigan was a state university and part of the state system of public schooling, its faculty was responsible for oversight of academic standards at the secondary level. In consequence, professors like Dewey were expected to visit local schools. Recalling the experience, Dewey claimed that the visits had had "a great influence in impressing upon me the significance of a democratic system of public education."[14] According to George Dykhuisen, one of Dewey's early biographers, the experience "sent Dewey in search of an educational theory which would reconcile the demands of education, psychology, and philosophy."[15] All

45

this notwithstanding, one must still recall that Dewey's interest in education was not primarily theoretical and did not have merely intellectual origins. George Herbert Mead, the philosopher who became one of Dewey's closest friends and colleagues at this time, once stated that "education was a problem that came to him with his children and that engrossed not only him but Mrs. Dewey."[16]

After ten years at the University of Michigan (with one year at Minnesota), Dewey was invited to join the faculty of the University of Chicago. Dewey was drawn to Chicago by its emphasis on research. Established in 1890 and opened in 1892, the University of Chicago was what classicist Paul Shorey described as "a college made to order . . . a university by enchantment."[17] President Harper was determined to recruit scholars who were "in love with learning, with a passion for research," and who were, at the same time, as committed to public service as he himself was.[18] Although Dewey certainly fit that mold, he found a place within Harper's grand plans more by default than by acclamation. Having been spurned by at least three more-established and better-known philosophers, Harper invited Dewey on the recommendation of Dewey's former junior colleague at the University of Michigan, James H. Tufts. "He is well known on both sides of the Atlantic for his [scholarly] activity," Tufts told Harper. Asserting that Dewey would be "an effective organizer of departmental work," as well as a good teacher, Tufts also noted that "as a man he is simple, modest, utterly devoid of any affectation or self-consciousness, and makes many friends and no enemies. He is . . . actively interested in practical ethical activity and is a valued friend of . . . Hull House."[19]

Accepting Tuft's nomination, Harper offered Dewey the chairmanship of the Department of Philosophy, but refused to pay him the $5,000 a year salary Dewey claimed his family would need "for living as we should want to live (and as the University would want us to live) in Chicago."[20] Disappointed about that, Dewey was nevertheless pleased that Harper was willing to allow him to subsume the university's work in education under the wing of the Philosophy Department. At a time of increasing academic specialization, this allowed Dewey and his colleagues simultaneously to pursue questions in three fields—philosophy, psychology, and education—that elsewhere were becoming more and more distinct. An unusual opportunity, this had great significance for the development of Dewey's thought.

Like Hall and others among the nation's early psychologists, Dewey had turned to psychology in the hope that, by doing so, he could help move philosophy from "general theorizing" to "an experimental science."[21] Whether and how philosophy could develop a new authority through science or itself become a science was a driving question for Dewey as well as for many of his peers.[22] As Hall, following William James, had initially done, many early psychologists sought a new basis for understanding mental functioning in physiology, often relying on laboratory experiments with animals. The hope was that the findings of this research could eventually be applied to practical problems, including those of education. By contrast, Dewey sought a laboratory in education. This aspiration made him highly unusual among his professional peers.

Dewey at the Laboratory School

Writing to Alice soon after he arrived in Chicago, Dewey lamented all the different educational theories being bandied about. Although he found merit in some of the ideas then in vogue in educational circles—agreeing with the Hegelians, for example, that education required "effort" and also agreeing with their opponents, the Herbartians, who claimed that education instead required "interest"—Dewey still complained that "general theorizing" was not "very edifying when our own children can't get even a poor school to go to." Feeling frustrated that talk about education was more abstract than concretely illuminating, Dewey confessed to his wife that he was "in a fair way to become an educational crank; I sometimes think I will drop teaching phil[osophy]—directly, & teach it via *pedagogy*." After all, he went on to explain, "the school is the one form of social life which is abstracted & under control—which is directly experimental."[23]

With that in mind—and to create a school to which he and his wife might send their own children—Dewey established an experimental school at the University of Chicago. It opened in January 1896 with an enrollment of sixteen children and two teachers. It reached its maximum size in 1902, with a student enrollment of 140 and a faculty of 23, supplemented by 10 graduate students. Throughout its existence, John Dewey served as its director.

The curricular focus of the Dewey School, as it was often called, was "occupations" rather than "studies." According to Dewey, this was because "the child comes to school to *do*; to cook, to sew, to work with wood and tools in simple constructive acts; within and about these acts cluster the studies—writing, reading, arithmetic, etc. Nature study, sewing, and manual training . . . are not introduced as some studies among others, but as the child's activities, his regular occupations."[24] Intended to offer the child a "simplified social life" that would enable him "to become gradually acquainted with the structure, materials, and modes of operation of the larger community," the school sought to allow each student "individually to express himself through these lines of conduct, and thus [to] attain control of his own powers."[25] Having arrived in Chicago when the city was still in the throes of the Pullman Strike, Dewey and his colleagues were deeply concerned about growing social divisions in American society. As demonstrated by the emphasis he placed on occupations and community life, they believed these could perhaps be lessened and conflict avoided through acceptance of "producerist" ideals, which valued skill in work more than the accumulation of wealth.[26]

Ambitious in prospect, the school was said to be an exciting place. Visitors reported in amazement that students talked seriously to one another about the problems in which they were engaged and that they seemed able to work on their own, without much adult supervision. Despite that, in its first years, the school was also said to be somewhat chaotic. In consequence, after the first few years, it was reorganized according to a departmental plan. This helped ensure that it would run "more systematically and definitely—free from a certain looseness of ends and edges," Dewey explained.[27] Along with Alice Dewey, the person most responsible for the reorganization was Ella Flagg Young, a longtime Chicago schoolteacher and administrator, who studied and worked with Dewey from 1895 until 1904 and who became the supervisor of instruction at the Laboratory School in 1899. Tough, savvy, articulate, and deeply intellectual, Young had a great deal of hands-on experience to offer Dewey and for a time was one of his most important teachers.[28]

While working closely with Young and others at the Lab School (the term "laboratory school" having been initially applied to the Dewey School by Young), Dewey began to articulate a distinctive view of educational study, which was built around three essential points.[29] First, Dewey believed that to be experimental, educational study had to be conducted in a school, a naturalistic setting. Such a school "does not aim to be impractical," Dewey explained in 1896, but its purpose was neither teacher training nor the direct and immediate improvement of school methods. Practice schools were to fulfill the first of those functions, and by demonstrating new curricula and techniques, model schools were to take care of the second. By contrast, the special function of a laboratory school was "to create new standards and ideals and thus to lead to a gradual change in conditions."[30] Without such a laboratory school, Dewey told President Harper, "the theoretical work [in education] partakes of the nature of a farce and imposture—it is like professing to give thorough training in a science and then neglecting to provide a laboratory for faculty and students to work in."[31] Echoing this point in a talk to the University of Chicago Pedagogy Club soon after the Laboratory School was established, Dewey explained that such a school should bear "the same relation to the work in pedagogy that a laboratory bears to biology, physics, or chemistry." Like a chemistry laboratory in a university that was devoted to "chemical truth" as opposed to "work in dyes or drugs of direct commercial import," a laboratory school was to focus on "scientific theory of the practical organization of educational forces."[32]

Undertaken in a laboratory setting, educational study, Dewey also believed, should both advance and link scientific and social innovation. On the scientific side, this involved trying out new ideas about teaching, learning, and child development. On the social side, it required finding ways to overcome the divisions that had emerged between families and schools, nature and daily life, and, most important, different classes of people, especially those classified as "cultured" and as "workers."[33] Keenly troubled by the increasing inequalities of American society, Dewey believed that pedagogies powerful enough to socialize and liberate the potential of all children had to be discovered if theoretical claims to equality were to have meaning in the modern world.

Finally, Dewey was convinced that educational inquiry should be directed toward finding ways to increase educational efficiency via the creation of a more cohesive, interrelated social system, in which teaching and learning would go on within and across a variety of institutions, and not be considered as narrowly defined, exclusive school functions. "The great problem in education on the administrative side is to secure the unity of the whole," Dewey wrote in *The School and Society.*[34] He meant that isolation between levels and types of schooling and between schools and other social institutions should be reduced. This would increase efficiency, he noted, by allowing children to utilize in school what they had learned in other institutions, especially the family, and by enabling the school to enliven its activities through close contact with the business, academic, cultural, and natural worlds. If the special function of the university was to generate new knowledge, that knowledge, Dewey reasoned, rather than old, outdated knowledge, should be rapidly made available to schoolchildren; similarly, if, say, mathematical skills were of special importance in the business world, that realm of application should be tapped to add interest to school instruction.

By testing the value of scientific discoveries in the social microcosm of an experimental school, Dewey thus hoped to discover ways to promote harmony and mutuality between and among different disciplines, institutions, and groups of people. As he explained in his 1899 presidential address to the American Psychological Association, he genuinely believed that "educational science is first of all a social science."[35] It was a means to discover "the *conditions* which secure intellectual and moral progress and power," a description Dewey claimed to have adopted from Ella Flagg Young.[36] If Dewey's belief in direct school experimentation as opposed to laboratory experimentation followed by school application made him unusual among university scholars beginning to study education, so did his insistence on the social side of education. While most of his peers now looked to psychology as the basis for research in education, Dewey looked to psychology modified by insights derived from philosophy and the social sciences. Instead of approaching education as a means for training inborn capacities, Dewey approached education as a means for nurturing new social capacities, especially the skills, orientations, and knowledge necessary to building and sustaining a democratic community.

Dewey's social view of education fit better with a distributed, collaborative approach to educational study than with a narrowly professional one. For Dewey, the study of education necessitated a partnership between and among many different people—a wide range of scholars and citizens as well as teachers, administrators, and parents; it could not be advanced through a hierarchy that differentiated among scholars, practitioners, and parents.

In important ways, this belief had grown out of Dewey's daily engagement in the life of a school, which had led him to become deeply interested in the conditions under which teachers worked. Unwilling to acquiesce in the increasingly common belief that an educational researcher should be "the middleman between the psychologist and the educational practitioner," Dewey became more and more convinced that educational scholarship and educational practice should be fused not merely in the same institution, but also in each and every person who worked in a school.[37] Viewing "science" as the "freed activity of mind," he went so far as to argue in 1903 that progress in education depended on getting rid of the bureaucratic structures that prevented teachers from reflecting on their work.[38] Instead of having "one expert dictating educational methods and subject-matter to a body of passive, recipient teachers," Dewey argued for "the adoption of intellectual initiative, discussion, and decision throughout the entire school corps." Freedom combined with intellectual cooperation provided a better way to ensure effective teaching than "close supervision," he maintained.[39]

At a time when the elaboration of administrative functions was generally seen as "progressive," Dewey's experience led him to oppose the growth of central supervisory personnel in the schools. Beyond that, in the face of arguments concerning the greater need for training among high school teachers, he insisted that primary teachers needed the same freedom and, presumably, therefore the same training. The implication of Dewey's position, which was best expressed in an essay entitled "Democracy in Education" (1903), was that education could become a science only if and when schools as they existed were transformed into communities built on freedom of action and freedom of thought. His position was very much at odds with the hierarchy then developing among educational institutions, a hierarchy in which mostly male university scholars of education would generate the knowledge needed by mostly male school administrators, who would, in turn, be responsible for dictating and supervising the instructional methods to be used by teachers in schools, especially the mostly female teachers involved at the elementary levels.

A Creative Community: The Social Sources of Dewey's Thought

Though out of step with many of his national professional peers, throughout his years in Chicago, Dewey lived and worked within an extraordinary community of close acquaintances who understood, shared, supported, and helped further develop his ideas. It is striking, for example, to realize the degree to which Dewey's ideas were reflected in and, in turn, shaped by those of Ella Flagg Young. In 1901, Young wrote a dissertation under Dewey's supervision that was entitled *Isolation in the School*. Following Dewey, it adopted some Herbartian ideas, notably the idea that interest is critical to education, while ignoring others, especially the Herbartian argument that the building up of ideas could be measured mathematically. If Young's dissertation supported Dewey's claim to have helped her find a more systematic way of thinking, his arguments against centralization and in favor of cultivating the intellects of all teachers derived from her. Stated most directly in an essay he titled "Democracy in Education," which was written while Dewey was working closely with Young, those ideas were given much less emphasis in his writings once he and Young lost contact.[40] "Upon the whole, the forces that have influenced me have come from persons and situations more than from books," Dewey once said, and his relationship with Young certainly verified the observation.[41]

As head of a new department in a university that had opened its doors only two years before his arrival, Dewey had been able to recruit his own colleagues, and the five men he had selected had proven to be "a congenial group."[42] All had been former colleagues or students of his. George Herbert Mead and James H. Tufts had been on the Michigan faculty with him, Tufts leaving before Dewey and Mead, after. James R. Angell had been a graduate student in psychology at Michigan, and Addison W. Moore and Edward Scribner Ames were graduate students in the new Chicago department before gaining faculty rank. "There was . . . no thought . . . of building up what William James was later to dignify . . . [as] a 'Chicago School' of Philosophy," Tufts maintained, though, in retrospect, it is not at all surprising that such a school did emerge.[43] Compatible, but not identical intellectually, the work of the Chicago philosophers was focused by what Tufts described as "the powerful analytic mind of Professor Dewey," who was reported to have been "a rarely stimulating colleague and chief."[44]

Thus surrounded by departmental colleagues who were at once sufficiently different and like-minded to think in counterpoint to him, Dewey was especially influenced by George Herbert Mead. Of relatively similar temperament and background, and only three years apart in age, the two had established a relationship of respect, affection, and trust while working together in Ann Arbor. Mead later claimed that Dewey was "the philosopher of America," while Dewey, for his part, said that Mead possessed "the most original mind in philosophy in America of the last generation."[45] As Mead's chief, Dewey concerned himself constantly with Mead's professional advancement. Writing to his wife, Mead reported, for example, that "Mr. Dewey has been at the President about Jimmie Angell's and my advancement. His nibs stuck first at the fact that we have no Ph.D's. Mr. Dewey spoke lightly of the honor and the President was pained at the lack of feeling for the degree—Well, said Mr. D., they might take an hour off someday and take it. And the President was shocked at Mr. D's levity."[46] Reveling in Dewey irreverence, Mead was hinting at the spontaneity, candor, and humor the two could express to each other, despite a tendency to great reticence in public. Not coincidentally, both were reported to have been so shy and stiff in the classroom that they would stare at the ceiling while speaking their thoughts in nonstop monotones. However that may have been, Dewey's efforts on Mead's behalf did not go unmatched. Mead served as an indispensable ally in the Laboratory School. Along with the Dewey children, the Mead children were enrolled there, and Mead worked tirelessly as a fund-raiser for the school. Beyond that, it was thanks to Mead and his wife that Dewey's lectures to the parents of the Lab School were subsequently edited and published as *The School and Society.*

The personal connection that joined Dewey and Mead served as a conduit for the wholesale transfer of ideas. From Dewey, Mead gained a better sense of the social significance of psychological study, which was profoundly liberating to him, since he, no less than Dewey, remained Protestant and evangelical in felt obligation to the world even as he moved away from the formal religiosity of his youth. From Dewey's study of the reflex arc (1894), Mead also learned the importance of approaching psychology in terms of behavioral units or "acts" rather than as discrete stimuli and responses. Able, as a result, to conceive of behavior holistically, Mead could perceive that relationships between an individual's behavior and his or her environment were dynamic, reciprocal, and interactive. From there, it was but a relatively short step to understanding the origins of the self and of thought as social, formulations that Dewey, in turn, accepted from Mead without modification or elaboration and, according to his daughter, "made . . . a part of his subsequent philosophy."[47]

Helped, encouraged, and stimulated by Mead and surrounded by a circle of sympathetic and devoted departmental colleagues, Dewey also engaged in very productive exchange about education with other University of Chicago scholars, especially, but not exclusively, the so-called "Big Four" of the Chicago Sociology Department, Albion W. Small, Charles R. Henderson, George E. Vincent, and W. I. Thomas.

Like Dewey, the early Chicago sociologists were charting a new field of university study. Although William Graham Sumner had begun teaching sociology at Yale in 1876, sociology did not become well established in universities until the 1890s, and even then it was often joined to one of the other social sciences, most commonly anthropology or political science. Still tinged with the social meliorism so essential to its origins, early Chicago sociology resembled work proceeding at other universities in that it was concerned with formulating generalizations about social problems and society. This distinguished it from sociology as carried out at settlement houses like Hull House, where greater attention was placed on reform and where, not coincidentally, women were more likely to hold leadership positions. More than at many universities, however, sociologists at Chicago grounded efforts to develop theory in empirical investigations. In this way, early Chicago sociology resembled Dewey's approach to educational study.[48]

The Chicago sociologists were deeply interested in education and, hardly by chance, given their approach to sociology, were also inclined to see it in ways that were compatible with Dewey's views. Certainly that was evident in Albion Small's 1897 essay, "Some Demands of Sociology upon Pedagogy." "The prime problem of education, as the sociologist views it," Small argued, "is how to promote the adaptation of the individual to the social conditions, natural and artificial, within which individuals live, and move, and have their being." Careful to state that he did not wish to trespass into the domain of "pedagogical technology," which, he said, involved questions having to do with the relative importance and proper sequence of action and information in education, Small acknowledged the increasing need for professional courtesies across specialized fields of university work. And yet he was still willing to set forth questions for education research.[49]

Small's essay presented ideas that were echoed in subsequent writings by Dewey, which suggests that Small's thought was yet another stimulus for Dewey's. So was that of biologist Jacques Loeb, who joined the Chicago faculty in 1891. To claim, as Philip J. Pauly has, that "Loeb was the single most important model for Dewey's image of the scientific inquiry in the 1890s" is to ignore the variety of mutually reinforcing models Dewey found within the creative community the University of Chicago provided him.[50] However, there is no doubt that Loeb and Dewey were close friends, that their wives and children were pals, and that there was lively and significant interchange between them. In addition, the roster of Lab School advisors included some of the university's most prominent scholars—botanists Thomas C. Chamberlain and John M. Coulter, zoologist Charles O. Whitman, anthropologist Frederick Starr, geographer Rollin D. Salisbury, and ecologist Henry C. Cowles, among them—and Dewey was in frequent conversation with them all.[51] However great Dewey's originality of mind, part of his brilliance derived from a capacity for systematizing and synthesizing what was "in the air."

The University of Chicago during its early years was an institution whose boundaries were still highly permeable. This would become less true as professionalization, standardization, and bureaucracy were translated into clear, often hierarchical definitions of institutional function—put otherwise, as universities like Chicago came to be seen as preeminent sources of expertise different from once-kindred centers of social inquiry and cultural dissemination. Not coincidentally, however, this was a development that followed Dewey's Chicago years. Indeed, some of the relationships that most influenced his thinking about education bridged the university's walls. Dewey's friendship with Jane Addams, which ranked in import for him with his relationship with Mead, is a well-known example.

Having had contact with Addams and Hull House before moving to the University of Chicago, Dewey took part in settlement clubs and classes on a regular basis and joined Hull House's first board of directors when the settlement was incorporated in 1896. According to Dewey's daughter, who was named after both Jane Addams and Addams's close friend Mary Rozet Smith, Dewey's understanding of "democracy as a guiding force in education took on both a sharper and deeper meaning because of Hull House and Jane Addams."[52] Addams understood democracy as a matter of lived social relationships based upon mutual regard across boundaries of race, class, and gender. She exemplified this in her life at Hull House and explained it in a variety of writings, including *Democracy and Social Ethics* (1902), which Dewey used as a teaching text in a course in which he invited Addams to lead class sessions with him.[53] Described by Chicago political scientist Charles Merriam as "a great professor without a university chair, a great statesman without a portfolio, a guiding woman in a man-made world," Addams no less than Dewey was searching for ways to transform social relations and establish patterns of thinking so that increasing numbers of people, from increasing numbers of cultural traditions, could live together in crowded, urban conditions and still maintain a sense of harmony, order, beauty, and progress.[54]

Despite the extraordinarily rich personal and professional life he found within his extended circle of colleagues at the University of Chicago and Hull House, Dewey abruptly resigned from the university in April 1904. His action resulted from complicated administrative problems involving the merger of the Dewey School with a neighboring school earlier established by Francis W. Parker and a series of misunderstandings between Dewey and President Harper concerning Alice Dewey's role in the Lab School. With the help of his former fellow graduate student James McKeen Cattell, Dewey was able to secure a new appointment in the Philosophy Department at Columbia, where he remained until his retirement in 1939.

Even though Dewey achieved increasing fame and continuing intellectual productivity after 1904, his rapid departure from Chicago extracted a very high price. Although he would continue to write about education and to be active in educational organizations and causes for the rest of his life, his days of direct experimentation in education came to an end in 1904. Not surprisingly, most of his subsequent educational writings, including most notably *Democracy and Education,* his magnum opus published in 1916, were based on insights derived from work in the Chicago Lab School.[55]

Cut off from daily contact with his Chicago colleagues and embittered toward the university where for a time he had found such great intellectual excitement, Dewey never engaged in what his friend Harold Rugg described as "a systematic and critical appraisal" of what had been accomplished in the Laboratory School. This was unfortunate for many reasons, not least because it limited the degree to which his conception of educational inquiry could take hold. If Dewey had evaluated the Laboratory School, he might have commented further on the difficult problem of transforming experiments in an unusual school, with an unusual clientele (most of the students were faculty children), into common, public school practice. While still in Chicago, he often described laboratory schools as similar to experiment stations that could help guide education reform by translating into practice and thereby testing new approaches to organizing school learning. He also frequently stated that he believed that school reform was dependent on general changes in public opinion because these shaped the actions of school boards, superintendents, and teachers. Although he would reiterate the latter point in *Individualism Old and New* (1930) and *Liberalism and Social Action* (1936), he never indicated how the "wider change" was to be encouraged, let alone assured, and he never spelled out the means by which laboratory schools were to be linked to other institutions.[56] Instead of pressing forward with his thinking along these lines, Dewey, as Harold Rugg observed, now turned from "educational reconstruction to 'reconstruction in philosophy.'"[57] Even though he would occasionally lecture at Teachers College, after 1904 Dewey did not make the study of education a central, daily part of his life.

Edward L. Thorndike: "Conquering the New World of Pedagogy"

As things turned out, Dewey left Chicago for Columbia in the same year that Edward L. Thorndike published *An Introduction to the Theory of Mental and Social Measurements* (1904), which helped popularize a conception of educational study that was at odds with Dewey's approach. Unlike Dewey, Thorndike favored the separation of philosophy and psychology. Despite considerable disdain for educators and an extremely imperialistic view of psychology, which he thought supreme for studying and controlling human affairs, Thorndike formulated ideas that were also more suited to translation into formulas for educational practice. A conservative person whose prose was clear, to the point, humorless, and colorless, Thorndike was about as different from Dewey as two men could be.

Known as the "father of the measurement movement," Thorndike believed, as he put it some years later, that "whatever exists at all exists in some amount. To know it thoroughly involves knowing its quantity as well as its quality."[58] Like some other psychologists (including his fellow behaviorist John B. Watson) who saw the mind as nothing more than a physiological entity, Thorndike was reported to have exclaimed: "I just cannot understand Dewey!"[59] Beginning in 1904, the two men worked in relatively close geographic proximity, Dewey in the Department of Philosophy at Columbia and Thorndike at Teachers College; they had close friends in common, including James McKeen Cattell, who had been one of Thorndike's teachers and was Dewey's old friend; and they agreed on some matters, not least the incompetence of G. Stanley Hall, whom Thorndike once described as "a mad man," whose study of *Adolescence* (1904) was "chock full of errors, masturbation and Jesus."[60] Despite all that, the gulf between the two men was vast, Dewey often criticizing the kinds of studies Thorndike engaged in (though, to my knowledge, never commenting directly on Thorndike himself) and Thorndike, for his part, always insisting that, at best, Dewey's educational writings were primitive. "What physical science has to do in comparison with the cosmologies of the early philosophers," Thorndike announced in 1911, "the science of education has to do in comparison with the first generalizations of Herbart, Spencer, or Dewey."[61] More than the post-Chicago reorientation of Dewey's activities, Thorndike's rise to prominence made it unlikely that educational scholarship would develop along the lines Dewey had advocated.

Fifteen years younger than Dewey, Thorndike had graduated from Wesleyan in 1895 and had then gone on to Harvard to study English literature. While at Wesleyan he had read William James's *Principles of Psychology* (1890), which he had found "stimulating, more so than any book that I had read before, and possibly more so than any read since."[62] In consequence, he had enrolled in a course with James, which had turned him from English literature to psychology and had prompted his transfer to Columbia University. At the time, Columbia was the leading institution in developing experimental psychology, which was important to a young man who had already begun to study the intelligence of young chicks by observing changes in their behavior and their apparent capacity to learn. More important to Thorndike, at Harvard, psychology was still regarded as a branch of philosophy, and as Thorndike recalled, "under no circumstances, probably, could I have been able or willing to make philosophy my business."[63]

As a doctoral student at Columbia, Thorndike was able to cultivate what he later described as his penchant for "factual material [which] seems to benefit me more than what is commonly called discussion and criticism."[64] He had studied statistics with anthropologist Franz Boas, worked closely with James McKeen Cattell, and written a dissertation on animal intelligence. Upon completion of his doctorate, Thorndike had taught for a year at the College for Women of Western Reserve University in Cleveland, Ohio, and had then joined the faculty of Teachers College in 1899. As he was well aware, education offered a growing field of application for psychologists. "In the United States more than one hundred and fifty million dollars, collected by enforced taxation, is spent annually on public schools in the attempt to 'change human natures,'" his mentor, James McKeen Cattell, had reminded his colleagues in the American Psychological Association in 1895.[65] This augured a large opportunity for what Cattell, avoiding the less prestigious term "applied psychology," called "experimental psychology." Having missed out on an appointment at the New York University School of Education, which went instead to his rival and former Wesleyan acquaintance Charles Hubbard Judd, and having chosen Western Reserve because the only alternative was the Wisconsin State Normal School at Oshkosh, Thorndike was eager to return to New York. As he told his future wife, he also saw the opportunity at Teachers College as auspicious, since he expected to enjoy "conquering the new world of pedagogy."[66]

To do that, Thorndike quickly set about developing a psychology that could, he hoped, be of direct use to educators. Focusing on learning, defined as making connections between stimuli and responses, he called attention to the importance of individual differences based on inherited traits and characteristics and argued that these largely determined one's capacity to make connections—put otherwise, to learn. "What anyone becomes by education," Thorndike maintained, "depends on what he is by nature."[67]

Having thus clarified the limits of education, Thorndike identified the ways in which connections were made, emphasizing three laws: the "law of readiness," which held that it was pleasurable to make a connection when "a conduction unit" was ready to do so; the "law of exercise," which posited that after a connection was made, it was likely to be made again in a similar situation unless a great deal of time elapsed in between;

and the "law of effect," which said that when a connection was rewarded, it was strengthened.[68] This suggested that drill was meaningless in education, since only rewards could enhance learning. In addition, Thorndike's early work showed that special training in, say, Latin or the natural sciences had little influence on the general development of one's mental capacities, as manifested, for example, in one's powers of reasoning or of observation. That there was no scientific basis for what had been commonly called "transfer of training" thus also became a hallmark of the new "educational psychology" Thorndike created during his first years at Teachers College.[69]

Along with these substantive psychological findings, Thorndike called attention to the importance of basing educational studies on controlled experimentation and precise quantitative measurements. Because his conception of educational psychology was built around identifying individual mental traits and understanding how those changed in response to various stimuli, he was far more interested in tests of simple variables than he was in observation within naturalistic settings. He also thought that what he called "direct experiment" was more important.[70] During his first year at Teachers College, Thorndike had spent considerable time in schools, but having found this to be a "bore" and unnecessary for the kind of investigations he wanted to do, he subsequently urged his students not to waste their time in school visits except to administer some test or experimental device.[71] It was much more important, he thought, to advance one's competence in statistics. "To have in education the real benefits of quantitative science," he observed, "we must spend arduous years in devising, testing, and standardizing units of measurement, in searching for convenient arbitrary zero-points, and eventually for . . . the errors of measurement."[72]

Thorndike favored precise, numerical measurements of anything and everything relevant to education—mental capacities, changes in behavior, and even the aims of education. Writing in 1905, he explained: "We are no longer satisfied with vague arguments about what this or that system of administration or method of teaching does, but demand exact measures of the achievement of any system or method or person."[73] Unlike many of his peers, however, Thorndike was not interested in the collection of numbers as an end in itself or even for the fulfillment of censuslike purposes. Rather, he was concerned with using statistics to analyze relationships vital to education as he understood it, for example, the relationship between progress in spelling (as demonstrated through the increase in words spelled correctly after a specified period of study) and the relevance of the words, which would make learning them more pleasurable (relevance was to be measured by the occurrence of the words in a specified set of well-known books, like the Bible). Investigating that kind of relationship might identify ways to increase the likelihood that a stimulus would be connected to the appropriate response, which Thorndike hoped could lead to a better understanding of chance and probability in education.

Relative to many of his peers, Thorndike was willing to encourage the professional advancement of graduate students who were women. But he also believed that by natural ability men were better suited to the most challenging and responsible occupations. This was because he thought the variation in ability among men was greater than that among women.[74] Hence, more men would be among the most gifted, and it was from their ranks that, ideally, school superintendents, education researchers, and other leaders would be drawn. Even if "women should capture the teaching profession," he observed, "they would hardly fill its most eminent positions . . . [and] even should all women vote, they would play a small role in the senate."[75]

In light of these attitudes, it is not surprising that Thorndike thought teachers should come to understand their subordinate place in the educational hierarchy. "It is the problem of the higher authorities of the schools to decide what the schools shall try to achieve and to arrange plans for school work which will attain the desired ends," he asserted in a 1906 text, *The Principles of Teaching*. "Having decided what changes are to be made they entrust to the teachers the work of making them. The special problem of the teacher is to make these changes as economically and as surely as is possible under the conditions of school life."[76] By defining teaching as a technical, subordinate task, Thorndike was implicitly elevating not only school administrators, but also educational psychologists like himself to a superordinate place relative to teachers. Prophesying that, as educational psychology garnered more and more knowledge, "it would tell the effect of every possible stimulus and the cause of every possible response in every possible human being," Thorndike was suggesting that as educational psychology became more exact and therefore more powerful as a strategy of prediction, teaching would, in a sense, be increasingly de-skilled.[77]

Thorndike's gender-related, hierarchical model for how different kinds of workers should relate to one another in education certainly reflected his belief that biological factors—"human nature"—ideally should be the primary source of guidance for social practices and policies. In addition, his model for the education profession insulated scholars like himself from the direct application of knowledge, which fitted nicely with established patterns of status in the academic world. Even though psychologists like Thorndike were eager to tap the markets for their services that were opening up in schools, factories, hospitals, and advertising firms, they were aware that their more "pure" academic colleagues often looked down upon their research. Because, in William James's words, applied psychologists were bent on devising "practical rules" to offer educators, jail wardens, doctors, and clergymen, they were presumed to "care little or nothing about the ultimate philosophic grounds of mental phenomena." [78] Having strayed from the scholar's "pure" search for the truth, applied psychologists were seen as inferior.

Even though this attitude may seem peculiar in such a utilitarian culture as that of the United States, the fact is that a reverence for asceticism had been helpful in distinguishing academics generally from their peers in other professions, and this attitude continued to carry prestige as advancing specialization spawned more and more special fields, including some that were "pure" and some that were "applied." Aware of this, as G. Stanley Hall also had been, Thorndike always described himself as a psychologist and never as an educator. More important in the long term, the model he projected for the education profession presumed that the education researcher was the searcher for truth and the practitioner was merely the person concerned with application.

This kind of displacement of status concerns would complicate differences in perspective between scholars of education, on the one hand, and teachers and other school personnel, on the other. Increasingly, too, as differences in perspective were institutionalized in a hierarchical ordering much like that already evident between doctors and nurses, a segmentation came to characterize relationships between "thinkers" and "doers" in education, the former being predominantly male university professors of education or school administrators and the latter being predominantly female school teachers. Foreshadowed by the gender-related hierarchy between female teachers and male supervisors that had emerged in the nineteenth century, social relations within education would become increasingly complex as more and more grades and levels became important to the field, but gender-related rankings between and among educational workers remained highly resistant to change. Really as a sideline of his more important investigations, Thorndike's work provided scientific sanction for a division of labor based on this sexual template.

Obviously, Thorndike's approach to the study of education was the antithesis of Dewey's. Thorndike's psychology was narrowly behaviorist. Eliminating all consideration of consciousness, it reduced human actions to little more than responses to stimuli. After reading William James's *The Principles of Psychology,* Dewey had formulated a conception of behavior that, contra Thorndike, was both holistic and purposive. He had first presented this in "The Reflex Arc Concept in Psychology" in 1896.

In addition to that fundamental difference, Thorndike's approach presumed that educational practices should be grounded in psychology rather than being informed by and, in turn, informing psychology, philosophy, and other social studies. It presumed, further, that education was relatively powerless in the face of "human nature," a central purpose of educational science being to identify realistic educational purposes. Unlike Dewey, who believed that educational study should be directed toward making education a primary method for achieving planned, deliberate social change, Thorndike thought it should help people see that education could not promote equality or lessen differences between individuals or within and across groups of people. Thorndike's view of educational study presumed, too, that education in general, and teaching in particular, could be improved by scientific knowledge generated outside of schools and totally apart from the idiosyncratic circumstances of particular teachers, children, and classrooms.

In essence, Thorndike's approach to educational study accepted and presented as both inalterable and beneficial all the distinctions Dewey found problematic and troublesome, including distinctions between learning and doing, knowing and undergoing, experience and nature, thought and action, school and society, child and curriculum, and, last but not least, people classified as "workers"—teachers—and as "cultured"—supervisors. Most important, perhaps, Thorndike's views provided a logic for university schools of education as well as a disciplinary base for educational research that fit well within the patterns of organization increasingly evident throughout the educational world. Whereas Dewey's approach to educational study favored synthesis across disciplines and open communication and collaboration across roles and was therefore in opposition to advancing professionalization, Thorndike's approach advocated reliance on specialized expertise and fostered efforts to promote educational study as a professional science.

Thorndike and Teachers College: A Reciprocal Relationship

In light of its value to advancing professionalization, it is not surprising that James Earl Russell, dean of Teachers College from 1897 until 1927, should have found Thorndike's approach congenial and supported his work, the result being that Thorndike's rise to prominence was inseparable from Teachers College's increasing institutional prominence among university-based or -affiliated schools of education. By contrast, Russell described Dewey's work at the Chicago Laboratory School as one of the old "methods of experimentation."[79] In 1897, when it was first announced, Dewey had thought Russell's appointment as dean would bode well for Teachers College. However, the circumstances that surrounded the appointment did not bode well for the approach to educational scholarship Dewey was then still developing at the University of Chicago.[80]

According to Russell, in 1897, Teachers College was "a private normal school with sixty-nine regular students of junior-college grade and a demonstration school of some four hundred pupils . . . [and] an annual deficit in current expenses of $80,000."[81] Arriving to head the Department of Psychology and General Method, Russell had discovered that Benjamin Ide Wheeler, one of his undergraduate teachers at Cornell, had reversed himself and declined appointment as president of Teachers College. The college's trustees were therefore anxiously searching for another candidate, and Russell had suggested that the college would not need a president if it were to become a full and equal faculty of Columbia University. At the time, the trustees had already established an affiliation, albeit one that was strained and unequal. More than Russell may have realized, having himself attended coeducational Cornell University and taught at the University of Colorado, the faculties of older, exclusively male institutions like Harvard and Columbia found it difficult to accept the possibility that a feminized field like teaching could require advanced study and professional preparation on a par with male-dominated fields like medicine, law, and engineering.[82] Harvard President Charles W. Eliot spoke for Columbia as well as for Harvard when he said: "The faculty in common with most teachers in England and the United States feel but slight interest or confidence in what is ordinarily called pedagogy."[83]

Overcoming a long history of resistance to both coeducation and the possibility of university-level educational study, Seth Low, president of Columbia from 1890 to 1901, managed to convince the Columbia trustees to concur in Russell's suggestion and bring Teachers College within the Columbia orbit, though not, as Russell put it, as "a professional school on a par with the others . . . [but] as the stepchild of the University Department of Philosophy and Education," which would oversee all Teachers College courses leading to degrees.[84] Low had also managed to convince Russell to become dean. Having thus assumed responsibility for an institution that was caught between a university's demands for high standards in a field many of its faculty did not consider worthy of professional status and its own need for tuition income to cover perennial deficits, Russell became one of the nation's foremost advocates for a professional science of education. He believed that professional knowledge and training could improve teaching, which would, in turn, foster a more generous attitude toward education among both academics and the public at large.[85] When Russell later said that Thorndike had "shaped the character of the College . . . as no one else has done and as no one will ever again have the opportunity of doing," he was testifying to the degree he had needed and relied on Thorndike to try to help him legitimate Teachers College to Columbia and pedagogy to the world.[86]

Convinced that "the science of education . . . needs to be developed and made over to fit modern conditions," Russell chided Thorndike when he publicly belittled the importance of practical studies and school observations.[87] As a psychologist working in a teachers college, Thorndike evidently felt quite contemptuous of the college's professional programs. An ambitious man, he seems also to have recognized, however, that the college's professional focus was important to his influence beyond his own circle of psychological colleagues. It was probably for this reason that he refused to transfer to Columbia when he was invited. Doubtless, too, however, Russell's support for his teaching and research was important.[88]

Having been recruited in 1899 to teach child study and genetic psychology (which was really the history of human evolution), Thorndike helped convince the dean to reorganize the college in 1902. In the process, five distinct departments were established, including one for educational psychology. At the time, only two institutions offered any work officially called educational psychology, and none had a separate department.[89] If the novelty of this organization advanced Russell's ambitions for the college, the new arrangement also advanced Thorndike's plans for "conquering the world of pedagogy." A separate department of educational psychology would allow Thorndike to teach Columbia University psychology students who wanted some familiarity with this new special field, and it would also allow him to present work in educational psychology as the basic science for educational practitioners. Soon after the department was created, courses there become mandatory for all Teachers College doctoral students.[90]

To make money and to spread the word, Thorndike also began to write textbooks. *Notes on Child-Study* appeared in 1901, *Educational Psychology* was published in 1903, and *An Introduction to the Theory of Mental and Social Measurements* was first printed in 1904. Enrollments at Teachers College, which numbered just under 1,400 students by 1899 (including summer school and extension sessions), created a large and growing market for these and others of Thorndike's books. In fact, by 1913, when Thorndike's three-volume *Educational Psychology* appeared, Teachers College's enrollment exceeded 3,000, and sales of Thorndike's book were, of course, not restricted to Teachers College audiences.[91] Introducing his narrowly behaviorist and deterministic view of learning, as well as his belief in the importance of quantitative measurements and statistical analyses, into the college's required courses, Thorndike spread his message further with books such as these. According to a close colleague, his 1904 text, *An Introduction to the Theory of Mental and Social Measurements,* was "based on the view that non-mathematical investigators in psychology and education should be enabled to make intelligent use of statistical methods, understanding the principles involved and appreciating both the great need for quantitative study of human behavior and the inherent difficulties of such an enterprise."[92] The text helped establish statistics, a science originally developed in connection with physics and mathematics, as a vital new method of education research.[93]

From the beginning of his deanship, Russell wanted Teachers College to engage in the training of leaders. Echoing the sentiments of many advocates for the university study of education, he had always insisted that normal schools should not aspire to this, since they could not offer the breadth of study that was necessary for self-direction, which, to Russell, was the quality that separated leaders from all the rest.[94] Deliberately and effectively intending to make the college a training ground for a new elite, Russell established a journal, *Teachers College Record,* to report on the special ways in which education was treated at the college. He also created an "appointment committee" to help graduates find appropriate employment.[95] Ever mindful of the institution's financial problems, he also initiated summer sessions, which brought teachers and administrators to the college from all over the nation, especially from the South, and then sent them home again with knowledge and experience—and texts like Thorndike's—that set them apart from their peers.

Well before he resigned in favor of his son, William F. Russell, in 1927, the results of these efforts were clear. To generate income from student fees, Teachers College had become the largest school of education in the world. Aggressively placing its graduates, it had also come to dominate the job market for educational leaders. By 1923, for example, Teachers College graduates filled twelve of the eighteen full (university) professorships of education in California, and students of Teachers College graduates filled another four. In addition, of the 145 professors or heads of departments of education in the California normal schools, 55 were Teachers College graduates, and 80 were students of Teachers College graduates.[96] As Elmer Ellsworth Brown, the chancellor of New York University (NYU), remarked a little wistfully, since NYU's school of education had continued to serve a clientele of mostly New York City teachers, Teachers College had "come to be preeminently not a college for teachers, but a college for the teachers of teachers and for the directors of teachers. As a natural accompaniment, it has ceased to be mainly a school of instruction and has become, in increasing measure, a school of research."[97] If, as was certainly the case, Thorndike helped Russell realize his ambitions for Teachers College, the achievement of those ambitions, in turn, lent influence to Thorndike's ideas. Long before his retirement in 1941, former Thorndike students had moved into prominent positions at most of the nation's normal schools and schools of education and, in doing so, had taken Thorndike's ideas about education and his conception of education research with them.

Dewey Displaced: Charles Hubbard Judd at the University of Chicago

As this was happening, Charles Hubbard Judd, John Dewey's successor at the University of Chicago, was also working to professionalize the study of education. Second to Teachers College in student enrollments and prominent graduate placements, Chicago was home to not one, but two journals, *School Review,* which tended to deal with matters relevant to secondary education, and *Elementary School Record.* No less than Teachers College, Chicago was coming to be known as a prominent center for education research.

Like Thorndike, Judd was a Wesleyan graduate and a psychologist. Unlike Thorndike, however, he had gone to Europe after graduation, where he had worked in the laboratory of renowned German psychologist Wilhelm Wundt. Exposed through Wundt to a complex, social conception of the mind, Judd's work in psychology avoided the narrowly behaviorist template that undergirded all of Thorndike's research. In fact, experiments conducted by Judd in 1908 demonstrated that, contra Thorndike, there could be transfer of training if students were offered principles to link what they learned in one situation to what they needed to know in another.[98] For Judd, the so-called higher mental processes that enabled people to participate actively in learning were more important than the kinds of simple stimulus-response connections Thorndike focused on.[99] Beyond that, unlike Thorndike, Judd did not see learning as an invariant process. As early as 1915, when he published *Psychology of School Subjects,* he argued that it was rather a process that varied according to the task or subject at hand.

Despite such very important differences between their psychologies, Judd shared Thorndike's keen interest in fostering the scientific study of education, which, to Judd, meant "the application of laboratory methods to the study of . . . educational problem[s]."[100] As Ralph W. Tyler, a prominent student of Judd's said at the time of Judd's death, Judd deeply believed "that a sound foundation for educational policy and practice must be based on facts and tested principles rather than on speculation or collections of 'best practices.'"[101] In addition, he thought that schools could be effective only if their curricula were set with aims and content derived from both an analysis of society and a study of learning. More social in perspective than Thorndike, Judd was essentially conservative in outlook, expecting schools to prepare students for the world as it was rather than, as was the case with Dewey, for the world as it ought to be.

Having accepted a job early in his career at the New York University School of Pedagogy, Judd had discovered that, despite his mastery of psychology, he was "ill prepared to teach teachers." As he later recalled, he had decided this while lecturing on "Weber's Law," which held that discrimination between two stimuli depended on their relative rather than their absolute differences. His audience had been a group of New York City teachers "who were seeking increases in their salaries by listening to me," he remembered, and his lecture had been interrupted with the question: "Professor, will you tell us how we can use this principle to improve our teaching of children?"[102] Unable to answer, he had begun to interest himself in school problems and how those might be studied directly and in a scientific manner. That interest again separated him from Thorndike, who was happy to leave the study of school problems to his more "professional" colleagues, his own concern being the psychological basis for educational practice. No less than Thorndike, however, Judd was committed to the development of an educational science that would be based on controlled experimentation and precise quantitative measurements.[103]

Judd was eventually dismissed from NYU not because he lacked pedagogical knowledge, but because he joined several colleagues who "agitated reform" by widely and loudly expressing their belief that the academic standards in the School of Education should be higher. He then taught briefly at the University of Cincinnati and at Yale University before moving to Chicago to assume the work in education that Dewey had left five years earlier.[104] No less convinced than James Earl Russell of the importance of university support for professional training in education, Judd set out with similar zeal to develop a program of research and advanced study that would win approval among his faculty colleagues.[105]

A few years after Judd's arrival, the Department of Pedagogy was separated from the Department of Philosophy. Judd believed education deserved autonomous status, and as he told his student George S. Counts, he also regarded philosophy as an "enticement" that should be avoided, since, as a field of study, it was "too easy."[106] The only faculty member to evidence an interest in philosophy during Judd's thirty years as chair was denied promotion to a full professorship.[107] Whatever the methods of philosophy, they were not the same as those of "the science of education," Judd insisted, which were "statistical" and "experimental."[108]

In an effort to professionalize the study of education at the University of Chicago, Judd discontinued all undergraduate programs, placed the training of secondary school teachers under the control of a universitywide committee that could strengthen work in the subject matter teachers were preparing to teach, and created a new course of study for students in the department, which was now entirely devoted to research and research training. In lieu of the previous courses in the history of education and psychology, two new ones were instituted, one called "Introduction to Education" and the other called "Methods of Teaching." The change, Judd claimed later, had been prompted by demand for "a scientific discussion of methodology" and for "a general introductory discussion of educational problems from a scientific point of view."[109]

Over the years, Judd also recruited a faculty that was as supportive of his views as the Dewey group had been supportive of the views of their chief. The Judd group included many men—there were, by conviction, no women—who became well known in the so-called scientific movement in education. Among them were Franklin Bobbitt, Frank E. Freeman, Walter Dearborn, William S. Gray, William C. Reavis, Guy T. Buswell, Newton Edwards, Karl Holzinger, and Leonard Koos. Active outside the university as well as within, the Judd group gained a commanding position in important professional organizations like the National Society for the Study of Education, a membership organization founded in 1895 (originally as the National Herbart Society) to promote the study of education, and the Cleveland Conference, an invitational group of school leaders organized at the time of World War I. They also served on the editorial boards for the *School Review* and the *Elementary School Record,* both of which Judd himself edited for many years.[110]

In addition to developing a program that fit well with the slowly growing belief that the university study of education should be aligned with the social and behavioral sciences, rather than philosophy, Judd quietly but effectively distanced himself and the new Department of Education from people who had been close to Dewey. He did this by banishing Dewey's former colleagues. Not coincidentally, a philosophy of education course that had been taught by George Herbert Mead was dropped, and one dealing with "principles of education" was adopted in its stead.[111] Not coincidentally, either, Judd's suggestion to the president that "the ordinary member of the faculty, who has not dealt with the problems of education" should in the future not be allowed to recommend candidates for jobs as school superintendents was prompted by a letter written by biologist John Coulter, who had been a close friend of Dewey's and had helped develop the science curriculum at the Laboratory School.[112]

Testifying to the chill that came to surround all that Dewey had tried to do, Harold Rugg, a Teachers College professor who taught at Chicago for a time under Judd, claimed that he had never heard the former chairman "spoken of except with derision or scorn."[113] More telling still, one of Judd's departmental colleagues claimed that, until 1909, the Lab School had provided ineffective basic instruction because it "was conducted largely on the basis of incidental drills."[114] At Chicago, the fulfillment of Judd's professional aspirations seemed to require denial of the possibility that the study of education might have become "scientific" in a very different way.

That may not be surprising in light of the fundamental differences that existed between Dewey and Judd. Although both thought experimentation was necessary in education, Dewey saw the school as the laboratory of education, whereas Judd saw the school as primarily the place for the implementation of real laboratory findings. One might study problems of "efficiency" via a school survey, and one might evaluate the value of a test in the same way, but the actual work of formulating guiding principles was to be done by academics in the university. Differences between Dewey and Judd concerning the proper locus for experimentation arose from two additional points of divergence. Whereas Dewey saw teachers and researchers as more alike than different, wanting both to be skilled students of education, Judd believed that the improvement of education required the professionalization of education, which, in turn, necessitated that teachers and researchers fulfill distinct roles. Teachers should teach, in the process transmitting subject matter, organizing classrooms, and approaching children according to knowledge generated by researchers. In accord with these differences of function, Judd believed there should also be differences of gender—teachers should be female and researchers, male—and differences in levels of education—teachers should not be required to pursue graduate training, while researchers should possess the Ph.D. It was telling that Chicago teacher leader Margaret Haley admired Dewey, but described Judd, whom she apparently saw as an enemy, as a "ventriloquist" with a "portly form and stentorian voice." [115]

Whether or not the differences that existed between Judd and Dewey necessitated purposeful efforts to eclipse Dewey's perspective within the Department of Education at Chicago, Judd's support for the scientific study of educational problems throughout his long tenure at Chicago, which extended from 1909 until 1938, had a somewhat ironic and perhaps positive effect. Pushed toward canons of objectivity and rigor that were increasingly evident across the social sciences, even in Chicago sociology, which became increasingly quantitative throughout the 1920s, the status of educational study was probably higher at Chicago than at Columbia, where it proceeded in a separate faculty affiliated with, but not a part of, the university per se. The standing of education at Chicago was also higher than at Harvard, where a distinct graduate school of education was not established until 1920. That notwithstanding, because the reputation of educational study at Chicago was heavily dependent on Judd's leadership as well as on his own high personal and professional stature, as Judd moved into retirement, the Department of Education fell victim to skeptical, if not hostile, administrative scrutiny. In the long run, then, the University of Chicago proved no more friendly to educational scholarship than its kindred eastern universities, and, subsequently, in the 1990s, it would prove to be less so.

Relative rankings aside, Judd's efforts at Chicago combined well with Thorndike's efforts. Even if the two men were rivals, together they were critical in gaining acceptance for controlled experimentation and statistical measurements as essential methods of educational study.

Technologies of Influence:
Testing and School Surveying

Writing in 1920, Paul Hanus, Harvard's first professor of the history and art of teaching, celebrated what he considered a major victory. Whereas twenty years earlier it had not been clear that there was a science of education, he could now report that "we are no longer disputing whether education has a scientific basis; we are trying to find that basis."[1] To Hanus, earlier claims that a science of education could be derived from history and philosophy did not make sense. While emphasizing psychology, William H. Payne had claimed this at the University of Michigan, insisting that, among other things, history's status as a "culture subject" would help gain acceptance for educational study as a legitimate university pursuit.[2] Even though some of his colleagues believed the university study of education represented "the substitution of method for academic attainment," Payne insisted that theory was important.[3] Hanus disagreed. He thought the application of precise quantitative measurements to the problems of school management was what mattered most. Slowly, but surely, this was leading, he thought, to the accumulation of sufficient data concerning instructional techniques, curriculum construction, personnel policies, and building management so that principles of efficient administration could be formulated. In light of Hanus's active championship of this approach to educational scholarship, as well as his active involvement in school surveying—Hanus led a major survey of the schools of New York City in 1911–12, for example—Charles Eliot's refusal to change his title from professor of history and art of teaching to professor of education was more than a little ironic.

Of course, Eliot's position reflected the extreme resistance to developing educational scholarship that existed at Harvard and many other elite eastern universities early in the twentieth century. Hanus had endured this not only in his relationship with Eliot, but also in slights from faculty colleagues. Joining the Harvard faculty at the time Eliot had pushed William James and others to begin offering courses for teachers,

Hanus had been scorned from the first. Reflecting this sentiment, philosopher George Herbert Palmer had even gone so far as to say that "when professor Hanus came to Harvard, he bore the onus of his subject."[4] In spite of that, Hanus had invented courses for undergraduates interested in teaching that were quite original. Leaving William James to lecture on psychology, Hanus had focused on the "Organization and Management of Public Schools and Academies." Instead of texts about practical methods, he had had his students read original documents like the report of the National Education Association's Committee of Ten, which had been chaired by President Eliot. Thus trying both to please Eliot, who wanted Harvard to be involved in school reform, and to avoid the narrow vocationalism so distasteful to his colleagues, Hanus nevertheless became the brunt of a faculty protest.

Led by Hugo Munsterberg and a few other faculty members, the protest was against Eliot's long-standing preference for student course election and interest in professional education. In the face of that, Hanus had been forced to give up courses for teachers and to turn his attention instead to the education of administrators, especially school superintendents. The Harvard faculty was willing to admit that administrators, unlike teachers, did need special training.[5] According to Munsterberg, "psychology is a wonderful science, and pedagogy, as soon as we shall have it, may be a wonderful science, too, and very important for school organizers, for superintendents and city officials, but the individual teacher has little practical use for it."[6] Hanus had therefore taken up the work about which he spoke so hopefully in 1920 less from preference than from pressures generated by antieducationist forces, which were exceptionally strong at Harvard.

Regardless of the ironies involved, Hanus's interest in applying scientific methods to the problems of educational administration was widely shared among both professors of education and school administrators during the first decades of the twentieth century. By building a science from the data generated by the administrators, the professors could participate in the widely announced public interest in education reform, while also justifying a niche for themselves among the professional faculties of the university. Equally important, they could offer the administrators principles of efficient practice, the enunciation of which could lend authority to the administrators' decisions and set them apart from both the teachers they supervised and the school board members to whom they reported. The hierarchical but reciprocal relationship that grew up between the two groups created a professional community and the beginnings of a professional knowledge base.

Beneficial in that way, close linkages between early university educationists and their allies in the field also had disadvantages. Scorned by their more "academic" colleagues and welcomed by their practice-based brethren, the early educationists created models for research that tended to limit the continuing elaboration of the theory and research methods so essential to any science. University schools and departments of education grew up at a time when school administrators were being asked to organize their schools in ways that might serve increasing numbers of ever more diverse students. They were also under constant pressure from a tax-fearing public, which wanted more for less. In consequence, there was scant demand for theory and high demand for practical techniques that might yield new "efficiencies" in the delivery of instruction as well as the general management of a school system. Responding to this, scholars of education sought to develop more professionally useful versions of traditional fields of scholarship and adapted techniques from social and psychological research for use in the schools. Even though this advanced their immediate interest in developing a professional knowledge base for school management, the tilt toward practical service that resulted would prove constraining as well. Indeed, one can argue that the emphasis supported a managerial orientation at the expense of perspectives that might have encouraged leadership in considering large questions concerning education and its purposes.

The History and Philosophy of Education:
From Center to Periphery

At the turn of the century, efforts to develop research methods for education were not confined to psychology. Although psychology came to provide the most important early frameworks for education research, at the outset, philosophy and history had been central. As I have indicated, for example, at the University of Michigan, William H. Payne had counted on history and philosophy to provide the theory that would distinguish the university study of education from study at a normal school. Critical of normal schools for embracing an excessively utilitarian conception of what knowledge would be most useful to educators, Payne had seen great value in historical study. Even if one could "not expect to learn from it how to stop whispering, or to prevent tardiness, or to teach subtraction, or any one of the thousand things that a teacher must know," Payne had insisted that the history of education had "uses which are general and comprehensive." It exposed one to "trends of thought on educational questions through the centuries, . . . discussion of complex problems, wisdom in dealing with systems and methods that have once been put on trial, etc.," he had maintained.[7] The history of education, he had therefore argued, "should be made the counterpart and proof of the science of education."[8]

With Payne's backing, the history of education had become a staple subject at universities across the country. Typical texts from those early years were J. K. F. Rosenkranz's *Die Padagogik als System,* which was translated into English as *The Philosophy of Education* (1886), and two volumes by Gabriel Compayré, entitled in translation from the French *Lectures on Pedagogy, Theoretical and Practical* (1887) and *The History of Pedagogy* (1885). Robert Herbert Quick's *Essays on Educational Reformers* and major works by Plato, Rousseau, Pestalozzi, and Froebel completed the list. Believed by many to reveal the unfolding of the human mind or the progress of the human race, education history-cum-philosophy was an essential ingredient in establishing education as a special field of scholarly investigation and professional study.

Given the importance of historical and philosophical studies at the turn of the century, it is hardly surprising that Teachers College should have aspired to leadership in that domain as well as many others. Partly because it was an independent institution affiliated with, but not part of, a university and partly because its early founders and early leaders were exceptionally determined in pursuit of the goal, the faculty at Teachers College was zealous in its efforts to develop every corner of what might become a professional knowledge base for education. Edward Thorndike may have been Teachers College's leading light, but among his faculty colleagues were many who pioneered the development of a wide range of special fields. To that end, while nurturing Thorndike, Dean James Earl Russell had also encouraged Paul Monroe, who had been hired by Teachers College in 1897 immediately after finishing his doctorate in sociology at the University of Chicago, to shift his focus from history as a school subject to history as a field of education research. Monroe had begun teaching the history of education in 1898 and had published his first book, a lengthy *Source Book of the History of Education for the Greek and Roman Period,* in 1901.[9] By 1905, he had produced a number of other books, including a *Text-Book in the History of Education,* the chief "merits" of which he had announced as the avoidance of unsubstantiated generalizations through resort to "a body of historical facts" and the description of relationships between educational theories and actual educational practices, past and present.[10]

Monroe's aim had been to seek a scientific basis for educational scholarship in historical "facts." Publication of his *Text-Book* represented a turning point in the relation of history and philosophy to educational scholarship. Thanks to Monroe's efforts, history had become the subject of most dissertations completed at Teachers College during the first two decades of the twentieth century.[11] Works such as Henry Suzzallo's *The Rise of Local School Supervision in Massachusetts* (1906), William Heard Kilpatrick's *The Dutch Schools of New Netherland and Colonial New York* (1912), Edgar Wallace Knight's *The Influence of Reconstruction on Education in the South* (1913), and Robert Francis Seybolt's *Apprenticeship and Apprenticeship Education in Colonial New England and New York* (1917) created a literature for the field that was intended to be "factual" and therefore, according to the then-prevailing norms of the historical profession, "scientific."[12]

Despite this focus, during the early years of the twentieth century, the history of education declined in popularity with students. In response, education scholars called for an even further narrowing of focus to those influences that had shaped education in the United States in the twentieth century. The filtering that resulted was evident in the differences between Monroe's *Text-Book,* which began with the (unnamed) "primitives" and ran through Oriental, Greek, Roman, and European history to end in "The Present Eclectic Tendency," to which a mere 14 out of 761 pages were devoted, and Ellwood Patterson Cubberley's 1919 classic, *Public Education in the United States,* which began with a brief initial chapter on "Our European Background" and then chronicled the "battles" fought and won on the way to a variety of "new"—that is, then-current—ideas, developments, and "fundamental principles."[13]

No longer suitable for use in general "culture courses," texts in the history of education became less and less comprehensive and more and more professional and presentist. Not surprisingly as a result, historians increasingly disregarded the history of education in general. Indeed, during their first decades in print, neither the journal of the American Historical Association nor that of the Mississippi Valley Historical Association (later renamed the Organization of American Historians) published a single article about the history of education.[14] As Henry Johnson, who had a long career at Teachers College teaching methods of instruction to would-be history teachers, explained forthrightly in a memoir, "real" historians increasingly shunned historians of education. As Johnson recalled, just after he was appointed to the Teachers College faculty, he had "stepped into the office of Professor Dunning, head of the Graduate Department of History, Columbia University to pay my respects to him. He rose from his desk to shake hands and in the midst of a waiting group of students asked with a twinkle: 'Be yo' the guy what teaches them methods at Teachers College? Well, . . . I recommended you but don't you ever dare to say pedagogy or pedagogical to me.' I knew from of old that behind his mockery was serious questioning of the right of an institution like Teachers College to exist; I met other scholars whose disapproving comments lacked the grace of humor." [15]

To Paul Monroe, the "very general skepticism on the part of university faculties and of the departments of long standing, concerning the possibility of the scientific study of educational activities, either of exact, comparative, or historical character" was troubling.[16] But his students were more concerned with their standing in the ever more clearly defined and distinct community of professional educators and, with that audience in mind, continued their efforts to professionalize historical writing about education. Despite that, with students rating the history of education poorly, offerings in educational history declined, while offerings in other subjects multiplied.[17] Even at Teachers College, history eventually lost its initially premier place as the method of choice for doctoral dissertations.[18] By the 1920s, it had been replaced by studies based on school surveying, which was increasingly seen as a technique essential for administrators in training. "Why not every superintendent an educational surveyor?" had become the call of the day.[19]

Dignity amidst Disdain: Ellwood Patterson Cubberley and the First Generation of Scholars of School Administration

Known for decades as the author of the standard history of American education, Ellwood Patterson Cubberley was nonetheless a leading figure in promoting the development of school surveying and in linking surveying to educational administration conceived as a field of university study. As his younger Stanford colleague Jesse Brundage Sears once remarked, Cubberley belonged to a generation of educationists that had shared an "almost fanatical belief in the possibilities of developing a science of education."[20] This belief colored all aspects of Cubberley's long and influential career.

Dean of education at Stanford from 1917 until 1933, Cubberley had first arrived in Palo Alto to become an assistant professor of education in July 1898. Having opened its doors seven years earlier, Stanford had had an Education Department from the first. Initially called the Department of the History and Art of Education, the department offered courses about child study and the "Comparative Study of City and State School Systems in the United States" as well as about the history of education and educational theory. Cubberley's appointment signaled a move toward a more practical emphasis. Building carefully, Cubberley presided over a small department (the full-time faculty eventually numbered around a dozen), which came to include a number of leading educationists. Even before Cubberley retired, the department had become a major supplier of school administrators for northern California. Eventually, beginning in the mid-1950s, that focus gave way to one that placed greater emphasis on educational study conceived as a branch of social research. Not coincidentally, the shift boosted Stanford into a leadership position among schools of education, high national rankings tending to correlate with an emphasis on theory rather than practice.[21] But that was later, and at the time Cubberley arrived, he hoped the department could "strive to train principals and superintendents who should be leaders in the future more than teachers for high schools."[22]

To Cubberley's great surprise and dismay, however, he had quickly discovered that his new colleagues did not share his own "high conception" of education.[23] Indeed, soon after Cubberley's arrival, Stanford President David Starr Jordan told him that, if the decision had been left to the faculty, the Department of Education would have been terminated. Having come to admire Cubberley when, ten years earlier, Cubberley had been a student at Indiana University, where Jordan had then been president, Jordan was apparently counting on his new recruit to make education a "respectable" field of university work.[24]

Having been a teacher and a school superintendent, as well as president of Vincennes University, a small Baptist college in Ridgeville, Indiana, before joining the Stanford faculty, Cubberley was determined to meet Jordan's challenge, and if stability and growth were the only measures, he would have to be judged successful in the effort. By 1917, the Stanford department had become a distinct school of education, over which Cubberley presided as dean, and before he retired fourteen years later, its permanent faculty had more than tripled in size.[25] That notwithstanding, faculty hostility persisted. As one colleague later confessed, among many Stanford faculty members, "Education" was hardly considered to have the dignity of either a "Science" or an "Art."[26]

In encountering skepticism and scorn from his peers, Cubberley was not unusual. And yet, in their autobiographical writings, Cubberley and other early educationists said relatively little about the disdain their faculty colleagues had expressed toward them. Having spent their careers striving to legitimate the university study of education, most educationists were not inclined to be candid concerning the degree to which scholars in other fields had scorned them. That notwithstanding, there can be little doubt that negative sentiments about education both within and outside academe added fuel to their collective quest to develop a science of education and to demonstrate its utility.

To equip themselves to do this, Cubberley and a significant number of other early students of educational administration went to Teachers College in New York City for graduate study. Encouraged by Stanford's Jordan, Cubberley arrived in September 1901. He was convinced that, if he were to undertake advanced study, the Stanford Department of Education might gain in standing and repute, which it certainly did within, if not beyond, the emerging community of professional educators. Cubberley completed the M.A. in 1902, returned to Stanford for two years of teaching, and then returned to Teachers College again, where, in 1905, he received the Ph.D.

Already inspired with a missionary's faith concerning the importance of building up the Stanford department so that it might "train principals and superintendents who should be leaders," at Teachers College Cubberley was introduced to a circle of professional colleagues, most of whom, like Cubberley himself, were men who came from middle-class, Protestant backgrounds and had been schoolteachers and/or administrators.[27] It also helped initiate him into several of the subfields cultivated by educationists, school administration and the history of education among them.[28] Cubberley's dissertation dealt with *School Funds and Their Apportionment*. It convinced him that "the question of sufficient revenue lies back of almost every other problem" and that professionalization was essential to an effective attack on that problem.[29] Although he had studied with both John Dewey and Edward Thorndike, he left Teachers College imbued with the belief that the scientific study of education involved the empirical, statistical analysis of problems having to do with the organization and management of schools. As his biographers observed, Cubberley's time at Teachers College led him to believe that "a scientific study of the phenomena of education must use the statistical method."[30] After receiving his doctorate, Cubberley set out to make Stanford the leading West Coast exponent of that point of view.

The shared orientation that developed among the Teachers College graduates of 1905 was, of course, also shaped by the larger social context in which they lived. Cubberley and his graduate school peers were ready converts to the ideas of scientific management.[31] Like contemporaries outside of education, they saw great promise in the work of Frederick Winslow Taylor, the world-famous engineer whose plan for piecework factory management became a model for the administration of many different types of institutions, including the nation's schools. First enunciated in an 1895 essay read before the American Society of Mechanical Engineers, Taylor's depiction of the piecework system quickly came to serve as a pervasive metaphor for the practical value of defining all kinds of "efficiency," industrial, social, or educational, according to precise input-output correlations. By 1910, if not before, this seemingly clear and certain formula for harmony and productivity had captured the imagination of businessmen and government officials throughout the Western world.[32] What is more, in education, input-output studies remained a staple of education research at least until James Coleman demonstrated their weakness in 1964.

Compelling to men like Cubberley because it appeared to have direct relevance to questions of educational administration, scientific management was attractive, too, because its emphasis on quantitative measurements fitted well with the increasingly popular belief that there was a need for "school facts as the basis for school policy."[33] To a considerable extent, this belief derived from the muckraking exposés Joseph Mayer Rice had written for the *Forum* in the 1890s. A pediatrician turned pedagogue via two years of study with Wilhelm Rein at Jena and Wilhelm Wundt at Leipzig, Rice had visited schools in thirty-six cities across the United States and talked with some 1,200 teachers, in the process concluding that most schools were failing to do their jobs well. By administering tests to schoolchildren, he had also undermined long-established assumptions about education, including the belief that by devoting more time to basic school subjects like spelling, one could achieve better results.

School administrators meeting within the clublike Department of Superintendence of the National Education Association (NEA) initially rejected Rice's findings. To the administrators, they had seemed "foolish, reprehensible, and from every point of view indefensible."[34] But Rice's claims had proven difficult to refute without countervailing "school facts," and they had raised questions in the minds of the business and civic leaders, who were increasingly represented on school boards nationwide. In consequence, as a defense, if not a preference, school administrators had become increasingly concerned with finding ways to gather precise information about the "efficiency" of the schools.[35] There was just no other way to answer Rice's claims that "up to the present time the science of pedagogy has been in its entirety a structure based on no stronger foundation than one of opinions . . . and no really sustained forward movement may be expected until the conflicting views are subjected to analysis in the light of clear and unmistakable facts." [36] In consequence, more and more educational reformers came to talk about the possibilities for educational progress through the accumulation of "school facts."

Leonard P. Ayres, the Russell Sage Foundation, and the School Survey Movement

Inspired with a common sense of purpose, many among the Teachers College graduates of 1905 became involved in school surveying. Often working in partnership with one another or with like-minded colleagues at other universities, they studied the operation of school systems and individual schools throughout the United States. Sometimes focusing on the adequacy of one aspect of a school, for example, its physical plant, and sometimes seeking to provide a more comprehensive evaluation of all aspects of a community's schools, school surveys provided a means for gathering data about school organization and practices and for building consensus and a sense of community among leading urban school superintendents and university professors of education. As more and more school surveys were completed—there had been 125 by 1917 and 625 by 1928—educational administration began to emerge as a distinct field of professional study. [37]

According to most contemporary accounts, the school survey movement began in the United States in 1911, when Paul Hanus of Harvard surveyed the schools of Montclair, New Jersey, and E. C. Moore of Yale surveyed the schools of East Orange, New Jersey. [38] Unlike earlier school studies, these surveys were carried out by "an impartial outside expert" instead of by local citizens and school authorities, and they relied upon "objective evidence . . . facts relating to the progress and achievement of pupils." [39]

Though school surveying was novel within education research at this time, it was a technique that had grown out of an increasingly important form of social research. It derived from research methods first put to use in England in Charles Booth's massive study *Life and Labor of the People of London* (1889–1903). These methods were subsequently refined in the United States by both settlement workers and urban reformers interested in improving the housing, health facilities, employment, and education available in different neighborhoods of large cities.[40] Then, beginning in 1906, a major survey of social conditions in Pittsburgh was initiated under the leadership of reforming journalist Paul U. Kellogg. First published in *Charities and Commons* and then, between 1909 and 1914, in six volumes, the Pittsburgh Survey concentrated on a city that symbolized both the new wealth and the degradation of industrial capitalism. It offered a model of social research tied to reform that was quickly picked up and copied elsewhere.[41] In important ways, this was a result of the Russell Sage Foundation, a trust created by Margaret Olivia Sage in 1907. Dedicated to "the improvement of social and living conditions in the United States," the Russell Sage Foundation early decided to pursue its mandate through social investigation combined with public advocacy.[42] The survey became one of its most important instruments.

According to Shelby M. Harrison of Russell Sage, the purpose of a survey was to identify and publicize the ways in which all the different elements of a community had changed and what those changes, in turn, required from the community in terms of new regulations, taxation, or institutional reform. The survey, he contended, represented a marriage between "the work of the scientist in adding to the sum of human knowledge and . . . the work of the journalist in so presenting the new knowledge that it may affect life and events."[43] Obviously, however, if the survey was a means for disseminating public information, it was also a device by which newly forming policy elites could advance their ideas in an "objective" and "scientific" way. The survey lent an aurora of disinterest to elite efforts to shape local institutions and politics. As was made clear by Abraham Flexner's famous report, *Medical Education in the United States and Canada,* published in 1910 by the Carnegie Foundation for the Advancement of Teaching, surveys also allowed outside authorities to demonstrate the need for new, usually national standards of performance. This was possible because they seemed to involve nothing more than the apolitical and disinterested collection and carefully targeted presentation of information.[44] As a purposeful means for disseminating information, mobilizing public opinion, and shaping public agendas, surveys were a quintessentially "progressive" technology.

Although the survey was initially intended as a means to study *all* aspects of a community, according to Shelby Harrison's analysis of surveys, "a tendency set in . . . after a few years, toward employing the survey to appraise [only] one major phase of community life."[45] A logical concomitant of ever-increasing specialization in government, the professions, and the academic world, the practice of surveying one sector of a community in isolation from the rest was encouraged by education professors eager to study the administration of schools. As Ellwood Cubberley once stated, they believed specialized school surveys would help stimulate "the growth . . . of a professional consciousness," while also making it possible to meet "public demand for a more intelligent accounting by school officers for the money expended for public education."[46]

Eagerly embraced by professors of education, the survey movement was promoted by the officials of some of the newly founded philanthropic foundations. Leonard P. Ayres was the most important among them. He joined the Russell Sage Foundation in 1908. From then until 1920, Ayres served as chief of both the Department of Statistics and the Department of Education, whose mandate was "'to discover facts, develop methods, and formulate procedures' that would 'aid educators to substitute knowledge for opinion, and to base action on evidence rather than on tradition or speculation.'"[47]

A lifelong bachelor with two known passions in life, bicycle racing and statistics, Ayres had taught school and been superintendent of schools for Puerto Rico before joining the Russell Sage staff; while at the foundation, he completed a doctorate in statistics at Boston University. Ayres's time in Puerto Rico had been as formative for him as similar experiences had been for Cubberley and other early professors of education. However, in Ayres's case, it had taught a different lesson. Whereas Cubberley had been impressed by the relative powerlessness of superintendents, Ayres had become convinced that "in education . . . we have little definite knowledge, many theories, much speculation, and a heterogeneous mass of practice which differs widely in different localities."[48] That had appalled him. Too oriented toward factual precision to believe that educational improvements could come through "the slow processes of philosophy, nor . . . the stirring words of voice or pen of any educational prophet," he became committed to improving education via the collection and analysis of comparative information about different schools and school systems.[49] Having early parted company with Thorndike over the causes for school leaving, Thorndike characteristically tending to locate such problems in individual competence and Ayres tending to see them in curricula geared to the "unusually bright one," Ayres was determined to find ways to identify and gain public support for more effective school practices.[50]

At Russell Sage, Ayres pursued this interest in a number of ways, the most important having been school surveying. Although, according to

Ayres, the foundation's education program was based on the principle "that progress in education is the result of the discovery of truth," he was well aware, as he put it, that the "truth does not disseminate itself."[51] It was for this reason, in fact, that he believed the technique of surveying could be useful in education. The purpose of school surveys, he once said, was "to educate the public . . . to tell the people in simple terms all the salient facts about their public schools."[52] Were school surveys conducted by "trained and experienced educators and investigators," rather than "mothers' clubs, chambers of commerce, newspapers, or college students," Ayres was confident they could win public support for the recommendations offered.[53]

Even though Ayres's priorities were not identical with those of education professors like Harvard's Paul Hanus, Stanford's Ellwood P. Cubberley, Teachers College's Edward L. Thorndike, and Chicago's Charles H. Judd, his priorities were supportive of theirs. Among contemporaries, he was admired for "his discriminating use of statistical methods in school research, and his constant subordination of the exhibition of statistical form to clearness and simplicity of presentation."[54] During his tenure at Russell Sage, Ayres led or participated in thirteen major school surveys, including a survey of the Cleveland schools that was intentionally designed to be "the most complete inquiry into a city school system up to that time."[55] The Cleveland Survey gave a large boost to the mission to which the pioneers of research in educational administration were committed.

The Cleveland Survey

Initiated by the Cleveland Foundation, a federation of small funds and bequests, the Cleveland Survey grew out of long-standing concern with high rates of pregraduation school-leaving in many Cleveland schools.[56] Unclear as to what should be done about the problem, Allen Burns of the Cleveland Foundation had asked Leonard Ayres to come to Cleveland early in 1916 to discuss school surveys with local organizations and school officials. Soon thereafter Ayres had agreed to serve as the survey's director and had assembled a team of thirty professional educators and statisticians to work with him. Many members of the team, including Charles H. Judd, were students or faculty members from the University of Chicago.

Individually or in groups, the survey staff studied every aspect of education in Cleveland, eventually publishing twenty-five separate reports

Table 5 Staff and Publications of the Cleveland Survey

Staff Member	Affiliation	Publication(s)
Leonard P. Ayres	Russell Sage Foundation, Director, Division of Education and Division of Statistics	*Child Accounting in the Public Schools; The Cleveland School Survey (Summary); The Public Library and the Public Schools* (with A. McKinnie); *School Buildings and Equipment; School Organization and Administration*
May S. B. Ayres	Columbia University, Graduate Student (Ph.D. pending)	*Health Work in the Public Schools*
Franklin Bobbitt	University of Chicago, Professor of Educational Administration	*What the Schools Teach and Might Teach*
Alice C. Boughton	Columbia University, Graduate Student	*Household Arts and School Lunches*
Edna Bryner	Russell Sage Fondation, Special Agent	*Dressmaking and Millinery; The Garment Trades*
Earle Clark	Russell Sage Foundation, Statistician	*Financing the Public Schools*
Ralph D. Fleming	Alexander Hamilton Institute, Author	*Railroad and Street Transportation*
Shattuck O. Hartwell	Muskegon, Michigan, Superintendent of Schools	*Overcrowded Schools and the Platoon Plan*
Walter A. Jessup	University of Iowa, President	*The Teaching Staff*
George E. Johnson	Harvard University, Assistant Professor of Education	*Education through Recreation*
Charles H. Judd	University of Chicago, Director, School of Education	*Measuring the Work of the Public Schools*
R. R. Lutz	Russell Sage Foundation, Special Agent (education)	*The Metal Trades; Wage Earning and Education (Summary)*
Adele E. McKinnie	Columbia University, Graduate Student	*The Public Library and the Public Schools* (with L. Ayers)

Table 5 *continued*

Staff Member	Affiliation	Publication(s)
Herbert A. Miller	Oberlin College, Professor of Sociology	*The School and the Immigrant*
David Mitchell	University of Pennsylvania, Assistant Professor of Psychology	*Schools and Classes for Exceptional Children*
Iris P. O'Leary	Department of Public Instruction, New Jersey, Special Assistant for Vocational Education	*Department Store Occupations*
Clarence Arthur Perry	Russell Sage Foundation, Director, Department of Recreation	*Educational Extension*
Frank L. Shaw	General Education Board, Educational Statistician	*The Building Trades; The Printing Trades*
Bertha M. Stevens	United Employment Bureau of New York City, Director	*Boys and Girls in Commercial Work*
George S. Counts	University of Chicago, Graduate Student	
Joseph F. Gonnelly	University of Chicago, Graduate Student	
William S. Gray	University of Chicago, Graduate Student	

SOURCE: Leonard P. Ayres, *The Cleveland School Survey* (Summary Volume) (Cleveland, Ohio: Survey Committee of the Cleveland Foundation, 1917).

(see table 5). Each report was based on extensive fieldwork: tests administered to schoolchildren; interviews with teachers, parents, and local citizens; classroom observations; and visits to school buildings. After the survey team discussed initial drafts, the reports were presented to local school authorities in order to clear up "questions of fact and questions of form," but not to settle "differences of opinion with respect to interpretation and recommendation."[57]

After they were completed, the reports were released to the public and the press at open luncheons ($.60 admission was charged to the first 300 people wanting to attend) held at one of the city's leading hotels. Continued on a weekly basis for most of a year, the lunches were well attended and, according to Ayres, very effective in encouraging newspaper coverage, so much coverage, in fact, that education displaced war news on the front pages of the Cleveland papers. To Ayres, this public relations process

> constituted a new development in educational practice and in the technique of the school survey. It might be called bridging the gap between knowing and doing, or it might be termed a process of carrying the community. It was a method of educating the public concerning its educational problems. Its object was to make the entire school system pass in complete review before the public eye. It made the schools and the public pay attention to each other. . . . Its aim was to place before the citizens a picture of the schools, a picture so accurate that it could not mislead, so simple that it could not be misunderstood, and so significant that it could not be disregarded. The Cleveland experience demonstrated that it was entirely possible to arouse the public to this sort of interest in their school problems and then to sustain that interest.[58]

As a result of this newly crafted, purposively compelling style of public communication, the survey's recommendations were difficult to resist. Having found that "the community genuinely wants good schools and is determined to have them" and having determined through careful testing that the school plant was excellent, the teaching staff was of "inherently good quality," and the business management was "honest and efficient," the survey zeroed in on problems of "professional" leadership.[59] According to Ayres and his colleagues, the city needed to hire a school superintendent who could create a "system of scientific general supervision," and to do this, the school board had to be reformed. Currently, it was too bogged down in the daily management of the schools and should concentrate instead on "deciding what it wants done, selecting people to do those things, studying results to see how well they are being done, and . . . telling the public about problems faced and progress made."[60] What the Cleveland Survey suggested was that educational progress required a professional superintendent capable of providing scientific management for the schools and a school board willing to restrict itself to general questions of purpose, competence, and communication. By implication, the survey was recommending a clear division of labor between those possessing scientific expertise and those possessing general knowledge. The former required professional training in educational administration, the latter merely a general education.

Not surprisingly, the conclusions reached by the Cleveland Survey were protested by the incumbent school superintendent and by some members of the board of education. The board president even accused the Cleveland Foundation of having fallen victim to the "cult of surveying" and compared the survey it had sponsored to "a clinic run by surgeons and students, not for the good of the patient, but for the operators."[61] But resistance was of little avail, and the surveyors prevailed. In January 1917, Frank Spaulding, then superintendent of schools in Minneapolis, was chosen to lead the Cleveland schools. Spaulding was a model of the modern school manager and a close ally of the professors who were developing educational administration as a field of professional study. In time, he would himself become a professor in the Department of Education at Yale University.

Soon after Spaulding's appointment in Cleveland was announced, Ayres went to work as a statistician for the Council of National Defense; then, in early 1918, he became head of the Statistics Branch of the Army's General Staff. After World War I, he left the Russell Sage Foundation and school surveying behind and became vice-president of the Cleveland Trust Company. By 1920, as Paul Hanus observed, educators were "no longer disputing whether education has a scientific basis."[62] With surveying becoming an increasingly routinized aspect of school administration and measurement techniques well established as essential to the evaluation of educational problems, there was little to hold Ayres's interest.

It is important to note, too, that after World War I, owing to the specialized focus of their studies and to their interest in profession building, school surveyors did not generally participate in the continuing development of methods of community research. Even though this remained a central preoccupation of other social scientists until at least World War II, educationists tended to remain aloof from efforts to advance theory or methods. Rather, having identified a service for which there was high demand, school surveyors were content to engage in a form of research that is best described as "social bookkeeping," the censuslike description of social data.[63] Already regarded as inferior academically, education scholars were further isolated from colleagues with whom they shared substantive, if not professional, interests. What is more, by shunning theoretical, methodological, and philosophical questions, educationists limited the capacity of their "science" to generate new knowledge.

Lewis M. Terman and the Testing Movement

In *Public School Administration* (1916), Ellwood P. Cubberley stated that he and his educationist colleagues nationwide had been determined "to change school supervision from the ranks of an occupation to that of a profession,—from a job dependent upon political and personal favors to a scientific service capable of self-defense in terms of accepted standards and units of accomplishment."[64] If the school survey movement appeared to help them do that, so did the testing movement, the two having supported one another. In fact, when Paul Hanus had surveyed the New York City public schools in 1911–12, he had used a standardized test invented by Stuart A. Curtis, one of Thorndike's students at Teachers College, to measure mathematics achievements. This was believed by contemporaries to have "firmly established the principle that in conducting school surveys scientific tests must be utilized where they are available."[65] In consequence, after 1911, as school surveying became increasingly common, measurement experts found a growing market for their wares.

Presaged by the spelling tests administered by Joseph Mayer Rice in the 1890s, but really growing out of work done by Thorndike, achievement tests were designed to gauge individual performance on a wide range of tasks, everything from spelling to reading, grammar, handwriting, and Latin vocabulary. They were usually not geared toward stated classroom objectives, though, of course, individual teachers created their own achievement tests all the time. Rather, standardized achievement tests, which were tests always administered in the same fashion, were intended to measure differences in individual capacity to handle words, passages, and the like that had been ranked according to some measure of difficulty. The proliferation of achievement tests was phenomenal: between 1917 and 1928, some 1,300 achievement tests were developed in the United States; by 1940, there were 2,600.[66] The explosive growth of these tests was fueled by the simultaneous development of "intelligence" tests.

Initial efforts to use what James McKeen Cattell first called "mental tests" to gauge mental functioning had not been successful. Cattell had hypothesized that the strength of one's hand squeeze, the number of consonants one could repeat after one hearing, the accuracy with which one could guess weight differences in identically shaped boxes, and other similar "mental tests" could provide an index of one's mental power. However, Clark Wissler, one of Cattell's graduate students at Columbia, had discovered that there was no positive correlation between the results of such tests and the grades of more than 300 Columbia and Barnard undergraduates.[67] In many ways, this was not surprising, since Cattell's interests had been more descriptive than predictive.[68] That notwithstanding, Wissler's disappointing research had ended Cattell's research into mental measurements.

Despite that, psychologists in France and Great Britain continued to search for viable tools to describe and measure intelligence. Far more than Cattell, whose interests harkened back to nineteenth-century, Baconian conceptions of science more than they presaged the increasingly instrumental conceptions of the twentieth century, they hoped testing could serve important social-engineering purposes. In 1905, Alfred Binet and Theodore Simon invented a scaled series of tests, based on chronological age, that measured a wide variety of separate mental functions.[69] Often based on knowledge—for example, definitions of a house and a horse or the capacity to arrange 3, 6, 9, 12, and 15 gram objects in order—the tests established what Binet and Simon called an individual's "mental age." Their work was facilitated by Francis Galton and Karl Pearson's formulation in the late nineteenth century of "correlation coefficients," which allowed precise description of the degrees of similarity and dissimilarity between phenomena.[70] At roughly the same time as Binet and Simon were developing their first tests, Charles Spearman was describing a two-factor theory of intelligence, in which "G" represented a "general intelligence," which transcended specific factors ("s"). Spearman's conception of intelligence differed significantly from Binet and Simon's more multifaceted concept, and it was Spearman's conception, along with Binet and Simon's scaled tests, that was transferred to the United States.

Two of the most important individuals involved in the transfer were trained at Clark University, which remained a leading center of the new psychology during the early decades of the twentieth century. Although G. Stanley Hall "strenuously opposed" mental measurement, it was one of his students, Henry Herbert Goddard, who first translated the 1905 version of the Binet-Simon tests into English.[71] As director of the Training School for the Feebleminded in Vineland, New Jersey, Goddard used the Binet-Simon tests to classify children. A eugenicist who invented the term "moron" and helped popularize fears of genetic retardation through publication of a popular and admittedly exaggerated case study entitled *The Kallikak Family: A Study in the Heredity of Feeble-Mindedness* (1912), Goddard also became an early popularizer of mental tests. After translating the Binet-Simon tests in 1910, he organized summer schools to train public school teachers in their use.[72] By 1915, he had distributed more than 22,000 copies of his translation of the Binet-Simon tests and 88,000 copies of the answer sheet.[73]

While Goddard was thus engaged in popularizing knowledge about the importance of mental testing, another Clark graduate, Lewis M. Terman, was at work transforming the Binet-Simon tests so that they could be administered to a group rather than to individuals. This was a crucial step in making the tests suitable for general use, including use in the schools.

Terman had been born in Johnson County, Indiana, on January 15, 1877. The twelfth of fourteen children, he seems to have been a bright, ambitious, and self-assured young man, who always lived in a hurry. He graduated from Central Normal College, taught school, and served as a high school principal before enrolling at Indiana University in Blooming-ton for an A.B. and an A.M. in psychology. Thereafter, he won a fellow-ship for graduate study at Clark, where he earned a Ph.D. in 1905.

Terman had been introduced to psychology at Central Normal Col-lege. Looking back on his education there, he recalled that he had "found *Dewey* obscure" and been "fascinated by *James*," whose "*Talks to Teach-ers* greatly intensified my interest in the psychological aspects of educa-tion."[74] Then, at Indiana, he had begun to read works in experimental psychology, especially those dealing with "mental deficiency, criminality, and genius."[75] When he had arrived at Clark, Terman had therefore be-come keenly interested in mental testing. His decision to follow this inter-est in his dissertation cost him G. Stanley Hall's direct supervision, since, as Hall told him "very emphatically," Hall disapproved of mental tests and thought the "quasi-exactness of quantitative methods" could be mis-leading.[76]

Even though he would have liked to work with Hall, Terman's disser-tation was important to him. Entitled "Genius and Stupidity: A Study of the Intellectual Processes of Seven 'Bright' and Seven 'Stupid' Boys," it afforded Terman his first opportunity to create tests, which ranged from tests of language mastery, to be displayed by solving anagrams, to tests of "the interpretation of fables," to be demonstrated by deriving morals from twelve proverbs. Although the tests had revealed few significant dif-ferences between the "bright" and "stupid" boys, the dissertation solidi-fied Terman's lifelong belief in genetic determinism. Confessing that the study offered few data relevant to the point, Terman had nevertheless concluded that "the study has strengthened my impression of the rela-tively greater importance of *endowment* over *training,* as a determinant of an individual's intellectual rank among his fellows."[77] Like Goddard, Terman seems to have enthusiastically imbibed the determinist perspec-tive then so unfortunately prevalent at Clark.

Suffering from tuberculosis, Terman moved to California. Initially re-turning to his earlier work as a principal, he eventually secured a post teaching pedagogy and child study at the Los Angeles State Normal

School (later UCLA) and, finally, in 1910 was recommended to Cubberley by E. B. Huey, another Clark graduate, for an assistant professorship in educational psychology at Stanford. In a memoir, Terman claimed that Stanford was "the university that I would have chosen before any other in all the world."[78] He would remain at Stanford for the rest of his long career, though not in the School of Education. He retired in 1942 and died in 1956.

Acting on a suggestion of Huey's, Terman began working on a modification of the Binet-Simon tests soon after he arrived at Stanford. He was convinced, as he wrote in 1911, that "tests must be developed which will enable us to differentiate all degrees of intellectual ability and all kinds of intellectual unevenness."[79] Previously, intelligence tests had been used primarily to identify people who were retarded—the so-called defectives. But in Terman's vision, these tests could and should become a means "for measuring the intelligence of [all] school children."[80] In pursuit of that possibility, Terman published a test in 1916 that quickly became known as the "Stanford-Binet." Because the test was standardized—the material on the test did not vary, and it was always to be administered and scored in the same way—and because the test was tied to norms of performance that allowed one to compare individual scores to the average score of the general population, it was widely adopted for use in schools. Building on the work of William Stern, a German psychologist, Terman used a new term—I.Q.—to describe an individual's intelligence or intelligence quotient. Determining a person's I.Q. involved the application of a simple formula: an individual's so-called mental age (i.e., his or her score on the Stanford-Binet) would be divided by his or her chronological age, and then, to avoid fractions, that sum would be multiplied by 100.

Until 1916, Terman had worked in relative isolation at Stanford. As he later explained, "between 1910 and 1916 I made no trips East and did not even apply for membership in the American Psychological Association."[81] Then, in the spring of 1917, he was invited to join the Committee on the Psychological Examination of Recruits, chaired by Robert Yerkes, president of the American Psychological Association, which was working to develop tests that could be used to screen and classify army recruits. The committee was a "Who's Who" of the new psychology, and participating in its work led Terman to confess that after the war he "no longer felt isolated."[82]

Working under the War Department's Committee on Classification of Personnel, this group of psychologists developed and administered two group intelligence tests: the Army Alpha for literate recruits and the Army

Beta for those who were illiterate. By the end of the war, the tests had been given to some 1,750,000 men. Even though the test results were rarely actually used in assigning soldiers to jobs, the work of the committee greatly heightened public awareness of the new technology of testing.[83] It was a notable example of what historian John Carson has called "persuasion across boundaries," the psychologists convincing military personnel that something called "intelligence" had an effect on performance and the military personnel pushing the psychologists to find ways to modify existing testing instruments to suit the practical demands of organizing an army that grew to seventeen times its initial size between March 1917 and November 1918.[84] More important even than that, as James Reed and others have suggested, "the war changed the image of testers and of the tested."[85] Once thought of as relevant primarily to "morons," mental tests now appeared relevant to everyone. The results for the nation's schools would be prodigious.

At the war's end, earlier efforts to introduce testing to the nation's schools continued apace. Facing ever-increasing enrollments—total enrollment in the schools increased 20 percent between 1910 and 1920, and 22 percent between 1920 and 1930—and growing ethnic diversity, more and more schools were looking for seemingly fair and objective ways to differentiate students.[86] The assumption was that student achievement could be enhanced and greater efficiency achieved through homogenous grouping. Testing seemed to fit the need, though teacher-designed tests were generally believed to be unreliable. Recognizing this, many school surveys recommended that school systems create bureaus of research, which were sometimes called "departments of psychology and efficiency" or "departments of testing."

If the needs of the schools, highlighted by school survey evidence, created a demand for standardized tests, the increasing availability of tests made it possible to meet the demand. Terman himself created a variety of intelligence and achievement tests that were adopted by many schools. After the war, he and Robert Yerkes received funds from the General Education Board, a foundation created by John D. Rockefeller, to develop a National Intelligence Test for children in grades three through eight. In addition, Terman developed an intelligence test known as the Terman Group Test for grades seven through twelve as well as the Stanford Achievement Test for students in all grades. All of Terman's tests were published and marketed by the World Book Company, and all sold extremely well. During the first ten years of distribution, for example, the Terman Group Test sold 775,000 copies, which, according to Paul Chapman's study of the Terman tests, meant that nearly one-fifth of all U.S. high school students took the test.[87] Encouraged by his success with intelligence tests, Terman also developed achievements tests, which also sold well. For example, the Stanford Achievement Test, which was first published in 1922, had annual sales of 1,500,000 by 1925.[88]

As the undisputed leader among psychologists focusing on school testing programs, Terman achieved national renown during the 1920s. He became editor of a World Book series on "Measurement and Adjustment" and served on many editorial boards. In 1921, he inaugurated a large longitudinal study of gifted children, 1,500 California elementary and high school students, reports of which appeared in 1925, 1930, 1947, and posthumously in 1959. In 1922, he left the Stanford School of Education to become chair of the Stanford Department of Psychology—note the change in affiliation success could bring. With new endowment money to recruit new colleagues, Terman was able to boost the standing of that department from last place in national rankings before the war to one of the highest-ranked department by the middle 1920s. In 1922, he was also elected president of the American Psychological Association (APA).

That office allowed Terman to offer his own assessment of the testing movement. Lamenting that mental tests were better recognized "as a mere practical device" than as a tool for research, Terman suggested that fundamental understanding of race differences, mental growth, genius, and insanity awaited continuing test-based research.[89] Whether he was right, by 1922 testing was a well-established means by which educational psychologists could help shape school practices and educational policy. Often located in one of the "research bureaus" that grew up as more and more cities underwent school surveys, by the mid-1920s, educational psychologists had found an expanding market for their expertise. Much in demand, they tended to ignore Terman's advice. As one contemporary explained, they usually found it "necessary to forego the more theoretical and technical aspects of educational research for the sake of being *a bureau of service.*"[90]

Like their colleagues who conducted school surveys, educational psychologists were thus, in a sense, the victims of their own success. From the mid-1920s on, they became more involved in the continued invention and refinement of tests and less engaged in searching for fundamental new insights into the nature of learning. They took for granted and helped perpetuate plans for school improvement that relied on ever more sophisticated schemes for differentiating between and among individuals. But having found a technology that could be applied and tinkered with endlessly, they generally avoided questions concerning the value and necessity of sorting students in the first place.[91]

Consensus and Community: A Science for School Administration

By 1922, the year in which Terman gave his APA presidential address, it was readily evident that a professional community had emerged among university-based educationists and their allies in school research bureaus and administrative offices. One sign of this was the existence of several new professional groups that had grown up in conjunction with the survey and testing movements. These were self-consciously intended to advance "the scientific movement in education."

One was the Cleveland Conference, a clublike organization that was formed at the end of the Cleveland Survey. Its founders included Leonard Ayres, Charles Judd, W. A. Jessup, and Edward C. Elliott. In Judd's words, the Cleveland Conference represented "an effort to get together a small group, all of whom are known to be interested in the development of scientific studies in education."[92] In addition to holding annual meetings to share information, the Cleveland Conference served as a placement and referral network for school administrators and researchers. In fact, one of the Cleveland Conference's first unofficial acts had been to lobby on behalf of Frank Spaulding's appointment as superintendent of the Cleveland schools.

Another professional group to emerge from the survey and testing movements would have much greater significance over the years. Known initially as the National Association of Directors of Research, this group evolved eventually into the American Educational Research Association (AERA). Organized at a meeting of the NEA Department of Superintendence in 1915, the association was initially made up of men who were all (with one exception, Leonard Ayres) affiliated with research bureaus in the public schools. As one founding member put it, they "were all measurers" and shared a commitment to the "use of educational measurement in all educational research."[93] Then, in 1921, membership rules were changed, and "ability as a research worker," rather than professional position, became the standard for admission. Even though this began what Robert Travers has described as AERA's long, slow detachment from practice, in its early years, the association represented and advanced the practical application of testing and measurement techniques within the public schools.

If organizations such as these testified to new professional linkages between school administrators and education scholars, so did the consensus that had emerged concerning the design of university curricula for school administrators. Two points were essential in this. The first was that quantitative measurements were necessary for the study of educational problems, and the second was that administrative study should be both clinical and empirical.

Of course, statistics had earlier become part of the education curriculum. Because he was convinced that all students of education "should be enabled to make intelligent use of statistical methods," Edward L. Thorndike had actually begun to offer a course at Teachers College dealing with the application of statistics to education as early as 1902.[94] Two years later he had published the first edition of his *Introduction to the Theory of Mental and Social Measurement,* which contemporaries universally cited "as the beginning of the application of statistical methods to educational problems."[95] Before the decade was out, arguments concerning the importance of precise educational measurement had even migrated from manuals of research methods to works like Samuel T. Dutton and David S. Snedden's *Administration of Public Education in the United States* (1908). Soon thereafter Thorndike and George D. Strayer published *Educational Administration: Quantitative Studies* (1913), which became a standard text in the field.

Some educators were critical of increasing reliance on numbers to frame problems of school administration. William H. Maxwell, for example, who served as superintendent of schools in Brooklyn and New York City from 1887 to 1918, described advocates of quantification as "our friends of the standard-test-scale-statistical theory . . . [who] proclaim their theory as a panacea for all educational ills."[96] Maxwell insisted that the results of education should be measured in life rather than in school tests. He therefore found that educationists of this persuasion, "particularly [those] of the closet or university type," were "unmindful of the lessons of education history," insensitive to "the universal rules of logic," and carried away by the current "mania for collecting statistics."[97] Even in the face of such criticism, however, by the middle 1920s, quantitative measurements had been generally accepted as an essential part of the professional study and practice of school administration.

If the importance of statistics was controversial, the centrality of empirical data derived from clinical settings was even more so. This was evident in debates within the National Society of College Teachers of Education, an organization established in 1902 to bring together "individuals offering Education courses in colleges and universities."[98] In March 1910, for example, there was a heated debate triggered by an address delivered by Frank Spaulding, then superintendent of the Newton, Massachusetts, public schools. According to Spaulding's autobiography, Paul Hanus, who was president of the society at the time, had invited his address. Hanus had complained to Spaulding that recent meetings had been "very dull," and having heard Spaulding give the same address earlier, Hanus had counted on him "to stir things."[99]

Claiming that the administration of public education was "grossly inefficient," Spaulding had blamed the situation on inadequate professional education. Every school administrator needed to develop his own "working philosophy of education," he claimed, by which he really meant a conception of how a good school ran. Taking aim at the traditional curriculum's emphasis on history and philosophy, Spaulding went on to insist that a philosophy "borrowed or adapted from Hegel or Herbart, Harris, or Hall" would not do. Instead, Spaulding ventured, school administrators needed knowledge that would be of practical value in fulfilling their most essential task, which was convincing the public to provide the financial wherewithal required by expanding school systems. For that, instruction in business principles, especially "the simple, business principles of *efficiency*," was vital.[100] Auguring new possibilities for collaboration between superintendents and university educators, Spaulding had suggested finally that all professors "form a limited working partnership with at least one school superintendent, better with several" in order to "carry on continued studies of the actual plans and problems of administration."[101]

Two academics were asked to comment on Spaulding's address. Although one of the two, Edward C. Elliott of the University of Wisconsin, was in essential agreement with Spaulding, the other, William Paxton Burris of the Dean College for Teachers at the University of Cincinnati, was not. Objecting to the discount Spaulding had placed on the formal study of philosophy, Burris's statement apparently unleashed a torrent of argument from people who disagreed with Spaulding's insistence on a practical as opposed to an academic approach to educational study. "A cynic, listening to the discussion at the meeting, might have said that most of us were not yet ready to study school administration," Hanus reported in an unabashedly partisan summary, which supported his fellow professionalizers and demeaned the more academic traditionalists.[102]

There was much talk of the sciences—economics, sociology, ethics, philosophy, psychology . . . but there was comparatively little reference to the study of school administration itself. . . . On further reflection it seems clearer than ever that the way to study school administration is to study school administration, and not to study the social and philosophical sciences, however great the value of a thorough study of these sciences may be—and it is very great—as a preparation for the study of school administration.[103]

Whether Spaulding had persuaded the members of the National Society of College Teachers of Education in 1910, by the mid-1920s, it was widely accepted that administrators in training needed the kind of hands-on, practical, business-oriented instruction he had recommended. By that time, Spaulding had served as superintendent in five cities—Ware, Massachusetts; Passaic, New Jersey; Newton, Massachusetts; Minneapolis, Minnesota; and Cleveland, Ohio—and had moved on to become Sterling Professor of Educational Administration at Yale. There, he had organized one of the first seminars to be built around close collaboration between students and school superintendents. Over the years, more and more similar courses were established, and they quickly gained popularity, since, as Henry W. Holmes of Harvard put it, "such study has the tang of reality and wholeness."[104] By 1925, such "professional courses," which had been unknown a quarter century earlier, were the norm at schools of education across the country. "Exact investigations which carry knowledge beyond conventional opinions, no matter how sagacious," were now seen as the necessary basis for professional school administration.[105]

Having thus entered the curriculum of university schools and departments of education, educational administration would remain a major field of professional training in the decades ahead. Despite that, owing to its almost exclusively applied or service orientation, educational administration did not develop high standing as an academic field within universities. At most institutions, it remained isolated from kindred specialization in business or public administration. What is more, one would be hard pressed to suggest ways in which the field of educational administration contributed to scholarly or public understanding of the place of schools and schooling in the social order. To the extent that such insight emerged, it was more likely to come from sociologists than school administrators and even more likely to come from college presidents speaking in the public interest. Not in the mid-1920s, but roughly two decades later, after World War II, that would be troubling to Cubberley's heirs.

CACOPHONY: CURRICULUM STUDY DURING THE INTERWAR YEARS

The scientific task preceding all others is the determination of the curriculum.

Franklin Bobbitt

In the school the aim has been to have no extra curricular activities, since every activity of the pupil, whether at school or at home, is considered a part of the general educative process.

The Staff of the Elementary Division of the Lincoln School

"Evaluation" . . . involves the identification and formulation of a comprehensive range of major objectives of the curriculum.

Ralph W. Tyler

If, by 1920, there appeared to be increasing consensus among education-ists concerning the problematics of their field and the founding of profes-sional associations augured well for the emergence of a close-knit, self-regulating professional community, during the next two decades harmony gave way to dissonance and multiple voices. Indeed, having been sidelined earlier, Dewey's ideas became popular again, although, more often than not, theories and practices that were labeled Deweyan had little, if any, actual connection to Dewey's writings. Still, developments during the 1920s and 1930s demonstrated that, even if education was now well es-tablished as a distinct academic specialization, there was little coherence to the field. The purposes of education were very much in dispute. So were the norms governing the professional roles assigned to teachers, ad-ministrators, and scholars of education. Needless to say, too, there was nothing resembling standards to distinguish scholarship from careful ob-servation or thoughtful reflection or, on the other end of the spectrum, from rank speculation and ideological pronouncements. In part, the dis-agreements and confusions evident among scholars of education were a reflection of general puzzlement about the foundations of social scholarship. As dictatorships emerged in Europe and the world was plunged into a severe economic depression, questions concerning possibilities for re-integrating ethics and values into "objective" scholarship arose across the social sciences. More important, however, the lack of regulation govern-ing education generally also encouraged disagreements and dispute among educationists.[1]

Nowhere was the cacophony louder than in discussions of the curric-ulum. In the United States, shifting social priorities have always been manifested in changing school arrangements, and during the 1920s and 1930s, the spotlight landed on the curriculum. After several decades of profound change in the ecology of educational institutions, attention now turned to what should be taught. Interest in curriculum was stimulated by the interplay of a number of distinct forces.

First, interest in curriculum change represented an extension of the reform efforts generally known as "progressive education." Often difficult to distinguish, the two terms having become almost synonymous, "exper-imental schools" and "progressive schools" were increasingly giving up traditional subject-focused curriculum in favor of problem- or project-focused activities. Especially evident at the elementary level, this shift re-flected growing acquaintance with theories suggesting the importance of engaging children in learning through their own interests as well as a widespread, popular wish to promote greater freedom and creativity in the classroom. With World War I over and, during the 1920s, the econ-omy booming, many people were eager to explore ways in which they could escape what were now seen as the illiberal constraints of Victori-anism. Jazz, radio, and the airplane dominated the era.[2] Within that con-text, it was almost inevitable that experimentalism would also creep into the course of study. While it is true that many schools remained quite traditional in curriculum and organization, it is also the case that child-centered, active modes of teaching and learning now acquired a currency they had not had before World War I.[3]

In addition to this general move toward pedagogically progressive practices, demographic circumstances stimulated interest in curriculum reform. School enrollments grew throughout the first decades of the twen-tieth century. With immigration rates high until passage of restrictive leg-islation in 1921 and 1924, school populations were continuing to grow and diversify. With this in mind, one California educator went so far as to insist that schools were now "to undertake the assimilation of the Ne-gro, the Indian, the Creole, the Filipino, the Porto Rican, the Alaskan, the natives of Haiti, San Domingo, Virgin Islands, Hawaii, in addition to

Mexicans, Chinese, and other Asiatics, the isolated whites of Kentucky and West Virginia, and the descendants and defectives of the New England hinterland."[4] Combined with a trend toward enforcement of compulsory education laws that had started early in the century, as well as efforts to relax academic standards in order to make high schools more appealing to all youth, these demographic realities accelerated the move toward curricular diversification that had begun before World War I. No longer were reading, writing, and arithmetic the common core of all school curricula. Now, those subjects were surrounded by many others. What is more, with growing numbers of students continuing on to high school, the sequence of courses one might pursue after elementary school was likely to be set according to professional predictions of a student's postschool life prospects.

If demographic factors encouraged interest in efforts to broaden school offerings, so did publication of the report of the NEA's Commission on the Reorganization of Secondary Education. Entitled *Cardinal Principles of Secondary Education,* the 1918 report argued that high schools should direct their efforts toward promoting growth in seven different areas: health, command of the fundamental processes (the 3 R's), worthy home membership, vocation, citizenship, worthy use of leisure time, and ethical character. Unlike the earlier report of the NEA's Commission on Secondary School Studies—commonly known as the Committee of Ten—*Cardinal Principles* did not recommend an essentially uniform academic core. Instead, it pushed for a curriculum that included many different kinds of subjects, more flexibility in academic requirements, and increased student guidance and testing.[5] Critics of American education have often viewed the report as triggering a slow and steady decline in academic standards that has yet to be entirely reversed over eighty years later.

Whether that is a fair appraisal, in the wake of the *Cardinal Principles* report some school systems reorganized their curricula, while others ignored the report entirely. As Edward A. Krug has argued in his classic history of high schools, local autonomy was "one of the main principles of the curriculum revision movement" of this era.[6] This resulted in wide variation among different systems. Generally, however, reorganization meant adding subjects—usually commercial studies, social studies, industrial arts, the physical and biological sciences, and home economics—and dropping others—most often Latin, ancient history, French, and advanced mathematics.[7]

As the purposes of schooling became more directly linked to the practical activities of adult life, a trend accelerated by the Great Depression, "life adjustment" became a goal for students in many schools. In some instances, this led to exciting new approaches to instruction. This was the case, for example, with some of the work sponsored by the Progressive Education Association in the 1930s. In other instances, however, an emphasis on life adjustment resulted in courses that were so far from academic as to be absurd. The best-known (and most-exaggerated) example of this came a little later, in 1947, in the courses in "basic living" that were backed by the U.S. Office of Education's Commission on Life Adjustment Education for Youth. Focusing on "problems of youth" and "group problem-solving," such courses might incorporate traditional subject matter, but many offered little more than discussion of boy-girl relationships or information about "manners, speech, dress, universal military training, use of alcohol, mental hygiene, and communism and democracy."[8]

Once seen as primarily important in terms of educating individual students, schools were now expected to fulfill a host of changing social purposes. Whatever the cause—vocational education and citizenship in the 1920s, social reconstruction in the Depression years of the 1930s, patriotism and preparedness thereafter—schools, having become institutions that were expected to provide social as well as individual benefits, became hosts to frequently changing, ever-diversifying curricula.

Finally, along with all this, curriculum diversification was given a boost by university-based scholars of education. Initially as part of school administration and then as a distinct subfield, curriculum study now assumed greater importance. During the 1920s and 1930s, psychologists produced more and more standardized tests, which could be used to assess students and match them to curricular tracks. "Have you measured the minds of your pupils?" a World Book Company advertisement queried. "Do you know that it is now as easy to measure the mental ability of a child as it is to weigh him or to measure his height?"[9] In addition, new specialists in curriculum study began to generate approaches to course development, especially at the elementary and secondary levels, that lent an aura of "science" to curriculum reform. This, too, led accountability-minded school boards dominated by administrative progressives to become involved in curriculum change.

In attempting to assume a leadership role in curriculum making, educationists were, of course, embroiling themselves in an intense politics. They were challenging the primacy in curriculum matters that had long been held by subject-matter specialists, the very arts-and-sciences scholars who already viewed them with such contempt. Not only that, but also, even though vague slogans like "social efficiency" and "progressivism" were rampant, educationists, like Americans generally, lacked clear and agreed-upon conceptions of educational purposes. In consequence, different educationists held fundamentally different views of how school curricula should be organized. Finally, in addition to professional turf issues between and among academics and educationists, there were many other parties—parents, foundation patrons, and college presidents, not to mention schoolteachers and advocacy groups—who believed they had the right to determine what should be taught in the nation's schools. Such groups often held the power necessary to support, modify, or undermine the theories of curriculum generated and, in some instances, translated into policies and practices by the educationists. As was the case of the developmental perspectives beginning to emerge in the 1930s, different groups sometimes lined up on different sides of an issue, with one foundation or lobbying group supporting reform and another trying to thwart it. As a result of all this, the story of curriculum study during the interwar years is one of constant struggle, frequent reform often followed by a restoration of the status quo ante, and relatively little fundamental change.

Regardless of the lasting overall effect of curriculum change in the nation's schools, throughout the period scholarship in education continued to grow. Doctoral enrollments moved upward, journals expanded in volume and number, and specialization increased. By 1930, more doctorates were given in education than in any field other than chemistry. By 1940, 14.3 percent of all doctorates given in the United States were given in education, and the numbers would continue to rise.[10] Well before the end of World War II, education was firmly institutionalized within the nation's research universities, and the transformation of normal schools into teachers colleges, and then state colleges, and eventually state universities was well under way. Indeed, as Geraldine Jonçich Clifford and James W. Guthrie noted in their study of education schools, by the 1920s most private normal schools had been closed, and by 1940, virtually all of the surviving state normal schools had become teachers colleges, with the result that "the century-old term 'normal school' disappeared into educational history."[11] At the same time, the growth of high schools and the resulting need for high school teachers facilitated the steady growth of university schools and departments of education even during the Depression years of the 1930s.

CHAPTER FOUR

Politics, Patronage, and Entrepreneurship:
The Dynamics of Curriculum Change

In 1927, the National Society for the Study of Education (NSSE) published its *Twenty-Sixth Yearbook*. It was the first volume the organization had devoted entirely to "curriculum-construction." Earlier there had been volumes considering the teaching of discrete school subjects. In 1906, for example, there had been one on *The Teaching of English in Elementary and High Schools* and, in 1921, one on *Silent Reading*. But the *Twenty-Sixth Yearbook* was the society's first effort to focus attention on the variety of methods and approaches that were now available to educators interested in studying problems of curriculum more generally and apart from the particular concerns of specialists in reading, math, science, or history. According to its editor, Guy M. Whipple, the *Twenty-Sixth Yearbook* had grown out of a suggestion made by Harold Rugg of Teachers College in 1924. As chair of the committee responsible for that particular yearbook, Rugg had urged that consideration be given not to "what the content of the curriculum should be, but . . . [to] how that content should be selected and assembled." This was needed, he maintained, because there was wide interest in curriculum reform at the time as well as a good deal of actual school experimentation.[1]

As Rugg was aware, however, there were considerable differences of opinion between and among the new curriculum experts. Some believed curriculum should be built around "the scientific study of society"; others believed "child interest" should provide the organizing principle. Rugg's goal therefore was to bring advocates of these different positions together in order to formulate a "synthesis" of their views. Overcoming "*divergences* in theory [that] have been overstressed at the expense of *agreements*" was important, Rugg believed, because curriculum change needed to be approached as a "comprehensive, all-embracing, and continuous" process. Heretofore, most curriculum revision had been mobilized by national committees studying one or another subject. In Rugg's view, such committees were not capable of closing "the gap between school and society, and between curriculum and child growth."[2]

What Rugg implied in introducing the *Twenty-Sixth Yearbook* he stated more boldly in the lengthy history of the curriculum he wrote as section I of the volume. Having reviewed the work of a number of influential national curriculum committees, he observed that the staffs of these ventures "contained not a single professional student of curriculum-making, not an educational psychologist, not a sociologist, not a critical student of society."[3] As a result, he maintained, they "used subjective and *a priori* methods in arriving at their recommendations and . . . ignored the results of curricular research." His goal, in light of that charge, was to offer "great praise . . . to the hundreds of university men and school administrators" who had served on such committees and to transfer responsibility for curriculum making to less traditional, more progressive elements—"in addition to technically trained students of education, disinterested students of contemporary civilization—analysts aloof from the academic formulae of education—the poet, the novelist, the dramatist, the architect, critics of economic, political, and cultural life, students of the development of society, specialists in contemporary industry, business, government, population, community, and international affairs."[4]

In fact, however, as Rugg confessed, the *Twenty-Sixth Yearbook* was put together by a committee whose members were "all professional students of the curriculum."[5] Seeking to advance the professional powers of educationists, the *Twenty-Sixth Yearbook* represented an effort to take control of curriculum making away from discipline-based scholars and to give it to scholars of education. Even teachers were left out, which Rugg justified in a footnote. "Under proper conditions . . . the true educational intermediary between the immature child and adult society is the teacher," he asserted. "But under the current hampering conditions (better, of course, than in earlier decades and improving slowly) of inadequately trained teachers of large and numerous classes, heavy teaching programs, insufficient facilities and lack of educational perspective . . . my allegiance [is] to the curriculum rather than to the teacher as the effective educational intermediary between child and society."[6] Reflecting a new sense of empowerment among increasingly secure scholars of education, Rugg's bold assertion of educationist expertise belied the variety of views and the difficulties associated with curriculum change. Relatively unchallenged during the interwar years, such assertions would be widely criticized and condemned thereafter.

The Scientific Study of Society

One of the earliest scholars to formulate a "scientific" approach to curriculum design was John Franklin Bobbitt. A Ph.D. graduate of Clark University, Bobbitt had initially been interested in the application of eugenics to education.[7] Then, in 1909, he had been hired as a lecturer in the history of education at the University of Chicago. Arriving there in the same year Charles H. Judd had become chair, Bobbitt had soon discovered that the subject he had been recruited to teach was being dropped as part of Judd's reorganization of the department. Dewey had thought the history of education important; Judd did not. He wanted psychology to provide the framework for educational science. In consequence, Bobbitt had become Judd's assistant, covering the chairman's classes when he was on the road leading school surveys, giving speeches, or attending professional meetings.[8]

Through his work with Judd, the focus of Bobbitt's interests had shifted to scientific management. With Judd's help, he had become involved in the school survey movement. In connection with that, he had studied the writings of Frederick Winslow Taylor and had urged their application to the administration of schools.[9] In addition, he had developed a popular new course on "the curriculum," out of which came the first text to set forth "*principles of curriculum-making*." Entitled *The Curriculum,* the 1918 volume was intended "to present some of the theory needed for the curriculum labors of this new age."[10]

According to Bobbitt, society had become more and more complex as specialization and democracy had increased. In consequence, a new education was required that could go beyond "filling the memory with facts" to training "thought and judgment in connection with actual life-situations." This meant, Bobbitt maintained, that schools should devote themselves to "the function of training every citizen, man or woman, . . . for proficiency in citizenship." Following from that, the task of the curriculum maker was to identify "that *series of things which children and youth must do and experience* by way of developing abilities to do the things well that make up the affairs of adult life; and to be in all respects what adults should be." Surveying society as it was, not as it could or should be, was, in Bobbitt's view, the best way to define curriculum objectives.[11]

Widely read at the time, Bobbitt's book was especially important to another early scholar of the curriculum, Werrett W. Charters. Having studied with John Dewey at Chicago, where he had received the Ph.D. in 1904, Charters had originally focused on teaching methods. Then, after becoming director of the Research Bureau for Retail Training at the Carnegie Institute of Technology in Pittsburgh in 1919, he had begun to conduct job analyses. This was a technique for analyzing the components of different occupations that had been developed in conjunction with Taylor's formulation of scientific management. Following publication of Bobbitt's *The Curriculum*, Charters had set out to explore the viability of using job analysis to develop school curricula.[12] The result was a volume entitled *Curriculum Construction* (1923), in which Charters argued that developing a curriculum should involve studying community life to identify educational objectives of both the vocational and the extravocational types; then, determining in detail which ideals and activities would allow one to reach those objectives and which meshed well with the interests of children; and, finally, arranging the selected activities in instructional order according to what was known about child psychology.[13]

From 1919 until his retirement in 1942, Charters worked in partnership with a long list of graduate students at several different universities to analyze adult occupations and to develop curricula appropriate to them. In 1929, for example, he published (with Douglas Waples) *The Commonwealth Teacher-Training Study*, which tried to identify "the [83] traits of teachers." As depicted by Charters and Waples, these ranged from "accuracy" to "wittiness." Having identified teachers' traits, Charters and Waples then ascertained how important each of them was for teaching at different levels of the school system. Finally, they enumerated all "the activities of teachers," which, once again, covered an enormous range from "complying with social conventions" to "exercising initiative in useful ways." Designed to provide schools of education with a standard against which they could review and revise their curricula, the Charters and Waples's study reduced what many still called the art of teaching to charts, lists, and formulas of minute behaviors.[14]

Like Charters, with whom he is usually associated, Bobbitt devoted most of his career to developing the principles of curriculum construction he first formulated in 1918. His best-known book, *How to Make a Curriculum* (1924), which reported a curriculum development project in Los Angeles, offered a guide that was widely read and used. Based on the demands of adult life, it delineated general educational objectives as well as the specific abilities to be fostered through the teaching of many different subjects, some traditional and academic (for example, Latin and mathematics), others less so.[15] True to the Taylorism that had inspired him, Bobbitt's prescriptions were precise and detailed with nothing left to chance and little left to the teacher's discretion.

Eventually, Bobbitt became disillusioned with the approach to curriculum making he had pioneered. In his contribution to the NSSE's *Twenty-Sixth Yearbook,* he reversed his earlier claims having to do with the purposes of education, now stating that education should be regarded as an end unto itself and not as preparation for life.[16] By 1941, when he retired from the University of Chicago, he had gone even further. According to his young Chicago colleague Philip W. Jackson, by then Bobbitt had concluded that his earlier efforts had nothing more than antiquarian value. "Curriculum 'making' belongs with the dodo and the great auk," Bobbitt claimed.[17] Earlier, however, Bobbitt's ideas had been in wide circulation. During its first years in print, *The Curriculum* had sold more than 3,000 copies annually, and even in 1929, its last year in print, it was still selling approximately 1,000 copies.[18] Important in promoting utilitarian conceptions of school purpose, Bobbitt's ideas provided a powerful spur not only to curricular diversification, but also to the decoupling of the curriculum from traditional academic subjects. Beyond that, his writings encouraged educationists to claim special expertise in matters pertaining to the course of study.

Child Interest

In *The Struggle for the American Curriculum, 1893–1958,* Herbert M. Kliebard hypothesized that the change of heart Bobbitt revealed in the *Twenty-Sixth Yearbook* was a result of the influence of William Heard Kilpatrick, who had become "completely mesmerizing" to him.[19] The suggestion is certainly plausible; Kilpatrick was a man of powerful charisma and honed skill as an entrepreneur. He was also associated with a very different approach to curriculum organization from the one Bobbitt had promoted. Kilpatrick was an advocate for "the project method," an approach to curriculum that emphasized how one went about teaching and learning more than what one sought to teach and learn. If this differed from Bobbitt's emphasis on relating content to tasks, it nevertheless also tended to render unimportant the grounding of school curricula in traditional academic subjects.

A southerner whose initial career as a teacher at Mercer University in Macon, Georgia, had been brought to an end by charges of irreligion, Kilpatrick had moved to New York in 1907 to study at Teachers College. He had been encouraged to do so by Edward L. Thorndike, whom he had met when he and Thorndike had served on the summer faculty at the

University of Tennessee. Despite that, it was John Dewey whom Kilpatrick proudly and publicly claimed as his mentor and guide. Joining the Teachers College faculty in 1913, Kilpatrick remained on that faculty until 1937, when Dean William F. Russell insisted that, having reached the age of sixty-five, he should retire. Faced with mounting public criticism of the Teachers College faculty's bent toward radicalism, the Teachers College dean was apparently worried about the continuing influence of Kilpatrick and others of the group that had come by then to be known as "the frontier thinkers."[20] That was a subsequent development, however, and in the 1920s, Kilpatrick's preoccupation was the project method.

In the same year that Bobbitt had published *The Curriculum*, Kilpatrick had published an article called "The Project Method." The article advocated encouraging "wholehearted vigorous activity" and making this the goal of any and all school curricula. The term "project method" was useful, Kilpatrick claimed, because it gave emphasis to three important aspects of the learning process. The first was the necessity for actually undergoing an experience. Presumably, this was derived from Dewey's belief that one learned best through purposive activity and mindful, self-conscious doing. The second feature of learning that Kilpatrick thought essential was the law of effect that had been formulated by Thorndike. This posited that a bond created by connecting a stimulus to a response would be strengthened or weakened depending on the satisfaction or annoyance of the situation in which that bond was created—put otherwise, the more enjoyable the experience was, the more learning there would be. Finally, Kilpatrick claimed the project method focused attention on the importance of ethical conduct, since a purposeful act had to proceed within a social context.[21]

A philosopher, rather than a psychologist, Kilpatrick set forth ideas that were eclectic in origin and more formulaic than profound in explication. Even though his grasp of Dewey's thought seems to have been partial and simplistic, he cast himself as a disciple who would translate Dewey's ideas into an approach that teachers could actually use in their classrooms. By emphasizing a simple how-to-do-it plan, Kilpatrick hoped to persuade teachers to adopt his ideas. To that end, he worked zealously to gain followers who would endorse his approach. Having initially described the project method in the 1918 article, he then arranged to have the essay distributed in pamphlet form. It sold over 60,000 copies.[22] In addition, Kilpatrick, who was known as a brilliant and very popular teacher, lectured to some 35,000 students during his quarter-century career at Teachers College. As they were for Thorndike, the lecture halls at Teachers College were a major medium for the dissemination of Kilpatrick's ideas. In addition, he spread his belief that "wholehearted purposeful activity in a social situation" should be "the typical unit of school procedure" all across the country on the public lecture circuit.[23]

Beyond all that, with Kilpatrick's encouragement, the project method provided a platform for what Kilpatrick himself described as "a project [method] propaganda club . . . an informal relatively secret organization."[24] Initially convened in conjunction with the March 1921 meeting of the Department of Superintendence of the National Education Association (NEA), the organization was called the National Conference on Educational Method. According to the call sent out for its first meeting, it was designed to serve the interests of "those directly concerned with the actual work of teaching" and to advance the belief "that on the laws of learning and the principles of democratic group life all educational procedure should be based, both in teaching and in the supervision of teaching."[25] This was, of course, a thinly veiled challenge to school administrators and their allies in university schools and departments of education. In addition to holding annual meetings, the conference sponsored *The Journal of Educational Method,* which claimed in its first statement of editorial position to be "moderately progressive" and devoted to "the improvement of teaching." In actuality, however, the journal served as an unabashed promoter for the project method and for Kilpatrick himself.[26] Kilpatrick wrote articles for most of the early issues—his series on educational method eventually becoming his book *Foundations of Method* (1925); most of the other articles described the ways in which Kilpatrick's ideas were being used in schools across the country.

Eager for influence and savvy in its pursuit, Kilpatrick became one of the best-known educationists of his era. His views were troubling to many of his contemporaries who worried that he was presenting the project method as a panacea for all curriculum problems and, in so doing, was jeopardizing the standing of educationists generally. This concern led Bobbitt's confrere, W. W. Charters, in a 1922 speech to the NEA's Department of Elementary Education, to charge that the project method was fine as a method of instruction, but misleading if treated as a universally valid principle for organizing the curriculum.[27] Ernest Horn of Iowa State University echoed the point. Rightly reminding easy converts that the project method had originated among teachers of agriculture and domestic science who wanted to distinguish practical, task-oriented activities from other kinds of school work, Horn maintained that the project method gave too much emphasis to the whims and wishes of the child and too little to "social utility."[28]

Never one to turn a deaf ear to critics, Kilpatrick responded *sotto voce.* James Hosic, his close and admiring friend who served as editor of *The Journal of Educational Method,* wrote an editorial suggesting that professors of education like Horn and Parker, who objected to building curricula around projects, were really objecting to teacher initiative in education reform.[29] Even if the charge had some truth in it, appearing in a journal that was directed at teachers, it was a nasty claim. With acrimony mounting and advocates of "the scientific study of society" becoming increasingly alienated from advocates of "child interest," Harold Rugg sought to lead the "field" in one of its first ventures in synthesis. The result two years later was the *Twenty-Sixth Yearbook,* but consensus concerning the goals of schooling and responsibility for curriculum design still proved elusive. With decision-making power still vested in local authorities and with so many different parties vying for priority in curriculum construction, achieving consensus was probably not a realistic possibility. Regardless, the fact was that decisions concerning which curricula one or another school district would follow continued to have more to do with the entrepreneurial skills and determination of different reformers than with settled principles or clearly articulated aims. What is more, without agreement among curricularists, champions of traditional, discipline-driven curricula could rather easily assert the benefits of curricula aimed solely at mastery of subject matter.

The Teachers College "School System"

In addition to chapters describing different approaches to curriculum construction, the NSSE's *Twenty-Sixth Yearbook* featured essays presenting the way curriculum was generated at private progressive schools like Lincoln, a laboratory school at Teachers College. Lincoln had opened in September 1917. The moving force in its founding had been Abraham Flexner, who had written the famed report *Medical Education in the United States and Canada* for the Carnegie Foundation for the Advancement of Teaching in 1910. Thereafter Flexner had gone to work for the Rockefeller philanthropic trust known as the General Education Board (GEB), where he had become involved in school surveying. Seconded by former Harvard president, Charles W. Eliot, Flexner's quest now was to reform precollegiate education.

Like Eliot, Flexner believed that the amount and style of instruction in most school subjects were a product of tradition rather than careful current consideration of the most appropriate aims and methods of "modern" education. As he explained in a pamphlet describing *A Modern School,* which he wrote in 1915 for the GEB, he thought a "modern school" should be organized around four subjects—science, industry, aesthetics, and civics—with other subjects like reading, writing, spelling, and figuring becoming "instrumental studies." Drawing heavily from his own experience running a school in Louisville, Kentucky, Flexner also urged that abstraction be replaced by more concrete experience, that local cultural and scientific organizations be tapped to supplement school studies, and that the school be "tentative and experimental" in all its "attitudes," thus allowing for "gradual improvement through readjustment." As Flexner summarized it, "The Modern School should be a laboratory from which would issue scientific studies of educational problems—a laboratory, first of all, which would test and evaluate critically the fundamental propositions on which it is itself based, and the results as they are obtained." The education offered its students should be "the least of the services rendered. . . . More important would perhaps be its influence in setting up scientific as against dogmatic educational standards."[30]

With that as its initial blueprint and with promises of support from the GEB, Flexner had approached James Earl Russell to see if Teachers College would be willing to sponsor the venture. Flexner would have preferred to establish an independent laboratory school, organized as a freestanding institution like the Rockefeller Institute for Medical Research, where Flexner's older brother, Simon Flexner, was the director. But his colleagues at the GEB had insisted on the alliance with Teachers College, and Russell, who was always in search of funds and hopeful that the venture could advance ends in which he was interested, had been eager to enter into the partnership. In retrospect, it is evident that Russell had a rather different conception of the venture than the one Flexner held. Russell wanted to find ways to allow "experts" to conduct experiments that could be useful to school systems whose weaknesses had already been exposed in a school survey, while Flexner was interested in experimentation for its own sake and wanted the experimentation carried out by the teachers themselves.[31] Despite this critical divergence, the two men did apparently agree "to do our work in such a way that no scientifically minded man can dispute the results. We can't afford to spend so much money as is contemplated in getting personal opinions even of a staff of good men. The public wants the truth, and we should be able to tell them what is fact and what is opinion in education."[32]

There was another concern behind Russell's interest in Flexner's proposal. Owing to the kinds of cross-pressures that often undermined curriculum experimentation at private schools, the Teachers College "school system" was in flux.[33] This made Russell especially eager for the affiliation. Lincoln was not the first K–12 school to be established by Teachers College. In 1887, Teachers College had opened what was described as "a school of observation and practice." Called Horace Mann, the school had quickly become "a grand object-lesson to all who come to Columbia University for the study of education," or so at least Samuel T. Dutton, a faculty member who also carried the title of "Superintendent of the Teachers College Schools," claimed.[34] Beginning in 1887 with only four students and growing to sixty-four kindergarten and elementary students the following year, Horace Mann added a high school in 1890. Thereafter its enrollments grew rapidly, from 253 children in 1890 to 639 children in all departments by 1900–1901. During roughly the same period, its tuition charges were also significantly increased, from $10 in 1889 to $60 for the kindergarten, $125 for the primary grades, $150 for the grammar grades, and $200 for the high school in 1896.[35]

Because Horace Mann drew a rather elite clientele, which was willing to pay highly for outstanding education, there was strong parental pressure to offer nothing but the best.[36] By 1901, it had its own five-story building, which ran for a full block on Broadway. It was replete with a large auditorium, a gym, art studios, a library, and classrooms and was topped with a weathervane shaped like a pen—"a model school house," Hopkins President Daniel Coit Gilman once said.[37] The Horace Mann curriculum was rigorous, and an unusual portion of the school's graduates went on to college. Any initial ambitions toward experimentalism had thus been thwarted by the ambitions of the parent body, who wanted a school James Earl Russell described as "the conventional type" and quite "conservative."[38]

In 1901, Teachers College had therefore created the second school in its "school system."[39] The new institution was an amalgam of a local, church-sponsored kindergarten and an elementary school founded by a Teachers College graduate and former Horace Mann teacher. According to Teachers College's dean, it was to be a practice school for the college as well as an experimental school. Harkening back to the origins of Teachers College in the Industrial Education Association, a charitable venture to provide manual and industrial training for poor New York City youngsters, the new school was especially directed toward neighborhood outreach. According to an early description, "a special effort will be made to interest the children of the neighborhood in the industrial and domestic arts, in the fine arts, and in those occupations and recreations which make for upright moral character and good citizenship."[40] Subsequently, this aspiration was solidified when a Teachers College trustee, James Speyer, and his wife gave $100,000 to construct a building for the school. According to a press release issued by Teachers College at the time, "the Speyer School will be in a very real sense an Experiment Station. It will give an opportunity not only to test theories applicable to public school work . . . but it will strive to utilize for educational purposes the best that is offered by social settlements."[41] To accommodate this aim, the new building featured classrooms, a gym, a library, a rooftop garden, and apartments for staff residents, at least two of whom were to be trained settlement workers, nominated by the University Settlement on the Lower East Side, where James Speyer was also a trustee.

Unlike the University of Chicago Laboratory School, where many Chicago faculty children were enrolled, and unlike the Horace Mann School, where the students tended to come from "professional" families who expected them to continue on to college, the Speyer School purposefully sought students whose fathers were "shop-keepers, teamsters, janitors, policemen, and street-car conductors." Like a hospital clinic where new doctors-in-training treated charity patients and new therapies were tried out, attendance at the Speyer School was free, and it was therefore deemed appropriate to "allow much more practice teaching and experimental work."[42] Unlike Horace Mann, the Speyer School was also meant to be "a model public school" that would serve the mostly newly arrived German residents of the Manhattanville neighborhood just north of the Teachers College campus at 120th Street and Broadway. To do this, it sought to prepare its students not for college, but for entry into existing low-level occupational roles. "America has as great need as any other country of intelligent workmen and skilled housekeepers, perhaps a greater need," a Teachers College press release announced, "and it is a part of the policy of Teachers College to experiment along these lines for the benefit of American schools. The Speyer School will attempt to show what is practicable under the actual conditions of the public school system."[43]

With ever-mounting public interest in having public schools that operated under "actual conditions" engage in tracking students into vocations for which they were best suited by family background and intelligence, the Speyer School quickly evolved into a demonstration site rather than a setting for experimentation. People visiting the Horace Mann

School on 120th Street often traveled six blocks north to visit it. If the steady stream of visitors helped limit the testing of innovations, so even more powerfully did the interest—or lack of interest—of the Teachers College faculty. Even though faculty members were engaged in research, often with graduate students, few were interested in school-based experimentation. Edward Thorndike, for example, who was indisputably Teachers College's best-known and most influential researcher, scorned such inquiry, and to James Earl Russell's regret, his attitude was quite widely shared in the faculty. As was the case in this instance, despite the seemingly great promise of allowing educationists and teachers to work collaboratively on problems of curriculum in action, laboratory schools often failed to sustain their initial experimental purposes.[44]

All this, compounded by advice indicating that, owing to many other experiments, experimentation was now less necessary in the early grades than in the high school and the upper grades of the elementary school, led Dean Russell to end Teachers College's involvement in the school, where only the lower grades were available. Operated for a time by the New York City Board of Education with some minor assistance from Teachers College, the school was discontinued in 1924, when its building was renovated to become the Teachers College Institute of Child Welfare Research.[45] This, too, was funded by Rockefeller philanthropy, this time in the form of grants from the Laura Spelman Rockefeller Memorial Fund. In several sometimes ironic ways, private wealth, not only in the form of high tuition incomes but also in the form of philanthropic gifts, helped make school-based experimentation problematic at Teachers College.

Initially located on Park Avenue between 66th and 67th Streets, Lincoln resembled the Chicago Laboratory School during the Dewey years in that it was an enormously exciting, innovative, and happy place. With an unusually able faculty that was committed to experimentalism and keenly interested in curriculum change—"Try anything once and see if it works" was their motto—the school developed a curriculum built around "units of work," each of which combined a variety of traditional school subjects.[46] The first and second grades studied community life; the third grade was devoted to a unit on boats that combined history, geography, reading, writing, arithmetic, science, art, and literature. Even in the high school, the traditional subject-matter divisions disappeared. Students in the tenth and eleventh grades studied "ancient and modern cultures" and students in the twelfth grade undertook a unit on "living in contemporary America."[47] Eager to share what they were trying out and learning, the

Lincoln School faculty published many remarkable books and pamphlets—for example, Hughes Mearns's *Creative Youth* (1925) and *Creative Power* (1929), which included many selections of student writing, and Satis N. Coleman's "A Children's Symphony," which reproduced a four-movement symphony that had been composed and performed by Lincoln students. Unlike the initial Dewey School, Lincoln insisted on the frequent testing of student achievement, which demonstrated that Lincoln students scored somewhat above national norms though a little lower than other students in eastern independent schools.[48] In this way, it combined "science" and child centeredness.

Despite its remarkable achievements during its thirty-one-year history, Lincoln was troubled from the first. Although the school was part of the Teachers College "school system," its relationship with Teachers College was less than ideal. In considerable measure, this was a result of the different hopes James Earl Russell and Abraham Flexner had held for the school from the first. Typically, for example, Russell wanted experimentation to be carried out by acknowledged "experts."[49] This fit with his wish to generate knowledge about education that would be sufficiently authoritative to be transferred to other schools. If, instead of highly talented but little-known teacher-researchers, someone like Kilpatrick or Thorndike had made Lincoln the setting for his work and the focal point of his teaching and writing, things might have been different. However, as things actually turned out, Flexner provided a strong second to the views of Otis Caldwell, Lincoln's first director, who wanted all experimentation to be done by teacher-researchers. Disenchanted with the possibilities this offered the Teachers College faculty to pursue the kind of research he thought important (even if they apparently did not agree), James Earl Russell did not make cooperation between Teachers College and Lincoln a high priority.

In addition to these problems, a central difficulty at Lincoln had to do with its capacity for influence. Transferring their innovations to other schools, which usually had fewer resources and less highly selected students, was often impossible for private laboratory schools like this one.[50] In planning the Lincoln School, Flexner had assumed that it could do for education at the elementary and secondary levels what the Johns Hopkins Medical School had done for medical education. As James Earl Russell realized, however, the challenges involved in influencing educational practice were much more complex at the elementary and secondary levels than they were at the professional level. Whereas the Hopkins model needed to be adopted at only slightly more than 100 institutions to become the national paradigm, the Lincoln model would have needed to gain acceptance within well over 100,000 local school districts, where authority for curriculum design resided. As Russell had realized from the first, this would have required that Lincoln "be a fairly typical American school."[51]

Whatever Lincoln was, however, it certainly was *not* a typical school. As had also been the case at Horace Mann, Lincoln was a tuition-charging independent school operated by Teachers College. It was also college preparatory. The presence of tuition-paying parents with college entrance expectations did not preclude experimentation, but it did encourage its concentration in the lower grades. Hence, even though Lincoln was especially intended to focus on curriculum innovation at the secondary level, the curriculum for the last four years was much less innovative than that for the earlier years.

Although Lincoln was a successful model of innovation, its unusual qualities sealed its fate. Declining during the Depression, Lincoln came under scrutiny from Teachers College at the end of the 1930s. Soon thereafter a decision was made to merge it with the Horace Mann School, which, since 1920, had admitted only girls, a separate school for boys having been established in Riverdale, New York. Then, in 1946, a decision was made to close both schools by the end of the 1947–48 academic year. Driven by financial pressures, these decisions were predicated on arguments concerning the irrelevance of private schools to the problems of public education. As Hollis Caswell, the Teachers College president who oversaw Lincoln's closing, explained, very few people now believed that "a private tuition school is the most suitable means for the College to employ in the years ahead in developing its program of school experimentation."[52] After the school's termination, the endowment the GEB had provided for Lincoln was transferred to a research institute, first known as the Institute for Educational Experimentation and eventually renamed the Horace Mann Lincoln Institute. Thereafter what was probably the nation's best-known school of education did not operate a school of its own.

Denver, Colorado, Teachers Study the Curriculum

Along with chapters devoted to curriculum construction in private experimental schools like Lincoln, the *Twenty-Sixth Yearbook* described curriculum reform projects in a number of public school systems. One of these was Denver, Colorado, during the seven-year superintendency of Jesse H. Newlon. Having earned a master's degree at Teachers College in 1914, while serving as principal of the Decatur (Illinois) High School, Newlon had made teacher-led curriculum revision a centerpiece of his superinten-dency from his arrival in Denver in 1920. Newlon had focused on curricu-lum reform because he believed that "curriculum making is a first consid-eration in the successful administration of any school system." That was true, he explained in a 1923 resolution to the Denver Board of Education, because curriculum revision could eliminate "nonessentials and mis-placed materials" and therefore save about 10 percent of the annual bud-get. More important, it could help ensure that the schools were effective in their state-mandated function of "raising each individual as nearly as possible to the maximum of his capacity for functioning as a citizen."[53] Keenly aware of the interest curriculum development was generating at places like Teachers College, Newlon saw curriculum development as a way of incorporating new research into daily school practice. By "culti-vating a scientific spirit" among teachers, he also believed it would im-prove instruction.[54] Unlike Russell at Teachers College, who was eager for laboratory schools to generate general principles that could be widely disseminated and used, Newlon was concerned with improvement in one location.

Operating in a school district that had a tradition dating from the 1890s of teacher participation in curriculum revision, Newlon, with the assistance of Assistant Superintendent A. L. Threlkeld, established teacher-led committees to review different subject areas. Realizing after a year that "it is impracticable to expect teachers to carry on all of this work after school hours," he had then convinced the board of education to provide money for teachers to have time released from classroom re-sponsibilities to concentrate on the curriculum work.[55] In addition, he had convinced the board to hire two full-time administrators to work with the curriculum committees and to provide additional funds for out-side consultants. Before he left Denver in 1927 to succeed Otis Caldwell as director of the Lincoln School at Teachers College, Newlon had se-cured more than $100,000 of public funds for curriculum studies that had involved over 600 teachers, approximately one-third of all those em-ployed. He had also brought many noted educationists to Denver to ad-vise the teachers, his eclectic list including, among others, Harold Rugg from Teachers College, W. W. Charters from the University of Chicago, and Ernest Horn from Iowa State.[56]

Doubtless helped by the fact that he had served as president of the NEA in 1924–25, Newlon's efforts in Denver captured the attention of school people across the nation. Thousands of the Denver curriculum re-ports were ordered, and in many cases, they became the basis for curriculum reform in other communities. This, of course, pleased Newlon, though it was the boost curriculum study gave to teachers that intrigued him most. Writing in 1933, he even ventured that "the printed course of study, unless used with caution and understanding, may defeat our purposes. The printed course of study is not our main objective. Our major purposes are a broader concept of education, and more enlightened, alert teachers."[57]

As seemed always to be the case with curriculum work, Newlon's views about curriculum revision and the approach he had followed in Denver were controversial. Although Newlon saw positive benefits for teachers in participation in curriculum reform, teachers were not so sanguine. As one Middletown teacher told Robert and Helen Merrell Lynd, "We live in such a clutter of 'revising the curriculum' and 'keeping records' that the teaching of the better teachers is suffering."[58] Not only that, but also Newlon's views were at odds with those of some of his fellow educationists, for example, with those of Chicago's Charles Judd, who favored expert-generated curriculum reform. While arguing that more money should be devoted to education research, Judd had once stated that "the kind of curriculum research that I have been advocating cannot be carried on by untrained people, nor can it be performed as a trivial addition to a major task of teaching." It required training to ensure that those involved understood that "the use of scissors and paste is not research," and it necessitated a significant commitment of time.[59] Unlike Newlon, who believed teacher-led curriculum revision could promote staff development as a necessary first step toward educational improvement, Judd believed educational improvement depended on formal, "scientific" research and what he once described as teacher supervision "in a fashion which is at once direct and scientific."[60]

The Emergence of a New Specialization: Curriculum and Instruction

Despite Judd's opposition, Newlon's emphasis on curriculum study as a means for encouraging the continuing education of teachers was picked up by many educationists involved in curriculum projects. As Hollis L. Caswell once explained, the emphasis made sense to them because "just writing courses of study and distributing them to schools" had proven to be a futile exercise.[61] Having received a doctorate in educational administration from Teachers College in 1929, Caswell had arrived at this conclusion while serving on the faculty of the George Peabody College for Teachers in Nashville, Tennessee. When he had arrived there, Peabody had just been chosen by the GEB to be its field office for school survey work in the South, and Caswell had been asked to work with Frank Bachman of the GEB in directing the office. In that capacity, Caswell had served as a consultant to many state curriculum projects, the best known probably having been the Virginia State Curriculum Program, which ran from 1930 to 1937. As he recalled later, his experience in the field led him to believe that "the improvement of instruction rather than the writing of courses of study" should be the goal of curriculum reform.[62]

In pursuit of such improvement, Caswell had recommended that teachers, working in collaboration with local supervisors, be asked to read selections from a broad range of theoretical works—Kilpatrick and Bobbitt were both included in his bibliographies—and then encouraged to discuss questions like "What is the curriculum?" and "What is the place of subject matter in education?"[63] Having once hoped to involve discipline-based university faculty members in these conversations, Caswell had discovered that doing so was well-nigh impossible. Although "they often would comment that the schools did not teach pupils to read and write and spell before they came to college," he recalled, "when we would go to the mathematics faculty or like department and ask if they would designate some member of their staff to go out with a person from the education department to work with curriculum committees of public school teachers we did not get an overwhelming acceptance."[64]

In spite of that, Caswell continued to insist that curriculum making, a process he conceived more expansively than writing a course of study, should be a widely collaborative enterprise. As he explained in a text he wrote with his Peabody colleague Doak S. Campbell, "when the curriculum is defined to include all elements of experience, curriculum development becomes a complicated process." It was a process, he explained, in which "teacher, research worker, subject matter specialist, psychologist, sociologist, philosopher, educator, administrator, and supervisor must all make contributions."[65]

Caswell's writings about the curriculum established him as a leader in educational circles and led to his election as president of the Society for Curriculum Study. This little-known group evolved out of informal meetings of university faculty members concerned with curriculum and especially with "scientific" approaches to curriculum construction. Having begun to meet in the mid-1920s, the society was formally organized in 1932. Although some people belonged to both groups, the society's membership was smaller, more university based, and more male than that of the Kilpatrick Conference on Educational Method, which, by 1930, had evolved into the NEA Department of Supervisors and Directors of Instruction.

Becoming president of the society in 1936, Caswell was eager to professionalize a distinct curriculum "field." With that in mind, he convinced people in both groups that a merger of the two organizations would help gain recognition for curriculum workers as specialists distinct from administrators and might even promote consensus concerning the conflicting aims and procedures that had pitted different factions against one another. To advance prospects for a merger, Caswell and Rudolph D. Lindquist, director of university schools at Ohio State, who was then serving as president of the NEA group, established a joint committee in 1936 to explore the possibility of bringing the two organizations together. Unlike the earlier Rugg *Yearbook* committee, this group did not aspire to "synthesis." Its report on "the changing curriculum" was very frank about disagreements between curriculum thinkers, which resulted, the report claimed, in "efforts at curriculum development . . . marked by contradictory, conflicting, and inconsistent thought and practices."[66] However, collaboration within the committee did eventually result in 1943 in a merger of the two groups, the combined organization taking the name Association for Supervision and Curriculum Development.[67]

Having thus helped found the leading professional organization of curriculum specialists and, earlier with Doak Campbell, having written a text that in its purposeful combination of different theorists and practitioners was as formative for the "curriculum field" as Bobbitt's books had been earlier, Caswell became chair of the Teachers College Department of Curriculum and Instruction in 1937. This was the first distinct curriculum department established in the United States, curriculum up to this point having been considered within the domain of educational administration. Seven older departments that had dealt discretely with problems of curriculum, supervision, teaching materials, and methods for different levels of schooling were now combined into a new umbrella configuration that focused on all aspects of curriculum for both elementary and secondary schools and colleges.[68]

Many years earlier Caswell had engaged in heated debate with his graduate mentor, George D. Strayer, concerning the wisdom of this separation. Strayer, who chaired Teachers College's programs in educational administration and its Division of Field Studies, would have preferred to have curriculum remain in that domain.[69] By the late 1930s, however, curriculum revision had become so ubiquitous—70 percent of cities with populations over 25,000 had organized curriculum development programs by 1937, and approximately 50 percent of smaller cities had similar endeavors—that demand for training was sufficient to warrant a distinct department.[70] Caswell's conception of curriculum and instruction thus allowed Teachers College, responding to market forces, once again to extend the purview of educational studies. Previously defined as a function to be supervised by school superintendents, curriculum study was becoming a specialty in its own right.

Social Reconstructionism and Its Transformation

In the same year that Teachers College created the Department of Curriculum and Instruction, William Heard Kilpatrick retired from the Teachers College faculty, and Jesse H. Newlon succeeded him as chairman of what was called Division I, the Division of Educational Foundations. Even before that division was officially created in 1934–35, however, many of the scholars who would become its members had begun to formulate a common position concerning the responsibilities of public education during a time of severe economic depression. Led by Kilpatrick, a group consisting of Harold Rugg, George S. Counts, John L. Childs, R. Bruce Raup, Goodwin Watson, Edmund deS. Brunner, Jesse H. Newlon, Harold F. Clark, F. Ernest Johnson, Donald P. Cottrell, and a few others had held twice-monthly dinner meetings since 1927, "canvassing informally, without programs planned in advance, the roots of every phase of our culture."[71] By the time the new division was created, they had reached consensus on a fairly wide range of controversial issues: they had aligned themselves with Deweyan instrumentalism, with the belief that "the school should reflect life and not remain isolated from it," with the view that there should be an activist role for teachers to facilitate social reform, and with the assumption that "education should be centrally involved in social reconstruction."[72] In that year, they also decided to publish a new journal, *The Social Frontier,* and selected George Counts to be its editor.

Having grown up in a fairly strict Methodist family on the Kansas frontier, Counts had graduated from Baker University, taught school, and served as a high school principal and athletic coach before enrolling for graduate study at the University of Chicago in 1913. He had initially planned to major in sociology, a field in which Chicago was achieving renown, but had switched to education on the assumption that this would lead to a more secure living. Charles Judd became his advisor. Even though, according to Counts, Judd "didn't want any philosophy in [the] School of Education," Counts had managed to go his own way. He had even persuaded Judd to let him minor in sociology rather than psychology, which was a first for a Judd student.[73]

Between his graduation in 1917 and his appointment to the Teachers College faculty in 1927, Counts had held appointments at five different universities, including Yale and Chicago, and had published three pioneering works in the just-developing field of the sociology of education. *The Selective Character of American Education,* which documented a close relationship between parental occupation and persistence in secondary school, was published in 1922; *The Social Composition of Boards of Education,* which demonstrated that "the dominant classes in our society dominate the board of education," appeared in 1927; and *School and Society in Chicago,* which focused on Chicago as a case study of "the play of social forces upon the school," came out in 1928.[74] Although the three books were extraordinarily incisive, pioneering analyses of the relationship between schooling and social class in the United States, it was for a speech he gave at the convention of the Progressive Education Association (PEA) in Baltimore in 1932 at the height of the Great Depression that Counts became famous. Entitled "Dare Progressive Education Be Progressive?" the speech was subsequently published with two other speeches by Counts as *Dare the School Build a New Social Order?* A tract for its time, the volume offered a conception of the teacher's role that few of Counts's fellow scholars of education, including John Dewey, would have fully accepted. Though quite idiosyncratic, the Counts volume made many people believe that educationists, especially those at Teachers College, were left-wing radicals. Like so much else associated with curricular change during the interwar period, this association would later be used to criticize educational scholarship.

Tapping his long-standing belief that psychology had been overemphasized in the study of education, Counts began by criticizing the tendency among progressive school people to focus too exclusively on the child. Moving from there to the claim that "there can be no good individual apart from some conception of the character of the *good* society," he chided progressive school people for having failed to articulate a "theory of social welfare." The result, Counts claimed, was not only that progressive education tended to reach only a small segment of society, particularly the children of "the liberal-minded upper middle class," but also that it was missing the opportunity to forge a new tradition in American life. To be progressive, he concluded, it would need to "become less frightened than it is today at the bogies of *imposition* and *indoctrination.*" Not only that, but also teachers would need to lead the way to change. As Counts put it:

> Teachers, if they could increase sufficiently their stock of courage, intelligence, and vision, might become a social force of some magnitude. About this eventuality I am not over sanguine, but a society lacking leadership as ours does, might even accept the guidance of teachers. Through powerful organizations they might at least reach the public conscience and come to exercise a larger measure of control over the schools than hitherto. . . . That the teachers should deliberately reach for power and then make the most of their conquest is my firm conviction.[75]

When he finished the speech, the audience was apparently spellbound and silent.

Subsequently, Counts further explored his ideas concerning the role of teachers in social reconstruction via *The Social Frontier*. With Counts at the helm, the journal committed itself to "considering the broad role of education in advancing the welfare and interests of the great masses of the people who do the work of society."[76] While he was editor, it published an extraordinarily lively and provocative collection of essays on topics like "Freedom in the School," "The Youth of America," "W.R. Hearst—Epitome of Capitalist Civilization," "What Sort of a School Is a CCC Camp?" and "Liberalism and Civil Liberties." Its authors included, among others, John Dewey (who wrote an essay for a special "John Dewey's Page"), Charles Beard, Sidney Hook, Merle Curti, George A. Coe, Lewis Mumford, Norman Thomas, Roger Baldwin, and Harold Laski. Winning 6,000 subscribers by the end of its first year, *The Social Frontier* thrived through 1937, when Counts retired as editor. Thereafter financial problems forced its editorial board to surrender control of the journal to the PEA, which, in 1939, changed its name to *Frontiers of Democracy*.[77]

The decline and demise of *The Social Frontier* coincided with the waning of other social reconstructionist efforts. One of these was Harold Rugg's attempt to move the nation's public schools toward a social studies curriculum that would help nurture critical, freethinking citizens. In a sense, what Rugg aspired to do was to help youngsters acquire the kind of understanding of American society that he had not himself acquired until he was in his mid-thirties.

Having been educated initially as an engineer, Rugg had begun his professional career in education in full sympathy with the measurement movement mobilized initially by Edward Thorndike and Leonard Ayres. After receiving his Ph.D. at the University of Illinois, he had joined the faculty of the University of Chicago. There, between 1916 and 1918, he had published several monographs that were characteristic of such study. *The Experimental Determination of Mental Discipline in School Studies* had appeared in 1916, *Statistical Methods Applied to Education* in 1917, and *Scientific Method in the Reconstruction of Ninth Grade Mathematics* in 1918.

Testifying to the notice those volumes had brought him (and the power of a recommendation from Judd), Rugg had been recruited to serve on the army's Committee on Classification of Personnel. Service on that committee or on the Committee on the Psychological Examination of Recruits, chaired by Robert Yerkes, president of the American Psychological Association, increased most members' zeal for testing and measurement—recall the impact of such service on Lewis Terman. For Rugg, by contrast, wartime service had offered exposure to new and startling ideas. Through two fellow committee members, Arthur Upham Pope and John Coss, both of whom were psychologists, he had discovered the work of Van Wyck Brooks, Waldo Frank, Randolph Bourne, and other contemporary social critics. The result, as he described it later, was an introduction to "what the social-economic-political to-do was all about" that would eventually transport Rugg from the science of education to studies of creativity.[78] More immediately, however, the new perspective Rugg gained during the war led him to leave what he later dubbed "Judd's ordered team of 'scientists'" at the University of Chicago for a new "company of creative individualists" at Teachers College.[79]

In January 1920, Rugg became a professor of education there as well as director of research at the Lincoln School. Finding himself surrounded by exponents of progressive education, as well as by the avant-garde artists and writers of Greenwich Village, Rugg became an advocate for the child-centered school, about which he wrote a well-known book with Ann Shumaker (the second of his three wives) in 1928. Through his work in social studies, he also became an influential and controversial proponent of social reconstructionism.[80]

Soon after arriving at Lincoln, he convinced Otis Caldwell to allow him to develop experimental units, combining history, geography, and community studies, for the fifth and sixth grades. For these, he wrote and mimeographed hundreds of pages of teaching materials, which, in pamphlet form, were subsequently offered for sale to three hundred principals and superintendents who had previously been students of Rugg's at Chicago or Teachers College. Nine years later he wrote and distributed several social studies pamphlets that had a total distribution of over 750,000.[81] He did this with the assistance of his brother Earl and a growing number of research assistants. Thereafter Rugg expanded the effort into a fourteen-volume textbook series entitled *Man and His Changing Society*, which was published by Ginn and Company between 1929 and 1940.

According to the introduction repeated in each volume, the series had been written so that "young Americans can be given an appreciation of the significant contemporary problems of living together." It combined previously separate courses in history, geography, and civics, the assumption being that these subjects were best approached in an integrated fashion that would fully illuminate contemporary cultures. Yet again, of course, the social purpose of schooling was central, and traditional disciplinary considerations were given a back seat. As Rugg explained, however, the new approach was not intended to cause "a reduction in the amount of history or of geography included in the course. Rather, it has produced a sharp increase in the amount of these subjects . . . [and] a wealth of new material."[82]

Sales of the Rugg textbooks were phenomenal. Between 1929 and 1939, 1,317,960 books in the series were sold, along with 2,687,000 workbooks.[83] The controversy they stirred was equally great. Bertie Forbes, publisher of *Forbes Magazine*, claimed he would personally "insist that this anti-American educator's text books be cast out."[84] Responding to a chapter that claimed that advertising contributed nothing but higher consumer costs to American society, the American Association of Advertisers asked every one of its local members to pressure their local school boards not to buy the books. Even though Rugg found many defenders who thought the books presented a fair portrait of the United States and would help students learn to form independent judgments, the criticism of the books, combined with the patriotic fervor of World War II, sealed their fate. Ginn discontinued them in 1940.

By that time, one of Rugg's former colleagues at the Lincoln School, Paul R. Hanna, had developed an alternative series with Scott, Foresman and Company that tells much about the fate of social reconstructionism in the 1940s and 1950s. The Hanna series was self-consciously intended to carry on Rugg's interdisciplinary, social emphasis, but in a much more moderate way.[85] While at Teachers College, first as a student (Hanna received the Ph.D. in 1937) and then as an assistant professor and research associate at Lincoln, Hanna had participated in the Kilpatrick discussion group and had become well acquainted with Rugg, Counts, Newlon, and the rest. He lamented their lack of interest in elementary education, although he himself had, in fact, refused to become involved in preparing an elementary social studies series for Macmillan with Counts and Charles Beard because he was convinced they would not do their share of the work.[86] But he recalled later that Newlon in particular had always given him very good advice. Apparently Newlon had told him: "Never behave in such a way that you have the platform from which you speak jerked out from under you."[87] That was what Rugg had done with his social studies texts, Hanna believed, and with Rugg's public pillorying in mind, he framed his series in a much less critical way.

Tied in with the Scott, Foresman "Dick and Jane" reading series, which was edited by William S. Gray, a prominent reading specialist at the University of Chicago, the Hanna elementary social studies series sold over 8 million copies in its first thirty years in print. According to Hanna, the series carried on the social emphasis of "the frontier thinkers" because it was intended to describe typical human activities. More telling, however, was that the series was meant to solve what Hanna called the problem of "scope and sequence."[88]

Hanna had been critical of curriculum making at Lincoln because there was no overarching rationale other than teacher interest and competence to provide focus and order for the different curriculum units. Echoing a phrase also used by Harold Rugg, he described the Lincoln faculty as a group of "prima donnas."[89] Subsequently, he had developed the concept of "scope and sequence" while working with Hollis Caswell on the Virginia State Curriculum Program. The concept was meant to ensure that students would be introduced to the full range of human relations. Not only that, but with everything preplanned, the curriculum would be "teacher proof." That phrase may have been invented later, but like John Franklin Bobbitt, Hanna seems to have seen the curriculum as a means for preventing teacher initiative.

If social reconstructionism was a radical effort to enlist schools in purposive social change, social studies as conceived by Paul Hanna was merely a means to acquaint students with the activities of their world: first the family and then the local community, the state, the nation, and the international community. Equally important, if social reconstructionism had been an effort to help teachers assume important roles in social reform, social studies as developed by Hanna tried to guarantee that teachers would not be able even to set the parameters of the curricula they taught. Regardless of Hanna's terminology in describing the series, the social reconstructionist aspirations of the Rugg series were gone from it, and gone, too, was the Rugg series's grounding in the writings of historians like Charles Beard and James Harvey Robinson. Through self-conscious divergence from the more radical views of his progressive mentors, Hanna developed a bland series that pleased the school boards of middle America throughout the 1940s and 1950s and even thereafter.

The demise of *The Social Frontier,* the discontinuance of the Rugg textbooks, and the steady sale of the Hanna social studies series came as the United States was entering World War II and leaving behind the economic suffering and intellectual radicalism of the 1930s. The nation's movement away from the social and intellectual ferment of the Great Depression years toward a war-related rise in patriotism yet again changed the social context for curriculum making. Even as curricularists elaborated special concepts like scope and sequence, which would become the building blocks of their particular branch of professional study, it was evident that changes in national goals and shifts in public opinion would have at least as much to do with curriculum change as theories spun by professional educators. What is more, however variously they may have been expressed, the assertions of expertise and aspirations to leadership in matters pertaining to curriculum that had run through the varied efforts of educationists between the two wars would have a boomerang effect after World War II.

CHAPTER FIVE

Developmental Perspectives: Critics Challenge Determinism in Education

If the emergence of curriculum and instruction as a distinct field of professional specialization was one important result of interwar interest in curriculum change, another had to do with challenges to prevailing conceptions of intelligence and educational achievement. Mounted by diverse sets of scholars, from both within and outside the educationist camp, as well as by "progressive" school leaders, these challenges involved efforts to study child and human development and to develop teaching materials and approaches to curriculum consistent with that research. In addition, they involved efforts to find ways to link achievement testing to the improvement of education rather than the sorting of students. In important ways, these interwar developments challenged fundamental assumptions about teaching and learning as well as practices and policies derived from these assumptions.

As was becoming increasingly the case, philanthropic foundations played an important role in shaping the events that surrounded interwar interest in new developmental perspectives. Thanks to grants from various Rockefeller philanthropies, research opened new possibilities for extending education to more and more people. However, those possibilities were quickly foreshortened by World War II and the renewed support for established approaches to testing and tracking that was provided by the launching of the Educational Testing Service (ETS) in 1947, an event that was brought about through the intervention of the Carnegie Corporation and the Carnegie Foundation for the Advancement of Teaching.

At this time, there were subtle but important differences in orientation between the various Carnegie philanthropies, on the one hand, and the various Rockefeller trusts, on the other. The Carnegie philanthropies were still guided by the social vision introduced into the Carnegie Foundation for the Advancement of Teaching and, to a lesser extent, the Carnegie Corporation by the Carnegie Foundation's first president, Henry S. Pritchett. This presumed that progress was dependent upon the training of talent in a hierarchically organized system of institutions, admission to which would be more and more limited the higher one went. One's competence as judged by standardized tests of ability and achievement was to be the basis for admission. Even though it was widespread in American society, officials at the Rockefeller philanthropies held this view less commonly. Whether this was a result of Rockefeller interest in the education of African Americans, of John D. Rockefeller Jr.'s personal involvement in the family's philanthropy, or of Abby Aldrich Rockefeller's quite liberal concerns for working women, modern art, and progressive education, the subtle differences in view between the Carnegie and Rockefeller philanthropies during the interwar years translated into quite different roles in education policy. While the Rockefeller funds served as patrons to researchers interested in developmental perspectives, the Carnegie organizations tended (with important exceptions) to take the side of older, more academic, and more narrowly behaviorist models. Carnegie support for the establishment of ETS marked the culmination of this orientation.

The Laura Spelman Rockefeller Memorial Fund

Rockefeller interest in child and human development was largely the result of the thinking of two unusual men. The first was Beardsley Ruml, a psychologist who is best known for having invented the withholding tax. Ruml was a charming, brilliant, self-indulgent *wunderkind,* who had completed the Ph.D. at the University of Chicago with psychologist James R. Angell in 1917. Like many of his professional colleagues, he had served with the Committee on the Classification of Personnel during World War I. Thereafter he had gone to work briefly for the Scott Company, a short-lived consulting firm made up of psychologists interested in adapting the new technology of mental testing to the personnel requirements of the nation's growing industrial firms. In 1920, he had joined his mentor at the Carnegie Corporation during the year Angell had been its president (1920–21). Then, on Angell's recommendation, he had been hired to lead the Laura Spelman Rockefeller Memorial Fund, a trust established by John D. Rockefeller in October 1918 to honor his first wife, Laura ("Cettie") Spelman Rockefeller. In addition to funding a number of major memorials to Mrs. Rockefeller, the fund was intended to carry forward her interest in the welfare of women and children. Floundering during its first years, the Memorial finally found direction when Ruml presented the trustees with a brilliant memorandum explaining that "the practical attack on social problems is the scientific attack broadly conceived." This led to a three-pronged program in the social sciences, child study and parent education, and interracial relations.[1]

The person most closely associated with Ruml in developing the Memorial's program was Lawrence K. Frank. If Ruml was known among contemporaries as a man of lavish tastes, Frank was known as a matchmaker who constantly sought to introduce the various members of his wide and ever-widening circle of acquaintance to one another. Having grown up mostly in New York City, where he had graduated from DeWitt Clinton High School and Columbia University, Frank had worked at the New York Telephone Company for seven years before World War I. This had fostered the interest he had initially developed at Columbia in statistical economics and had led to his wartime service with the War Industries Board. There, Frank had worked especially closely with Wesley Mitchell, the Columbia economist who helped found both the New School for Social Research and the National Bureau of Economic Research. During the war and thereafter, Frank also became a close friend of Mitchell's wife, Lucy, who had founded the Bureau of Educational Experiments (later Bank Street College of Education) in 1916. She introduced him to the world of progressive preschool education. Between the end of the war and Frank's appointment to the staff of the Memorial in 1923, he had served as the business manager at the New School and had begun to write occasional articles about education. These had helped shape the ideas Frank would offer Ruml when Ruml asked him to help plan how the Memorial might spend approximately $1 million a year to help children. The result in the spring of 1923 was an outline for research in child development coupled to a plan for disseminating the research through parent education.[2]

Although Frank's thinking shifted from an essentially behaviorist perspective on child development in the 1920s to a more cultural orientation in the 1930s, as early as 1922 several key features of his mature thought were clear.[3] Most important perhaps was his belief that even if "intelligence is born, not made . . . we may still maintain that native intelligence may be, and is, hampered and thwarted, chiefly by social life and the process of formal schooling, and that it is the office of education to assist in the emancipation of intelligence."[4] Viewed this way, education was society's primary vehicle for freeing people from the beliefs, values, norms, customs, and behaviors that stood in the way of the free expression of their "intelligence," a word that Frank, following John Dewey, used often to describe a deliberative, scientific approach to the problems of life. Reflecting the romance with psychoanalytic ideas that was so *au courant* among progressive intellectuals in the 1920s, Frank called this process of enlightenment "psychoanalysis."[5] As historian Hamilton Cravens has aptly noted, as Frank's thinking matured over the years, he eventually "turned psychiatry into cultural analysis."[6]

In addition to believing that psychoanalysis, so defined, was central to education, Frank insisted that education should be based on an understanding of children's growth and development as organic beings. This meant that one should not be concerned about one aspect of a child's life apart from other aspects, the intellectual, for example, being integrally related to the physical and moral.[7] In Frank's view, the meaning of "child welfare" also needed to be reconceived. Rather than connoting the care of children with special needs, it was now necessary, Frank insisted, to approach child welfare as having to do with the well-being of all children. Today, he wrote in 1931, it is generally recognized that "'The Problem Child' has . . . become 'The Problems of the Child.'"[8]

As Frank was well aware, of course, to ground education in a scientific understanding of the child would require research into child development. Though supportive of it, Frank believed lay organizations of mothers like the Child Study Association, which had originated from the earlier child-study movement championed by G. Stanley Hall, were more effective as agents of dissemination than as centers of research. The kind of research he hoped to stimulate would be more rigorous and objective than the kind of research Hall had encouraged, and unlike that earlier research, it would not fit within a genetically determinist mold.

Possibly hoping to create a mediating agency analogous to the Social Science Research Council, which had been nurtured into being by Beardsley Ruml to help organize the Memorial's activities in the social sciences, Frank financed a Committee on Child Development within the National Research Council (NRC), the research arm of the National Academy of Sciences. Initially chaired by Bird T. Baldwin of the Iowa Child Welfare Research Station, the committee came to life when Robert Woodworth, chair of the Department of Psychology at Columbia and a member of the committee, wrote a letter to some 1,200 psychologists to ascertain their interest in child development. Woodworth discovered that of the one-third who responded, some 129 said they were involved in research about child psychology. Tapping into that group, the committee convened four conferences between 1925 and 1933. It also distributed Memorial money in the form of fellowships, launched a bibliographic journal, and in 1933 transformed itself into the independent Society for Research in Child Development, an organization that today has a membership of almost 5,000.[9]

In addition, between 1922 and 1933, the Memorial made major grants to establish five centers of child development research, at Teachers College, the University of Iowa, the Merrill-Palmer School (later Institute), the University of Minnesota, and the University of California at Berkeley. Testifying to Frank's belief in cross-professional, cross-disciplinary study, all were freestanding and affiliated with several different faculties. The first center was at Teachers College. Called the Institute of Child Welfare Research, the venture was not very successful. Although Helen Thompson Woolley, probably the nation's best-known female psychologist at the time, was recruited to be its director, the Teachers College Institute suffered from some of the same problems that plagued the Lincoln School. Most important in this case, its research remained an ancillary activity in which few regular Teachers College faculty members participated. Housed in the old Speyer School building, the institute was therefore discontinued in 1936, when the Memorial grants ran out.[10]

Nature versus Nurture: The Iowa Child Welfare Research Station

The other Memorial institutes were longer lived, and one in particular, the Iowa Child Welfare Research Station, played an important role in the history of education research. Founded initially in 1917 through the efforts of a leader of the Iowa Congress of Mothers named Cora Bussey Hillis, the Iowa station was located at the University of Iowa in Iowa City and was initially funded by the state legislature and the Women's Christian Temperance Union. During its first years, under the direction of Bird T. Baldwin, the station opened an experimental nursery school, which served as both a demonstration center and a laboratory in which to study "normal" children. This set research at Iowa on a different track from research involving either "defective" children or "geniuses." So did Baldwin's early recognition that more than I.Q. was involved in the school achievement of young children. That early insight led him to criticize the adequacy of the I.Q. as a measure of a child's cognitive capacities, which placed him squarely at odds with Lewis M. Terman and most measurement experts.

As soon as Baldwin had learned of the Memorial interest in child development, he had begun to seek its support for the Iowa station, and just before his sudden and unexpected death in May 1928, he had finally secured a promise of financing. Worrying that the grant might be jeopardized by Baldwin's death, Iowa President Walter A. Jessup moved promptly to find a successor. At the time, Iowa was self-consciously and effectively transforming itself into a national research university, and foundation support for research was regarded as essential to the effort.[11] Because the candidate suggested to Jessup by Ruml was unavailable, he turned to George D. Stoddard, a young psychologist already serving on the Iowa faculty. Appointed acting director in 1928, Stoddard became permanent director in 1929 and remained in that post until 1942. As things turned out, it was an appointment that would have important consequences for education research, policy, and practice.

Although Stoddard himself believed that Jessup had turned to him because he was desperate, Stoddard proved to be a brilliant choice. Graduating from Pennsylvania State University in 1921, Stoddard had then studied with Alfred Binet's colleague Theodore Simon at the Sorbonne; thereafter he had done his doctoral work in psychology at Iowa. Under the supervision of Giles M. Ruch, he had devoted most of his doctoral career to analyzing ways to predict college achievement. Discovering that group intelligence tests and reading comprehension tests were not effective predictors and that high-school class standing was effective, he had decided to develop "training tests, which tested for knowledge acquired before college." These became the Iowa Placement Examinations, and as Stoddard recalled, they helped shift the purpose of college placement testing from prediction to "helpfulness," the aim being to support student academic success.[12]

Stoddard's time at the Sorbonne, combined with work on his doctoral dissertation, had made him perhaps even more skeptical of I.Q. testing than his predecessor had been. With ample Rockefeller funds to support the work, Stoddard therefore encouraged the station's researchers to pursue the investigations of hereditary versus environmental influences on intelligence that Bird Baldwin had begun. The resulting output was extraordinary in quantitative terms: whereas 144 research publications had been produced under Baldwin's leadership between 1917 and 1928, 603 were produced between 1928 and 1942, 586 under Stoddard's direct supervision.[13] More important, work done at the Iowa station during Stoddard's years as director posed a direct challenge to the idea that I.Q. was a fixed entity, fully determined by inheritance. As Stoddard reported in 1939, studies by Harold Skeels demonstrated that when "the illegitimate children of dull or feeble-minded mothers and out-of-work or laboring class fathers" were placed in "good homes" early in infancy, their test scores equaled those of "bright children," and investigations carried out by Beth L. Wellman showed that children enrolled in the station's preschool laboratories gained twenty points between pre- and postenrollment I.Q. tests. "These projects," Stoddard explained, "are revising scientific and popular viewpoints regarding the fixity of intelligence. Reliable evidence indicates that large influence must be assigned to environmental impact." [14] Unlike many of their peers, the Iowa researchers were rejecting a determinist position in favor of the view that intelligence was an interaction between hereditary and environment.

During Stoddard's years as director, German Gestalt psychologist Kurt Lewin was also recruited to the Iowa station. Having met Lewin in Berlin in 1928, Frank helped support him when, in 1933, a group of prominent psychologists convinced the Emergency Committee in Aid of Displaced German Scholars to bring Lewin to Cornell University for two years. At Cornell, Lewin taught in the School of Home Economics, which had been a site for one of the Memorial's major child-study and parent education programs. [15] Following this introduction to research in child development, Frank engineered a meeting between Stoddard and Lewin, which led to Lewin's appointment on Rockefeller funds at the Iowa station.

Frank's belief that Lewin would flourish at Iowa proved correct. During the nine years he spent there—Lewin moved to MIT in 1944—Lewin had remarkable graduate students and postdoctoral fellows, many of whom became outstanding figures in social psychology. With Dorwin Cartwright, Leon Festinger, and Ronald Lippitt, among others, he carried out important research about frustration and aggression in children and the social organization of classrooms. His work demonstrated not only that children could not really be understood apart from the social situations in which they lived, but also that democratically organized classrooms were more conducive to learning than autocratic environments. [16] With characteristic humor and irony, Stoddard later recalled that Chicago's Charles Judd had underscored the importance of this insight for education reform when he visited the station and told Lewin that he had been impressed that the experimental classroom he had just observed seemed to be "a faithful representation of the standard American classroom." According to Stoddard, "Lewin, looking pinker than usual, replied, 'But Professor Judd, that happens to be our version of autocracy in action!' " [17]

The perspective developed at the Iowa station was definitely more social and interactionist and less hereditarian and determinist than the perspectives held by most American psychologists doing research about children at the time. In consequence, as the Iowa research became known among psychologists via publications and presentations at professional meetings, it caused controversy. As early as 1928, Lewis Terman had chaired a National Society for the Study of Education (NSSE) yearbook committee that had been organized on his suggestion "to answer the question whether educational effort can or can not make bright children out of dull ones." The volume, which became known as the *Terman Yearbook,* had been planned to settle questions concerning the relative importance of "nature versus nurture," and, not surprisingly, it came out strongly on the "nature" side of the debate. Most contributors suggested that I.Q. was a limiting factor in child development.[18]

Owing to work at the Iowa station, however, the *Terman Yearbook* had not laid the "nature versus nurture" controversy to rest. In consequence, Guy M. Whipple, the general editor of the NSSE yearbooks, had suggested that another yearbook be commissioned, this one to be edited by George Stoddard. Known as the *Stoddard Yearbook,* the volume, according to Whipple, "was intended to be 'a more positive study' than the '*Terman Yearbook,*' and 'not so much a debate upon controversial issues as an exploration of possibilities.'" In spite of that intention, as Whipple also noted, the *Stoddard Yearbook* demonstrated that "the discussion of nature and nurture in 1940 is just as controversial as it was in 1928—more so, indeed."[19]

Whether that was actually true is difficult to know. According to Hamilton Cravens, who has written extensively about the controversy, most psychologists who were asked to contribute to the *Stoddard Yearbook* refused to do so on the grounds that they were not involved in research on the issues involved.[20] Even Terman's old graduate school friend Arnold Gesell told Florence Goodenough, who studied gifted children at the Memorial-supported Minnesota Institute for Child Welfare, that "we are trying to get somewhat away from a fixed dichotomy of Nature vs. Nurture."[21]

However, because Whipple, avowedly seeking fairness and balance, appointed Lewis Terman and several of Terman's closest allies to the committee that edited the *Stoddard Yearbook,* the Iowa point of view was presented as controversial. Having run the committee in what he believed to be a democratic fashion, Stoddard had allowed all committee members to solicit contributions. Terman and Goodenough had done so with great determination. In private, Terman said that he thought "the Iowa stuff" was "bunkum."[22] And both he and Goodenough apparently saw the new volume as offering an opportunity to win the "research battle with Beth Wellman," next to Stoddard, the Iowa station's most prominent student of intelligence.[23] In consequence, most of the articles debated questions related to the "nature vs. nurture" controversy, rather than exploring "new possibilities," and most of the published "personal reactions" of committee members continued the debate. Claiming that the years between 1928 and 1940 had "not been as fruitful of crucial research as one could have hoped," owing to "retrogression in the methodological procedures that have been employed," Terman, for example, accused Stoddard and Wellman of being "biased and uncritical." According to Terman, "the Iowa claims regarding the influence of schooling on mental development are subject to the gravest doubts."[24]

After the *Stoddard Yearbook* appeared, one of Terman's Stanford protegés, a statistician named Quinn McNemar, went further in attacking the methods involved in the Iowa research. Charging that the Iowa studies contained "gross statistical flaws," his article dealt a severe blow to the Iowa point of view.[25] Recognizing the damage this article had done, Stoddard published *The Meaning of Intelligence* in 1943. The book circulated widely and reached audiences that scholars like McNemar, who published in rather esoteric professional journals, never reached. Reviewing all the relevant research literature, the book made a clear and forceful case for efforts to nurture human capacity through education. Its final chapters, analyzing the educational and social implications of a social view of intelligence, also linked the research to current policy questions concerning problems of adolescence and youth.

Written after Stoddard left Iowa to become president of the University of the State of New York and its commissioner of education, *The Meaning of Intelligence* was important in disseminating the Iowa perspective, even though the views associated with that perspective came to be increasingly disassociated from the Iowa name. Beyond that, a belief that intelligence was importantly shaped by one's environment, including one's educational opportunities, became a major hallmark of Stoddard's frequent public presentations. These tended to stress the need to increase educational opportunities of all kinds, from nursery school through college, and via all possible media, including film and television. Last, but hardly least important, Stoddard's post-Iowa career was a prominent one. It included stints as president of the University of Illinois and of Long Island University, dean of the Department of Education and then chancellor and executive vice-president of New York University, and chair of the board of the American Council of Education, among many other affiliations. In all those roles, Stoddard's actions were planned, however indirectly, to advance the perspective he had acquired and helped develop at the Iowa station.

The Progressive Education Association's Eight-Year Study

During the 1930s, the Progressive Education Association (PEA) became an important vehicle for the support and dissemination of developmentalist perspectives like those emanating from the Iowa station. Established in 1919 as a membership organization and initially dominated by leaders from private experimental schools who wished to advance the "new education," the PEA came increasingly over the years to be an organization led by reform-oriented educationists. In 1929, for example, Harold Rugg was elected to the PEA Executive Board. He and his colleagues pushed the PEA to go beyond promoting progressive ideas through publicity, chiefly in the form of reports published in *Progressive Education,* to engage in actual study and experimentation.[26] Concerned that innovation at the high school level was being unduly constrained by college admission requirements, the PEA therefore established a commission in 1930 to investigate what could be done to improve the situation.

Called the Committee on the Relation of School and College (four years later it became a commission instead of a committee), the group would be especially important in pushing to improve measurement practices by aligning them with increasingly diverse and complex school purposes and objectives. This seemingly minor, rather technical change, in fact, led to the development of what was called evaluation to distinguish the approach from mental measurement, and evaluation directly challenged several beliefs that had been essential to the scientific movement in education earlier in the century. By insisting that achievement be tested in relation to clear statements of instructional objectives, evaluation countered the belief that "achievement" could be measured apart from a clear conception of what one had been taught. By focusing on instruction, it opposed the presumption that achievement correlated with "ability" more powerfully than with instructional effectiveness. And by emphasizing instruction, it contradicted the belief that curriculum making could be separated from teacher development. Even though the new beliefs associated with evaluation would take decades to seep fully into educational policy and practice, they began to foment change during the 1930s when possibilities for nurturing experimentalism at the high school level were under active consideration.

Wilford Aikin of the William Burroughs School in St. Louis chaired the PEA Commission on the Relation of School and College. It had twenty-eight members, mostly drawn from public and private schools that were considered progressive, and was initially funded by several of the schools and then by the Carnegie Corporation of New York. To test whether students could do well in college even if they did not meet standard entrance requirements, the commission set out to have those requirements waived for the graduates of the thirty schools that would participate in the study. After two years of preliminary planning and another year of negotiating with colleges, the plan went into effect in 1931. Three years later the first graduates entered college, with the next five classes having also been freed of college entrance requirements. Because the plan was to be in place for at least eight years, the project came to be known as the Eight-Year Study.[27]

Even though graduates of the thirty Eight-Year Study schools were freed from standard college entrance requirements, admission for them was dependent on high school achievement. This was to be gauged by a recommendation from the student's school principal, supplemented by "a carefully recorded history of the student's school life and of his [or her] activities and interests, including results of various types of examinations and other evidence of the quality and quantity of the candidate's work, also scores on scholastic aptitude, achievement, and other diagnostic tests given by the schools during the secondary school course."[28] From the very start, this made questions concerning record keeping and student assessment crucial to the project's success.

During the first years of the project, while the PEA Committee on Records and Reports devoted itself primarily to inventing new forms for record keeping, the schools were asked to administer existing tests. This pleased some members of the commission, notably William S. Learned of the Carnegie Foundation for the Advancement of Teaching and Ben D. Wood, a former Thorndike student who was director of the Columbia University Bureau of Collegiate Educational Research. Learned and Wood were interested in the PEA experiment and helped secure Carnegie Corporation funding for it because they hoped it might be linked to a study they were then conducting of college students in Pennsylvania. That study was designed to find out why students in Pennsylvania enrolled in high school and college and how one might predict which high school students would excel in college. For that study, Learned and Wood were in the process of developing a variety of tests, including intelligence, achievement, and "comprehensive" tests that were intended to measure a student's "general culture" rather than his or her grasp of a specific field. Learned and Wood hoped that Eight-Year Study schools would also use these tests to satisfy the conditions necessary for their students' college admission.[29]

To many other members of the commission, Learned and Wood's position was anathema. They saw the two men as determined conservatives who believed the purpose of schooling should be nothing more than the acquisition of knowledge and intellectual skill. By contrast, commission members were trying to move away from such narrowly academic views in order to link schools more effectively to both student interests and social need. To these more progressive members of the commission, tests of the kind Learned and Wood were piloting in Pennsylvania were threatening because they would probably stifle all possibilities for introducing more freedom and creativity into high school curricula.[30]

Although differences between the more conservative and more progressive factions within the commission were kept in check for the first years of the project, they came to a head at a meeting of the Directing Committee in Princeton, New Jersey, in July 1934. When the progressive faction threatened to leave the project if the Pennsylvania tests were used, Boyd H. Bode, a philosopher of education from Ohio State University, suggested they ask Ralph W. Tyler to come and talk with them about how he might solve the assessment problems of the venture. Tyler was immediately summoned and after a relatively brief discussion was hired to become director of evaluation for the commission. Thereafter Learned resigned from the study, and Carnegie support for it was discontinued. In its place, the General Education Board (GEB), a Rockefeller philanthropy, provided the study with very generous funding until its completion. The GEB's new assistant director, whose special responsibility was education, was Robert J. Havighurst, who had worked with Tyler at Ohio State. His appointment assured easy cooperation between the GEB and the PEA.[31]

Ralph W. Tyler: From Mental Measurements to Evaluation

At the time Tyler joined the Eight-Year Study, he was thirty-two years old and well launched on what was to be a remarkable career. A short, wiry man with twinkling eyes (hidden behind thick glasses) and a sometimes quite boisterous sense of humor, Tyler held an insistent commitment to down-to-earth, practical thinking. Having grown up in rural Nebraska, he was also a "small-d democrat," who wanted to improve educational opportunities for all people. Beginning his career as a teacher of mathematics and science, Tyler had then enrolled for graduate study at the University of Chicago, where Charles Judd had become his advisor. Describing Judd as "a hard-nosed New Englander," Tyler had admired his mentor's psychology, especially his ideas about the so-called higher mental processes, which helped one carry learning over from one situation to another.[32] At Chicago, however, Tyler had actually been closer to W. W. Charters, with whom he had worked as an assistant for statistics on the Commonwealth Teacher Training Study. Still, the approach that came to be known as evaluation would blend the ideas of both of Tyler's Chicago mentors, drawing from Judd to take seriously objectives more complex than simple recall and drawing from Charters to think about objectives in terms of practical "real world" skills, knowledge, and competencies.

After completing his doctorate at Chicago and serving briefly on the faculty of the University of North Carolina, Tyler joined W. W. Charters as a research associate in the Bureau of Educational Research at Ohio State, where Charters had moved in 1928. Tyler thought of himself as "a curriculum person" at the time, but Charters had prevailed upon him to accept an appointment that required that he work with other faculty members on problems of instructional effectiveness and measurement.[33] Although his new direction had not initially been of his choosing, the work Tyler did at Ohio State enabled him to help shift the focus of educational measurement from mental testing to evaluation.

During his time at Ohio State, Tyler discovered that professors were unable to respond to questions concerning what they hoped their students would learn, the professors apparently presuming that students should simply learn whatever the text had to offer. This discovery led him to conclude that formulating objectives was instrumental to instructional success. Keenly aware as well that most tests tested little more than the retention of information and that well-formulated educational objectives often included more than that, Tyler concluded that to be effective educational objectives should be formulated in behavioral terms.[34] As he explained in one of the many essays he published during those years, "a satisfactory test or examination in any subject is an instrument which gives us evidence of the degree to which students are reaching the objective of the subject." Because there were often a variety of objectives, examinations, he continued, should be designed to indicate "the degree to which students are attaining all of the important goals which instructors are trying to reach in a given subject."[35] As formulated by Tyler, testing became a means to discover when teaching resulted in the acquisition of the desired objectives and to improve instruction that had not achieved the objectives sought. No longer simply a means to measure the acquisition of information, testing could now serve as a major catalyst for improving education.

When tapped to work on the Eight-Year Study, Tyler was ready to implement ideas about student assessment that he had been working on for at least six years. His first task was to hire a staff that could work with him in helping the thirty Eight-Year Study schools plan and carry out their evaluations. The evaluation staff was also responsible for a follow-up study of the college achievement of graduates. The group he gathered consisted mostly of men and women who were young, untrained in techniques of measurement, and deeply committed to Tyler. As one of them recalled later, "We were convinced that Ralph Tyler was right and that getting measures of these objectives beyond knowledge and simple skills would work a revolution." [36] With headquarters first at Ohio State and then at the University of Chicago, where Tyler transferred in 1938, the evaluation staff included a number of people who would go on to prominent careers in education, Hilda Taba, Bruno Bettelheim, and Lee J. Cronbach among them. As one member of the Tyler team explained, they were "apostles and evangelists" for the new approach to testing Tyler was developing, and they became important in disseminating and further developing his approach to educational improvement through evaluation. [37]

After hiring a staff, Tyler had the Eight-Year Study schools establish committees of teachers that would work with his staff to describe the objectives they were pursuing. Beginning during the summer of 1935, he also organized summer workshops to help teachers identify ways to measure whether students were meeting the objectives they had set. According to a PEA pamphlet Tyler helped write, these differed from typical summer schools in that "there were no formal classes or lecture courses. The needs of the individual student, school, and community determined the program, and a staff of consultants fresh from contact with new developments in evaluation, curriculum, guidance, and the study of adolescents, were on hand to serve as needed." [38] The workshops were unprecedented in the latitude and autonomy they granted teachers. Whether or not the teacher knew the origins of the ideas, participation in these workshops, and more generally in the Eight-Year Study, familiarized hundreds of them with Tyler's thought.

Even though new ideas about testing began to make their way into both education research and practice in these ways and discussions about the value and feasibility of developing tests that could measure more than the recall of information began to appear in professional journals during the late 1930s, the beginnings of World War II overshadowed the Eight-

Year Study. By the time Tyler and his staff had sifted all the data they had collected and written up their findings and approach, the war had begun. The volumes that were published to describe the Eight-Year Study's innovations in testing, as well as in other areas, sold poorly—some as few as 1,000 copies; the best-seller of the five-volume series sold only 6,400 copies.[39] Despite that, the Eight-Year Study initiated a challenge to beliefs about human capacity and educational purpose that had governed educational practice since at least the nineteenth century and that, during the early twentieth century, had been supported by the scientific movement in education. Even if circumstances limited the immediate impact on educational scholarship of this challenge, like the Iowa perspective on intelligence, ideas concerning assessment and educational improvement would again become prominent in the 1960s.

Human Development: The PEA's Commissions on Curriculum and Human Relations

While the Eight-Year Study zeroed in on relations between high schools and colleges, two other PEA commissions set out to investigate the capacity of high schools to serve non-college-bound youth. The first of these was the Commission on the Secondary School Curriculum, and the second was the Commission on Human Relations. Both were supported by the GEB, and, indeed, officials at the GEB were important in shaping them. Worried that approximately one-third of American youth were neither working nor in school at the height of the Great Depression, GEB representatives were actively trying to understand why this was the case and what could be done to increase the holding power of the high schools.[40] By the time the PEA commissions were initiated, the Laura Spelman Rockefeller Memorial Fund had been folded into the Rockefeller Foundation, Beardsley Ruml had left the Rockefeller offices to become dean of social sciences at the University of Chicago and then treasurer of R. H. Macy's, and Lawrence K. Frank had become associate director for education of the GEB. From this new position, Frank was able not only to infuse developmentalist perspectives into discussions of education policy, but also to introduce a greater emphasis on culture into developmentalist thought.

The Commission on the Secondary School Curriculum was launched in May of 1932. Vivian T. Thayer of the Ethical Culture Schools chaired it. According to Thayer, the new study group was necessary as a counterweight to the Eight-Year Study. He and others within the PEA were concerned that the Eight-Year Study's emphasis on college admission would "encourage preoccupation with college work alone."[41] To think of secondary education only or even primarily in connection with college would be unfortunate, Thayer thought, because high schools should organize their curricula around adolescent interests. "Utilizing the educational experiences of pupils and the so-called subject-matter fields to stimulate what John Dewey has termed the reorganization and the reconstruction of pupils' experiences" was the purpose of secondary education, he contended.[42] The commission was clearly at odds with what it would later describe as "'scientific education' under the guidance of a behavioristic or mechanistic psychology." Describing such education as little more than "habit training, intended to adjust the individual to external conditions," the commission advocated synthesizing intellectual training with the emotional and social sides of adolescent development.[43]

In line with its experiential approach to subject matter, the Thayer commission insisted that the various school subjects should be approached as part of what it called "general education," a term the commission used to describe the education people needed to realize their own potential and to participate effectively in a democratic society.[44] With an eye on increasing their ability to hold young people until graduation, the group insisted that high schools should now help young people develop "a working philosophy of values which will give meaning, zest, and purpose to living." This was now necessary, it was claimed, because "life outside provides too little opportunity for participation and affords too little direction toward establishing young people in a rightful place of their own."[45] Beyond that, the commission insisted that this was an appropriate orientation for secondary education.

In addition to reconceptualizing what subject matter meant within "general education," the group maintained that high schools needed to make "guidance of young people as they orient themselves in the basic and essential relationships of living within their culture" an important aspect of secondary education.[46] In order to do this, the PEA maintained, there needed to be an in-depth study of adolescence. As explained to the GEB, there had been a great deal written about adolescence, but not from the point of view of "young people themselves."[47]

As originally constituted, the Thayer commission included, in addition to Thayer, W. W. Beatty, superintendent of the Bronxville Schools; Boyd H. Bode of Ohio State; Elliot Dunlop Smith of Yale; and Katherine Tayler of the Shady Hill School in Cambridge, Massachusetts. Subsequently, Caroline B. Zachary, an educational psychologist; Helen M. Lynd, a professor at Sarah Lawrence College; and Margaret Mead, a Columbia anthropologist, joined the group. All were close friends of Frank, who, according to Mead, provided "the whole intellectual background of the Commission."[48] By 1936, however, Bode, Smith, and Tayler had resigned because, at least for Bode, the commission was "far too sentimentally child-centered" and "dominated by the attitude of 'the psychiatrist.'"[49]

Bode's impression made considerable sense in light of the Thayer commission's decision to sponsor a special committee on adolescence, to be led by Caroline B. Zachary. Talented and charismatic, if somewhat unsystematic in her thought, Zachary had had an unusual education.[50] After graduating from the Spence School for Girls in New York City in 1914, she had spent ten years at Teachers College, studying with William Heard Kilpatrick and teaching at the Lincoln School. Soon thereafter she had left for Vienna, where she had studied with Freud's divergent disciple Carl Jung. Upon her return to the United States, Zachary had become director of the Mental Hygiene Institute at the New Jersey State Teachers College in Upper Montclair, an institution whose faculty she had initially joined while still a doctoral student at Teachers College. In that capacity, she had written frequently about the importance of "personality adjustment" among teachers, her argument being that teachers could not educate the whole child and deal well with the problems of children unless they themselves had been helped to become personally and socially self-reflective and autonomous.[51] Viewing teachers in training as the adolescents most of them still actually were, Zachary had really been studying adolescent development even before she was asked to chair the special committee established by the Thayer commission. As Bode had apparently feared would be the case, her views came to dominate the Thayer commission's work.

With Zachary at the helm, the committee she led set out to observe adolescents and to compile case studies that would reveal all that was involved in "a student's adjustment to school" other than "native intelligence."[52] All told, Zachary and her committee developed case studies of more than 650 young people, who were not only students at progressive secondary schools, but also, to ensure representativeness, students at a city high school that was self-consciously nonprogressive, a trade school, and a camp run by the Civilian Conservation Corps. Zachary was convinced that "there is no significant correlation between a high IQ and the ability to develop live interests, to sustain them, and to work concentratedly and conscientiously on a given task."[53] Her goal in the adolescent study was to learn enough about young people so that the school could fulfill its "chief duty," which, according to her final report, was "to give the help young people need in order to make socially constructive adjustments in the course of their growth—that is, the school is mainly concerned with their social development."[54] Whether it would be accurate to call this view child centered, it certainly was on the extremely social, life adjustment end, as opposed to the academic end, of any continuum of school purposes.

If Zachary's committee brought a psychological perspective to the commission's work, the Committee on Intellectual Development, a second committee set up under the auspices of the Thayer commission, brought a more anthropological perspective. According to Margaret Mead, this committee grew out of Thayer's participation in a monthlong seminar Frank had organized in Hanover, New Hampshire, during the summer of 1934. The seminar was intended to advance what were known as personality and culture studies by fostering conversation between and among scholars in different fields related to human relations. In fact, however, the meeting was heavily weighted toward anthropology with Franz Boas, Edward Sapir, A. R. Brown, Ruth Benedict, Robert Lowery, and Mead all in attendance. W. Lloyd Warner was also invited as a critical observer of the group. Subsequently, Thayer asked Mead to provide advice to the PEA's commission and then actually to become a member of the group. She did so, she claimed, because she wanted the commission to undertake research into "the structure and function of school, [and] the actual role of the teacher and the significance of intra-school relationship."[55]

After the 1934 Hanover Seminar on Human Relations, it was also decided that yet another commission was needed, this one to develop teaching materials based on the materials developed for and discussed at the seminar. The seminar materials dealt with "human relations" from the perspectives of psychology, biology, anthropology, sociology, mental hygiene, sex research, child development, and literature. As described by the PEA, "the significance of these source materials and those extended materials to be prepared, is derived from the fact that they deal with an area of problems long neglected or avoided in the education of the adolescent . . . his own behavior, the behavior of those around him, . . . [and] his emerging and constantly more difficult sex problems. Of even more significance, . . . the school also fails to give him awareness of and insights into the culture which impinges on his every decision."[56]

The convenor of the seminar and the behind-the-scenes organizer of this third PEA commission was once again Lawrence Frank, who secured GEB funds to support the new venture.[57] Alice Keliher, another former Kilpatrick student, became its chair. After finishing her doctorate at Teachers College in 1929, Keliher had been awarded a Grace Dodge Fellowship to study children's programs in Europe. She had taken a movie camera with her on the trip and had filmed many of the centers she visited. Returning to the United States at the height of the Great Depression with her films, Keliher landed a job doing research for Arnold Gesell at Yale. Gesell had, of course, been trained by G. Stanley Hall at Clark and had become imbued with his mentor's belief that human beings unfolded in invariant stages. At the time Keliher worked for him, he was engaged in a "naturalistic study of infant behavior" that was funded by the GEB. Although Keliher found Gesell's approach to research artificial and constraining, her job at Yale brought her to Frank's notice.[58] In consequence, when Frank was looking for someone to lead the PEA's Commission on Human Relations, which was officially constituted in 1935, he turned to her.

The Thayer and Keliher commissions were not identical in purpose, the Thayer group hoping to demonstrate an approach to school reorganization and the Keliher group hoping to disseminate materials that would help young people, including those not in school, surmount problems of adolescence. In the end, however, the differences between them were far less important than the fact that both groups produced some extraordinary works and both threw their weight on the side of expressive, naturalistic, youth-centered approaches to education. One of the outstanding volumes to emanate from the Zachary committee of the Thayer commission was *The Adolescent Personality: A Study of Individual Behavior* by Peter Blos. At the time Blos wrote the book, he had recently fled to the United States from Nazi Europe. He had been born in Karlsruthe, Germany, and had studied education at the University of Heidelberg (he subsequently also received a Ph.D. in biology from the University of Vienna). Intending to become a science teacher, he had been recruited to tutor the four children of Dorothy Burlingham (the daughter of glass artist Louis Comfort Tiffany), a wealthy American who had taken up residence in Vienna in order to be analyzed by Sigmund Freud. Through her, he had met both Sigmund and Anna Freud. Anna Freud was apparently impressed with him because at the end of two years, when Blos was ready to move on, she had helped Burlingham convince him to remain by promising to make it possible for him to open his own school. Recruiting Erik

Homburger (later Erik Erikson), an artistic friend from his gymnasium days, to assist him, Blos created a school that was very much like an American progressive school. The curriculum was organized around projects and ranged in an interdisciplinary way over many different subjects—Eskimos, American Indians, geography, mythology, and German history among them. Children were encouraged to choose what they would study in their free time.[59] According to the psychoanalyst Robert Coles, Blos and "Herr Erik," as Erikson was then called, "wanted the children to feel 'free,' that is, unafraid of school, and in many respects their own masters."[60]

However romantic her thought may have seemed to some contemporaries, Zachary was able to attract Blos to her committee's work along with a number of other unusually talented young professionals interested in children, including pediatrician Benjamin Spock, who subsequently stated that Zachary had had "the 'broadest, deepest influence' on his thinking."[61] Blos's *The Adolescent Personality* was an attempt to explain and demonstrate how teachers could analyze the personality of the adolescents with whom they worked in order to meet the needs of those young people more effectively. "Histories like the ones presented in this volume," Blos explained, "are intended as materials for study, useful in advancing the basic understanding of personality development. Although the teacher must of necessity put his emphasis on the practical demands of the immediate situation, his teaching will be immeasurably enriched . . . if he learns to view day-to-day classroom behavior in terms of the light it sheds upon the fundamental trends of his pupils' personalities and their developmental needs."[62] Becoming something of a classic among progressive educators, Blos's book launched the young psychologist on a prominent and influential career as a child analyst and expert on adolescence. As one of his former colleagues wrote in an obituary in 1997, "Dr. Blos was 'Mr. Adolescence' for many, many years."[63]

Another outstanding book to emanate from the PEA commissions, this one from Keliher's Commission on Human Relations, was Louise Rosenblatt's *Literature as Exploration*. Having become involved in the commission through Margaret Mead, one of her Barnard College roommates, Rosenblatt combined a profound knowledge of comparative literature—she held a doctorate from the Sorbonne—with insights into culture and personality acquired through postdoctoral study with Franz Boas and Ruth Benedict at Columbia. This unusual combination enabled her to present the teaching of literature as teaching about "human relations . . .

the experiences of human beings in their diverse personal and social relations."[64] Not only that, but building on Dewey's ideas about experience, Rosenblatt insisted:

> There is no such thing as a generic reader or a generic literary work. . . . The novel or poem or play exists, after all, only in interaction with specific minds. The reading of any work of literature is, of necessity, an individual and unique occurrence involving the mind and the emotions of some particular reader. . . . The teacher's job, in its fundamental terms, then, consists in furthering a fruitful interrelationship between the individual book or poem or play and the individual student.[65]

Rosenblatt's book was quickly recognized as a pioneering work, and it established its author as a leading figure among scholars interested in the teaching of English. From 1948 to 1972, she taught at the New York University School of Education. Over the years, her perspective became increasingly influential and is widely credited with establishing what is called the reader-response approach to the teaching of literature. Despite that, as Rosenblatt herself was aware, a return to conservatism after World War II limited the influence of the kind of pedagogy she advocated. Equally important, few of her professional colleagues in English departments were willing to participate in professional organizations like the National Council of Teachers of English. Lamenting that, Rosenblatt acknowledged that they did not share her sense that finding ways "to promote an educational process aimed at developing critically minded, socially productive individuals" was of "paramount importance."[66]

Class, Caste, Mobility, and Cultural Bias: The University of Chicago Committee on Human Development

In addition to the Iowa studies and the PEA commissions, during the interwar years the Rockefeller philanthropies provided major financial support for research into questions of social stratification and education conducted under the auspices of the Committee on Human Development at the University of Chicago. Important for many reasons, this research greatly magnified the assault on the I.Q. initiated at Iowa, while also reinforcing the importance the PEA had assigned to the education and socialization of youth.

The Committee on Human Development was created in 1940, when an earlier Committee on Child Development was enlarged and renamed. The earlier committee had been organized in 1930 with Rockefeller funds. It had been an intentionally more flexible and not necessarily permanent alternative to an institute of child development like those at Iowa and Teachers College. By the late 1930s, however, it had apparently lost focus as a research unit and had become almost exclusively a teaching program. As a result, when Ralph Tyler became its chair in 1939, he had decided to reorganize it. Recall that Tyler had left Ohio State for Chicago in 1938, taking the evaluation staff of the PEA's Eight-Year Study with him. Chicago President Robert Maynard Hutchins had invited Tyler to assume the post of university examiner, an office required by the fact that Chicago granted degrees based on examinations rather than course units completed. To ensure that Tyler would be sufficiently enticed to accept that offer, Hutchins had also promised him the chairmanship of the Department of Education, a post that was open owing to the impending retirement of Tyler's mentor, Charles Judd.[67]

At the time of Tyler's return to Chicago as a faculty member, the Department of Education was under scrutiny, since Robert Redfield, Chicago's dean of social sciences, believed its reputation had declined. A careful, principled, and very astute politician on behalf of education, Tyler probably reorganized the Committee on Child Development in order to bring the faculty from the Department of Education into closer relationship with prominent researchers in other departments, which, in actuality, it managed to do. Such a move could forestall the kind of severe action against the department that was later taken when, in similar circumstances, in 1997 the University of Chicago Education Department was unfortunately closed. To help him with the reorganization, Tyler invited Robert J. Havighurst, who had been working on education for the GEB, to serve as the committee's executive secretary.[68]

For most of the next twenty years, one of the central members of the new committee was W. Lloyd Warner, who joined the University of Chicago faculty in 1935. Trained at Berkeley, Warner had begun his career in social anthropology by studying one of the aboriginal tribes of northeastern Australian. Then, after securing an appointment as an assistant professor at Harvard, he had met Elton Mayo, the Australian organizational theorist who was serving on the faculty of the Harvard Business School. Since 1924, Mayo had been involved in a study of productivity at the Hawthorne Works of the Bell System's Western Electric Company. Described in an unpublished biography as "a man with a dream of research that would be a comprehensive study of man in society," Warner joined Mayo in this work, in the process helping to shift the Hawthorne Study from its original psychological orientation to one that was more social.[69]

Warner believed that the key to understanding human behavior lay in understanding social relationships not only or even primarily between individuals, but also more important, between different social groups. As he told one of his colleagues on the Hawthorne Study, he believed this to be the case "whether you study the Australian totemic clans, the gangs of Chicago, or your departmental groups."[70]

As an extension of the Hawthorne work, Warner planned to study a neighboring community to ascertain the social relationships of the workers when not at work. For a variety of reasons, however, he decided not to choose a site near the Midwestern plant that Mayo was centering on, but rather grounded his investigation of community social relationships in Newburyport, Massachusetts, which he dubbed "Yankee City." With a staff of thirty people and an ample research budget (much of which came from the Rockefeller funds supporting Mayo's work), Warner and his colleagues eventually produced a series of monographs that established the concept of social class as essential to social analysis.[71] Though Warner's understanding of class was later criticized as too broad to be meaningful—C. Wright Mills for one claimed that Warner's concept was like a "sponge" that had absorbed three distinct social categories having to do with economics, status, and power—it provided a framework that was extremely generative for subsequent fieldwork.[72]

Even before the Yankee City Studies were published between 1941 and 1947, Warner's approach to community analysis had been adopted in a number of important works of social research that were highly relevant to education. Among these were four volumes sponsored by the American Youth Commission (AYC) of the American Council of Education: *Children of Bondage: The Personality Development of Negro Youth in the Urban South* by Allison Davis and John Dollard; *Negro Youth at the Crossways: Their Personality Development in the Middle States* by E. Franklin Frazier; *Growing Up in the Black Belt: Negro Youth in the Rural South* by Charles S. Johnson; and *Color and Human Nature: Negro Personality Development in a Northern City* by W. Lloyd Warner, Buford H. Junker, and Walter A. Adams.[73] All used Warner's six-class framework (upper-upper, lower-upper, upper-middle, lower-middle, upper-lower, and lower-lower), and some won wide acclaim as daring, innovative works. Among these, none was more widely recognized than Davis and Dollard's *Children of Bondage*. It was praised for its courageous challenge to racial stereotypes. "The book blasts the absurdity of the 'convenient ideology that all colored people are identical,'" a reviewer for the *Journal of Negro History* announced.[74] It was also saluted for its effort to combine a Warner-like approach to the analysis of social class with the more psychological approach John Dollard had been developing at the Institute for Human Relations at Yale.[75]

In addition to these volumes, Warner's approach was used in *Deep South: A Social Anthropological Study of Caste and Class* by Allison Davis, Burleigh B. Gardner, and Mary R. Gardner. Based on more than a year of fieldwork in Natchez, Mississippi, during which Allison Davis; his wife, Elizabeth Stubbs Davis; and St. Clair Drake lived in and studied the black community and Burleigh and Mary Gardner lived in and studied the white community, the book demonstrated the ways in which both class and caste ran through all the social groups of the community and shaped every aspect of life, including politics and the law. It also embodied Warner's ambition to encourage social anthropologists to scrutinize their own societies in the same way they had previously scrutinized distant societies like that of the indigenous peoples of New Guinea and Australia. Its authors were all students of Warner's, and one, Allison Davis, followed him from Harvard to the University of Chicago. There, Davis, as well as Warner, turned his attention to the study of education. If, for Warner, education was of interest because it had clear importance to matters of social stratification, for Davis, it was of interest because it was directly linked to his personal experience of race and class.

Having grown up in Washington, D.C., Davis had graduated from Dunbar High School, a segregated school with exceptionally high academic standards, and (summa cum laude) from Williams College. Thereafter, he had received an M. A. in English from Harvard. Unable to return to Williams as a teaching assistant—the president had claimed "there were too many Southern students" already in that position—he had become an instructor at Hampton Institute in Virginia in 1925. There, he later recalled, he had acquired his "first insights into cultural and social class differences and educational efficacy."[76] Having come of age in comfortable circumstances and received an education rarely available to black Americans of his generation, he had felt unprepared to reach his Hampton students, most of whom came from backgrounds very different from his own. This had led him back to graduate school at Harvard in 1931, where he had begun to study social anthropology with Warner. With time out to study with Bronislaw Malinowski at the London School of Economics, to do the fieldwork for *Deep South,* to write *Children of Bondage* with John Dollard, and to teach at Dillard and Atlanta Universities, Davis followed Warner to Chicago in 1935, where he became a research associate for the Committee on Child Development. After completing the Ph.D., Davis was appointed to the faculty of the University of Chicago in 1942, becoming the first African American to hold full faculty status with teaching duties in an American university that was not traditionally black.[77] He remained at Chicago until 1978, when he retired as the John Dewey Distinguished Service Professor in the Department of Education.

Among the many important works to emanate from the Committee on Human Development, two were especially significant for scholarship in education. The first was *Who Shall Be Educated?* by W. Lloyd Warner, Robert J. Havighurst, and Martin B. Loeb. Warner and Havighurst had first met in 1934, when Lawrence Frank had organized the seminar on human relations out of which the PEA's Commission on Human Relations had grown. As they became reacquainted through the Chicago committee, they agreed that Warner's approach to social class analysis had implications for education that should be explored. During the next few years, therefore, they co-taught the course "Social Status and Learning" during two quarter terms a year. In connection with that course, they realized there actually was a lot of material on the subject and decided to write it up in book form. They asked Martin Loeb, a graduate student, to help them.[78]

Who Shall Be Educated? followed Warner's belief that class (defined as social status) was a prime axis for community organization. In addition, it presented education as one of the most powerful "elevators" that kept the American class system fluid. In line with that, Warner, Havighurst, and Loeb maintained that education was a primary means by which American society could regulate itself, adjustments in the educational system producing the "degree and kind of social mobility that is within the limits which will keep the society healthy and alive."[79] Widely debated by scholars, *Who Shall Be Educated?* was translated into popular discussions of education policy when Harvard President J. B. Conant adopted it as his own, first in lectures he gave at Teachers College in 1945 and subsequently in the many lectures he gave and books he wrote in connection with the studies of the high school he conducted for the Carnegie Corporation between 1956 and 1964.[80] Perhaps equally important, *Who Shall Be Educated?* helped launch studies of status attainment within the sociology of education, which subsequently became a staple in this growing subfield of educational study.[81]

The second study associated with the Chicago Committee on Human Development that had enduring influence on American education, this time primarily as a result of the challenge it posed to universalistic "culture-free" views of intelligence, was *Social-Class Influences upon Learning* by Allison Davis, which was based on the 1948 Inglis Lecture he delivered at the Harvard Graduate School of Education. In this brief volume, Davis brought together the results of several years of research undertaken by a group of committee members under his direction. The book's message was starkly simple. According to Davis, "the relative success of two persons in solving a given test-problem . . . depends not simply upon their hereditary equipment, but also upon their relative familiarity with the cultural situation and symbols in the problem, their relative degree of training with similar problems, and the relative strength of their motivation." [82] With wide-ranging and significant empirical evidence to support the statement, Davis's argument directly challenged previous claims concerning the supposedly unbiased character of intelligence tests.[83] The book was very widely read—in fact, it was constantly reprinted for thirty years—and, along with the detailed research studies from which it drew, helped stimulate efforts to find less-biased means for assessing aptitude, intelligence, potential, and achievement.[84]

The Educational Testing Service

Ironically, just one year before Davis delivered the Inglis Lecture, a long campaign to establish "a general examination board" had finally achieved success with the establishment of the Educational Testing Service (ETS). The original proponents of such an organization were William S. Learned and Ben D. Wood, the directors of the Carnegie Foundation's Pennsylvania Study. Recall that they had opposed the development of new methods of assessment in connection with the PEA's Eight-Year Study. With an eye on that venture, they had been lobbying for a merger of the College Entrance Examination Board, the Cooperative Test Service of the American Council on Education, and the Graduate Record Examination sponsored by the Carnegie Foundation since 1937. Threatened by the PEA's success in getting colleges to waive standard entrance requirements for students in the Eight-Year Study schools, Learned and Wood hoped a general examination board would help ensure the continued use of standardized tests for college admission. They believed this was essential to maintaining high academic standards and to ensuring that those, rather than a variety of often vaguely defined, more social purposes, continued to guide the programs of American high schools.

In the late 1930s, Learned and Wood's lobbying might have achieved its goal if Carl Brigham, a College Board psychometrician who had helped invent the Scholastic Aptitude Test (SAT) and was now working to improve the SAT and other tests, had not intervened. In an article published in *School and Society*, as well as in correspondence with J. B. Conant, whom Learned and Wood had enlisted to help their cause, Brigham had expressed grave concern about two matters. The first was "premature standardization"—developing norms to give meaning to test results before the full significance of what had been tested was fully understood. The second concern was that there had been a lack of research into questions that were essential if tests were to be meaningful. As Brigham explained, "the literature of pedagogy is full of words and phrases such as 'reasoning,' 'the power to analyze,' and 'straight thinking,'" none of which is understood. Unless there was more research into such fundamental processes, Brigham insisted, testing would interfere with efforts to develop reasonable objectives for education. Claiming that the demands of the market and the claims of "educational politicians" had stunted the development of a valid science of education, Brigham feared that sales would overwhelm the research functions of a large permanent testing service. As he put it, "although the word *research* will be mentioned many times in its charter, the very creation of powerful machinery to do more widely those things that are now being done badly will stifle research, discourage new developments, and establish existing methods, and even existing tests, as the correct ones."[85] Brigham's opposition had scotched the plan temporarily, but discussions were revived after World War II and, with the Carnegie Corporation acting as broker (and Brigham dead), the Educational Testing Service was chartered in 1947. Just as World War I had done earlier, World War II had demonstrated the usefulness of testing and other psychological services. What is more, thanks to passage of the G.I. Bill, there were huge numbers of veterans returning home eager to apply to college. With few alternative ways available to match them to different institutions, college entrance testing seemed newly necessary.

Regardless of the quantity or quality of the research it supported, as Brigham had feared would be the case, the very existence of ETS helped perpetuate existing educational practices. Its establishment was important in supporting the belief that standardized tests should play a central role in college and graduate school admission, and that belief, in turn, supported conceptions of educational purpose that gave priority to academic rather than social aims. In addition, belief in the value of admissions testing was essential to the idea that schools and colleges should serve selective as well as educational functions. Certainly J. B. Conant believed they should help allocate access to educational opportunities and so did (and do) many other Americans. But some of the people most deeply involved in research about child and human development—George Stoddard, Lawrence Frank, and Ralph Tyler among them—were pushing for ever-increasing access to more and more levels of education for more and more people. They wanted to improve the effectiveness of instruction, rather than perfecting instruments of selection, and were able to advance that view through research during the 1920s and even more so during the Depression years of the 1930s. Their successes notwithstanding, the conceptions of educational purpose that were advanced by the establishment of ETS and then by the advent of the Cold War for a time turned scholarship in education away from the progressive purposes that had been so central to it during the interwar era.

EXCELLENCE AND EQUITY: THE CONTINUING PROBLEMS AND POTENTIAL OF EDUCATION RESEARCH

By accepting the unfounded pretensions of so-called professors of education, we have permitted the content of public school instruction to be determined by a narrow group of specialists in pedagogy, well-intentioned men and women, no doubt, but utterly devoid of the qualifications necessary for the task they have undertaken.

Arthur E. Bestor

I want to change this bill [the Elementary and Secondary Education Act of 1965] because it doesn't have any way of measuring those damned educators. . . . We really ought to have some evaluation in there, and some measurement as to whether any good is happening.

Robert F. Kennedy

During the years following the end of World War II, public education in the United States came under intense scrutiny. Popular critics lambasted the schools for tolerating mediocrity and "life adjustment" and for failing to identify and nurture high levels of intellectual talent. If modifying school curricula to appeal to student interest had been the rallying cry before the war, now the call was for rigor and excellence. Gone was the prewar concern with "the general education" of all youngsters. The topic of note now was the education of the most able. Not coincidentally, it was in 1955 that the College Entrance Examination Board introduced advanced placement testing to encourage the acceleration through college of especially well prepared students.[1] Important, too, of course, especially to the dynamics of the next decade, was the Supreme Court ruling the previous year in *Brown v. Board of Education* that segregated schools could not be equal and were therefore unconstitutional.

The new emphasis on high levels of academic achievement—excellence—especially for the best students reflected popular attitudes resulting from the war. Sometimes called a "physicists' war," World War II had brought the "hard" sciences the same kind of acclaim that psychology had won during World War I.[2] Believing that the atom bomb had won the war and knowing that university scientists had been the bomb's chief inventors, Americans looked at scientists and scholars with new-found respect. Their admiration made them eager to ensure that the country would have a continuing supply of scientific manpower. This inevitably raised questions concerning the schools and whether they could produce young people well enough prepared at the high school level to take up collegiate and graduate studies in science.[3] Especially after the Russians launched Sputnik in 1957, that question became inseparable from anxieties about national defense. As editor Mortimer Smith explained in the *Bulletin* of the Council for Basic Education, an organization founded in 1956 to strengthen "the academic curriculum" of the nation's schools, Sputnik provided "a potent pep pill" to reformers committed to higher academic standards.[4]

Within this climate, it was perhaps not surprising that scholars of education were blamed for having encouraged the prewar trend toward "mushy education."[5] According to University of Illinois historian Arthur Bestor, professors of education were purposefully ridding the public school curriculum of both the disciplines and disciplined thinking. Describing them as a "fifth column" of people who had had "only the most fleeting glimpse of the great world of science and learning," Bestor waged a multifaceted campaign to return responsibility for school content to the disciplinary specialists.[6] As he implied in his 1953 book *Educational Wastelands,* Bestor was convinced that, under the guidance of educators trained in pedagogy, rather than traditional subject matter, the public schools had become intellectually arid institutions.

Of course, some contemporaries disagreed with Bestor. Philosopher Sidney Hook was one of them. He chided Bestor for believing that "the life of the mind is lived only in the liberal arts college" and that "schools of education constitute a kind of intellectual underworld." Unlike Bestor, Hook believed teachers needed to feel responsible not only for the subject matter they might be teaching, but also for each student and his or her different interests and needs.[7] Such defenses notwithstanding, Bestor's criticisms were echoed by popular writers like James D. Koerner, who blamed school failure on the "intellectual caliber of the education faculty."[8] They were additionally reinforced by publicly prominent individuals like Admiral Hyman Rickover, who was much revered for his involvement in the development of nuclear submarines. He insisted that the only way out of "the present educational chaos" was to create a "council of scholars" that would set national standards for high school graduation and for "the scholastic competence of teachers."[9]

The critics' belief that the schools were mediocre because educationists were intellectually vapid carried the day. During the 1950s, as the prestige of discipline-based academics, especially scientists, rose, that of educationists declined. Even Francis Keppel, dean of the Harvard Graduate School of Education from 1948 until 1962 and then U.S. Commissioner of Education until 1966, was ready to claim that "education is too important to be left solely to the educators."[10] Not surprisingly, therefore, discipline-based scholars came to dominate efforts to strengthen curriculum. Beyond that, discipline-trained scholars increasingly found themselves being sought after by schools of education. In educational administration, as well as in the so-called foundations of education, one now found growing numbers of faculty who were philosophers, sociologists, political scientists, economists, and historians. Fostering a move away from narrowly defined professional concerns, the turn toward disciplines introduced a new source of criticism of education research. Even though disciplinary research gained in academic standing, it was now said to be less directly relevant to the field.

If pervasive antieducationism and a concern for academic rigor were the most persistent themes of educational discourse during the 1950s, increasingly during the 1960s attention centered on equality of opportunity. In a brilliant analysis of the differences between the New Deal and the Great Society, historians Harvey Kantor and Robert Lowe have argued that in searching for ways to increase equality, the federal government did not choose to develop a strategy built around reducing unemployment and guaranteeing minimum levels of income, although it might have done so. Instead, education became the tool of choice. As Kantor and Lowe aptly noted, "seldom has education occupied so central a place in the minds of those responsible for planning social and economic policy."[11] This emphasis on education was due to the labor movement's acquiescence in the individualistically oriented consumerist policies of the New Deal, which eclipsed the larger issues of social democracy that had often been bundled under the label "the labor question."[12] In addition, because school desegregation appeared to be the most successful aspect of the initially broad attack by the National Association for the Advancement of Colored People (NAACP) on problems of racial inequality and civil rights, that group concentrated more and more of its efforts on education. Even though many black leaders, including W. E. B. Du Bois, objected to the policy, NAACP priorities fostered a new link between school desegregation and the fulfillment of civil rights for black Americans.[13]

Of course, there were also more proximate reasons for the Great Society's emphasis on education. Lyndon Johnson believed in education. So did John W. Gardner, the Carnegie Corporation president who chaired the task force Johnson charged with planning his administration's initial education policies and who subsequently became secretary of health, education, and welfare in 1965.[14] Education was also popular politically, far more so than possible alternative policies such as income supports. For all these reasons, during the 1960s, the federal government became a major player in a domain of social policy that heretofore had been largely left to the states and localities. Since the founding of the Republic, the federal government had provided general assistance to education, often via land grants. But now it became directly involved in establishing policy goals, and the amounts of funds it distributed increased manyfold.[15]

As part of the new federal role in education, authorities in Washington became more involved in education research. Much of this research had to do with the evaluation of new federal programs, which became a major growth industry beginning in the late 1960s. In turn, as demands for program evaluation increased, not only universities, but also the nation's proliferating think tanks—the Rand Corporation, the Stanford Research Institute, and the American Institutes of Research among others—grew apace.

Much that was discovered through evaluation was worrisome to policy makers in education. Mandated under the Civil Rights Act of 1964, James S. Coleman's massive study of the nation's schools discovered that, contrary to common expectations, equality of resources did not necessarily result in equality of results. Three years later an evaluation by the Westinghouse Corporation showed that the early interventions provided by Head Start had only ephemeral effects on school achievement. Not surprisingly, Great Society planners defended the programs they had designed. For example, Edward Zigler rightly claimed that Head Start had been intended to foster "greater *social competence* in disadvantaged children" rather than the cognitive skills measured by the Westinghouse evaluators.[16] Head Start was, in fact, built around the kinds of insights into environmental influences on intelligence that had first been discovered by the researchers at the Iowa Child Welfare Research Station. Beyond that, subsequent evaluations—in the case of Head Start, studies carried out in the 1970s and 1980s by David P. Weikart of the High/Scope Educational

Research Foundation in Ypsilanti, Michigan—often confirmed the confidence of Great Society planners. Regardless, evaluation studies provided important grist for the increasingly powerful conservative movement that would finally triumph with the election of Ronald Reagan to the presidency in 1980.

Even before that happened, however, retrenchment set in, and the expanded federal role of the 1960s had begun to diminish. The irony, of course, was that even as this was occurring, scholars were engaged in studies that would profoundly enrich understanding of the policy-making process in education. At the time Johnson launched the War on Poverty, little was known about how one might improve education through federal legislation. As Robert Haveman observed in his study of poverty policy research, "the president could call for a War on Poverty, but nobody—economists, sociologists, social critics, and least of all policymakers—knew how to wage it effectively."[17] However, thanks to provisions insisting on the evaluation of virtually all programs, researchers slowly began to scope out the dynamics involved in planned change.

As had not been true in the 1950s, educationists contributed to this alongside social scientists. Indeed, many of the important advances in evaluation research resulted from the work of educationists. Throughout the 1970s, the ideas of educationist evaluators about the differences between "formative" and "summative" evaluation and the significance of "stakeholders," among other things, began to find their way into the new journals and professional meetings devoted to evaluation and policy studies and to set the mold for new awards and professional standards.[18] As Ernest House, an evaluator from the University of Colorado, observed, this was "an unusual accomplishment for researchers in education," who had rarely been "accorded equal status with social scientists."[19]

In addition to increasingly sophisticated knowledge about policy making, beginning in the 1970s and accelerating during the 1980s and thereafter there were other indications that researchers were moving toward more powerful understandings of and approaches to research. This was most evident in the application of cognitive science to the classroom, in the initiation of interpretative studies of educational processes that brought culture more centrally into view, and in varied efforts to link scholarship more closely to practice and policy.

Despite gains in knowledge and perhaps in status, education scholarship was placed in jeopardy as severe cuts in funding, followed eventually by the abolition of the National Institute of Education in the late 1980s, shrank the federal role in research to next to nothing. While education research began to mature, thanks to the development of cognitive science, a greater appreciation of the centrality of culture in education, and a new openness to qualitative approaches to educational study, federal support for it dwindled drastically.

CHAPTER SIX

Contested Terrain: The Disciplines versus Education

Beginning in the 1950s, scholars outside education became leaders in a variety of well-funded projects to revise the subject matter of the nation's schools. This had not occurred since at least the 1920s. Thanks to pride in America's wartime successes, combined with anxieties associated with the Cold War, the reluctance to participate in curriculum improvement that Hollis Caswell had encountered among his arts and sciences colleagues in Virginia in the 1930s seemed suddenly to give way to eagerness to join one of the so-called course improvement projects sponsored by national organizations like the American Association for the Advancement of Science, the American Chemical Society, and the College Entrance Examination Board and funded initially by foundations and then much more lavishly by the newly created National Science Foundation (NSF) or, less often, by the U.S. Office of Education. The result was an alphabet soup of new curricula.

In addition, though this was somewhat less noticed, there were self-conscious efforts to increase the disciplinary or academic rigor of many subfields of education research. For example, in the history of education, two very different revisionist thrusts were intended to remove the anachronistic and Whiggish orientation of most existing literature. In educational administration, an effort to nurture a theoretical emphasis borrowed from the social and organizational sciences was intended to help students of school administration better understand the nature of research, conceived as scientific inquiry as opposed to social bookkeeping. The goal of these various disparate efforts was to better align scholarship in education with scholarship in other fields.

Much heralded during the 1950s and early 1960s, all of these movements initiated changes that are still evident in scattered ways to this day. That said, none of them was able to promote thoroughgoing, sustained change in educational scholarship. Funding for the curriculum projects came to an end in the late 1970s as claims mounted that NSF was attempting to impose a national curriculum on localities. Unable to ignore a press for relevance that coincided with enrollment declines in the 1970s, historians of education turned again to more applied approaches. And in the case of the theory movement in educational administration, the continuing attraction for scholars of educational administration of work as consultants to school systems and then, increasingly, to the federal government undermined efforts to nurture new styles of research. Compounding all this, as the climate of opinion shifted in the middle 1960s from one in which excellence was the key word to one in which equality of opportunity was the nation's primary goal in education, the academic emphasis that became so notable in education scholarship during the 1950s gave way to more applied styles of education research.

The "New Math"

The curriculum reforms of the 1960s began in mathematics. Despite claims that professors of education were responsible for the mediocrity of the nation's schools and despite the large role played in course improvement by discipline-based scholars, curriculum reform was strongly supported by the teachers and scholars of mathematics education who belonged to the National Council of Teachers of Mathematics (NCTM). Founded in 1920 to help improve the content and methods of mathematics instruction, NCTM was the most important professional association for mathematics educators. Like most organizations in education, however, it represented one part of the field better than others. Scholars and teachers of K–12 mathematics who were relatively academic in their orientation were more in evidence than were more socially or developmentally inclined, "progressive" mathematics educators. However representative, sentiment expressed within the pages of its journal, *The Mathematics Teacher,* was distinctly on the side of high academic standards and rigor. Columns in *The Mathematics Teacher* frequently lamented the failure of most states to require mathematics for high school graduation and expressed dismay about "'functional mathematics' devoid of algebra and geometry." The assumption that most high school students ("the other 85%" who were not outstanding) needed only the "mathematics of daily life" or "of life situations" was frequently challenged.[1]

The first project to attempt a reform of mathematics instruction was led by Max Beberman, a professor of mathematics education at the University of Illinois. Having studied mathematics as an undergraduate at the City College of New York, Beberman had received both a master's and a doctor's degree from Teachers College. Thereafter he had given up teaching at the secondary level to become an assistant professor at Florida State University and then in 1955 an associate professor (and later full professor) at the University of Illinois, where he was also affiliated with the University High School.[2] In response to a request from the deans of education and engineering to lead a committee to investigate how secondary school mathematics instruction could be changed to guarantee that entering freshmen would be able to master calculus, Beberman became director of the University of Illinois Committee on School Mathematics (UICSM) in 1951.[3]

With funds provided by the Carnegie Corporation of New York, UICSM was intended "to bring mathematics into the teaching of mathematics, and to encourage the learner to discover as much of the subject as time and circumstances will permit."[4] Beberman and his colleagues believed that mathematics (and other sciences) had developed a great deal during the twentieth century and that the new knowledge had not been included in the high school curriculum. Their goal was to align high school mathematics with that work.[5]

In the process of their work, the Beberman group developed two key principles of instruction. Because, according to Beberman, the goal of mathematics education was comprehension and not merely the manipulation of numbers, his group came to insist that studying mathematics had to involve "discovery and precision in language." Discovery drove students to derive principles as they worked on solving problems rather than simply memorizing them from "the book." This would not obviate drill in manipulating numbers, Beberman explained, but it would help to ensure that students' understanding was sufficient to allow a principle learned in one situation to be applied in another. In addition, language was important because it allowed communication about mathematical entities and this tended to deepen understanding. Convinced that abstractions were important in mathematics, Beberman believed that what mattered in mathematics instruction was communicating that the number seven was a symbol for a set of like entities and not itself a thing with an independent "real" existence.[6]

Beberman's ideas about the teaching of mathematics were derived from a careful testing of texts in the University of Illinois High School and a number of other schools. The UICSM teaching materials were developed by a committee made up primarily of university mathematicians; then they were piloted by specially chosen teachers, who had attended regional training conferences; and, finally, they were evaluated through student testing and the observations of teacher coordinators and, as necessary, revised. Publicly, Beberman described the project as a result of "the combined efforts of mathematicians and teachers."[7] Privately, however, he presented the project as an effort to develop materials that could not be corrupted by "the average teacher," who was less competent, he thought, than a "teaching machine."[8] Even though Beberman was himself a mathematics educator, he seems to have shared the disdain for educators that was so pervasive among academics at the time and so publicly paraded. As it did for so many others, this disdain seems to have energized his interest in reform. Some earlier curriculum development projects had involved a fairly complicated process for piloting and evaluating material, but few, if any, had begun with ideas about the essence of a discipline and derived pedagogical premises from efforts to teach those ideas.

The National Science Foundation

Initiated with funding from the Carnegie Corporation, the Beberman group subsequently received funding from the National Science Foundation, which supported not only UICSM, but also other course improvement projects like the Physical Sciences Study Committee and the social science project "Man: A Course of Study" (MACOS). Created in 1950, NSF was designed to advance the argument Vannevar Bush had presented in *Science—The Endless Frontier* concerning the nation's need for scientific research in peacetime as well as war. With prominent national figures like former Harvard President J. B. Conant arguing that "the future of science in this country will be determined by our basic educational policy," improving science education early became part of NSF's approach to supporting scientific research.[9] During NSF's first years in operation, however, it refrained from providing funds for activities involving what it called "pre-college education." Then, beginning in 1953, declining college enrollments in mathematics and science prompted NSF to begin deliberations concerning how it might increase the numbers of students undertaking the study necessary for scientific careers. Pressed repeatedly by college educators, NSF began to do this by funding summer institutes for K–12 teachers. In 1953, the Fund for the Advancement of Education, a spin-off of the Ford Foundation, had piloted such an institute at the University of Minnesota. NSF institutes began in 1954.

Starting with one summer institute in that year, the NSF precollege teacher education program grew rapidly and quickly, with the budget increasing from $150,000 in 1955 to a high of $125 million in 1966, 1967, and 1968. At the start, the institutes were intended to increase the subject-matter knowledge of individual teachers. As a 1969 evaluation noted, this might involve providing minimal knowledge "for the high school football

Table 6 NSF Funding for Summer Institutes
and Curriculum Development, 1951–75

Fiscal Year	Summer Institutes	Curriculum	Overall Education
1951	$0	$0	$0
1952	0	0	1,540,171
1953	9,500	0	1,407,188
1954	10,000	0	1,887,767
1955	147,350	0	2,099,496
1956	615,270	17,410	3,521,134
1957	5,216,501	629,840	14,698,298
1958	6,684,414	835,372	20,398,468
1959	22,108,287	6,030,325	64,355,784
1960	21,926,776	6,419,341	66,907,353
1961	21,118,610	6,410,871	66,824,249
1962	26,034,103	8,989,756	78,580,448
1963	26,595,245	12,632,408	90,987,376
1964	27,349,223	13,975,712	102,580,373
1965	27,140,880	14,551,867	120,414,677
1966	25,783,001	15,563,952	124,305,225
1967	24,330,296	18,355,444	123,360,166
1968	22,121,886	19,352,297	124,832,567
1969	21,311,510	18,133,320	115,297,494
1970	23,300,000	16,313,000	120,179,865
1971	23,307,148	15,644,000	98,811,231
1972	16,140,332	8,087,000	93,728,301
1973	10,410,989	5,267,000	62,233,405
1974	5,819,000	7,137,857	80,709,308
1975	—	7,379,837	74,350,000
Total	357,480,321	201,726,609	1,654,010,344

SOURCES: National Science Foundation, *The National Science Foundation and Pre-college Science Education: 1950–1975* (Washington, D.C.: U.S. Government Printing Office, 1975); National Science Foundation, *Annual Report* (Washington, D.C.: U.S. Government Printing Office, 1954, 1955, 1956, 1967, 1970, 1972, 1973, 1974, 1975, 1976).

coach who has just been shoved into a physics teaching slot" or offering experienced teachers advanced graduate work.[10] Some institutes focused on a single field; others were hybrids with names like "General Science" or "Multiple Fields." Eventually, in addition to the summer institutes, yearlong ventures were added, some organized as intermittent in-service programs for classroom teachers, others as full-time sabbatical projects.

NSF funding provided unprecedented dollars for research in education (see table 6). As Francis A. J. Ianni observed from his post at the Cooperative Research Branch of the U.S. Office of Education, even though Congress had become increasingly willing to supply "research funds for remedial programs for the deaf, the blind, the mentally retarded, the delinquent and even the gifted, appropriations for curriculum research and development in the area of the improvement of the quality of education have been difficult to obtain." According to Ianni, this was largely a consequence of "the lack of drama in educational research—no congressman's daughter has ever died of a split infinitive."[11] NSF funding—as well as smaller amounts of money from the program Ianni was affiliated within the Office of Education—proved his point. If the coffers were opened by the unusual drama associated with the external threat posed by the Cold War and then by the launching of Sputnik, the willingness of prestigious discipline-based scholars to involve themselves in education added to the effect. But drama is difficult to sustain, and funding for curriculum research declined as precipitously in the late 1970s as it had increased in the mid-1950s.

Jerrold R. Zacharias and the Physical Sciences Study Committee

NSF support for curriculum research followed the launching of the summer institute program. It moved in this direction on the urging of Jerrold R. Zacharias, an MIT physicist, who had played a leading role in the development of the atomic bomb. Zacharias had become increasingly dismayed at the conceptions of physics held by his MIT undergraduates. He was upset that they came to MIT with little comprehension that "physics was not just theory, that physics *really*—underline *really*—was what you do either in a laboratory or by observation."[12] To rectify this situation, Zacharias dreamed up a plan to create ninety short films to be accompanied by texts and other teaching materials that would demonstrate such basic physics concepts as vectors, velocity, force, and mass. Presenting this plan in a March 1956 memorandum to MIT President James R. Killian, Zacharias then discussed his idea with NSF Director Alan Waterman, an old professional acquaintance, during a summer visit to Washington, D.C. Waterman was apparently so taken with Zacharias's proposal that he immediately arranged a dinner at the Cosmos Club, where "Zach" was told: "You've got to do this. . . . A physicist from MIT, respected guy, boy, you're our man."[13]

As psychologist Jerome S. Bruner observed in describing Zacharias, "he was a man shaped by success."[14] Although much that had fed this was personal, Zacharias exemplified the self-assurance and inclination to assume leadership roles that was a shared characteristic among elite physicists of the World War II generation. Physics had expanded rapidly in the United States during the 1920s and 1930s—between 1920 and 1932, twice as many Ph.D.s had been awarded as between the end of the Civil

War and the beginning of World War I.[15] Already offering young white males of modest social background great opportunities for advancement, physics took on even more cachet as a result of the extraordinary research and development—especially, but not exclusively, in the domain of atomic physics—undertaken during World War II. The result thereafter for men like Zacharias was a sense of entitlement combined with public spiritedness that was really quite remarkable. One might note parenthetically that it is difficult to imagine that one could have found among educationists an efficacy similar to that which Zacharias apparently exuded. If the occupational culture of physics supported a sense of agency, the occupational culture of education did not operate that way. Unlike physicists, who had been given ample opportunities for national service during World War II, educationists by and large had been ignored. Once again, the discount placed on educational expertise extracted a price.

All that aside, having stumbled into such an enthusiastic reception for his school physics plan at NSF, Zacharias moved with dispatch. In August 1956, MIT sent an official proposal to NSF, which was approved in early September with an award of $300,000 and a promise of $1.5 million the following year if it were needed. Even before learning that, however, Zacharias had gathered the initial nucleus of physicists who would work with him in what they immediately named the Physical Science Study Committee (PSSC). Between then and the first PSSC conference in December 1956, the initial Zacharias group had added some more scientists to the committee as well as a few key people who could help broker the materials they planned to develop. These included, among others, Morris Meister, principal of the Bronx High School of Science; Henry Chauncey, president of Educational Testing Service (ETS); and Vannevar Bush, author of the report that had led to the founding of NSF and chairman of the MIT Corporation.

Many of the ideas to emerge from the PSSC resembled those of the Beberman group at the University of Illinois. Like the mathematicians, the physicists decided their goal was to nurture understanding. They were dissatisfied with the idea of having students engage in experiments as an end in itself. In addition, they wanted to drop the applications so commonly central to high school physics instruction in order to emphasize the fundamentals: atoms, molecules, stars, and planets. In addition, they initially emphasized the production of teaching materials because they thought improving instruction in other ways would run amok owing to the incompetence of teachers. Moving with enormous speed, the PSSC produced its first volume, *The Universe*, embodying these principles by the summer of 1957. Then filmmakers, high school teachers, and teacher educators were added to the project to produce the teaching materials that would accompany the text. By the early fall of 1957, most of these materials were finished in their initial form; only the films, which proved enormously difficult to produce, remained in preparation.

Then, on October 4, 1957, Sputnik was launched. Faced with considerable public hysteria, Eisenhower created the President's Science Advisory Committee (PSAC), and Congress passed the National Defense Education Act (NDEA), through which additional money for curriculum development was directed to colleges and universities. The increased drama Sputnik brought to matters of education resulted in even higher levels of financial support to the PSSC: $500,000 from the Ford Foundation, $250,000 from the Alfred P. Sloan Foundation, and $442,000 more from NSF. Between 1956 and 1960, a total of $8 million of federal funds would go to the project.[16]

Within two years, PSSC had produced four courses, "The Universe," "Optics and Waves," "Mechanics," and "Electricity and Modern Physics," each of which had its own text, laboratory apparatus and guides, films, teachers' guides, and examinations, the last having being produced for PSSC by ETS. In addition, there was a series of paperback books, the Science Study Series, to provide supplemental reading material.[17] All the materials were officially piloted and revised on the basis of teachers' comments and student exam scores. However, as one observer noted: "Scientists were usually hesitant to accept the criticism of their 'science' from school teachers."[18] Regardless, beginning in 1960, the PSSC materials were distributed by a new nonprofit company, Educational Services, Inc. (ESI—it later became the Educational Development Center, Inc., or EDC), which was created to fulfill NSF requirements concerning the independent distribution of materials developed with NSF funds. Even though the course was considered extremely difficult, sales were steady and significant. As early as 1962, PSSC physics was being taught to approximately 80,000 students by some 2,000 teachers, many of whom had themselves studied PSSC physics in NSF-funded summer institutes. Eventually roughly 30 percent of all high school students studying physics used PSSC materials, and by the twentieth anniversary of the completion of the first set of materials, 1 million volumes had been sold.[19]

The Process of Education: "St. Jerome's Gospel"

Zacharias's interest in course improvement did not stop with physics. As a member of PSAC, Zacharias encouraged many other ventures, including a 1959 National Academy of Sciences study group that was asked to ponder links between various new curricula and what psychologists knew about teaching and learning. This was led by Jerome Bruner, a Harvard psychologist who was well acquainted with Zacharias and other Cambridge-based physicists involved in PSSC.

Candidly confessing that "psychologists, in the main, are embarrassed by education," Bruner organized the study group to contemplate topics like motivation, intuitive thinking, and the cognitive factors involved in curriculum design.[20] Conversation had centered on three ideas, he recalled later: first, the idea that "you don't think *about* physics, you think physics"; second, the belief derived from the work of the Swiss psychologist Jean Piaget that a person's understanding of an idea would be framed by the level of intellectual operations that person had reached; and, third, the notion that the way knowledge is put together or structured is essential to learning.[21] Summarized in a short but eloquent "chairman's report" called *The Process of Education,* which was known to insiders as "St. Jerome's Gospel," the book provided a popular rationale for discipline-driven curriculum projects like UICSM and PSSC.[22] Simply stated, the rationale was that "any subject can be taught effectively in some intellectually honest form to any child at any stage of development."[23]

The Process of Education placed Bruner at the center of the curriculum reform movement and led to his involvement in "Man: A Course of Study" or MACOS. As was frequently the case, this new course development project evolved out of a Zacharias-inspired, ESI-organized study group intended to improve the teaching of social studies. MACOS was the elementary school part of the project that emerged from that. It was to be a course about human evolution. Assuming leadership of the project appealed to Bruner because he was eager to see whether a group of historians, social scientists, and teachers could, in fact, teach young children about the nature of man in an intellectually honest way.

To do that, Bruner posed three questions that provided structure for the course: "What is uniquely human about human beings? How did they get that way? How could they be made more so?"[24] Thereafter the group developed films, texts, and teaching materials; piloted and revised the course; and, beginning in 1966, established a rather elaborate system of distribution. This involved regional centers where teacher trainers were taught to teach the new course; the teacher trainers then, in turn, trained others in school districts and individual school buildings. The distribution system was necessary, as participants noted with more than a little Cambridge bias showing, in order to get the course from the Widener

Library at Harvard to Wichita, Kansas.[25] Based primarily in anthropology and employing films and artifacts as well as texts, MACOS was designed to engage children in exploring life among Eskimos and Bushmen in order to help them understand how culture conditions human behavior. The course captured the imagination of many teachers, and for his part in its development, Bruner won awards from both the American Educational Research Association and the American Educational Publishers Institute.

Despite these successes, Bruner and his colleagues were unable to find a commercial publisher for the course materials. Most publishers were worried because the course was based on material unfamiliar to teachers. They were concerned, too, about the commercial viability of producing materials for a single course rather than an entire series. The recommended pedagogical techniques—using induction, small-group instruction, and multiple sources of information and teaching through participation—were new and complex, and that was additionally worrisome since the techniques would be difficult for a salesman to present in a short sales meeting. Even more than all that, publishers shied away from the project because it presented topics that might be controversial and get them into trouble. MACOS included films of Eskimos skinning baby seals and described the ways in which, in some societies, old people were expected to go off by themselves to die. Last, but hardly least important, in the late 1960s, the average expenditure for elementary social studies materials was $1 per pupil, and the multimedia MACOS materials were projected to cost $8 per pupil.[26]

MACOS's inability to find a commercial publisher testified to the severe constraints commercial text development imposed on educational innovation. In addition, as the project's materials made their way around the country, the political storm the course engendered demonstrated the degree to which local control of curriculum decisions could undermine research-based educational reforms. Like so much else about education in the United States, local decision making had a yin and yang effect—on the one hand, preserving important elements of democratic participation in educational politics, while, on the other, making it difficult to introduce innovations.

The furious reaction to MACOS was phenomenal. In Lake City, Florida, the Citizens for Moral Education waged a campaign to have MACOS barred from the schools because it was "godless, humanistic, evolution-based, socialistic, and 'sensual in philosophy.'"[27] In Montgomery County, Maryland, the curriculum developer for Citizens United for Responsible Education argued that the inventors of MACOS "were using public funds to teach their own private philosophies and value systems." Claiming that the course "had eliminated 'man's spiritual and moral dimension' from a consideration of what is human about human beings," she maintained that public funds could not have been spent to develop a curriculum to teach about "the development of Christian culture" and therefore should not have been used to develop MACOS.[28] Similarly, journalist John Steinbacher told a meeting of Citizens for Quality Textbooks in Vermont that MACOS was "teaching Deweyism, pragmatism, behaviorism, psychic manipulation, and humanism" and was "paving the way for a communist takeover and the destruction of the religious faith of the younger generation."[29] As more and more teachers and principals learned about MACOS and pushed for its adoption in their schools, comments like these were repeated all over the country at meetings of parent-teacher associations (PTAs), school boards, and education lobbying groups.

Subsequent public opinion surveys taken in the 1990s have documented that educators tend to be much more "progressive" in their views of "good education" than parents or members of the public at large.[30] The inclination of educators to accept MACOS and the public's disinclination to accept it may well indicate that difference existed earlier. More important, the persistence of different views may indicate the importance of combining curriculum innovations with systematic efforts to educate the public about them. Rarely have educators seen public education about education as a necessary part of their professional responsibilities, which may have had the unintended consequence of undermining education reform.

However that may be, predictably local-level complaints about MACOS found their way to Congress. In the spring of 1975, John B. Conlan, a conservative Republican congressman from Arizona, proposed eliminating support for MACOS from the NSF appropriation. His proposal was defeated, but shortly thereafter an amendment to the NSF authorization was brought to the floor of the House by Robert Bauman of Maryland, and this time the amendment passed. It mandated that Congress review all NSF grant proposals every thirty days and that NSF be required to submit documents explaining "to the maximum extent practicable the manner in which the national interest will be fostered by the approval of such grants."[31] As Philip Handler, president of the National Academy of Sciences, argued, the amendment was "a giant leap backward by a supposedly egalitarian House which voted to adopt a procedure appropriate only to authoritarian regimes." He angrily observed that it had turned the House into the "censor of the National Science Foundation."[32]

Thereafter debate also spilled into the Senate. By the summer of

1975, no fewer than three groups were investigating MACOS and, more generally, NSF support for curriculum development. Although the reports that were eventually generated tended not to support the charges of MACOS's critics and also failed to support the claims of those who believed NSF had been egregiously negligent in its oversight of its curriculum development grants, the fracas brought NSF funding for MACOS to an end. More important, what one NSF official described as "the worst political crisis in NSF history" brought the entire agency under assault.[33]

Worried about the credibility of NSF in Congress, Richard C. Atkinson, who became acting director of NSF in August 1976, carefully scrutinized all future NSF grants to be sure they would not stir congressional ire. He also appointed James Rutherford, a science educator from Harvard, to lead NSF's work in education. Rutherford favored President Carter's interest in strengthening the federal role in education by creating a cabinet-level department and decided that curriculum development could be more appropriately fostered through the new department, created in 1979, than through grants from NSF. In consequence, NSF gave up curriculum development in favor of studies of science teaching practices and preadolescent learning patterns.[34]

A brief era of adequate funding for curriculum reform was thus brought to an end. Slowly, but surely, "first-team scientists" also drifted away from education in order to resume their disciplinary agendas.[35] The coincidences and concerns that had given birth to curriculum reform had been powerful enough to draw the attention of discipline-based scholars to education for a time, but long-standing traditions of disrespect for educational scholarship, reinforced by discipline-based interests, militated against lasting commitments. Beyond that, reforming education proved far more difficult than discipline-based scholars had anticipated. Generally lacking a deep appreciation of the complexity of educational politics, discipline-based scholars had not expected their work to be subjected to the kind of public outbursts that greeted MACOS. Nor had they fully appreciated the twists and turns involved in disseminating new ideas from the center. Understanding that would present policy makers in education with continuing challenges.

From the History *of* Education to History *and* Education

During the 1950s and 1960s, there were other attempts to infuse discipline-based research into educational scholarship. There was, for example, a notable effort to reform the history of education initiated by the Committee on the Role of Education in American History. Sponsored by the Ford

Foundation's Fund for the Advancement of Education, the committee was intentionally organized to include only historians, none of whom was "a 'specialist' in American education." Finding that "for almost three quarters of a century the history of American education has had a promising future and a disappointing present," the committee recommended a number of correctives. It urged a broadened focus for historical studies: "For the historian . . . an agency need not be labeled a school. The embodiment of the intent to teach or otherwise to influence attitudes is in our sense an educational agency." It advocated efforts "to examine education as a creative force in United States history" and "thoughtful interpretation of the role of educational forces in certain great movements of American history." [36]

Then, in 1960, Bernard Bailyn, a historian at Harvard who was a member of the committee, published a critical needs and opportunity study about the history of colonial education. According to Bailyn, most historical writing about education was anachronistic because it had been written with professional purposes foremost in mind. Bailyn maintained that this had led to the confusion of education and schooling and that the confusion had to be corrected by new efforts to study the history of education more broadly. He conceived of history as "the entire process by which a culture transmits itself across the generations." [37]

Subsequently, Lawrence A. Cremin of Teachers College seconded Bailyn's views. Cremin was the author of *The Transformation of the School* (1961), a brilliant study of progressivism in education, which coincidentally modeled the kind of history the Committee on the Role of Education in American History advocated. He was an educationist who was widely respected by historians. Dissenting from Bailyn's claim that the weaknesses in the field were the fault of the professional biases of educationist authors, Cremin insisted instead that historians had shared their myopic vision. Other than that, however, he agreed with Bailyn's call for a broader focus and in a three-volume history, *American Education* (1970, 1980, 1988), set out to exemplify a broadened approach. [38] As Cremin described it in a definition that became more expansive over the years, he believed the history of education should be understood as "the deliberate, systematic, and sustained effort to transmit, evoke, or acquire knowledge, values, attitudes, skills, and sensibilities, as well as any learning that results from that effort, direct or indirect, intended or unintended." [39]

Stimulated by these public pleas for a new focus, the history of education began to attract attention from scholars in departments of history and, for a time, became one of the most exciting subfields of historical study. Although questions about schooling remained central, calls for a broader focus encouraged innovative work on the role of religion in the history of education and on questions having to do with attendance at and access to institutions of higher education as well as on a number of other topics. In addition, especially after the appearance of Michael B. Katz's *The Irony of Early School Reform* in 1968, studies of schooling took on a newly critical edge that linked the history of education to the concerns of historians and social scientists. Questions concerning mobility and the effects on life chances of ethnicity, gender, social class, and race now moved to the fore. This second revisionist thrust was not a response to the historiographical statements of Bailyn and Cremin. It was instead a reflection of growing public interest in equality of educational opportunity and the problems of poor, urban schools. Nevertheless, both streams of revisionism brought the history of education newfound respectability within university history departments and professional associations of historians. As had not been the case earlier when history journals failed to review works pertaining to the history of education, now the *American Historical Review* and the *Journal of American History* regularly covered such works.

Despite that, education did not long remain a center of interest for historians generally, and by the 1980s, if not before, new subfields like labor history and the history of the professions were displacing it as "hot" topics for historical inquiry. Beyond that, the shift to a more disciplinary focus did not strengthen the place of the history of education within the curricula of education schools. As Paul Monroe and other leaders in the effort to generate a professional history had discovered earlier, unless students could see the applied relevance of historical study, they voted against it with their feet. Enrollment declines in the early 1980s therefore presented historians of education and those of their colleagues in others of the humanities and social sciences who were based in schools of education with a difficult situation. Even in the 1980s, schools of education tended to be tolerated by university authorities not out of scholarly respect, but for the income they generated and the semblance of public service they offered their host institutions. Especially in light of their marginal status, enrollment declines could not be tolerated by administrators in schools of education for very long. Under severe pressure to please their "clients," historians of education found themselves facing a situation in which they often had to make their historical work subsidiary to other, more sustainable lines of teaching and research, policy studies being central among these.

Once again, the chances for rigorous discipline-driven research were diminished by the long-standing constraints that have always defined educational scholarship. When educational scholarship was professionalized, it was viewed with contempt by noneducationists; when it was discipline-based, it was shunned by students, who had wanted "recipes for practice" even when William H. Payne became the nation's first university-based professor of the science and art of teaching at the University of Michigan in 1879. Being torn between these opposing forces seemed to be an enduring dilemma for scholars of education.

The Theory Movement in Educational Administration

A similar situation prevailed within the field of educational administration. In the middle 1950s, thanks to the converging agendas of several groups, a new movement to infuse behavioral science theory into the study of educational administration made significant inroads at the nation's premier institutions of professional study.

Known as the "theory movement," this effort grew out of Kellogg Foundation interest in helping school administrators better direct their schools toward the improvement of community life. Not coincidentally, one of Kellogg's major advisors at the time was Ralph W. Tyler, who, as dean of social sciences at the University of Chicago, was an unusually successful promoter of interdisciplinary study owing to his insistence that collaboration would best emerge from cooperative projects.[40] Not coincidentally, too, Chicago was home to community studies conducted by W. Lloyd Warner, Allison Davis, and Robert J. Havighurst, among others, which, unlike specialized school surveys, were helping to reveal the value of the social sciences for educational inquiry.[41]

The Kellogg Foundation's interest in education and community life meshed well with concerns expressed within the American Association of School Administrators (AASA), an organization of academicians and practitioners founded in 1937 as the successor to the National Education Association's (NEA's) Department of Superintendence. By the late 1950s, leaders in the AASA were aware that the proportion of students in schools of education who were choosing to study educational administration was in decline.[42] They also knew that new approaches to leadership were taking hold in other fields and were being actively pursued by teams of researchers at institutions ranging from the Graduate School of Business Administration at Harvard University to the Research Center for Group Dynamics at the University of Michigan to the NEA's National Training Laboratory in Bethel, Maine. Sharing with others in education an eagerness to be associated with developments that might raise their status, the AASA approached the Kellogg Foundation for funding, and the two eventually collaborated in the organization of the Cooperative Program in Educational Administration (CPEA), a ten-year, $5 million venture whose most important purpose was to improve training programs for educational administrators. The CPEA was launched in 1950 at eight regional centers: Chicago, George Peabody, Harvard, Ohio State, Stanford, Teachers College, the University of Oregon, and the University of Texas.

One of the professors recruited to educational administration as a result of the new initiative was Jacob W. Getzels, a psychologist who had done his doctoral work in the Harvard Department of Social Relations, where he had been influenced by Talcott Parsons's interest in "grand theory."[43] Asked to join the faculty of the Department of Education at the University of Chicago in 1951, Getzels had not had previous exposure to the professional study of education. When he had ventured into his first classes at Chicago, he had "tried to find out from the students . . . what conceptual stance they took."[44] That the students had not seemed to know what he was talking about had been startling to the young psychologist, who had been schooled in the power of the self-conscious and purposive use of distinct theoretical perspectives. In consequence, he had read "a couple of texts in educational administration," but had found them also to be of little use. As he recalled later, "they seemed more like training manuals than conceptual or research treatises."[45] Unable to identify a theoretical basis for studying educational administration, Getzels had then delivered a lecture that was subsequently published to wide acclaim in the *Harvard Educational Review.* The lecture challenged the atheoretical empiricism that had become a hallmark of administrative studies in education and helped substantively to initiate the theory movement in educational administration.

"Systematic research requires the mediation of theory—theory that will give meaning and order to observations already made and that will specify areas where observations still need to be made," Getzels announced in the essay. Because there was "a dearth of theory-making, and such theories as do exist have thus far proved unequal to the task of stimulating research," there was, he maintained, "a conspicuous lack of systematic research in the field of educational administration." Charging that knowledge about school administration had heretofore been derived from nothing more than "surveys, *ad hoc* testimonials and untested principles," Getzels proceeded to describe what he called "A Psycho-Sociological Framework for the Study of Educational Administration." Maintaining that "the functioning of the administrative process" would depend on the character of the interaction that occurred between a person initiating administrative action and the one receiving it, Getzel argued that studies in administration should focus on the ways in which both individuals perceived their relationship.[46]

Soon thereafter Getzels, accompanied by Andrew Halpin of Ohio State and Arthur Coladarci of Stanford, attended a meeting of the National Conference of Professors of Educational Administration, a small, informal spin-off of the AASA whose purpose was to provide academics with an exclusive forum for discussing the education of educational administrators. According to one participant in that 1954 Denver meeting, the three scholars were

> highly articulate and, in many cases, charismatic . . . [and they] had a message to give:
> 1. Better research into educational administration was needed.
> 2. The research must be theory based.
> 3. Social science was the source of the theories.
> 4. The social scientists were the ones who could guide the professors of educational administration.[47]

Because their charm and persuasiveness appear to have mitigated possible feelings of resentment among the professors of educational administration present, the three psychologists carried the day, and their criticisms led to significant realignment in the field.

Evident in the volume *Administrative Behavior in Education* (1957) edited by Roald F. Campbell and Russell T. Gregg, which had been planned at the Denver meeting, this realignment involved a shift in emphasis from principles of management to the analysis of leadership and administrative behavior. It encouraged four new lines of research: administration as a social process, administration as a process for solving mutual problems, administration as decision making, and schools as formal organizations.

More general and abstract than empirical and concretely descriptive, the new studies that appeared after the 1954 Denver meeting tended to treat administration as a generic phenomenon, thus avoiding the highly specialized, narrowly professional focus of earlier scholarship in education. In addition, they tended to avoid prescriptive statements, the assumption being that good research was theory driven and that "scientific theories treat phenomena as they are."[48] They were deeply influenced by the separation between factual and ethical statements that Herbert Simon depicted as central to administrative science in his study *Administrative Behavior* (1947).

More like the pioneers of administrative study than they seemed to realize, advocates of theory in educational administration also directed their attention to creating structures that might sustain the reforms they had initiated. In 1956, they organized the University Council for Educational Administration (UCEA) to support cooperative research projects having to do with problems of instruction in educational administration. In 1964, they also launched the *Educational Administration Quarterly,* which was sponsored by the UCEA to disseminate theory-based studies.

Looking back on the theory movement, its proponents claimed it had had a significant impact on the field. Daniel E. Griffiths was one of the first professors of educational administration without formal training in the behavioral sciences to make a notable contribution to the movement. He claimed that it had "moved educational administration from the status of a practical art toward, if not altogether to, the status of an academic discipline."[49] Jacob Getzels stated more modestly that the movement had fomented a shift "from conceiving of educational administration as a domain of action only to conceiving of it as a domain of study also."[50]

Doubtless true at least at those universities that had been regional CPEA centers, according to Andrew W. Halpin and Andrew E. Hayes, two of Getzels's confreres at the 1954 meeting, the theory movement nevertheless failed. It could not win "acceptance at the grass roots within the professorate," they explained. Basing their claim on a 1973 survey of the professorate in educational administration, Halpin and Hayes concluded that even though the theory movement had sparked "a kind of intellectual excitement that previously had been conspicuously missing in the field of educational administration," most professors were "just not interested in research or in the *study* of administration." Their primary identification was "'with the field,' not with the university."[51]

The long-established profession-building focus of administrative study in education was reinforced by major changes in U.S. policy. After the 1954 *Brown v. Board of Education* decision and, even more, after passage of the Elementary and Secondary Education Act (ESEA) of 1965, the federal government assumed an unprecedented activist role in the formulation of education policy. According to Halpin and Hayes, this meant that there were abundant funds for "airport professors" willing to engage in contract research and that "the search for concepts with social concerns" was replaced by efforts to find "solutions instead of understanding problems."[52] Federal priorities thus promoted a return to the kind of collaborative relationship between professors and school superintendents that had first been established through the school survey movement. Eventually, this would yield insights into the policy-making process in education. More immediately, however, it helped undermine concentrated work on matters of theory.

Without major foundation funds to sustain and extend the movement toward a theoretical base for research in educational administration and with major government funds supporting a return to the practical as opposed to the conceptual, to empiricism as opposed to theory, the theory movement waned roughly fifteen years after it began. Although it clearly changed the focus of scholarship at some institutions, especially Chicago and Stanford, a 1974 canvass of the literature of educational administration indicated that the field as a whole had not changed its essential character—apparently it was still "far from being research oriented," what research there was tended to exhibit "a practical emphasis," and "interest in educational administration by other disciplines [was] at best limited."[53]

Having been oriented from the first toward the problems and concerns of school leaders, scholarship in educational administration remained a service-driven mode of inquiry. Fulfilling the canons of social bookkeeping, it tended to be more descriptive than analytic and to be concerned primarily with data that could be quantified. With much to encourage a profession-building focus for the field, and little to encourage a more academic focus, scholarship in educational administration did not generate or borrow consistent criteria for asking questions and making sense of data. Lacking a theoretical orientation, it was better able to help solve practical problems of school management than it was to advance understanding of educational purposes and the role of schools in relation to those. It did not provide adequate support to the assumption of leadership roles.

Although Ellwood P. Cubberley and other pioneers of educational administration as a field of university study had wanted to empower superintendents relative to nonprofessional school board members and others involved in educational governance, the field they had defined was not sufficient to that purpose. As had been the case early in the twentieth century, toward the end of the century school administrators tended to remain the servants of power—of school boards, mayors, and the policy researchers from disciplines like sociology, politics, and economics, who increasingly after 1965 shaped the public attitudes and framed the public choices to which educational administrators had to respond. Once again, tensions between theory and application, professionalized scholarship and discipline-driven research, had presented educationists with a dilemma they seemed unable to escape.

CHAPTER SEVEN

Gaining Ground and Losing Support:
The Federal Role in Education Research

Prior to 1954, when the Congress passed the Cooperative Research Act, the federal government's involvement in education research had been limited. Although a federal Department of Education had been created in 1867 to collect and disseminate "such statistics and facts as shall show the condition and progress of education in the several States and Territories," the department's early history had been troubled.[1] In characteristic nineteenth-century fashion, its proponents had hoped that by publishing statistics they would be able to convince all states to emulate those that provided the most support for education. Within two years of its establishment, however, opponents of the department, who feared federal intrusion into local affairs, tried to eliminate all of its funding. Unsuccessful in that effort, they nonetheless managed to have the department downgraded to an Office of Education within the Department of the Interior— subsequently, the name went back and forth between Office and Bureau, and its departmental home varied until it became an autonomous department with cabinet status in 1979. Opponents also refused to give the first commissioner, Henry P. Barnard, the full funding he had requested for the publication of circulars. According to Barnard, the denial was facilitated by the fact that the "schoolmen" seemed indifferent to the department's fate.[2] Even though its leaders were often eminent educators like William Torrey Harris, debates about the legitimacy and existence of the Department/Office/Bureau of Education have continued to this day, as have efforts to limit its budget. In consequence, until the 1950s, most of its reports were internally generated and offered little more than schematic compilations of raw data. Indeed, it was not until the mid-1950s that the federal government went beyond this to support research in significant ways.[3]

Stimulated by the Cold War, the civil rights movement, and the Johnson War on Poverty, the federal government finally provided for the development of a research infrastructure that included research centers, laboratories, a research dissemination center, and the National Assessment of Educational Progress. It also initiated and financed important inquiries into equality of educational opportunity and awarded contracts for evaluations that focused on the translation of policies into practice. Especially after the creation of the National Institute of Education in 1972, which was established in part to generate better educational research and development (R&D), it also played a role in encouraging basic research into teaching and learning.

Although to advocates of total freedom for field-initiated research, these efforts of the federal government to foster research directly and to bring greater cohesion to the field were controversial, both in terms of the research methods developed and the substantive knowledge gained, the scholarship that was initiated as a result of this new federal engagement was impressive. However much remained to be learned, in a rather short period of time a great deal had been discovered about ways to link policy and practice. Despite that, politics constantly jeopardized federal activities in education, especially those related to education research. In no other way were antieducationist attitudes more starkly revealed than in congressional debates about legislation pertaining to education research. What is more, neither a strong professional lobby nor a citizens lobby developed to provide the kind of constituency pressure usually required for positive congressional action. Although the American Educational Research Association (AERA) created a government liaison office in 1977, the most effective advocate, the Council for Educational Development and Research (CEDaR), was primarily interested in the organizations it represented, the federal centers and laboratories created in the 1960s.[4] In consequence, in the face of an impressive record of scholarly progress, there was a retreat from government support for education research. In a very real sense, therefore, the story of the federal role in education research was one of simultaneous promise and decline.

The Cooperative Research Program

Designed by U.S. Commissioner of Education Samuel Brownell, with help from his longtime friend from Nebraska Ralph W. Tyler, the Cooperative Research Program (CRP) initiated the federal government's move toward becoming an important contractor for education research. Having grown up in a family of educators and received both a master's and doctor's degree in education from Yale, Brownell wanted to upgrade the caliber of federal research. With that in mind, he worked hard to ensure that the CRP would allow the commissioner to contract with researchers at institutions outside the Office of Education. This was expected to increase available knowledge about education and to improve the quality of research. Funded with an initial appropriation of $1 million in 1956, the CRP was a bellwether for subsequent federal research programs. In order to secure an initial appropriation to fund the act that authorized the CRP, Commissioner Brownell had to agree to spend two-thirds of the funds for a particular purpose—in this case, research into the education of the mentally retarded.[5] Beyond that, during the first years of the CRP, there was a running struggle between Office of Education staff, which wanted the funds to be used to pay for surveys relevant to their own work, and the program's Research Advisory Committee, chaired by Ralph W. Tyler and other outsiders to the government, which worked determinedly to ensure that funds would go to field-initiated projects.[6]

Despite these problems, funding for the CRP grew at a rapid rate. In 1965, the CRP dispensed $17 million, a sum that was increased to $70 million the following year. In selecting research projects, the Research Advisory Committee favored those with a disciplinary orientation. In consequence, between 1955 and 1963, applications from discipline-based scholars quadrupled without a similar increase in applications from educationists. By 1963, noneducationists were the majority of applicants for CRP funds.[7] This inspired the CRP's director, David L. Clark, with great optimism. "By 1970 it may be possible to state that more was learned about education in the 1960s than had been learned in the previous history of education in this country," he announced hopefully in 1961.[8]

While many shared Clark's optimism, policy makers within the Office of Education were nonetheless worried that research was still "fragmented, non-cumulative, and inconclusive" and that it did not seem to translate into actual improvements in practice.[9] Many members of President Johnson's 1964 Task Force on Education, which was chaired by Carnegie Corporation President John W. Gardner, shared that view and recommended a further elaboration of the federal government's involvement in education research. In 1963, therefore, R&D centers were created to foster interdisciplinary studies and to ensure that a critical mass of scholars was investigating such major areas of federal interest as urban education and school administration. By design university-based, the R&D centers had to be organizationally free of schools of education. By 1967, there were nine centers in operation, with funding ranging from over $1,308,702 for the University of Pittsburgh Learning Research and Development Center to $172,717 for the Center for the Study of the Social

Organization of Schools and the Learning Process at Johns Hopkins University.[10]

Beginning in 1965, regional educational laboratories that would disseminate the centers' research were also established. As initially proposed by the Gardner task force, these labs were to be few in number and carefully designed and staffed. However, as they were actually created, officials within the Office of Education decided they had to ask Congress for the maximum possible by way of funding because, as one participant put it, "you'll never get more for labs. You can't grow [them] gradually."[11] In consequence, ten months after the creation of the labs was approved by Congress, eleven were beginning their work, and by September 1966, twenty were in development or operation. Located all over the country to satisfy the constituency interests of various members of Congress, the labs proved to be troubled institutions with high staff turnover and difficult relations with the Office of Education. By the end of 1967, John Gardner, now acting as secretary of health, education, and welfare, began the first of what would be many reviews of their organization and performance.[12]

To ensure better dissemination of research to teachers and other school personnel, the Office of Education also created ERIC, the Educational Resources Information Center. Intended to collect, abstract, and disseminate "exemplary information and research," ERIC operated through twenty clearinghouses established to screen documents to be included in its database along with all the research sponsored by the Office of Education. Mistakenly assuming that school and district personnel wanted the information thus made available, ERIC proved to be a masterful strategy for the central collection of information, but not for its dissemination to people in the field.[13] Practitioners tended not to be interested in education research. Whether this was a result of weaknesses in their training—either a lack of exposure to research or poor teaching in research courses—or a reflection of problems of quality and general public indifference, practitioners' lack of interest meant that there was very slight demand for the goods that ERIC had to offer.

During the late 1950s and early 1960s, while building this infrastructure for research, the federal government supported research through a number of pieces of legislation, notably (in addition to the CRP) the National Defense Education Act of 1958 and the Head Start provisions of the Economic Opportunity Act of 1964. Directed at children whose home environments might not provide optimal early opportunities for learning, Head Start, of course, built on the developmental research begun at the

Iowa Child Welfare Research Station many years before. Research relevant to education was also carried out by agencies like the National Science Foundation (NSF), the National Institutes of Health (NIH), and the National Institute of Mental Health (NIMH). Reaching unprecedented heights in the middle and late 1960s, funding for education research had become an important part of the federal role in education.[14]

The National Assessment of Educational Progress

Although the federal government had been involved in financing education research since 1954, under Francis Keppel, who became U.S. commissioner of education in December 1962, the federal role in education research grew in important ways. According to one of Keppel's subsequent Harvard colleagues, Patricia Albjerg Graham, "more than any other figure in America, [Keppel] eased the transition from pre-war progressive education, with its individualistic emphasis on the child and his or her adjustment, to the American educational agenda of the last half of the twentieth century, with its emphasis upon the needs of groups of children who were not well served by the existing educational structures."[15] As part of that, he also significantly increased the federal government's research capacity in education.

A former dean of the Harvard Graduate School of Education, Keppel had served during World War II as assistant to the chair of the Information and Education Division of the Joint Army and Navy Committee on Welfare and Recreation. Led by Samuel Stouffer, a pioneering survey sociologist, the Research Branch of the division had collected data about the attitudes of people serving in the armed forces. Then, on the basis of survey results, it had recommended solutions to tough management problems like how to handle demobilization at the end of the war.[16] The work of the Research Branch left Keppel with an enduring respect for the practical usefulness to policy makers of precise numerical data. Not surprisingly, therefore, he wanted to increase the capacity of the Office of Education to inform its own operations with research. With this concern in mind and cognizant of congressional interest in knowing that its investments could be shown to yield demonstrable effects, Keppel began to explore the feasibility of developing what became known as the National Assessment of Educational Progress (NAEP).[17]

During the early summer of 1963, Keppel consulted with Ralph Tyler about the feasibility of developing some kind of periodic assessment to describe improvements in education over time and to indicate by region or state the relative equality or inequality of education.[18] Since 1953, when the Center for Advanced Study in Behavioral Sciences in Stanford, California, was created by the Ford Foundation, Tyler had been its director. After meeting with Keppel in Washington, D.C., he returned to the center, where he discussed Keppel's query with three statisticians, John Tukey, Frederick Mosteller, and Clyde Combs. Soon thereafter he sent Keppel a memorandum explaining that existing tests distinguished among different individuals rather than measuring what people knew. As a result, Tyler explained, existing tests would not be useful in providing the kind of benchmark data Keppel wanted. Obviously enticed by the opportunity Keppel's proposal offered to extend his long-standing interest in developing means of assessment that could improve the effectiveness of education, Tyler went on to sketch a design for a national assessment.

Having learned from Tyler that his idea seemed actually to be feasible, Keppel then approached John Gardner in the hope of enlisting the Carnegie Corporation's support for developing a censuslike portrait of educational achievement nationwide.[19] Keppel believed that the development of a national testing program would proceed more smoothly if it was not dependent upon government funding. He knew, too, that under Gardner, as well as Alan Pifer, who succeeded him as president, the corporation was moving away from its earlier emphases and becoming a leading supporter of progressive innovations in education.[20] This was a result of changing views among corporation staff and trustees. Soon after receiving Keppel's request, Gardner authorized a discretionary grant of $12,500 to cover the costs of two meetings "to explore whether developments in testing and in methods of sampling now enable a fair assessment of the level of national educational attainment."[21] As a subsequent evaluation of NAEP pointed out, things moved very rapidly at this point, and there was relatively little discussion of the value of the endeavor. The questions in debate were largely procedural.[22]

In December 1963 and then again in January 1964, Keppel's proposal was discussed at meetings chaired by Gardner. The first meeting consisted primarily of psychometricians and the second, of prominent educators. Drawing on ideas he had already presented to Keppel, Tyler suggested at each gathering that a new assessment be created that would test general levels of knowledge. The assessment would not discriminate among individuals, he explained. Instead, it would attempt to gauge the levels of learning of the least-educated, average, and most-educated strata of U.S. society. Tyler also suggested that the assessment could be administered to a representative sample of the various important subgroups of the American school population by having different individuals complete only a few items and then combining their results with those of other individuals belonging to the same subgroup of the population. Tyler thought the tests should be given at the end of third and seventh grades and before students left high school. Although there would be discussion and debate about all sorts of design issues concerning NAEP over the next several years, as it actually evolved NAEP fit very neatly into Tyler's initial description of it.[23]

Following the two initial conferences and preliminary planning concerning how to proceed, Gardner asked Tyler to chair the Exploratory Committee on Assessing the Progress of Education, which was called ECAPE. Supported by roughly $2 million from the Carnegie Corporation and the Fund for the Advancement of Education, a spin-off of the Ford Foundation, the committee spent four years working with contractors chosen to develop different aspects of the assessment and meeting with citizens groups, educators, and politicians throughout the nation.

As Tyler described it, the committee's first task was to determine what skills and knowledge should be assessed. Because they wanted the assessment to be of interest to the public at large, Tyler arranged several levels of consultation. During weekend meetings held in each region of the country, Tyler and his colleagues met with groups of scholars who were knowledgeable about the subjects taught in schools, with lay people who could judge whether the items identified by the scholars seemed important to them, and with school people who could ascertain whether the items were, in fact, actually being taught in the local schools. Thereafter the Educational Testing Service and the American Institutes of Research developed the "exercises" that would determine what children knew about subjects ranging from writing and social studies to music. They called these instruments "exercises rather than test items," Tyler explained because the word "test" implied paper-and-pencil questions and the assessment might require observations, interviews, and other methods of data collection.[24] Finally, decisions had to be made about the ages at which children would be tested. Nine, thirteen, and seventeen were the initial choices.

To this point, work on NAEP had been largely technical. Now politics intervened. When Tyler wrote to a sample of school superintendents to seek their cooperation in the administration of a trial assessment, George Brain, a former president of the American Association of School Administrators (AASA), rallied that organization against NAEP and threatened to refuse cooperation in its development. According to a memorandum sent to the membership by the AASA Executive Council, "although labeled an 'assessment' program the NAEP project is a national testing program and as such it will be coercive."[25] As Tyler complained to the AASA staff director, the message was designed "to frighten rather than to inform."[26] Perhaps more than Tyler was willing to admit, the state superintendents of education—"chiefs," as they were called—were terrified that NAEP would open the door to national standards for education.[27] To their way of thinking, such standards would deprive them of a meaningful role in policy making. Eventually, when ECAPE was reconstituted as the Committee on Assessing the Progress of Education, its membership was expanded to include more administrators, and Brain was asked to become its chair. This reorganization overcame the opposition. The fact remains, however, that the fears of the state superintendents had almost brought NAEP to an end. Yet again, the introduction of an educational innovation faced difficulties owing to the multiple, overlapping administrative agencies that governed education in the United States.

Unsure about the ways in which NAEP data would be presented to the public and to Congress, Brain explained the state superintendents' position at the first meeting of the Committee on Assessing the Progress of Education. Indicating that the superintendents felt they had fallen under "criticism immediately after Sputnik" and had been "in the spotlight ever since," he pointed out that they had been charged with everything "from deficiencies in the teaching of science and mathematics to their ineptness in handling civil rights and poverty issues."[28] Not surprisingly, they were worried that NAEP would add fuel to the fire. However, if the Educational Commission of the States (ECS) managed NAEP, Brain suggested, the superintendents might feel more positively toward it. ECS was a new compact of the states that had been suggested by James B. Conant in his 1964 book *Shaping Educational Policy*. Convinced that it would be unconstitutional to develop national educational policy, but also of the opinion that more coherent and coordinated policies were necessary, Conant had suggested an organization like ECS in the hope that it might undertake the planning for nationwide education policies.[29] It was dominated by state education officials rather than by the federal officials and scholars who seemed so threatening to the state chiefs.

Still guided at least behind the scenes by Tyler and Gardner, negotiations were opened with ECS, and in June of 1969, ECS assumed responsibility for NAEP. Initially leery of doing this, ECS was convinced to do so by assurances that NAEP would not cause embarrassment for chief state school officers. As Michael Greenbaum and his colleagues have pointed out in a study of NAEP, this was a little ironic because, in the end, the

one member of ECS's steering committee who voted against the affiliation did so on the grounds that NAEP "was being designed so that there
would be nothing objectionable in it." The dissenter observed that ECS
was being guaranteed that NAEP would be "pablum."[30] Beyond that,
even though the assessment was under new management, its design was
unchanged. Initiated in April 1969, NAEP was essentially the assessment
Tyler had described to Keppel in the summer of 1963.

Surviving to this day, NAEP has frequently been criticized for captur-
ing data without linking those data to meaningful and publicly comprehensible suggestions concerning what they mean. In consequence, it has
been viewed as a weak instrument for stimulating improvements. Two
early critics complained, for example, that "at most NAEP can provide a
measure of educational progress analogous to the gross national product,
but not tools to affect it."[31] More recently a National Academy of Education panel monitoring new NAEP state assessments called upon NAEP to
"redefine education achievement in terms of what students will need to
know and be able to do to be productive and knowledgeable citizens in
the 21st century."[32] Urging a standard-setting function, though not using
those words, that recommendation was designed to push NAEP toward
a more active role in what had come by then to be called systemic reform.

However well grounded criticisms of NAEP may have been, it is important to appreciate that NAEP embodied a conception of assessment
that described general strengths and weaknesses. It offered data that were
at least intended to be useful to efforts to improve education generally. In
this way, it differed fundamentally from earlier approaches to assessment,
which had been based on tests that compared and ranked individuals, the
assumption being that sorting and tracking were the key to education
reform rather than general efforts to strengthen instruction.

In addition, it is important to bear in mind that at the time Tyler
formulated his initial conception for NAEP, the knowledge and techniques necessary to correlate inputs and outputs in education—put otherwise, to explain differences in achievement—were not well developed.[33]
Understanding that, Tyler had always held relatively modest expectations
for the assessment. Keppel, by contrast, had held bolder dreams. As he
had explained to the first Carnegie conference in December 1963, he had
wanted the assessment to generate "evidence that is clear, clear and de-
pendable on what you really mean by lack of opportunity."[34] At the time,
Keppel was eager to find hard data that would allow him to focus federal
educational policy on the promotion of "equal educational opportunity."
Not himself trained as a social scientist, Keppel seems not to have realized

that the meaning of opportunity could not be really "clear" until social scientists became more sophisticated in their understanding of outcome variables.

Although James Coleman's study *Equality of Educational Opportunity*, which was published three years after planning for NAEP began, would significantly advance such understanding, Keppel had wanted an assessment that really could not be. Whether or not more sophisticated techniques might have yielded different results, the data NAEP has collected have not made educational policy making more rational or scientific, as Keppel had once hoped might be the case. According to a 1977 evaluation of NAEP, this was largely a result of the diffuse character of the education research "community"—a community that would not be able to organize itself effectively to lobby Congress in support of its own interests. As the evaluators of NAEP aptly noted, "when social statistics are gathered by a community with a weak set of shared assumptions, the statistics fall into various traps, and therefore have little precise theoretical or programmatic use. However . . . this does not mean such statistics are not used at all. . . . They are used like any other political resource" to argue for one's established point of view.[35] Despite that, thanks to Tyler's astute sense of educational politics, as well as his continuing belief that improving techniques for assessment—assessment as opposed to testing—was the sine qua non of improving education, NAEP was created and the federal role in research relevant to educational policy further enlarged.

James S. Coleman and *Equality of Educational Opportunity*

If NAEP data have been used for all sorts of political purposes, the same must be said of the data and interpretations presented in James S. Coleman et al., *Equality of Educational Opportunity*, published in 1966.[36] Generally known as the Coleman Report, the study was mandated by section 402 of the Civil Rights Act of 1964. This stated: "The Commissioner shall conduct a survey . . . within two years of the enactment of this title, concerning the lack of availability of equal educational opportunities for individuals by reason of race, color, religion, or national origin in public educational institutions at all levels."[37]

Traditionally, such a survey would have focused exclusively on the "inputs" to education—measurements of school building quality, teacher-student ratios, laboratories, and libraries—since these were assumed to define equality of educational opportunity. However, while Keppel was commissioner, the Office of Education was quite purposefully being reoriented to be less dominated by traditional education lobbies like the National Education Association (NEA) and more oriented toward researchers based in the social sciences. Alexander Mood, a Rand Corporation mathematician whom Keppel had recruited to lead the National Center for Educational Statistics, was that kind of scholar; and when Keppel asked him also to assume responsibility for what was initially called the "402 survey," it quickly became evident that the study would not simply be a census of school resources. As Gerald Grant pointed out in his extensive study of the Coleman Report, even before Coleman was brought in to undertake the survey, Mood was convinced that "there must be some attempt to measure the equality of results. That is, were black or yellow or poor children learning to read and write as well as others, and if not, why? What were the factors that seemed related to school achievement? Were they facilities, curriculum, libraries, teacher abilities, home background, or some combination of these?" [38]

Much impressed by *The Adolescent Society,* a book published by Coleman in 1961, Mood turned to the Johns Hopkins sociologist to undertake the 402 survey. Born in rural Indiana and educated in Kentucky and at Purdue University, Coleman had begun his career as a chemical engineer at the Eastman Kodak Company in Rochester, New York. The former boxer had then had a change of heart and, in 1951, had begun graduate studies in sociology at Columbia, which, as his former teacher Robert K. Merton once recalled, was at the time "a place sparkling with intellectual excitement." [39] In an enormously talented cohort, Coleman had been *"primus inter pares,"* absorbing both Paul Lazersfeld's interest in methodology and mathematical sociology and Merton's interest in theory rooted in systematic empirical investigation. [40] From Columbia, Coleman had gone on to faculty appointments at the University of Chicago and Johns Hopkins, eventually returning to Chicago in 1973.

Extraordinarily prolific and from all accounts a workaholic to whom eighteen-hour days were no less familiar than occasional time-outs for beer, squash, and poker, Coleman wrote the book that drew Mood's attention under a grant from the Cooperative Research Program (CRP) of the U.S. Office of Education. Apparently, the hope of CRP designers to draw new, discipline-based talent into education research had been abundantly successful in Coleman's case. Not yet famous when Mood tapped him, Coleman went on to achieve great prominence as a policy analyst whose work illuminated some of the most controversial topics of the day, including school desegregation, busing, and the relative merits of public and private schools. Beyond that, as a social scientist, Coleman was a polymath, only one of whose many achievements would be to become the foremost sociologist of education of his generation. Coleman died in 1995.

Seemingly an incisive judge of talent, Mood had been drawn to Coleman's 1961 study of adolescents because, unlike most studies of school effects, which tended then still to focus almost entirely on the goals of the educators, *The Adolescent Society* focused on the goals and interests of the students.[41] This suggested an interest in the achievement measures Mood suspected might be important to the equality of educational opportunity survey. As Coleman remembered things, he was, in turn, drawn to the possibility Mood held out to him because it offered the chance "to demonstrate the value of social research for policy issues" and to contribute to "increased equality of educational opportunity for black children."[42] Personally, Coleman was deeply committed to civil rights, although, as Gerald Grant has observed, he exemplified "Max Weber's ideal of the social scientist whose values properly determine the kinds of questions he asks, but whose scholarship commits him to look dispassionately at the results."[43]

Beginning in the late spring of 1965, Coleman set about designing a study that was meant to be presented to Congress in July 1966. He expected to collect data by having superintendents, principals, and teachers complete lengthy questionnaires describing items such as school equipment, books, teacher training, guidance and counseling programs, curriculum, athletics, and expenditure per pupil. He also planned to administer specially designed tests to 900,000 selected students, half white and half black, in the first, third, sixth, ninth, and twelfth grades.[44] However, when Keppel and then Mood contacted chief state school officers and superintendents to request their cooperation, many refused to give it. Fearing invidious comparisons and worried about queries from Washington concerning matters of race, more than one-tenth of the school districts Coleman had planned to sample refused to participate. Once again, tensions within the nation's multitiered governance system for education exacted a price.

Despite that failure, Coleman was confident that the massive data collected would demonstrate "striking" differences between predominately white and black schools.[45] But his confidence turned out to be misplaced. Much to everyone's surprise, the survey instead discovered few meaningful interschool differences when predominately white and black schools were compared within the same region. Beyond that, the study determined that minority students (with a few notable exceptions like those who were "Oriental Americans") scored "distinctly lower" on achievement tests than their white peers and that this disparity between white and black test scores increased with years of schooling. As Coleman explained it, this meant that "whatever may be the combination of non-school factors—poverty, community attitudes, low educational level of parents—which put minority children at a disadvantage in verbal and nonverbal skills when they enter first grade, the fact is the schools have not overcome it."[46]

The study confirmed the presence of segregation not only in the South, but also in the urban North, West, and Midwest, and offered many other significant findings—for example, that minority students enrolled in predominately white schools were likely to achieve on a par with their white classmates. However, the point that hit home the hardest was the fact that schools seemed to be relatively powerless in overcoming disadvantage. This challenged some of the beliefs most cherished by Americans, notably the belief that schools could offer children from different backgrounds an equal chance in life and that schools in particular, and education more generally, provided a powerful means for rewarding merit and promoting equality.

Not surprisingly, as news of the survey's findings began to be known, the report created a firestorm within the Office of Education. Policy makers within the Johnson administration were eager to press hard for school desegregation at the time, one of their weapons being promises of funding for better facilities. Obviously, Coleman's findings were extremely threatening to that. What is more, most of the money allocated by Congress for the Elementary and Secondary Education Act of 1965—nearly $1 billion in 1965—went to Title I, which provided money for compensatory education programs. If Coleman was right, such programs would have very little effect on existing inequalities.

Then, in December 1965, Mayor Richard Daley of Chicago leaned on Lyndon Johnson to have the Office of Education cool the pressure it was putting on the Chicago schools to desegregate. When early in the new year Johnson, in turn, leaned on Keppel to ease up, Keppel resigned. Although his successor, Harold Howe II, was also a very strong and courageous supporter of desegregation, the shift came at a difficult moment in terms of the Coleman study.

Needing to get a report to Congress by July and knowing that the full report would not be finished by then, the Office of Education was beginning to develop a summary report. After several versions of the report were rejected, one was approved that greatly deemphasized the study's most important finding. Just before the summary was released to the press, Howe held a press conference, but refused to answer any questions. Normally easygoing and open, Howe recalled later that he had been very nervous "because I was dealing with something I didn't fully understand. . . . You couldn't read the summary and get on top of it. You couldn't read the whole damn thing [because it was not yet finished] so you were stuck with trying to explain publicly something that maybe had all sorts of implications, but you didn't want to say the wrong thing, yet you didn't know what the hell to say so it was a very difficult situation for me."[47] Howe's reasonable dismay aside, the summary and the press conference appeared to do what officials in the Office of Education wanted.

With apparently no new news to report, the press published stories that were more helpful than destructive of the administration's civil rights and antipoverty programs, and when the full report was released in August, it was totally ignored. There were few press reports, and, apparently, congressional staff members did not even read the report. What is more, what comment there was tended to be negative. Social scientists worried about methodological flaws—measurement errors, invalid test items on the achievement tests that had been administered to students, inadequate controls, and weakly supported correlations.[48] Others claimed there had been a mismatch between the survey's objective, increasing equality of educational opportunity, and the method employed, tests of individual achievement.[49] And outside of the academic community, the study was loudly and widely derided, as was its author. Coleman was "reviled" in the southern press as well as in speeches by such civil rights leaders as Floyd McKissick, director of Congress on Racial Equality (CORE), who claimed that Coleman had implied, "Mix Negroes with Negroes and you get stupidity."[50]

Things might have ended there had Daniel Patrick Moynihan, recently returned to Harvard from service in the Labor Department, not put the report to both political and scholarly use. In the spring of 1966, before the report was published, Seymour Martin Lipset, one of the coauthors of Coleman's first book, *Union Democracy* (1956), had encountered Moynihan at the Harvard Faculty Club and said: "You know what Coleman is finding, don't you?" According to Moynihan, he replied by asking "What?" and Lipset had countered, "All family."[51]

The chance encounter with Lipset came on the heels of Moynihan's bitter experience as the author of "The Negro Family: The Case for National Action," a memorandum he had written for Lyndon Johnson. The memorandum had argued that addressing problems of family disorganization in black families was the surest route to achieving equality. Even though the memo had prompted Johnson's famous 1965 Howard University speech, which was followed soon thereafter by passage of the Voting Rights Act of 1965, Moynihan had been scorched by civil rights groups and academics for his criticisms of the black family.[52] Given these circumstances, it was exciting to Moynihan to learn that there might now be additional evidence supporting his contention that family problems were related to all sorts of inequities and needed to be addressed before other kinds of reforms could be truly effective.

Outraged by the way the Office of Education had handled release of the report, Moynihan invited Coleman to write up his findings for *The Public Interest*, which Coleman did. He then sent the article to Senator Abraham Ribicoff, who chaired the Intergovernmental Affairs Subcommittee. Calling Coleman to testify before the committee, Ribicoff subsequently claimed the report had been "hushed up."[53] That began to stir public interest in the study, and to encourage scholarly interest, Moynihan recruited a group of Harvard colleagues to organize a seminar to debate and reanalyze Coleman's data. Funded by the Carnegie Corporation, the seminar met during the 1966–67 academic year and aroused such interest that some meetings seemed more like large conferences than a seminar. Eventually, in 1972, many of the papers from the seminar were published as *On Equality of Educational Opportunity*, edited by Frederick Mosteller, a Harvard statistician, and Moynihan.[54]

Although the various authors who contributed to the Mosteller and Moynihan volume pointed to some weaknesses in Coleman's methods and findings, they described the study as "a formidable achievement," "pathbreaking, a watershed."[55] They also succinctly captured the study's most important contribution to research about schooling: "Henceforth no study of the quality of education or the equality of educational opportunity can hope to be taken seriously unless it deals with educational achievement or other accomplishments as the principal measure of educational quality."[56] Last, but hardly least important, as seasoned social scientists, they demonstrated in their various essays and in their subsequent work what Mosteller and Moynihan eloquently explained in their introduction to the volume. "One may have to settle for something crude to get started," they observed as they reflected on some of the statistics used in the survey. But "the nation had to get started," they continued. "If one stops thinking of EEOS [Equality of Educational Opportunity Survey] as the once and only survey of education, and instead thinks of it as part of a larger process of appraisal (reconsider policy, get new information, then repeat), he can appreciate why we are going to pass over some things on a first round and hope to do them better another time."[57] In the end, that was, indeed, the chief significance of the massive survey.

After all, it would be difficult to demonstrate that the Coleman Report had a direct, linear influence on policy. Although, as Gerald Grant has argued, Coleman's ideas were picked up by President Nixon in his 1970 Message on Education Reform, they did not lead to an immediate cut in funds. Quite the opposite. Nixon's message was delivered one month before he reluctantly signed what the *New York Times* described as "the most expensive educational legislation ever passed by Congress— a bill authorizing $26.4 billion over three years for elementary and secondary education."[58] What is more, even though Moynihan, who championed the study, served as an advisor to Nixon on domestic policy, there is no hard evidence to show that Coleman's ideas actually influenced Nixon's thinking. More likely, they provided a convenient rationale for proposing budget cuts Nixon already wanted to make.[59] Clearly, therefore, like the NAEP findings, the use made of the Coleman volume depended more on politics than on the implications for policy logically to be drawn from the information it offered.[60]

It is also important to note that, in the domain of policy, where the Coleman Report did have a large effect, its influence was the result of what Coleman himself considered misuse. Coming at a time when the courts were seeking to define remedies for segregation, judge after judge referred to the study in mandating the busing of children. Although Coleman had found that the achievement of black children improved if they were enrolled in a majority white school, the study was taken as supporting desegregation generally.[61] This dismayed Coleman, who claimed in a 1972 interview that "judges have . . . used the results more strongly than the results warrant." Three years later he published a study indicating that busing contributed to so-called white flight.[62] Sorry that the study had been misused in this way, Coleman was also disappointed that it had been "underutilized" by legislators.[63] As Coleman became increasingly aware, it is difficult to control the trajectory of ideas, and it is especially difficult to do so in a domain of policy like education, where the authority to make decisions and implement policy is extremely diffuse.

Regardless of its influence on policy, the Coleman Report had an extremely productive influence on education research. In addition to equally generative reanalyses like Christopher Jencks's *Inequality: A Reassessment of the Effects of Family and Schooling in America* (1967), it stimulated a host of studies about school effects, which slowly began to chip away at the tough question of what may produce equal educational opportunity if it is not the simple injection of additional resources. Mosteller and Moynihan closed the introductory chapter of their book on the Coleman Report with a wonderful—and, today, sadly poignant—section called "Needs and Hopes." Lamenting "the great gaps separating the educational achievement of different ethnic/racial groups," they said: "It may be hoped that before the century is out the great gaps will have disappeared. It may also happen that in the process a general theory of education will have evolved, been tested, replicated, and accepted. Just possibly."[64] However grandly optimistic that hope proved to be, the Coleman Report advanced education research beyond where it was when planning for NAEP had begun.

Title I Evaluation Studies

During the years of the Harvard seminar on the Coleman Report, evidence mounted concerning the difficulties involved in effectively advancing equality of educational opportunity through federal policy interventions. Much of this evidence came from evaluation studies mandated as part of the Elementary and Secondary Education Act (ESEA) of 1965. Signed by Lyndon Johnson on April 11 in a one-room school that he had once attended, ESEA was composed of five discrete sections, one of which—Title I—provided aid to school districts with "educationally deprived children of low income families." This included 94 percent of the nation's school districts in 1965. The other titles of ESEA authorized funds to states to purchase educational materials and then to lend these to public and private schools, provided monies to establish special supplementary educational centers and services, made money available for research and innovation, and provided assistance to strengthen state education departments.[65] Even though the National Defense Education Act of 1958 had been "an important harbinger" of ESEA in that it had involved categorical aid, was substantial in volume, and had allowed funds to flow to religiously affiliated institutions, it was ESEA that broke the long-standing logjam that to this point had blocked federal aid to education.[66]

The person most responsible for passage of ESEA was U.S. Commissioner of Education Francis Keppel, whose determined politicking finally overcame "the three 'R's' of Race, Religion, and Reds (Federal control)," which had so long capped possibilities for using federal dollars for education.[67] One of the people Keppel had to appease in order to secure passage of ESEA was Robert F. Kennedy, then a senator from New York. Kennedy did not believe schools did a good job educating black students. He was also not convinced that aid alone would change that. In order to impose greater accountability on the schools, Kennedy therefore insisted that Title I, which involved the lion's share of ESEA funds, be evaluated to ensure that the schools did, in fact, change.

Kennedy's insistence on evaluation ran head on into opposition from educators. They claimed that evaluation was already occurring. More important, they asserted that evaluation would advance excessive federal intrusion into local educational affairs. To appease both sides, a three-tier plan was worked out, whereby local authorities would report to state authorities, who would, in turn, report to the U.S. commissioner concerning "objective measurements" of the "educational attainment of educational deprived children."[68] Such measurements had never been included in NAEP. Although the specifications concerning evaluation were purposefully left vague to appease the educators, as Stephen K. Bailey and Edith K. Mosher pointed out in their classic study of ESEA, the requirement concerning evaluation was "loud and clear, and unprecedented in scope."[69]

Carrying out the evaluation proved to be difficult. Although ESEA was passed in April 1965, the related appropriation bill was not passed until late September. In the interim, in August 1965, President Johnson had informed all cabinet officers that they were to implement the program planning and budgeting system that had been invented at the Rand Corporation and then further refined by Charles J. Hitch and Alan C. Enthoven, who worked for Robert McNamara in the Defense Department.[70] PPBS, as the system was called, required that one evaluate programs using cost-benefit analyses, which would help identify the most efficient means to reach stated goals. The adoption of PPBS within the Office of Education complicated efforts to develop an evaluation plan for ESEA. Whereas Kennedy had wanted an evaluation that would hold local education authorities accountable for the use they made of ESEA funds, thereby ensuring that the money actually reached and benefited poor children, the people responsible for PPBS within the Office of Education expected the evaluation of ESEA to help them understand which strategies were most efficient in boosting the academic achievement of disadvantaged students.[71] In the end, neither goal was satisfied.

As Harold Howe told the Senate Subcommittee on Education when, as U.S. commissioner of education following Keppel, he presented his first annual report on Title I of ESEA, the report he was delivering lacked "some of the specifics of a technical evaluation report." It described the extent of the program—17,481 of the nation's 26,983 school districts had met the requirements necessary for participation in Title I, and on average, $119 had been spent per pupil. It also made clear that the use of Title I funds varied tremendously from one locality to another—in a rural community in the Northwest, Title I funds had paid for two school nurses; in one Tennessee district, they had paid for wireless hearing aids for deaf children; and in one of the Texas districts served, they had paid for a liaison between school and families who could help evaluate children's needs. Summarizing the state reports, Howe made a variety of more general claims about the accomplishments attributable to ESEA. These included higher student achievement in reading, especially with younger children; new interest and new confidence "awakened among the educationally deprived"; a "new spirit of cooperation and coordination" among districts; and "big city school systems had benefited."[72]

Given that these were very general, vague, and subjective claims, it is not surprising that no one was happy with them. Kennedy was irate. "Do you mean that you spent a billion dollars and you don't know whether [the children] can read or not?" he asked Howe. Although Howe's answer was prudent—"You know this program has been operating for less than a year and it is just like planting a tree; you don't plant it one day and then pull it up every week and look at the roots to see if its growing"—Kennedy was not satisfied.[73] The first evaluation of ESEA apparently convinced him that officials at the Office of Education were not competent to evaluate ESEA.[74]

Others involved in the discussions of Title I evaluations were equally dismayed. Evaluators for the Urban Institute—evaluators of the evaluation—concluded that the local studies could not be aggregated, which might have satisfied the purposes of PPBS. There were just too many "noncomparable, unrelated" inquiries, they claimed.[75] Some educators within the Office of Education, especially the seasoned veterans who resisted the reforms introduced under Keppel and Howe, went so far as to say the state reports were "garbage." Knowing that, at the local level, Title I funds were really used as general support monies, they recognized that the evaluation was more like a public relations document designed to please the responsible authorities than an accurate accounting of what had been done.[76]

In the wake of the disappointing first round of evaluation of ESEA, it was decided to modify the original three-tier design. Now localities and states would collect data, but not interpret them; that task would be left to experts in Washington. The officials responsible for PPBS hoped this would improve the analytic power of the evaluation. By this time, of course, the Coleman Report had been released, and following its logic, Alice Rivlin and other analysts at the Office of Education designed a number of studies analyzing relationships between "inputs" and "outputs" based on ESEA data.

One such investigation, called "TEMPO," was published in two volumes in 1968. Its results were devastating. The study found that pupil achievement tended to decline in Title I schools and that schools with 40–60 percent black student enrollments showed the poorest response to compensatory education programs. What is more, local bookkeeping was so confused that it was almost impossible to determine which programs were supported with Title I funds. As policy analyst Milbrey McLaughlin observed in a review of the Title I studies, "in practice there seemed to be no real Title I program to evaluate."[77] Within the Office of Education, this was read as evidence of a methodological flaw: data collection had been left to local authorities. In the wake of the Coleman Report, however, journalists read the TEMPO results as suggesting that compensatory education did not work.[78] Their reading added fuel to arguments that schooling was not the best way to intervene in problems of disadvantage.

Within this context, the Office of Education set about designing a third-round evaluation of ESEA, which once again found that Title I funds did not equalize service for poor children. Beyond that, it showed that the poorest schools were the ones most likely to use Title I funds as general aid rather than as categorical assistance for those students who were poor. According to McLaughlin, the report demonstrated that "compensatory education programs were not 'closing the gap'; in fact, participation in compensatory programs seemed to be having no effect at all."[79]

Not surprisingly, this provided ammunition for Daniel Patrick Moynihan and others advising President Richard Nixon. In the Message on Educational Reform that Nixon sent to Congress in March 1970, the president claimed that "we must stop letting wishes color our judgments about the educational effectiveness of many special compensatory programs . . . , [and] we must stop pretending that we understand the mystery of the learning process." Instead, Nixon recommended the creation of the National Institute of Education (NIE) "to begin the serious, systematic search for new knowledge needed to make educational opportunity truly equal."[80] Congress, of course, contravened Nixon's subsequent request to cut Title I funds. Ironically, as an increasing army of social scientists both within the Office of Education and outside worked to invent evaluation tools that could more sensitively assess compensatory ed-

ucation efforts, Congress demonstrated that it tended to be more respon-
sive to politics than expert advice. Title I had become popular, and it was
the program's popularity that would protect it, not what evaluators could
demonstrate about its actual effects.

The National Institute of Education

Nixon's initial proposal to create the National Institute of Education was
advanced at a time when there was widespread interest among social scientists, educationists, and officials in the Washington policy bureaucracy
in improving education research. This had already led to at least ten major studies undertaken between 1964 and 1969.[81] If those studies suggested new interest and even confidence in the possibilities of developing
sound approaches to the study of educational problems, such interest and
confidence were not frequently evident in the U.S. Congress. There, Augustus Hawkins's comment that he wondered if education research was
not just "a lot of jive" was more in line with common sentiment. According to Hawkins, education research seemed never to have practical
results. Congress was always told answers would be found next year.[82] At
a time when it was becoming increasingly clear that the Nixon administration would be looking for places to cut the budget, education lobby
organizations like the NEA, which itself conducted research, but primarily research relevant to the occupational concerns of its members, and the
Council of Chief State School Officers were also worried about cuts in
areas vital to them and were more than ready to make education research
the sacrificial lamb.[83]

It was within this atmosphere that Nixon's proposal to create NIE
was developed and advanced. The idea emerged from a White House
working group guided by Daniel Patrick Moynihan, now counselor to the
president, that had been organized to examine elementary and secondary
education. The group slowly worked its way to three policy options that
could be presented to President Nixon. Reviewing evidence that compensatory education was a weak policy instrument relative to others and that
the Johnson education programs appeared not to be working very well,
the group also discussed the fact that "the nation's educational establishment" was not ready to give up on trying to tinker with the input side of
equalizing educational opportunity. In the face of mounting social science
evidence that did not seem to be changing perceptions about policy, the
group realized that Nixon could decide to ignore the social science evidence, try to discredit it in order to continue existing policies, or go back
to the drawing board, so to speak, and start to design new policies based

on new knowledge. Wanting policies that would bear his distinctive mark, rather than Johnson's, and wishing to trim the increasingly large education budget, Nixon chose the third option. As Chester E. Finn Jr., Moynihan's deputy at the time, put it, "the National Institute of Education was the drawing board that he proposed."[84]

Once that decision was made, several other considerations came into play. The White House working group was of the opinion, according to Finn, that research and experimentation were something the government did quite well, even though the research and experimentation that had gone on under the auspices of the Office of Education had generally been of low quality. They were keenly aware, of course, that the Coleman Report had not emerged from research initiated by the Office of Education, but had instead been mandated by Congress when it passed the Civil Rights Act of 1964.

With that in mind, the working group proposed a new independent agency, and Nixon accepted the idea. According to Moynihan, the goal of the institute was to "master the art of education to the point that achievement is more or less evenly distributed among the different groups in our society and not enormously varied within groups. Not just equality of opportunity . . . but something like parity of educational outcomes is what we must achieve."[85] Put otherwise, Moynihan hoped that the institute could find the means to guarantee not merely equality of opportunity in the traditional meaning of that term, but also equality in education defined in the post-Coleman sense of equity or equality of results. Because Nixon had already proposed the possibility of a "National Institute for the Educational Future" during the 1968 campaign, creating an institute would appear to be following up on that earlier proposal, which was important politically. In consequence, immediately after Nixon sent his Message on Education Reform to Congress in the spring of 1970, Secretary of Health, Education, and Welfare Robert Finch began to draft legislation to create NIE.[86] Still, it was another two years before NIE was established, a delay due both to indifference in Congress and to the turmoil that followed the decision to bomb Cambodia, a decision Nixon made roughly two months after delivering his education message to Congress.

In the interim, Roger Levien, an engineer who served as codirector of education research for the Rand Corporation, developed plans for NIE. Mindful of the working group's insistence that NIE sponsor research that would be more rigorous than that traditionally associated with the Office of Education, Levien's report incorporated suggestions drawn from close knowledge of R&D organizations that were considered more successful, including NSF and NIH. It described an agency, parallel to the Office of Education, that would report directly to the secretary of health, education, and welfare. The institute Levien imagined was to serve four very broad purposes:

> I. To help solve or alleviate the problems and achieve the objectives of American education.
> II. To advance the practice of education as an art, science, and profession.
> III. To strengthen the scientific and technological foundation on which education rests.
> IV. To build a vigorous and effective educational research and development system.

To fulfill these goals, NIE would pursue activities in four broad areas—solving major educational problems, advancing educational practice, strengthening education's foundations, and strengthening the research and development system. Like NSF, NIE would have various directorates. A National Advisory Council working with a director would set its overall policy.[87]

After Levien submitted his report, Harry Silberman, associate commissioner of education for the National Center for Educational Research and Development, was asked to continue the planning for NIE. Unlike Levien, Silberman was trained in education and recruited a staff that consisted entirely of educationists. As Lee Sproull and her colleagues observed in their analysis of NIE, this was problematic to critics of the Office of Education, who now worried that "in spite of all their efforts NIE might turn out to be less than the sparkling gem of rationality they had envisioned."[88] In the end, however, when legislation establishing NIE was finally introduced in Congress on June 23, 1972, the proposed plan was essentially Levien's.

NIE's champion in Congress was John Brademas, a Democrat from Indiana, who had recently been elected a deputy majority whip. Brademas, who held a B.A. from Harvard and a Ph.D. in social studies from Oxford, was known as "a friend of education," a designation he proved worthy of in securing passage of legislation establishing NIE.[89] When the Education and Labor Committee held hearings on NIE, few members attended many sessions, and no representatives from scholarly or professional associations of educators appeared to testify on the legislation's behalf. Only Brademas attended all the hearings. When an omnibus education bill, including plans for NIE, was introduced in the House, there was predictable opposition. Edith Green, a Democratic congresswoman from Oregon, reiterated her long-standing belief that aid for education should go directly to colleges and universities and then went on to claim: "If you want to improve education, and if you want to cut funds, this [NIE] is the place to cut them."[90] Then, insisting that the bill needed additional committee review owing to its plan to exempt NIE employees from civil service requirements, another opponent actually managed to have the section pertaining to NIE stricken from the bill. Thereafter Brademas proposed the establishment of NIE as a floor amendment to the bill, which saved the agency, though by a slim margin. Not only that, but a majority of the members of the House Appropriations Subcommittee on Labor and Health, Education, and Welfare, which held authority over NIE, voted against its creation.[91] It was hardly an auspicious beginning, even though favorable witnesses before Brademas's committee had predicted funding for NIE that might reach $500 million in its first three years.[92]

Established in June 1972, NIE did not have a director until Thomas K. Glennan Jr., formerly director of the Research Division of the Office of Economic Opportunity, was appointed the following fall. Despite that, $110 million worth of programs were transferred from the Office of Education to NIE in August, including the R&D centers, the regional labs, and ERIC. This deprived NIE of time to plan and recruit staff prior to beginning operations, and equally unfortunate, it made NIE responsible for programs that were already seen by some as problematic. Given all that, it was not surprising that when Glennan went to Congress in the spring of 1973 to justify his budget request of $162 million for 1974, he was sharply criticized for not being able clearly to articulate NIE's short- or long-term goals. Worse than that, the budget that was approved was less than half what he had requested, a mere $65 million. As an editorial in *Educational Researcher* aptly noted, "in one year, NIE . . . [had] moved from emergence to emergency."[93] Needing to cover mandated institutions and programs, the funds appropriated were so limited that virtually all latitude to develop new programs or to support field-initiated studies had been removed.

In the following year, NIE was reorganized, and Harold Hodgkinson replaced Glennan as director. In search of a strategy that might win NIE more approval in Congress, Hodgkinson determined that his main goal would be to create what he called "a success history." As historian Keith Melville has observed in a study of NIE, this meant that "short-term projects replaced long-term research. Particular concerns replaced broader ones."[94] Although this helped stabilize NIE, two years later an evaluation group made up of university-based scholars convened by NIE recommended a reversal of course again. NIE should avoid seeking "quick solutions to educational problems," the committee's report said.[95]

With an unclear mandate from the start, NIE underwent frequent shifts in direction throughout its troubled history. What is more, after 1974, its budget never again topped $80 million.[96] When compared with research expenditures in other fields, the sums allocated to it were paltry. In 1974, the NIH budget was almost $1.9 million, the NSF budget was $567 million, and the Agricultural Research Service budget was $205 million. By contrast, the NIE budget was $65 million (see figure 1).[97] Over time, too, a larger and larger proportion of NIE's money had to be spent for congressionally mandated projects. As Philip Phaedon Zodhiates wisely opined in a review of NIE's later years, this amounted to "management by legislation."[98]

NIE's financial problems were a result of many factors, including a general loss of faith in social science as a guide to social progress and, owing to the Vietnam War, a tightening of finances at the federal level.[99] According to one former director, congressional Democrats also tended to be hostile to NIE, even viewing it as a "Nixon trick" that directed money toward research in order not to spend it more directly on educational services.[100] Most important, however, was a lack of understanding of education research in Congress. There was frequent complaint about "mushy educational jargon that doesn't tell us a damn thing."[101] More important, there was little appreciation within the Congress of the importance of many of the studies NIE supported and great impatience with the difficulties involved in advancing fundamental knowledge about education. "If per chance you and I were around here 10 years from now would we still be . . . trying to find out ways of teaching," one dubious representative asked.[102] Another simply stated that "my people need answers now."[103] In comparison with other pressing needs, the significance of the kind of activities undertaken by NIE just was not clear to politicians in the Congress. As one aide said: "After all, not very many people die for a lack of educational research."[104]

If ignorance and indifference in Congress undermined support for NIE, so did a lack of interest in education research generally, and in NIE more particularly, on the part of educators. The supposed consumers of education research, especially teachers and administrators, tended to think they could use the money spent on NIE more effectively if that money were given to them to use in their own schools and classrooms.

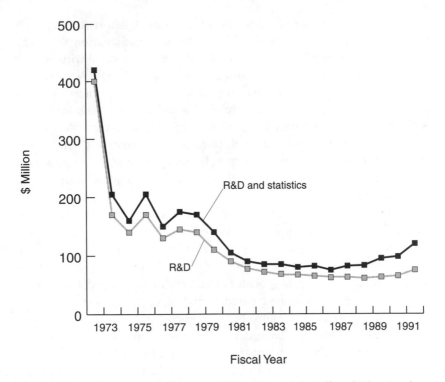

Figure 1 Funding for the National Institute of Education and the Office of Educational Research and Improvement, 1973–1991 (in 1990 constant dollars)
SOURCE: Richard C. Atkinson and Gregg B. Jackson, eds., *Research and Education Reform: Roles for the Office of Educational Research and Improvement* (Washington, D.C.: National Academy Press, 1992), 96.

What is more, like the "schoolmen" Henry Barnard had faulted for being indifferent to the Department of Education when it was founded, professional organizations like the NEA and the Council of Chief State School Officers did not lobby on behalf of the agency. Silent at its creation, they tended to remain silent at subsequent hearings concerning budget authorization. Even the American Educational Research Association did not testify in NIE's defense. According to Lee Sproull and her colleagues, this was because AERA was then an organization dominated by educational psychologists who were "uninterested in political lobbying." Until the middle 1970s, AERA had no procedure by which its officers or staff could make public statements on its behalf.[105]

The silence of the professional groups that might have helped Congress understand both the intellectual and the political significance of NIE deeply disappointed John Brademas. Acknowledging that some of NIE's problems lay at the door of Congress, which wanted "short-run payoffs" that were difficult, if not impossible, to achieve in education research, Brademas still insisted that the larger share of blame resided with educators. As Brademas charged in an article published in the AERA magazine, *Educational Researcher,* the "teachers, chief state school officers, educational organization and even researchers" who had remained aloof from NIE's travails had behaved like "county highway commissioners complaining that there was not enough pork in the barrel for them." They had failed in their "responsibility to help the country and Congress to a better appreciation" of the relationship between research and educational improvement.[106]

In his *Educational Researcher* essay, Brademas also suggested that NIE formulate a research agenda that might help it better demonstrate the relevance of the research it supported to well-recognized and urgent national priorities. He pointed out, for example, that congressional efforts to secure sufficient support for child development legislation would be greatly enhanced by a better understanding of "how and when children learn and develop, cognitively and non-cognitively." With Title I under attack in the House Committee on Education and Labor, he pleaded for research that might yield a better understanding of "educational disadvantage." And he urged greater attention to the meaning of "financial distress" among institutions of higher education without which future efforts to help fund colleges and universities might well come to naught. A savvy and unusual politician who truly believed that "on the skills, the imagination, the efforts of our educational researchers and developers depends, far more than perhaps even they realize, the capacity of American education to produce a free and civilized people," Brademas was pleading with the members of AERA to help build a constituency for education research.[107] He understood then the political reality that subsequent analysts have also captured. To be an effective agency supporting education research, NIE needed strong external support in order to overcome congressional indifference and hostility.[108]

Despite Brademas's admonitions, the various associations interested in education never managed to form an effective coalition in support of NIE. Compounding the problem was the continued indifference to research manifested by practitioners, which could be attributed in significant measure to a lack of emphasis on research in programs that educated teachers, administrators, and other school personnel. Given that situation, it was not surprising that, in 1985, NIE was reorganized out of existence as part of a reorganization of the Office of Educational Research and Improvement (OERI), which had been created when the Office of Education became a cabinet-level department in 1979. When it was officially disbanded by the Higher Education Amendments of 1986, NIE's functions were combined with those of the old National Center for Education Statistics and the Center for Libraries and Education Information.

The irony of NIE's fate was that its demise came as promising new directions were emerging in education research. However, in light of the funding cuts sustained between 1973 and 1986—cuts amounting to 79 percent in funds for education research—it was difficult to be optimistic.[109] What is more, as long-time policy analyst Chester Finn once observed, the U.S. government's main education research office, OERI, had so little discretionary money that it was hardly more than "a professional statistics and assessment agency, attached to a small check-writing machine that is programmed annually by Congress."[110] It had never been planned to be much more than a "holding company" for NIE, the National Center for Education Statistics, some library programs, and other miscellaneous dissemination projects.[111] Obviously, the federal role in education research was not commensurate with the contribution to educational improvement that education research might increasingly be able to make. The irony of the situation was stark.

CHAPTER EIGHT

Promoting Learning and Reform: New Directions in Education Research

By the time National Institute of Education (NIE) was disbanded, there were grounds for believing that education research was maturing. Long dominated by narrow, behavioral approaches to the study of teaching and learning, education researchers were beginning to apply insights emerging from cognitive science to problems of the classroom. Increasingly, too, they were using qualitative research methods to provide fine-grained analyses of educational problems. Among other things, this offered new insights into the centrality of culture in education. Last, but hardly least important, scholars bent on influencing both policy and practice were developing new ways to communicate and collaborate with the audiences they hoped to reach. By the 1990s, developments such as these augured well for education research.

Despite that, the field continued to face difficult problems. In 1995, for every dollar spent on education in the United States, less than 1 percent went to research.[1] What is more, as critics were quick to point out, to the extent that the program for the annual meeting of American Educational Research Association (AERA) was the measure, the field remained diffuse and lacking in focus, and there continued to be an abundance of studies that were flawed methodologically and insignificant in the questions posed. Even without going further, it should therefore be evident that turning new directions into sustained progress remained a challenge, one that would be made all the more difficult by continuing practitioner skepticism and public indifference.

The Beginnings of Cognitive Science

Undoubtedly, the development of cognitive science significantly improved chances for building a powerful science of education. Focused on understanding the ways in which people acquire, process, use, and represent knowledge, cognitive science is an amalgam of disciplines that together comprise a new science of mind.

In interesting ways, the thinking of Jean Piaget presaged the direction in which cognitive science would evolve. Breaking with the behaviorist assumption that an infant's "mind" was a blank slate, the famed Swiss observer and analyst of child development argued that cognitive structures, though not innate, developed through interaction with the environment during the first years of life. Using terms like "concrete operations" to describe the young child's need actively and even palpably to imagine a phenomenon under scrutiny and "formal operations" to describe the older child's increasing capacity for deductive thought involving the manipulation of symbols, rather than actual concrete objects, Piaget posited that child development was constrained by distinct, invariant stages of development.[2] Even though that belief would be seriously challenged subsequently, Piaget was very popular among American psychologists beginning in the 1960s. His ideas appealed because they helped make sense of the activity of even very young children. As psychologists Rochel Gelman and Ann L. Brown once put it, thanks to work stimulated by Piaget, "the mind of the young child has come to life."[3] Piaget's thinking promised to help free education from the dominance of behaviorism.

Behaviorism had, of course, developed at the beginning of the twentieth century as psychologists sought new methods for investigating the mental functioning of human beings. Rather than emphasizing mind, it had emphasized only what could be observed. This had been seen as a far more objective and scientific approach to the study of mental activity than investigations involving introspection, which might reveal the content of an individual's thought, though in an extremely subjective way. Behaviorism had been pioneered by psychologists like Edward L. Thorndike and John B. Watson, whose 1919 textbook, *Psychology from the Standpoint of a Behaviorist,* helped popularize the term. Relatively early in his career, Watson had given up psychology to work in advertising at J. Walter Thompson, but for a time he had been a forceful, if rather extreme, advocate for ignoring the study of consciousness and experience and focusing instead on stimulus-response patterns in rats, pigeons, and other animals as well as in human beings.[4] Among psychologists interested in education, behaviorism had encouraged the formulation of laws of learning like those Thorndike had enunciated as well as the invention of devices like teaching machines, which were given a significant boost in the mid-1950s by the endorsement of Harvard behaviorist psychologist B. F. Skinner.

As it turned out, however, behaviorism was a perspective that was relevant only to the mastery of relatively simple tasks involving short-term recall. For this reason, a few early students of education, notably Charles H. Judd, had not gone the behaviorist route. In addition, behaviorism had been criticized as narrow and mechanistic by other psychologists, including John Dewey and the more holistically oriented Gestalt psychologists who came to the United States in the 1920s and 1930s. Some educationists had also tried to find ways to help educators climb out of behaviorism's sway. Ralph Tyler had done this, for example, when he focused attention on complex educational objectives. Beyond psychologists, scholars like George S. Counts, Harold Rugg, and Margaret Mead had tried to introduce more social approaches to education that would free scholars of education from what they took to be an overemphasis on psychology generally. Despite such efforts to thwart its dominance, because behaviorism stressed the malleability of human beings and their responsiveness to external stimuli, it was an optimistic perspective that remained popular well into the 1950s.

Dominant for decades, behaviorism emphasized external stimuli and responses and deemphasized the internal, nonobservable aspects of mental functioning. It therefore obscured much that is involved in studying the "mind." This became increasingly apparent to scholars after World War II, when innovations resulting from the war allowed mathematicians, psychologists, and others to begin investigating cognition through analogy rather than through observation and presumed correlations between selected stimuli and behavior. Work along these lines was advanced by many different people. One was John von Neumann, a Hungarian-born mathematician at the Institute for Advanced Study at Princeton, New Jersey, who was an inventor of game theory and the builder of "a giant electronic brain known as MANIAC (mathematical analyzer, numerical integrator and computer)." Another was MIT mathematician Norbert Weiner, whose 1949 book *Cybernetics: Or Control and Communication in the Animal and the Machine,* called attention to similarities between the functioning of human beings and machines. Claude E. Shannon was also important. His work on the measurement of information was essential to what came to be known as information processing and led to the conception of the "bit." Herbert Simon, the Carnegie Mellon organizational theorist, must also be included in the list. An important figure in administrative theory whose work had been important to advocates of the theory movement in educational administration, Simon, in partnership with Allen Newell of the Rand Corporation, began in the early 1950s to study human problem solving via computer simulations.[5]

Beginning in the middle 1940s, these scientists and others of compatible interest began meeting regularly to swap ideas. Then, as Howard Gardner has described it in his history of "the cognitive revolution," there was a rather dramatic meeting called the Hixon Symposium at the California Institute of Technology in September 1948. Among papers by von Neumann, Gestalt psychologist Wolfgang Köhler, and a few others, one by psychologist Karl Lashley stood out as "the most iconoclastic and most memorable address."[6] Trained by none other than John B. Watson, Lashley challenged the most essential premises of behaviorism. "My principal thesis today," he announced, "will be that the input is never into a quiescent or static system, but always into a system which is already excited and organized. . . . Behavior is the result of interaction of this background excitation with input from any designated stimulus. Only when we can state the general characteristics of this backdrop of excitation, can we understand the effects of a given input."[7] This contravened the behavioralist insistence that what went on inside the mind was of little moment, there being a direct, unmediated link between stimulus and response. From there, Lashley moved on to assert that investigations of comparative grammar would be likely to provide insight into "cerebral life"—put otherwise, that anthropology and linguistics could assist in illuminating the working of the human mind and that such investigations should be accompanied by studies of physiology and neurology.[8] In essence, what Lashley did was to begin to catalog the disciplines that would eventually converge to define this new field.

After the Hixon Symposium, researchers interested in cognition continued to meet formally and informally, and in September 1956, there was another gathering that clarified for the participants that they were witnessing the emergence of a fundamentally new approach to questions about knowledge and the workings of the human mind. The gathering, officially called the Symposium on Information Theory, was held at MIT. Its program included papers by young linguist Noam Chomsky, who argued that language had just as precise regularities as mathematics, and by mathematical psychologist George A. Miller, who suggested that short-term memory in human beings was limited to seven entries. As Miller recalled subsequently, he had left the meeting "with a strong conviction, more intuitive than rational, that human experimental psychology, theoretical linguistics, and computer simulation of cognitive processes were all pieces of a larger whole, and that the future would see progressive elaboration and coordination of their shared concerns."[9]

The Center for Cognitive Studies at Harvard

Two years later Miller, who was at the time an associate professor of psychology at Harvard, left for a year at the Center for Advanced Study in the Behavioral Sciences in Stanford, California. While there, he developed plans for a new center for cognitive studies at Harvard, and with his appetite whetted by the California center's informal interdisciplinary environment, he returned to Harvard the following year, ready to move ahead.[10] His partner in the project was Jerome S. Bruner, author of *The Process of Education* and leader of the "Man: A Course of Study" (MACOS) project, which was just then in development. Bruner shared Miller's sense of alienation from the department to which he was officially assigned at Harvard. Although their intellectual interests were quite close, a departmental split that had occurred at Harvard in 1946 had placed Bruner in the Department of Social Relations and Miller in the Department of Psychology. For some years, the two had managed to collaborate in the teaching of a course called "Psychology 148: The Cognitive Processes," but Miller and Bruner were searching for a way to surmount the limitations of both departments.[11] As Miller later explained, seeking to establish a center with the word "cognitive" in its title was "an act of defiance" that protested the scientism into which both the Department of Psychology and the Department of Social Relations had fallen. "I came out of the closet," Miller explained.[12]

Early in 1960, Bruner and Miller took their idea to John Gardner at the Carnegie Corporation. Unbeknownst to them, Gardner had already begun discussing possibilities for corporation support for studies of communication and the cognitive process with Lloyd Morrisett, then a staff member of the corporation, and Caryl Haskins, a trustee.[13] For that reason, Gardner immediately invited a proposal from Bruner and Miller, which, when presented in March of that year, requested funds for an annual conference "to keep in personal contact with the workers at other institutions all over the world," a regular colloquium, and a "miscellaneous research fund" to support "small pilot projects," among the more routine expenses of operating a center that would host a handful of senior visitors each year as well as a number of junior faculty and graduate students. As Bruner and Miller told Gardner, they needed Carnegie Corporation support "in order to be spontaneous and flexible during the initial years while the Center is discovering what it should do and what it can be."[14] In style as well as substance, the proposal fit perfectly with the relatively laissez-faire style then prevalent at the Carnegie Corporation and Bruner and Miller were quickly awarded $250,000 over five years. They expected to raise additional money from the National Science Foundation (NSF) and the National Institutes of Health.

Opened in the fall of 1960, the Center for Cognitive Studies immediately became a beehive of intense intellectual activity. As Bruner recollected, it was the lunchtime seminars and the weekly colloquia that were most exciting. These ranged from linguist Roger Brown discussing "the acquisition of grammar" to Noam Chomsky talking about the "grammatical factors in the perception of sentences," Ulric Neisser discussing "a theory of intuitive thinking," David Page speaking about "teaching mathematics," and Walter Rosenblith describing "computer-aided electrophysiological studies in sensory communication."[15] According to two of Bruner's younger colleagues at the time, the seminars and colloquia were stimulating, but it was the informal daily interchange that made the center such an exciting place. As they remembered it, the center "gathered together a vibrant group of people with unconventional knowledge and interest, stuck them together in one place, gave them excellent research, meeting, and support facilities, and then allowed what was to happen to happen."[16] Less clear, they thought, about what cognitive studies was than about what it was *not*—it was *not* about behaviorist psychology— they pointed out that the center reconnected American psychology to the study of mental processes. This was a focus that had been lost in the United States through the triumph of behaviorism, even though study of mental processes had continued in Europe. To Europeans, therefore, the excitement attendant upon the center's revolt against behaviorism seemed a little odd. As one Dutch scholar explained, "it was somewhat like experiencing the American excitement over Heineken beer, which I had always thought to be just beer."[17] By contrast, to Americans, what was going on at the center was truly pathbreaking.

The Center for Cognitive Studies was tremendously important in stimulating work on all aspects of mental activities—memory, perception, grammar, artificial intelligence, sentence parsing, acoustics, learning, and much more. When Bruner and Miller returned to the Carnegie Corporation for a second grant in January 1965, they were able to tell John Gardner that the first grant had not only provided "initial encouragement," but also served as "a subsequent source of seed money." A budget that had begun at $150,000 had grown to just under $400,000 in 1964–65. Suffering, as they put it, from "the constraints of being 'successful,'" they wanted to continue to explore freely and to attract "'out-of-category' scholars" who could push the study of cognition into new and not yet understood channels.[18] Once again, the corporation provided the funds they sought.

The center was discontinued in 1970, when Bruner left Harvard for a protracted sojourn at Oxford. By then, the simple fact of its existence, combined with the discussions and research it had encouraged, had helped to ensure that initial excitement about new possibilities for studying cognition would be carried forward by a new generation of scholars. As Howard Gardner observed, "while the actual projects and products of the Center were probably not indispensable for the life of the field, there is hardly a younger person . . . who was not influenced by the Center's presence, by the ideas that were bandied about there, and by the way they were implemented in subsequent research."[19] Although some people point to 1972, when Allan Newell and Herbert Simon published *Human Problem Solving,* as the date when cognitive science began, others point to the year the Center for Cognitive Studies opened its doors.

Cognition and Education

The development of cognitive science was very significantly helped by more than $20 million of grant assistance provided by the Sloan Foundation between 1977 and 1987. In addition, beginning in 1987, the James S. McDonnell Foundation provided support for research that applied cognitive science to educational practice and offered postdoctoral fellowships to attract scholars to work at the interface of cognitive science and education. As Jill Larkin, director of McDonnell's Cognitive Studies for Educational Practice program explained, she and John T. Bruer, president of the foundation, were both convinced that cognitive science had significant potential to improve education. However, the chances of that happening were limited by scarce knowledge of cognitive science among scholars studying education and by the distance that separated education research from practice. The McDonnell program was designed to ameliorate both problems.[20]

Within less than a decade, practice-based research financed by the McDonnell Foundation was transforming classrooms from Providence, Rhode Island, to Nashville, Tennessee, and Berkeley, California. For example, recognition that the construction of knowledge is domain or subject specific led to cognitive studies of how historians actually reason, evaluate evidence, and construct interpretations, which, in turn, enabled Kathryn Spoehr to develop a hypermedia program for high school students that linked American history and literature. Via use of the program, students were able to acquire a better understanding of history by actually "doing" history.[21] An understanding of the importance of acquiring new knowledge in relation to the contexts in which it is to be used allowed John Bransford and the other psychologists, content specialists, and school personnel in the Cognition and Technology Group at Vanderbilt University to develop a series of videos showing Jasper Woodbury engaged in real-life situations that contained mathematics problems to be solved. Use of the videos not only improved mathematics achievement among middle school youngsters, but also enriched the group's understanding of the complex of factors involved in nurturing successful curriculum change.[22] Similarly, ideas concerning metacognition or learning about learning were essential to the development of "reciprocal teaching," a method by which Ann L. Brown and her colleagues improved the teaching of reading by modeling and giving youngsters opportunities to practice and talk about the processes that are necessary for comprehension.[23]

Work supported by the McDonnell Foundation demonstrated a point Robert Glaser, a cognitive psychologist at the University of Pittsburgh, made in 1988: cognitive science provided a theoretical basis that could enable the United States "to teach a far broader range of students and take them farther than ever before as modern society demands."[24] Beyond that, early work helped to clarify what John Bruer described as "the central theoretical and methodological issue in the future development of cognitive science": the question of "how cognition is, or is not, determined, supported, or constrained by sociocultural factors."[25]

Qualitative Methods and Interpretative Studies

The increasing awareness of "sociocultural factors" to which John Bruer referred came in part from what was being learned from studies that used qualitative methods to investigate educational processes. Eventually, qualitative research came to encompass pretty much any inquiry that was not quantitative, which would be seriously troubling to scholars concerned with more disciplined work, some of whom complained about what they termed "blitzkrieg ethnography."[26] Initially, however, qualitative research in education grew out of work in anthropology. Although it was variously labeled ethnographic, participant observation, case study, symbolic interactionist, phenomenological, constructivist, or interpretative, scholars who came to qualitative research through anthropology were insistent that interpretative studies were based not merely on "techniques" that allowed for "rich descriptions" or "continuous narrative descriptions." Qualitative research, they insisted, involved "methods" deriving from the work of Bronislaw Malinowski and a long line of anthropologists who had combined participant observation and interviewing to describe the "human meaning in social life."[27]

As early as 1928, Margaret Mead had argued that anthropologists could learn a good deal about educational processes in the United States by comparing them with those of "simpler" societies.[28] After that, a variety of anthropologists concerned themselves with educational questions, as the participation of Mead and other anthropologists in the interwar curriculum work of the Progressive Education Association demonstrated. Still, it was not until the 1950s that possibilities for systematically applying anthropological methods, especially ethnography, to education were formally discussed. This occurred at what is commonly called the 1954 Stanford Conference, which was actually held at the Carmel Valley Ranch in Carmel, California.

The organizer of the conference was George D. Spindler, who had received a Ph.D. in anthropology, sociology, and psychology from UCLA in 1952 and had then accepted a joint appointment in the School of Education and the Department of Sociology and Anthropology at Stanford. Funded by the Carnegie Corporation, the conference brought together twenty-two scholars, half anthropologists and half educationists, who spent four days discussing ten papers dealing with rationales for applying anthropology to education, what was meant by the phrase "the sociocultural contextualization of schooling," how anthropology could contribute to an understanding of education and the life cycle, and how intercultural learning and understanding might be enhanced.[29] Because they were aware that heretofore anthropological studies of education had been more dependent on individual interest and initiative than on institutional support, the group hoped to stimulate the development of the infrastructure necessary for more sustained work.

The timing of the Spindler initiative proved fortuitous. At the same time Spindler had accepted the post at Stanford, Solon Kimball, an anthropologist trained at Harvard, had accepted an appointment in the Department of Philosophy and the Social Sciences at Teachers College. Previously there had been a sprinkling of anthropologists in schools and departments of education, but this initiated formal training in educational anthropology (often called applied anthropology or anthropology and education). Although they never became very numerous, there were eleven training programs combining work in anthropology and education by the mid-1980s.

During the 1960s, as higher education expanded and funding for education research increased, NSF, the U.S. Office of Education, and other funding agencies provided increasing support for the application of anthropological methods to educational problems. The MACOS curriculum project, funded by NSF and led by Jerome S. Bruner, was grounded in anthropology, as were teaching materials developed specifically for inner-city schools by the Teacher Resources in Urban Education Project at Hunter College in New York City. More important perhaps, two U.S. Office of Education initiatives, the Culture of Schools program at Syracuse University and the American Anthropological Association's Program in Anthropology and Education, led to the organization of conferences and to research and publication by young anthropologists interested in education. As University of Florida anthropologist Elizabeth M. Eddy has observed, by the end of the 1960s "the institutionalization of educational anthropology as a legitimate specialization within the discipline almost was complete." Thereafter, in 1968, at the annual meeting of the American Anthropological Association, the ad hoc Group on Anthropology and Education was founded, which, in 1970, became the Council on Anthropology and Education. The *Newsletter* of this group evolved into the *Anthropology and Education Quarterly* in 1977.[30]

Although anthropologists of education shared with their colleagues in other hybrid education-and-social-science fields a partly status-related tendency to identify with their disciplines at least as, if not more, closely than with education, the methods they brought to educational scholarship offered tools that were important in broadening and enriching studies of classroom life. An important example is what was added to research on teaching. During the 1960s and early 1970s, most cutting-edge studies of teaching had fitted within a tradition known as "process-product" research.[31] Using observers to record predetermined teacher and student behaviors, process-product research attempted to correlate behaviors with student achievement, as measured by end-of-the-year tests. The hope was to identify effective behaviors that could then be applied as "treatments" that would enhance instructional effectiveness.

As more and more studies of this kind accumulated, critics charged that the process-product approach had failed to capture critical ingredients of effective instruction.[32] This became clear, they contended, as scholars realized that behaviors that fostered success in one year or one classroom did not necessarily have the same effect in the following year or another classroom. Ensuring that the same "treatment" was really the same was difficult, and even if one could do that, the supposedly same "treatment" could have different effects in different places. Searching for methods to capture some of the local and particular circumstances that might account for such differences, researchers increasingly turned to anthropology, more specifically to the ethnographic methods anthropologists had developed.

According to some proponents, the shift toward qualitative methods was generally inspired by recognition that there were severe limitations in the assumption "that 'what cannot be measured cannot be important.'"[33] In addition, the turn was facilitated by the disenchantment of some leading figures with older, more formal approaches to research and evaluation and by spreading awareness that education research had tended to this point to be undercontextualized.[34] Not insignificant, too, heightened interest in anthropology was further encouraged by the National Institute of Education, which in the middle 1970s began to support work on the "social contexts of cognition."[35]

Using ethnographic methods, anthropologists of education as well as educationists without formal anthropological training began to investigate patterns of discourse in classrooms.[36] They variously documented how peoples from different cultures regarded schooling, used language, and acted toward family members, nonfamily adults, and peers.[37] They also used theories of cultural differences to posit explanations of youth alienation.[38] The result was a much more nuanced and complex understanding of the factors that mediate instructional success. As Frederick Erickson, then of Michigan State, argued in 1988, by asking "What is going on here?" researchers had overcome the major weakness of process-product research, which was an overly narrow view of interaction, classroom process, and classroom product (school success as measured by end-of-the-year test scores).[39] At last, as the problematics of educational study broadened, the myriad complexities of classroom life were coming into view.

In addition, even though most education research continued to focus on schooling with too little awareness of the multiple contexts in which education can and does occur, scholars who were engaged in interpretative studies contributed important insights into the ways schooling operated as a social process in American life.[40] However controversial, critical and postmodern scholarship, which flourished throughout the 1980s, contributed to these insights. Although there were important differences among the scholars who wrote from these perspectives, there was a general concurrence in the belief that the failings of the U.S. education system were neither ironic nor accidental.[41] Especially from a Marxist perspective, these failings were seen as a logical and essential part of the inequities of capitalism. Although feminist scholars shared with critical and postmodernist scholars a belief in the oppressiveness of established school arrangements, they dissented from the latter's exclusive focus on race and class.[42] The merits of either perspective aside, growing acceptance for qualitative research had clearly opened the doors to many new debates about the social significance of education.

To what extent the new questions being asked and new research methods being employed were related to changes in demography is impossible to know with currently available data. Whereas almost all education researchers early in the century had been white males, by the 1980s women were receiving significantly more doctorates in education than men. In 1987, for example, women received 3,550 doctorates in education, while men received only 2,897.[43] Of course, many recipients of the doctorate in education did not become education researchers, and many education researchers held doctorates in other fields. Still, even though hard demographic data relevant to the point are surprisingly and unfortunately elusive, rising numbers of doctorates in education being awarded to women would probably correlate with increasing female representation among education researchers. If all education researchers were housed in university schools and departments of education, data to support the point might be easier to track. Clearly, however, many education researchers also went to work at the proliferating think tanks, operating foundations, and contract research companies engaged in educational study. Beyond matters of sex, members of minorities were also more visible in organizations like AERA by the 1980s. Even without hard data to support the point, therefore, one might venture as a hypothesis that changes in the problematics of education research were influenced in positive ways by increasing access for groups once underrepresented among education researchers.

New Links between Research and Practice

Throughout the 1980s, growing familiarity with qualitative research helped foster a variety of new relationships between education research and practice. Teacher research embodied one such relationship. Resembling the kind of inquiry teachers had carried out in the Laboratory School at the University of Chicago during John Dewey's years there and later in the Lincoln School of Teachers College, teacher research had been discussed intermittently in education journals throughout the century.[44] However, during the 1980s, owing to the expanding conceptions of research associated with qualitative studies, teacher research gained new standing.

Not surprisingly, one of the centers from which teacher research emanated during the 1980s was the Graduate School of Education at the University of Pennsylvania, which had earlier developed unusual strength in anthropology and education. Because ethnography and participant observation were often seen as unusually "democratic" modes of research, requiring little beyond what the thoughtful, reflective teacher did on a daily basis, it was a logical step for anthropologists interested in improving schooling to support teacher research. At Penn, such support was institutionalized within the Ethnography and Education Forum, which encouraged conversation among a broad spectrum of people interested in qualitative research, including both university- and school-based scholars and teachers.

According to two of the Penn faculty members who were active participants in that forum, teacher research represented an effort to create a more interactional relationship between university-generated research and school-based practice. As Marilyn Cochran-Smith and Susan L. Lytle explained, previously it had been commonly assumed "that knowledge for teaching should be primarily 'outside-in'—generated at the university and then used in the schools." Believing that this view discounted the degree to which teachers are themselves "knowers" and knowledge about teaching is embedded in the actual practices and contexts that characterize teachers' work, Cochran-Smith and Lytle argued that knowledge for teaching needed to be seen as both inside and outside.[45] Their work and that of other advocates of teacher research had been deeply informed by the views of Lawrence Stenhouse, who had established the Center for Applied Research in Education at the University of East Anglia in Great Britain in 1970. Deeply committed to the view that research should and could empower teachers, Stenhouse insisted that teachers should no longer be regarded merely as the objects of study, but now should actually be involved in carrying out "systematic, self-critical enquiry."[46]

Following in Stenhouse's footsteps, Cochran-Smith, Lytle, and others who shared their perspective increasingly sought opportunities to encourage teachers to engage in "systematic, intentional inquiry" as a means of learning about and improving their own practice.[47] Equally important, they wrote about teacher research, in the process explicitly addressing the kinds of questions concerning reliability and generalizability that more traditional researchers were likely to raise. Even though some educationists remained skeptical, this work convinced others that, beyond its value to the teachers so engaged, teacher research could help elaborate the knowledge base of teaching.[48]

While Cochran-Smith and Lytle wrote in support of teacher research, other researchers who were also teachers began to demonstrate the rich data that studies of one's own practice could yield. Magdalene Lampert, a teacher educator at Michigan State University and then the University of Michigan, was a leading example. Thus, in "How Do Teachers Manage to Teach? Perspectives on Problems in Practice," Lampert, drawing from her own work as a fifth-grade mathematics teachers (a position she held concurrently with her university appointment), presented the multiple, often conflicting demands of living and working in a classroom with children. One such demand had to do with considering where to stand in a classroom where the boys and girls had carefully arranged themselves on opposite sides of the room.[49] The essay demonstrated far more palpably than a traditional exposition could have done the importance of even seemingly minute contextual details, which sensitive teachers ignore at their peril. In another essay, Lampert described as "a kind of 'existence proof'" how she went about changing her own teaching of mathematics and, in turn, the way the students approached learning. In the process, she offered a beautiful exposition of the differences between formal theoretical justifications for certain behaviors and what she called a "teacher's practical reasoning."[50]

If during the 1980s some researchers tried to lessen the divide between theory and practice by combining teaching with research, others approached the same objective by undertaking what came to be known as "design experiments." This required that teams of people simultaneously engage in "designing learning environments, formulating curricula, and assessing achievements of cognition and learning," while also seeking "to contribute to fundamental scientific understanding."[51] According to Ann L. Brown, a Berkeley psychologist who was a leading practitioner of this new genre, her goal was to create innovative educational environments, while also studying them. This required first that the classroom function well; hence, Brown's simultaneous concern with curriculum, pedagogy, and assessment. This differed significantly from older styles of research, which focused on components of the educational process separately.[52] Beyond that, Brown's work was built on what she called "first principles"—for example, that learning is social in nature, that metacognition (or learning about learning) is essential to education, and that individual differences should be acknowledged and built upon.[53] All that went on in one of Brown's experimental classroom was intended to embody these principles within a concrete innovation, which she and her colleagues would introduce, and then constantly watch and modify before returning to the laboratory to consider how what they were learning did and did not square with established learning theory.

Systemic Research

At the same time that researchers were forging varied new ways to connect more directly and effectively to practice, students of policy making were moving closer to the politicians and policy makers they needed to reach, often at the state and local levels. In moving in this direction, policy researchers were building on what had been learned about the policy-making process since the 1960s. Most centrally, this had to do with the insufficiency of earlier belief in a simple linear model for the translation of research into policy, which had given way to much more nuanced views of knowledge utilization.

When the federal government was beginning to play a more direct and active role in pursuing national social goals through education, it had been widely assumed that research could be directly translated into policy, implemented at the state and local levels precisely as it was intended to be in Washington, D.C., and then evaluated after the fact. However, in the face of repeated evaluations that revealed that policies were significantly modified as they were interpreted and reinterpreted by administrators at the state, district, and school levels, evaluators began to scrutinize the policy process in new ways.[54] Adopting techniques pioneered in other areas of social policy, they moved away from simple outcome-focused evaluations carried out ex post facto and began instead to conduct experiments that were designed to put the spotlight on characteristics of the implementation process itself.[55]

Some experiments ended inconclusively. One of these was the "planned variation" strategy used in implementing Project Follow Through in the late 1960s. Intended to extend Head Start from preschool into the primary grades, Follow Through was not funded at sufficient levels to allow for a project as extensive as Head Start. As Michael Timpane, a policy analyst then at Rand, recalled, however, this constraint was immediately turned to advantage when "Follow Through was converted forthwith into an effort to vary education strategies systematically."[56] The hope was that observation of the working out of different programs in different settings would help analysts identify effective interventions and the circumstances that influenced them.

Although the Follow Through experiment seemed promising at first, to the surprise of many observers the variables involved were so difficult to identify and control that less was learned than anticipated. Even if one could identify gains and associate them with one rather than another plan for the delivery of Follow Through services, one could not be sure those gains were a consequence of the Follow Through program as opposed to a better teacher or some other variable. Partly as a result of such problems, scholars scrutinizing the same data reached different conclusions, some echoing Coleman's belief that differences in resources had little impact on results, others deciding that treatments that were well planned and assessed in appropriate ways could have positive outcome effects.[57] As education researcher David K. Cohen concluded, all the Follow Through experiment really demonstrated was that power in education was so decentralized that the controls necessary for experimentation were virtually impossible to maintain.[58]

Despite the frustration of experiments that did not fully clarify the questions posed, some experiments—for example, the Rand Change Agent Study, carried out from 1973 through 1978—did yield clear and important insights. Led by Paul Berman and Milbrey Wallin McLaughlin, the Rand study scrutinized 293 local innovations funded via the Elementary and Secondary Education Act (ESEA), the 1968 Vocational Education Act, and the Right-to-Read program in order to learn whether some were more successful than others and, if so, why that was so.[59] One important observation that resulted was, in McLaughlin's words, that "successful implementation is characterized by a process of mutual adaptation."[60] In order for teachers to change the way they taught, they had to learn new habits and patterns of behavior. In order to do that, they needed to be involved in shaping the reform through discussions and planning carried out over a fairly long period of time. Hence, to be adopted successfully, a reform would inevitably be modified as it was translated into practice.

Over the years, this initial insight was elaborated in many subsequent studies of policy implementation. Looking back on the Change Agent Study investigations ten years after they were completed, McLaughlin observed that effective change needed to be "systemic." Trying to modify one aspect of a school's instructional program would not work unless one assessed the ways in which change in one component would require related changes in other components. Having by now left Rand to become a professor of education at Stanford, McLaughlin also echoed the importance of viewing education reform as what she and Richard F. Elmore, then of Michigan State University, had called "steady work."[61] "We have learned that we cannot mandate what matters to effective practice," McLaughlin wrote with the modesty that more complex knowledge had brought. "The challenge lies in understanding how policy can enable and facilitate it."[62]

If post-1960s studies such as these resulted in significant new knowledge about federally initiated policy interventions, efforts to understand policies initiated at the state and local levels also brought new appreciation for the complexities involved in purposive educational change. State-level inquiries followed from the increase in state education policy making that was stimulated by publication in 1983 of *A Nation at Risk,* which one might note parenthetically was written largely by NIE staff. The message of that report was dire. It claimed that the United States had committed "an act of unthinking, unilateral educational disarmament" that had to be countered by a return to "excellence in education," defined primarily as higher academic standards.[63] In response to the report, governors and business leaders across the nation moved to raise standards, augment student assessment, increase teacher accountability, and improve staff salaries. This created a policy situation that raised a host of new questions and focused new attention on states and localities rather than on the federal government.[64]

Among the questions now in play, none was more important than figuring out why, in the face of thoughtful, well-planned reform efforts, fundamental school change was still so difficult to achieve. Realizing that part of the answer had to do with the complex, diffuse governance system under which public schools operated in the United States, policy researchers began to focus on identifying systemic barriers to reform; soon these researchers were moving from identifying the barriers to proposing how they might be overcome through "systemic reform." Marshall S. Smith, then dean of the Stanford School of Education, and Jennifer O'Day, then a graduate student there, developed the classic statement of this in the early 1990s.

Beginning with the premise that reform required a shared vision or set of values, Smith and O'Day suggested that for most Americans such a vision already existed at least generally. It involved both "the collective democratic values critical to our society: respect for all people, tolerance, equality of opportunity, respect for the individual, participation in the democratic function of the society and service to the society" and "the tasks and attitudes of the teacher and learner—to prize exploration and production of knowledge, rigor in thinking, and sustained intellectual effort."[65] In addition to further specifying this vision in terms of goals pertaining to teaching and learning, Smith and O'Day argued that systemic reform would require two different strategies to attain those goals. Systemic reform would require, first, a "coherent system of instructional guidance" to ensure that all students had opportunities to learn at high levels. In practice, this would mean that curriculum, pre- and inservice teacher education, and assessment would have to be coordinated. In addition, systemic reform would require reviewing all levels of governance to be sure each was working toward the same goals.[66]

Although Smith and O'Day wrote the essential description of what came to be called systemic reform, their work drew on studies carried out by researchers at many institutions, some of whom had organized themselves into a consortium to conduct policy research. Joining scholars at a shifting group of institutions (initially the institutions were Rutgers, the University of Southern California, Harvard, Michigan State, Stanford, and the University of Wisconsin at Madison), this consortium was named the Center for Policy Research in Education (CPRE). Led by Susan H. Fuhrman, then a senior research associate at Rutgers's Eagleton Institute of Politics, the group had sought and won a grant for $6.5 million from the U.S. Department of Education's Office of Educational Research and Improvement in 1985 to carry out collaborative research that was self-consciously designed to make research findings more readily available to policy makers.[67]

Fuhrman and her CPRE colleagues were aware that during the 1980s politicians and business leaders had been the primary initiators of education reforms and wanted to see if researchers could not collaborate with those groups in ways that would enhance the research base for their activities. With that goal in mind, members of CPRE decided to focus on research designed to provide what policy analyst Carol Weiss has called "enlightenment" or big-picture theoretical perspectives, to help clarify problem definition, and to offer advice concerning the feasibility of various policies.[68] Participants also concluded that they would need to approach the dissemination of their work as a continuous and multifaceted process that was integral to the investigations being carried out.[69] All this reflected increased knowledge of the ways in which knowledge has and has not exercised effective influence on policy making.

Able to demonstrate the value of education research to state education officers, governors, and business leaders, CPRE worked primarily on policy issues at the state and local levels. That notwithstanding, it is important to note that it could not have been started without federal funds. Beyond that, the sophisticated approach to policy making that CPRE embodied had grown out of several decades of federally funded research. Given the severe retrenchment in the federal role in education research that had occurred since the mid-1980s, possibilities for building on CPRE's success seemed sadly limited. With the notable exception of the Spencer Foundation, which provided major support for field-initiated studies and for fellowships that might strengthen the professional community of education researchers, most private funders had also pulled back from earlier support for education research. The apparent indifference this bespoke to a field in which there had been clear gains in knowledge was puzzling and troubling all at once.

CONCLUSION

Toward the Reconfiguration of
Educational Study

In 1929, at the age of seventy, John Dewey wrote a short, challenging, and important book about the study of education. Entitled *The Sources of a Science of Education,* the book originated as a lecture to the Kappa Delta Pi Society, an honor society in education. Perhaps for that reason, much that Dewey suggested was phrased in an extremely pithy fashion, which made the book rather difficult to digest. Combined with the inherent difficulty of the material Dewey was treating, the denseness of the argument may have accounted for the book's rather quiet reception. Although it received a few respectful notices when it was first published and isolated quotes have appeared from time to time since, *The Sources of a Science of Education* has not received the attention it deserves. Especially in light of the patterns evident throughout the last century of education research in the United States, *The Sources of a Science of Education* is an incisive and illuminating text.

In *The Sources of a Science of Education,* Dewey argued for a conception of educational scholarship that diverged significantly from the kind of scholarship that had developed in education after he had left the University of Chicago twenty-five years before. Insisting as he always had that theory and practice should be integral to one another, Dewey worried that research had developed at too great a remove from practice. It had become what he called "an arm chair science."[1] In addition, he feared that scholars of education did not interact frequently enough with their university colleagues in other schools and departments. In consequence, he suggested, "many professors in other lines in universities have not been awakened to the complexity of the educational undertaking," and scholars of education were increasingly likely to speak to each other in what he called "pedagese."[2]

Echoing views that he had explained many years earlier, Dewey also pleaded for a greater reliance on philosophy in educational study and a lesser reliance on quantification. He was worried that neglecting philosophy and focusing too exclusively on phenomena that could be measured would blind scholars to the larger meanings of education, for example, to the importance of the attitudes and orientations children developed while acquiring specific knowledge and skill. Finally, Dewey wisely noted that education was a new science, indeed, that the field was just beginning a transition from "empirical to scientific status."[3] That was important to keep in mind, he averred, because people must not expect too much of educational scholarship or give up on efforts to identify ways to improve it.

With uncanny prescience, Dewey thus pointed to problems that became central to educational scholarship during the first decades of the century. Despite the new directions of recent years, those problems have remained central until century's end.

Problems of Status, Reputation, and Isolation

The first problem has to do with the isolation of educational study from other branches of university scholarship as well as its relative remove from practice. Judging from the historical record, isolation within universities was in large measure a consequence of what historian Carl Kaestle has aptly described as the "awful reputation" of education research.[4] Since the earliest days of university sponsorship, education research has been demeaned by scholars in other fields, ignored by practitioners, and alternatively spoofed and criticized by politicians, policy makers, and members of the public at large.

In considerable measure, gender was the initial cause for the low status of educational study. Associated with teaching, which came to be seen as "woman's work" relatively early in the nineteenth century, the very term *education research* seemed to be an oxymoron to many notable university leaders. Men like Harvard President Charles W. Eliot prized good teaching, but were not at all sanguine that education could benefit from systematic investigation. Not coincidentally, Eliot was also unwilling to admit women to Harvard College, the result being the opening of the Harvard Annex (later Radcliffe College) in 1879, which, like the Harvard Graduate School of Education once it was organized in 1920, was located conveniently near, but outside the inner precincts of the university. Doubtless the low social rank of education research was further reinforced by issues of social class. Because it did not require a great deal of advanced training for entry, teaching was a profession that was relatively accessible to people of working-class or immigrant backgrounds. Associated with teaching, scholars of education were not generally presumed to have the social cachet attributed to lawyers and doctors.

If matters of gender and social class helped to define education research as a low-status pursuit, so did the fact that it was intended to be an applied science. Even though most observers of scientific work would now question whether there are significant and sharp differences between "pure" and "applied" study, the fact remains that more theoretical, less hands-on fields of investigation have tended to carry greater prestige.[5] Thus, physics may benefit from the practical inventions of engineers, but in any ranking of professional status, physics would exceed its more applied first cousin. In law, the law schools that have been most oriented toward theory and least oriented toward questions related to daily professional practice have tended to achieve the highest standing. Given this historical bias, scholarship in education, which has generally been intended to make teaching and school administration more effective, has suffered from a discount common among applied fields of investigation.

Clearly deriving from multiple sources, the low status that has plagued educational scholarship from the beginning has had several discernable and unfortunate effects, the most important having been the distance it has encouraged between educationists and their peers in the arts and sciences and other professional fields. Because the early educationists preferred to trumpet progress and quite understandably tried not to record the scorn they had endured, few wrote directly about the insults and innuendoes to which they had been subjected. That notwithstanding, one can recapture the shunning in fleeting statements. Henry Johnson's recollections of the spoofing he encountered when he ventured across 120th Street from Teachers College to the Columbia University Department of History were one example. Beyond that, one can observe the isolation of education institutionally. Although there may be logical historical justifications for the situation, it is nonetheless telling that the American Educational Research Association (AERA) did not become a constituent organization of the Social Science Research Council either when that organization was founded in 1923 or thereafter.

In multiple ways, a lack of regular and easy channels for conversing with scholars in other fields, sharing methods, and discussing problems has constrained the development of education research. That educationists continued to churn out school surveys long after sociologists and anthropologists had begun to develop more nuanced approaches to community study demonstrates the point. What is more, the important insights into education to emanate from the kind of cross-discipline, cross-field collaboration that went on under the auspices of the University of Chicago Committee on Human Development demonstrate the obverse. This was, of course, the group in which W. Lloyd Warner applied his ideas about social class and mobility to education and Allison Davis began his research into the cultural biases of so-called aptitude testing. More recently, educational study has clearly benefited from close relationships with anthropology. This has been evident in the significant knowledge gained from qualitative or interpretative research about teachers, teaching, classroom discourse, and cultural barriers to learning.

Taking many forms, the isolation of educationists could be seen quite differently depending on one's perspective. Indeed, from the perspective of practitioners, especially teachers, location in the university could be read as providing scholars with a powerful shield from the diurnal problems of practice. Ironically, in fact, although education was seen within the university as a low-status field, on the outside it could be said to have provided scholars with superior status to that of teachers. What is more, suffering disdain from colleagues within the university, scholars of education may have been more inclined to assume superior attitudes toward their colleagues in the field than would otherwise have been the case.

Like the segmented relationship that emerged between medical doctors and nurses, the relationship that grew up between scholars and practitioners of education was gender related and hierarchical.[6] As a scientist formulating the laws of learning, Edward L. Thorndike felt confident that he could enhance a teacher's performance without ever watching that teacher teach. Buoyed by a false sense of superiority and by then-common assumptions about linear relationships between theory and practice, scholars like Thorndike failed to heed the old adage that doctors could not cure if nurses did not care. Apparently, scholars like Thorndike did not appreciate what nurses have long understood about the professional status of doctors. They did not understand the degree to which medical success was dependent upon the knowledge, skill, and service provided by nurses. In consequence, they failed to realize that a science of education formulated apart from its elaboration in practice could not be powerful either as a set of systematic and criticized understandings and insights—a science—or as an instrument for changing behavior. Taking many forms, isolation resulting from low status has significantly weakened educational scholarship.

A Narrow Problematics

Viewed historically, it also seems clear that the narrow problematics that came early to characterize the field has acted as an additional constraint on both the scientific quality and the applied usefulness of educational scholarship. As with his warnings about isolation, Dewey was wise to suggest that excessive quantification, combined with a diminished emphasis on history and philosophy, would significantly limit educational study. Although he would not have been temperamentally inclined directly to criticize a colleague, his worries about the direction in which educational scholarship was developing were implicit criticisms of the emphases introduced into the field by Thorndike and other scholars of compatible view. Owing to his extraordinary prolificness and, even more important, to his location at Teachers College, Thorndike helped establish three of the most fundamental orientations of early educational research.

First, through his lectures and writings, Thorndike was pivotal in grounding educational psychology in a narrowly behaviorist conception of learning that involved little more than stimuli, responses, and the connections between them. Second, Thorndike's belief that "whatever exists at all exists in some amount" and that "to know it thoroughly involves knowing its quantity as well as its quality" supported an extreme emphasis on quantification in educational study.[7] It is not insignificant that one of the early textbooks for educational administrators, *Educational Administration: Quantitative Studies* (1913), which was written by Thorndike and George D. Strayer, was for all intents and purposes a manual of statistics. As *Social Diagnosis* by Mary E. Richmond demonstrated in social work, a text widely read in a newly emerging field of professional practice can go a long way toward standardizing views of role and approach.[8] Just as *Social Diagnosis* was vital in establishing casework as the modus operandi of social workers, so was the Thorndike and Strayer volume vital in making the quantitative analysis of school data a central responsibility of school administrators. Finally, Thorndike's deep-seated genetic determinism was an important factor in establishing an emphasis on testing and tracking in education and on test development and psychometrics in education research.

However important he may have been, Thorndike was not alone in establishing the methods and orientations of educational study. Many scholars participated in this, and it was via interactions between and among their ideas, within the context of early-twentieth-century American academic culture, that a problematics emerged. My purpose here, however, is not to further probe how the problematics of education developed, but rather to ponder the results.

People of good will certainly have differing opinions on the matter, but I find the early problematics of educational study deeply troubling. To look at the history of education research is to discover a field that was really quite shapeless circa 1890 and quite well shaped by roughly 1920. By that date, research in education had become more technical than liberal. It was more narrowly instrumental than genuinely investigatory in an open-ended, playful way. The field's applied emphasis had resulted in the marginalization of most subject matter that did not appear to be immediately "relevant" to the professional concerns of school administrators and, to a lesser extent, teachers. Useable knowledge, quite narrowly defined, had become the sine qua non of educational study. Equally important, the psychology that had come to stand at the core of educational scholarship was not only excessively and narrowly behaviorist, but also distinctly more individualistic than social. It simply ignored the degree to which multiple factors, including subtle interactions between and among individuals, groups, cultural traditions, and social structures, all combine to influence teaching and learning.

That the technical and individualistic character early grafted onto education research was unfortunate can be seen, I believe, in the impact this scholarship has had on professional educators working in the field. First, consider the situation of school administrators, who initially made up the target audience of many university departments and schools of education. It was to their needs that many of the first scholars of education addressed themselves. Among men like Ellwood Patterson Cubberley and Paul Hanus, the most common aspiration was to develop a body of knowledge that would help to empower school superintendents. Painfully aware of the degree to which administrators were the servants of the school boards that employed them, Cubberley and his colleagues wanted to help administrators achieve truly autonomous professional status. Did they succeed? Admitting the difficulties of a certain answer, I would still venture that the answer lies on the negative side of a continuum running from yes to no. In part, this was because early educationists like Cubberley and Hanus hoped to insulate school administrators from politics, which was neither realistic nor wise, since this would have contravened long-standing, deeply cherished, and important traditions of lay participation in school affairs. After all, for all that one might sometimes wish that scientific expertise could acquire the authority freely to govern in education, the fact is that education is about values and people appropriately disagree about values and should have opportunities to voice and work for their views. That notwithstanding, I would still argue that the continuing sub-servience of school administrators to school boards and other governing bodies is in part a result of the narrow problematics that quickly came to dominate educational study.

The technical, individualistic orientation of scholarship in education helped school administrators became competent managers, who could calculate budget efficiencies, formulate regulations, and otherwise over-see, regularize, and maintain the stability of a complex organization or complex system of organizations. But it did not provide them with the insights and self-confidence that might have helped them become leaders able to guide school boards as well as policy makers at all levels of gov-ernment.

Certainly, some school administrators did become important leaders in education, but more seemed able to identify the tipping point at which the hiring of a special teacher was economical than appeared skilled at framing larger matters of educational purpose and direction. One might argue that management skills rather than the more forward-looking, vi-sionary qualities associated with leadership were what school administra-tors required. However, if schooling was to serve as a powerful instrument for deliberate community re-creation and transformation, as many educa-tionists themselves claimed it should, then, in addition to competence as a manager, leadership was essential. What is more, since it was to the deference that accrues to leaders that Cubberley, Hanus, and their col-leagues aspired, the managerial emphasis that early came to characterize educational administration seems unfortunate.

Evident in limitations within the subfield of educational administra-tion, a narrow problematics also constrained educational scholarship in another way. Owing to the technical and individualistic orientation that was introduced into education as it became established in universities, scholars tended to investigate pedagogical, administrative, or policy ques-tions in education without taking up their social implications. Sociologist George S. Counts pointed to this shortcoming in a speech he delivered to the Progressive Education Association in 1932. Chiding progressive educators for paying too much attention to pedagogy and too little atten-tion to what might be called the demography of progressive education, Counts lamented the fact that the children of middle-class Americans were more likely to benefit from progressive education than were their working-class peers. To Counts, this undermined the essential progressive aim of creating greater equality and democracy through more social, "progressive" forms of education.[9]

In a variety of ways, the myopia Counts identified early in the century has continued. Even though recent work in the anthropology of education may have begun to lessen this emphasis, scholarship in education is more likely to view school-based teaching and learning as an isolated phenomenon than it is to view school-based teaching and learning as an aspect of a student's larger experience with education, including education within the family and community institutions. More often than not, too, matters of educational policy are taken up apart from matters of policy in such related domains as public health, social welfare, and economics. Among school reformers no less than scholars of education, efforts to improve learning are too often predicated on the assumption that improvements can be achieved through nothing more than school-based interventions. Although evaluations often indicate that such interventions have, at best, weak effects, such findings do not seem to propel scholars or activists to conceive of educational problems more comprehensively. Doing that seems an impossible leap. Obviously, this is not a phenomenon unique to education. It is a legacy of the modern trend toward specialization within all of the various disciplines and professions. Such general causes notwithstanding, within education it is traditions of scholarship that are deeply individualistic and technical in focus that have made it difficult to approach educational problems as multifaceted social problems.

Problems of Governance and Regulation

In addition to isolation and a constricted focus, the study of education has been limited by diffuse governance structures and a lack of professional community. It is startling to discover just how few regulations exist in education. It is similarly amazing to realize that publishers, test makers, and reformers of every color and stripe can "sell" their wares without prior piloting or evaluation. To be sure, some local or state school boards have required research before adopting a text, test, or school improvement project. But that is by no means always the case. In consequence, successful innovations in education are more dependent on entrepreneurship than on the validity of the research that supports them.

One could clearly see the importance of entrepreneurship in educational innovation in the case of William Heard Kilpatrick and the "project method." Because Kilpatrick championed the project method in front of the roughly 35,000 students he is said to have lectured to at Teachers College and because *The Journal of Educational Method*, which Kilpatrick helped launch, discussed it in down-to-earth ways that teachers found appealing, the project method became very well known in educational circles in the 1920s and 1930s. It was adopted in some schools, though how many schools actually tried to implement Kilpatrick's ideas is impossible to know for certain. Described by Kilpatrick in extremely vague terms, in actuality the project method became many different things to many different people. More an orientation than a method, it was really little more than an inclination toward active child-centered pedagogy. In consequence, of course, it could not be rigorously tested or evaluated. All that supported its value were random, anecdotal data; quotes taken from essentially incompatible educational theories (including those of both Dewey and Thorndike); and Kilpatrick's personal energy, charisma, and persuasiveness.

The example of Kilpatrick and the project method is an especially troubling one because there can be no doubt that the popularity of this innovation helped give progressivism writ large a black eye. Because it was so vague in description, extreme, Auntie Mame–like pedagogical experiments were often justified with references to it. In consequence, many people who were rightly critical of such experiments also became critical of progressivism more generally. They simply did not realize that to many of its advocates progressivism had less to do with child-centered pedagogies than with linking learning to important social issues. They were unaware that child-centeredness did not necessarily imply an antagonism to rigorous subject matter or to a central role for teachers. As in this instance, therefore, vaguely described innovations that are based on untested claims are worrisome. In the past they have undermined confidence in education reform generally, and unless things are changed, they are likely to continue doing so.

Kilpatrick's freedom to promote an untested innovation derived from the fact that there were and are very few filters of quality in education. There is neither a Better Business Bureau nor the equivalent of the federal Food and Drug Administration. Caveat emptor is the policy in this field. This is because education research has never developed a close-knit professional community, which is a prerequisite for the creation of regulatory structures that can protect both the welfare and safety of the public at large and the integrity of the profession. Such communities exist in some disciplines, for example, physics and, to a lesser extent, psychology; they also exist in some professions, notably medicine and law. But such a community has never developed in education.

In part, this is because education is a field that draws upon many different disciplines, each of which has its own canons and conventions. People who study education have therefore brought very different methods and standards to their work. The AERA, which is the largest organization of researchers in the field, is subdivided into 12 sections and 128 special-interest groups by both discipline and differing subjects of study.

In part, too, a strong professional community has never developed in education because the market opportunities are vast, at least as vast as all the materials and services the roughly 15,000 school districts that exist in the United States can absorb. This has meant that innovators and inventors have often had a stake in preserving the unregulated state of things. Regulation could interfere with their sometimes very lucrative free access to markets. For these reasons, as well as ones having to do with traditions of local control, which encourage disputes about matters of educational policy in which scholars inevitably become involved, educationists have never managed to organize themselves in support of creating greater coherence in the field.

On the one hand, making it possible to disseminate untested reforms, the lack of a strong professional community in education has, on the other hand, made it difficult to connect research efforts to the needs of potential consumers. Too often, for example, when policy makers or practitioners have wanted research on a particular topic, they have discovered that none exists. That was what John Brademas pointed out with frustration to the members of AERA in 1974, when he addressed that association about the National Institute of Education. Equally distressing, policy makers in search of expert guidance have often discovered that the research they needed did not exist or offered conflicting or indeterminate findings—or no findings whatsoever. It was this, after all, that led Robert Kennedy to excoriate Harold Howe II, when Howe, for good and understandable reasons, could not tell him whether Title I Elementary and Secondary Education Act funds had resulted in children actually learning to read. Even though many factors were involved, including conservative efforts to scale back the federal government, the erosion of federal support for research after the early 1970s was significantly caused by disillusion with the capacity of education either to improve education or to provide practical guidance for policy making.

Problems of linkage between needed and accomplished research have not been unique to education any more than problems of indeterminate or conflicting findings have been. However, few mechanisms have been developed, as they have been in some other fields, including health care and defense policy, to plan research agendas and then systematically to build the necessary infrastructure to carry those out. What is more, there have been no mechanisms for reconciling the differences that inevitably arise as scholars study difficult, complex problems. Lacking a single professional association, common patterns of research training, and shared standards for publication and grant awards, educational scholarship has been a field in which there have been many firecrackers, but none of the powerful illumination of a well-orchestrated fireworks show or a *son et lumière.*

What's to Be Done?

Given all this, what can be done to overcome the consequences of low status and isolation, of a narrow problematics, and of diffuse governance and authority structures that history reveals? Clearly, one place to intervene is the university.[10] Changes within universities might directly address some of the problems I have noted. Even more important perhaps, changes in universities might have an impact on general social attitudes, hopefully lessening the antieducationism that has been so pronounced in American society. In the end, public attitudes that deny the complexity, difficulty, and expense of education will have to change if education research is to be strengthened to the point where it can consistently and significantly contribute to both policy and practice.

To overcome the isolation of education research, more effective links must be created between educational faculties and the other faculties of universities. These could allow scholars of education better acquaintance with new developments in and across the disciplines and other professional fields of the university, while also encouraging discipline-based scholars with interests in education to collaborate in the study of education. In the past, distance and disdain have combined to make it difficult for scholars of education to transform cutting-edge disciplinary knowledge into curricula for schools and too often have also resulted in research ventures that have been dated in the methods used and in the ways they have been framed. Conversely, as Dewey noted, a lack of linkages between education and other faculties has deprived noneducationist scholars of the complex fascinations that can be had in studying educational problems. Last, but not least, too often in the past school reform efforts have run into trouble because scholars outside of education schools have tended to refuse to work with educationists—recall Hollis Caswell's failed efforts to recruit mathematicians and the way the leaders of the post–World War II curriculum projects circumvented most scholars of education. Some devices to link different university faculties already exist in the form of joint appointments or cross-faculty committees, and these should be encouraged. Others will have to be invented.

To sustain, strengthen, and enlarge bridges that can foster more communication between educationists and their colleagues, major university reforms will also be needed. First and most important, incentives will have to be developed to reward teaching much more highly than in the past, and along with incentives, there will have to be much more support to help people improve their teaching. Teaching is the central art of education. It involves knowledge and behaviors that can be studied and improved through research. Symbolically as well as actually, therefore, valuing teaching would provide an endorsement for educational scholarship that heretofore has too rarely been forthcoming from people who are not themselves educationists. Beyond that, discipline-based scholars who study education need to be rewarded for such work. Mechanisms must also be found to protect young discipline-based scholars who wish to study education, so that they can be assured that they will not be punished by their senior disciplinary colleagues, as is reported sometimes to have been the case in the past.

In addition to reforms designed to change faculty behavior, central administrations will have to monitor structures that promote cross-discipline, cross-profession collaborations to ensure that they remain genuinely cross-disciplinary and cross-professional as well as genuinely collaborative and well articulated with the challenges policy makers and practitioners outside the university face. Needless to say, too, central administrations must give high priority to promoting educational study as a shared, distributed function across the university, and they must sustain that commitment over time.

I should note emphatically that working to lessen the isolation of educationists within universities does not require, or in any way commend as a possibility, the closing of schools and departments of education. Quite the opposite is the case.

Claiming that its Department of Education had declined in quality (which incidentally did not fit the perceptions of most outsiders), the University of Chicago closed its department in 1997. As is frequently the case, the department did not enroll undergraduates, which, at a time of concern with strengthening Chicago's undergraduate college, may have been the true source of vulnerability. Even if it had fallen in national rankings, no university would consider closing its history or English department. Seen as essential, especially for undergraduates, a history or English department would instead be rebuilt. However that may be, at the time of the department closing at Chicago, the administration expressed concern about the quality of schools of education generally and promised that Chicago would find an alternative way to organize educational study. The implication was that Chicago might develop a new, improved model. That notwithstanding, a subsequent faculty committee was not able to win support for its recommendations. Although Chicago continues to offer master's-level degrees in education and is still home to some very fine scholars of education, most now housed in disciplinary departments, it would be difficult to argue that education research has been advanced by Chicago's action.

Departments like the one that used to exist at the University of Chicago and "ed schools" generally are important to the improvement of education and education research. Having been created to increase the effectiveness of teaching and school administration through the development and dissemination of systematic knowledge about education, these institutions are still essential to the achievement of that goal. Beyond the fact that education can all too easily slip off the research agenda of scholars with other primary professional affiliations, recent efforts to improve linkages between research and practice will founder without university departments that combine education research and the professional preparation of teachers, administrators, and other practitioners. Field-based research, oriented toward helping teachers and administrators perform their work more effectively on a daily basis or toward informing immediate and specific questions of policy, promises to help overcome long-standing difficulties associated with getting research to the front lines of education. However, such research will not help yield fundamentally new and deeper insights into the process of education unless the experiences of both researchers and practitioners working in the field are brought back to the university for more leisurely, theory-oriented consideration. Many years ago, a study group chaired by Stanford scholars Lee J. Cronbach and Patrick Suppes made essentially this point. The group was sponsored by the National Academy of Education, an honorary society of up to 125 scholars of education that frequently addresses matters of research quality. According to the Cronbach and Suppes group, there should be both decision- and conclusion-oriented inquiries in education. Decision-oriented studies are designed to help decision makers act intelligently; conclusion-oriented inquiries are designed to allow, through the free play of a researcher's imagination, for the discovery of new ideas, the description of previously hidden anomalies, and the investigation of relationships that had not been observed earlier.[11] Unless both types of inquiry are pursued, and pursued in close relationship to one another, efforts to better understand education and to improve it over the long haul will not be advanced.

Beyond that, both types of inquiry should be carried out in settings that allow direct and indirect student participation. If professional educators are trained in settings where they can learn to read, criticize, and themselves engage in research, they are more likely to become intelligent consumers of research (and perhaps participants in it) than would be the case if they are trained in an "ed school" where there is little or no research or in a disciplinary department. Today, of course, there is still too great a divide in schools of education between programs involving would-be teachers and administrators, on the one hand, and would-be researchers, on the other. Few students studying to be teachers or administrators are introduced to research. They do not receive sufficient help in becoming critical consumers of research, and they too rarely learn to engage in research to foster their own professional development. Hence, combining research and teaching functions in a specialized education faculty has the potential to benefit the enterprise not only by offering a laboratory setting to supplement field investigations, but also by providing faculty and students opportunities to bridge long-standing divisions between scholarship and practice.

I am aware, of course, that education schools have many problems and themselves need significant reform. What is more, I believe that, in addition to immersion in professional knowledge and concerns, educators-in-training as well as their faculty mentors need more exposure than has traditionally tended to be available to the people and ideas associated with other university faculties. Finally, at least as I read it, I think history indicates that education research will benefit if scholars holding diverse affiliations become more involved. All that notwithstanding, I am still convinced that education schools can offer a focus on the problems of education and education research that is not available in departments where education is not the central concern.

In addition to university reforms, to overcome the problems that have plagued education research, there will have to be continuing and increased effort to foster a stronger professional community in education. The importance of such a community has long been recognized by scholars, foundation leaders, and government officials among others, but interest in building community seems keener now than it was in the past. Of late, there have been active efforts within the U.S. Department of Education to strengthen the federal capacity to carry out and finance research.

Within private foundations like the Spencer Foundation of Chicago, there have been programs explicitly designed to help develop the infrastructure necessary for education research via fellowship programs, interventions in research training, and various programs intended to nurture conversations between and among different groups interested and involved in educational scholarship. Finally, within the National Academy of Education, the American Educational Research Association, and other professional associations, there is more and more willingness to work together in the interest of nurturing a more well developed sense of professional community.

Of course, it will be enormously difficult to sustain and augment what appears to be a growing wish to create greater cohesion among the different constituencies interested in educational scholarship. Translating interest into concrete, sustainable change will be even more challenging. The forces that have to this point encouraged fragmentation have not diminished. Many scholars who study education still hold diverse affiliations, and socially appealing as well as lucrative opportunities for solo entrepreneurship are still abundant in education. Admitting all that, one might also note, however, that the pressures that could encourage collaboration seem to have grown to the point where change actually has a chance of occurring. Most important, public and private monies for education research have dwindled significantly. With the enterprise thus in considerable jeopardy, action may finally be forthcoming. After all, if through collaboration more progress could be made toward understanding ways to act on problems considered essential to school improvement and more people could be alerted to the knowledge that already exists, that would be likely to encourage new investment. Were that to happen, possibilities to sustain the positive developments of recent years would be magnified, which would, in turn, help to ensure continuing change in the problematics of the field.

Within a strengthened professional community, scholars of education might also more commonly come to acknowledge their responsibility to educate the public about education and about education research. Doing that is essential if the currently weak demand for education research is to become more robust. The "hard" sciences did this in the 1930s with demonstrably positive effects. Thanks to various efforts to teach the public about the benefits of science, ordinary citizens came to believe that their lives would be bettered if investments in research were made. This is not the place to delve into the intricacies of the public relations campaigns that helped win public support for research in chemistry and physics; nor is it the place to detail the ways in which public awareness of infantile paralysis was awakened and, with that, a willingness to generate immense funds for research. However, it is crucial to be aware that unless scholars are willing and trained to talk with people who are not expert in education about the ways in which purposive, sustained inquiry can enhance the power of education, attitudes toward education will not be likely to change. It might therefore also be helpful if schools and departments of education could be encouraged to discuss how such training might be provided. Clearly, there is much to do.

Looking to history to understand the evolution of education scholarship is not an entirely happy or comfortable experience. With the benefit of hindsight, one can see the limitations of beliefs that once seemed indisputably true. Looking back, one can recognize wrong turns in what appeared as "progress" to earlier generations. What is more, with the distance a historical perspective lends, one can observe problems that are more difficult to grasp in their current manifestations. Needless to say, too, one can identify opportunities missed along the way. All that leaves one with the sense that the history of educational scholarship has been more flawed and troubled than one might wish were the case.

Of course, since all history is an imaginative reconstruction based on an inevitably partial and interpreted record of the past, one could write a different story than I have done. Rather than arguing that recent positive developments represent something of a break with the past, one could instead emphasize, as Dewey did almost seventy years ago, that the field is young and change slow. Although presenting that story would be possible, I believe that doing so would be less honest than telling the story I have told. It would fit the evidence less well. Still, the fact remains that one could present a less critical, more progressive account, which might be less discomforting. But going that way would be unfortunate, I believe, because recapturing the missteps and wrong turns may allow one not only to make sense of what happened earlier, but also to help reconfigure what can happen now and in the future.

Viewed as an accurate, yet purposive reconstruction, history can perhaps become an instrument of reform. Those elements in the history of educational scholarship that are troubling—everything from the attitudes revealed about education to the penchant shown for translating complex ideas into formulaic principles—may thus become guides to change. So conceived, an appreciation of history may in itself help strengthen the education research community and, through that, play a role in enhancing the capacity of scholarship to empower those who are involved in educating. Certainly, I very much hope that will be the case.

NOTES

Preface

1. Josiah Royce, "Is There a Science of Education?" *Educational Review* 1 (January 1891): 23, 24.

2. Ellen Condliffe Lagemann, "The Plural Worlds of Education Research," *History of Education Quarterly* 29 (summer 1989): 185–214.

3. Richard Hofstadter, *Anti-intellectualism in American Life* (New York: Alfred A. Knopf, 1962).

4. Robert E. Kohler, *From Medical Chemistry to Biochemistry: The Making of a Biomedical Discipline* (Cambridge: Cambridge University Press, 1982), 1.

5. For examples of this approach, see Dorothy Ross, ed., *Modernist Impulses in the Human Sciences, 1870–1930* (Baltimore: Johns Hopkins University Press, 1994); David K. Van Keuren and JoAnne Brown, eds., *The Estate of Social Knowledge* (Baltimore: Johns Hopkins University Press, 1991); and Alexandra Oleson and John Voss, eds., *The Organization of Knowledge in Modern America* (Baltimore: Johns Hopkins University Press, 1979), which is an older, less historiographically self-conscious, but still important collection.

6. Among the exceptions to this statement are Theodore R. Mitchell and Analee Haro, "Poles Apart: Reconciling the Dichotomies in Education Research," in *Issues in Education Research: Problems and Possibilities,* edited by Ellen Condliffe Lagemann and Lee S. Shulman (San Francisco: Jossey-Bass, 1999), chap. 3, and David F. Labaree, *How to Succeed in School without Really Trying: The Credentials Race in American Education* (New Haven, Conn.: Yale University Press, 1997).

Introduction

1. Lawrence A. Cremin, *American Education: The National Experience, 1783–1876* (New York: Harper & Row, 1979), 398 et passim.

2. Richard M. Bernard and Maris A. Vinovskis, "The Female School Teacher in Ante-bellum Massachusetts," *Journal of Social History* 10 (March 1977): 337.

3. Mason S. Stone, "The First Normal School in America," *Teachers College Record* 24 (May 1923): 263–71.

4. Samuel R. Hall, *Lectures on School-Keeping* (1829; reprint, New York: Arno Press, 1969), 28.

5. Kathryn Kish Sklar, *Catharine Beecher: A Study in American Domesticity* (New Haven, Conn.: Yale University Press, 1973), 147; Polly Welts Kaufman, *Women Teachers on the Frontier* (New Haven, Conn.: Yale University Press, 1984), 8–11; Keith E. Melder, "Woman's High Calling: The Teaching Profession in America 1830–1860," *American Studies* 13 (fall 1972): 19–32.

6. Catharine Beecher, *An Essay on the Education of Female Teachers* (1835), quoted in Sklar, *Catharine Beecher,* 114.

7. "Editor's Table," *Godey's Lady's Book,* January 1853, 176–77.

8. There are at least two views of what "professionalization" involves. In the older view, professionalization requires a progression through an invariant set of stages, after which an occupation becomes a profession (Abraham Flexner, "Is Social Work a Profession?" *School and Society* 1 (June 1915): 901–11, is the classic statement of this). In the newer view, professionalization is a more relational, continuous process through which various occupational groups vie with one another for autonomy, status, and jurisdiction over shifting fields of knowledge and service. I find the newer view more convincing. Among the many works that develop this perspective, my ideas have been most directly informed by Andrew Abbott, *The System of Professions: An Essay on the Division of Expert Labor* (Chicago: University of Chicago Press, 1988); Magali Sarfatti Larsen, *The Rise of Professionalism: A Sociological Analysis* (Berkeley: University of California Press, 1977); and Joan Jacobs Brumberg and Nancy Tomes, "Women in the Professions: A Research Agenda for American Historians," *Reviews in American History* 10 (June 1982): 275–96.

9. Quoted in Paul H. Mattingly, *The Classless Profession: American Schoolmen in the Nineteenth Century* (New York: New York University Press, 1975), 67. See also Edith Nye MacMullen, *In the Cause of True Education: Henry Barnard and Nineteenth-Century School Reform* (New Haven, Conn.: Yale University Press, 1991), 73–74, 131–34, 174–78.

10. George Frederick Miller, *The Academy System of the State of New York* (1922; reprint, New York: Arno Press, 1969), 171.

11. Cited in Theodore R. Sizer, *The Age of the Academies* (New York: Bureau of Publications, Teachers College, 1964), 12. The numbers of institutions and students given in Colin B. Burke, *American Collegiate Populations: A Test of the Traditional View* (New York: New York University Press, 1982), chaps. 1 and 2, are slightly lower, though the proportions are the same.

12. *National Survey of the Education of Teachers, Bulletin 1933,* no. 10 (Washington, D.C.: U.S. Office of Education, 1935), 5:12, 5:25.

13. M. A. Newell, "Contributions to the History of Normal Schools in the United States," in *Report of the [U.S.] Commissioner of Education for the Year 1898–99* (Washington, D.C.: U.S. Government Printing Office, 1900), 2:2270.

14. Jurgen Herbst, *And Sadly Teach: Teacher Education and Professionalization in American Culture* (Madison: University of Wisconsin Press, 1989), 95.

15. Quoted in Pamela Claire Hronek, "Women and Normal Schools: Tempe Normal, A Case Study, 1885–1925" (Ph.D. diss., Arizona State University, 1985), 83.

16. This anachronistic overemphasis on the women's colleges is evident, for example, in Barbara Miller Solomon, *In the Company of Educated Women: A History of Women and Higher Education in America* (New Haven, Conn.: Yale University Press, 1985).

17. Quoted in Newell, "Contributions to the History of Normal Schools," 2:2267.

18. Quoted in Herbst, *And Sadly Teach,* 69.

19. Quoted in ibid., 141.

20. Thomas Woody, *A History of Women's Education in the United States* (1929; reprint, New York: Octagon Books, 1966), 1:344–47; Anne Firor Scott, "The Ever Widening Circle: The Diffusion of Feminist Values from the Troy Female Seminary, 1822–1872," *History of Education Quarterly* 19 (spring 1979): 3–25.

21. Quoted in Bernard and Vinovskis, "The Female School Teacher," 337.

22. David Tyack and Elisabeth Hansot, *Learning Together: A History of Coeducation in American Schools* (New Haven, Conn.: Yale University Press, 1990), 80–89;

Myra H. Strober and David Tyack, "Why Do Women Teach and Men Manage? A Report on Research on Schools," *Signs* 5 (spring 1980): 494–503.

23. Sizer, *Age of Academies*, 44–45.

24. For the early development of high schools, see William J. Reese, *The Origins of the American High School* (New Haven, Conn.: Yale University Press, 1995).

25. Thorstein Veblen, *The Higher Learning in America: A Memorandum on the Conduct of Universities by Business Men* (1918; reprint, Stanford, Calif.: Academic Reprints, 1954), 248.

26. Edwin Grant Dexter, *A History of Education in the United States* (1906; reprint, New York: Lenox Hill, 1971), 386.

27. William W. Brickman, *Pedagogy, Professionalism, and Policy: History of the Graduate School of Education at the University of Pennsylvania* (Philadelphia: Graduate School of Education, University of Pennsylvania, 1986), 20.

28. Herbst, *And Sadly Teach*, 173–74.

29. David Felmley, "The New Normal School Movement," *Educational Review* 44 (April 1913): 409–10.

30. Ibid., 412.

31. Herbst, *And Sadly Teach*, 147–52.

32. Frederick E. Bolton, "The Preparation of High-School Teachers: What They Do Secure and What They Should Secure," *School Review* 15 (February 1907): 113.

33. Marjorie Murphy, *Blackboard Unions: The AFT and the NEA, 1900–1980* (Ithaca, N.Y.: Cornell University Press, 1990), 35.

34. For general discussions of this contest, see David John Hogan, *Class and Reform: School and Society in Chicago, 1880–1930* (Philadelphia: University of Pennsylvania Press, 1985), chap. 5, and Julia Wrigley, *Class, Politics, and Public Schools: Chicago, 1900–1950* (New Brunswick, N.J.: Rutgers University Press, 1982).

35. *Higher Professional Education for Teachers, School of Pedagogy, University of the City of New York*, pamphlet, n.d., Cubberley Library, Stanford University, Stanford, Calif.

36. *University of Buffalo, Circular of Information, 1895–96*, Cubberley Library, Stanford University, Stanford, Calif.

37. Henry C. Johnson Jr. and Erwin V. Johanningmeier, *Teachers for the Prairie: The University of Illinois and the Schools, 1868–1945* (Urbana: University of Illinois Press, 1972), 101.

38. *New York College for the Training of Teachers: Three Descriptive Articles*, pamphlet, n.d. (c. 1892), Cubberley Library, Stanford University, Stanford, Calif.

39. Geraldine Jonçich Clifford and James W. Guthrie, *Ed School: A Brief for Professional Education* (Chicago: University of Chicago Press, 1988), 53.

40. Ibid., 133–34.

41. Andrea Walton, "Women at Columbia: A Study of Power and Empowerment in the Lives of Six Scholars" (Ph.D. diss., Columbia University, 1995); Bette Weneck, "The 'Average Teacher' Need Not Apply: Women Educators at Teachers College, 1887–1927" (Ph.D. diss., Columbia University, 1996).

42. Ellen Condliffe Lagemann, "Experimenting with Education: John Dewey and Ella Flagg Young at the University of Chicago," *American Journal of Education* 104 (May 1996): 171–85.

43. For typical arguments along these lines, see William H. Burnham, "Education as a University Subject," *Educational Review* 26 (October 1903): 244; Edward Franklin Buchner, "Education as a College Subject," *Pedagogical Seminary* 18 (March 1910): 77; and Charles Hubbard Judd, "The Department of Education in American Universities," *School Review* 17 (November 1909): 593, 606.

44. Willard S. Elsbree, *The American Teacher: Evolution of a Profession in a Democracy* (New York: American Book Co., 1939).

Part One

1. Roger L. Geiger, *To Advance Knowledge: The Growth of American Research Universities, 1900–1940* (New York: Oxford University Press, 1986).

2. Julie A. Reuben, *The Making of the Modern University: Intellectual Transformation and the Marginalization of Morality* (Chicago: University of Chicago Press, 1996).

3. John Dewey, "My Pedagogic Creed" (1897), in *John Dewey: The Early Works, 1882–1898,* edited by Jo Ann Boydston (Carbondale: Southern Illinois University Press, 1972), 5:95.

4. Henry F. May, *The End of American Innocence: The First Years of Our Own Time, 1912–1917* (New York: Alfred A. Knopf, 1959).

5. Daniel T. Rodgers, "In Search of Progressivism," *Reviews in American History* 11 (1982): 124–27.

6. Geraldine Jonçich Clifford and James W. Guthrie, *Ed School: A Brief for Professional Education* (Chicago: University of Chicago Press, 1988).

7. JoAnne Brown, *The Definition of a Profession: The Authority of Metaphor in the History of Intelligence Testing, 1890–1930* (Princeton, N.J.: Princeton University Press, 1992), 127.

Chapter One

1. W. T. Harris, editor's preface to *The Intellectual and Moral Development of the Child,* by Gabriel Compayré, quoted in Robert B. Cairns, "The Emergence of Developmental Psychology," in *Handbook of Child Psychology,* vol. 1, *History, Theory, and Methods,* edited by William Kessen (New York: John Wiley & Sons, 1983), 91.

2. Quoted in Edward A. Krug, *The Shaping of the American High School, 1880–1920* (Madison: University of Wisconsin Press, 1969), 111. On the Herbartians, see Harold B. Dunkel, *Herbart and Herbartianism: An Educational Ghost Story* (Chicago: University of Chicago Press, 1970), and Kathleen A. Cruikshank, "The Rise and Fall of American Herbartianism: Dynamics of an Educational Reform Movement" (Ph.D. diss., University of Wisconsin–Madison, 1993).

3. John S. Roberts, *William T. Harris: A Critical Study of His Educational and Related Philosophical Views* (Washington, D.C.: National Education Association, 1924), 80–81, 102–4.

4. G. Stanley Hall, *Life and Confessions of a Psychologist* (New York: D. Appleton, 1923), 215, 379.

5. *Notable American Women,* s.v. "Shaw, Pauline Agassiz"; Barbara Beatty, *Preschool Education in America: The Culture of Young Children from the Colonial Era to the Present* (New Haven, Conn.: Conn.: Yale University Press, 1995), 73–74.

6. Beatty, *Preschool Education in America,* 73–74.

7. On precedents for Hall's questionnaire method, see W. Dennis, "Historical Beginnings of Child Psychology," *Psychological Bulletin* 46 (1949): 224–35.

8. G. Stanley Hall, "The Contents of Children's Minds," *Princeton Review* 11 (May 1883): 253.

9. Ibid., 271.

10. Ibid., 270.

11. G. Stanley Hall, "Child-Study: The Basis of Exact Education," *Forum* 16 (December 1893): 439.

12. G. Stanley Hall, "Child-Study and Its Relation to Education," *Forum* 29 (August 1900): 699.

13. [G. S. Hall], "Editorial," *Pedagogical Seminary* 1 (June 1891): 121.

14. Hall, "Child-Study and Its Relation to Education," 690; idem, "Child-Study," 429. See also James Dale Hendricks, "The Child-Study Movement in American Education, 1880–1910: A Quest for Educational Reform through a Scientific Study of the Child" (Ph.D. diss., Indiana University, 1968).

15. G. Stanley Hall, "The New Psychology as a Basis of Education," *Forum* 17 (August 1894): 718.

16. Quoted in Dorothy Ross, *G. Stanley Hall: The Psychologist as Prophet* (Chicago: University of Chicago Press, 1972), 40–41.

17. Quoted in ibid., 50–51.

18. Bruce Kuklick, *The Rise of American Philosophy: Cambridge, Massachusetts, 1860–1930* (New Haven, Conn.: Yale University Press, 1977), 180–81.

19. Ross, *G. Stanley Hall,* 70.

20. G. S[tanley] H[all], "College Instruction in Philosophy," *Nation* 23 (September 1976): 180.

21. G. Stanley Hall, "Philosophy in the United States," *Mind* 4 (1879): 92.

22. Hall, *Life and Confessions,* 215.

23. Quoted in Ross, *G. Stanley Hall,* 112.

24. G. Stanley Hall, "The High School as the People's College versus the Fitting School," *Pedagogical Seminary* 9 (March 1902): 65.

25. Charles Frances Adams Jr., "The Development of the Superintendency," quoted in Hendricks, "The Child-Study Movement," 40.

26. Quoted in Ross, *G. Stanley Hall,* 113.

27. Ibid. See also Arthur G. Powell, *The Uncertain Profession: Harvard and the Search for Educational Authority* (Cambridge: Harvard University Press, 1980), 42–43.

28. Quoted in Ross, *G. Stanley Hall,* 133.

29. Ibid., 134–36. On Gilman's logic, see John M. O'Donnell, *The Origins of Behaviorism: American Psychology, 1870–1920* (New York: New York University Press, 1985), 117–20.

30. Hall, *Life and Confessions,* 226.

31. David Tyack and Elisabeth Hansot, *Learning Together: A History of Coeducation in American Schools* (New Haven, Conn.: Yale University Press, 1990).

32. Ross, *G. Stanley Hall,* 165.

33. Dorothy Ross, "American Psychology and Psychoanalysis: William James and G. Stanley Hall," in *American Psychoanalysis: Origins and Development,* edited by Jacques M. Quen and Eric T. Carlson (New York: Brunner/Mazel, 1978), 43.

34. Mortimer Herbert Appley, "G. Stanley Hall: Vow on Mount Owen," in *One Hundred Years of Psychological Research in America: G. Stanley Hall and the Johns Hopkins Tradition,* edited by Stewart H. Hulse and Bert F. Green Jr. (Baltimore: Johns Hopkins University Press, 1986), 13.

35. William A. Koelsch, *Clark University, 1887–1987: A Narrative History* (Worcester, Mass.: Clark University Press, 1987), chap. 1.

36. Ibid., 146.

37. John Dewey to F[rederick T.] Gates, 15 June 1903, Letter #00903, John Dewey Papers, Center for Dewey Studies, Southern Illinois University, Carbondale.

38. Koelsch, *Clark University,* 40–41.

39. Von Holst quoted in ibid., 41; Laurence R. Veysey, *The Emergence of the American University* (Chicago: University of Chicago Press, 1965), 179.

40. Sara E. Wiltse, "A Preliminary Sketch of the History of Child Study in America," *Pedagogical Seminary* 3 (October 1895): 189–212. Sheldon H. White found that eighty-four publications based on questionnaire studies were published between

1894 and 1904. See his "Child Study at Clark University: 1894–1904," *Journal of the History of the Behavioral Sciences* 26 (April 1990): 134.

41. Beatty, *Preschool Education in America,* 78.

42. Koelsch, *Clark University,* 59.

43. *Clark University in the City of Worcester, Massachusetts, Summer School* [Catalog], 1895, p. 12, Cubberley Library, Stanford University, Stanford, Calif.

44. Theodate L. Smith, "Child Study at Clark University," *Pedagogical Seminary* 12 (March 1905): 93–96; Roberta Lyn Wollons, "Educating Mothers: Sidonie Matsner Gruenberg and the Child Study Association of America, 1881–1929" (Ph.D. diss., University of Chicago, 1983).

45. Ross, *G. Stanley Hall,* 281–82.

46. G. Stanley Hall, "Editorial," *Pedagogical Seminary* 3 (October 1894): 3–7.

47. William James, *Talks to Teachers on Psychology; and To Students on Some of Life's Ideals,* edited by Paul Woodring (1899; reprint, New York: W. W. Norton, 1958), 26, 27.

48. Jacques Barzun, *A Stroll with William James* (Chicago: University of Chicago Press, 1983), 13. See also R. W. B. Lewis, *The Jameses: A Family Narrative* (New York: Farrar, Straus and Giroux, 1991), chap. 3.

49. Howard M. Feinstein, *Becoming William James* (Ithaca, N.Y.: Cornell University Press, 1984), chap. 8.

50. William James to Henry James, 15 July 1865, quoted in Ralph Barton Perry, *The Thought and Character of William James* (Boston: Little, Brown, 1935), 1:220.

51. William James to Henry James, 3–10 May 1865, quoted in ibid., 1:219.

52. George Cotkin, *William James, Public Philosopher* (Baltimore: Johns Hopkins University Press, 1990), 21. For a more general discussion, see George Frederickson, *The Inner Civil War: Northern Intellectuals and the Crisis of the Union* (New York: Harper & Row, 1965).

53. William James to Henry P. Bowditch, 12 December 1867, quoted in Perry, *The Thought and Character,* 1:250.

54. Quoted in O'Donnell, *The Origins of Behaviorism,* 97.

55. Quoted in ibid.

56. O'Donnell, *The Origins of Behaviorism,* 97.

57. On James as a teacher and also on his introduction of biology to education, see Bird T. Baldwin, "William James' Contributions to Education," *Journal of Educational Psychology* 2 (1911): 369–82.

58. O'Donnell, *The Origins of Behaviorism,* 99–105 (p. 101 for the quotes).

59. Perry, *The Thought and Character,* 1:375.

60. William James to Henry James, 1 September 1887, quoted in ibid., 1:396.

61. Quoted in ibid., 2:53.

62. William James, *The Principles of Psychology* (1890; reprint, New York: Dover Publications, 1950), 1:113.

63. Ibid., 1:224.

64. Ibid., 1:297.

65. Ibid., vol. 2, chap. 26.

66. Powell, *The Uncertain Profession,* chap. 2.

67. Ibid., 48.

68. William James to [George H.] Howison, 27 October 1897, quoted in Perry, *The Thought and Character,* 2:131.

69. James, *Talks to Teachers,* chap. 1, "Psychology and the Teaching Art."

70. Ibid., 23–24.

71. Kuklick, *The Rise of American Philosophy,* 186.

72. Matthew Hale Jr., *Human Science and Social Order: Hugo Munsterberg and the Origins of Applied Psychology* (Philadelphia: Temple University Press, 1980).

73. Lewis M. Terman, "Trails to Psychology," in *A History of Psychology in Autobiography*, edited by Carl Murchison (New York: Russell and Russell, 1932), 1:314.

74. National Education Association, *Proceedings* (1911), 870. See also Edgar B. Wesley, *NEA: The First Hundred Years* (New York: Harper, 1957), 199–200; William H. Burnham, "The Problems of Child Hygiene, and the Contribution of Hygiene to Education," in National Education Association, *Proceedings* (1912), 1096.

Chapter Two

1. Quoted in Brian A. Williams, *Thought and Action: John Dewey at the University of Michigan* (Ann Arbor: Bentley Historical Library, University of Michigan, 1998), 16.

2. Ellen Condliffe Lagemann, "The Plural Worlds of Educational Research," *History of Education Quarterly* 29 (summer 1989): 202–4.

3. The various quotes are from Neil Coughlin, *Young John Dewey: An Essay in Intellectual History* (Chicago: University of Chicago Press, 1973), 3–5.

4. Quoted in ibid., 9.

5. John Dewey to Alice Chipman Dewey, 5 August 1894, Dewey Papers, Center for Dewey Studies, Southern Illinois University, Carbondale (hereafter Dewey Papers).

6. Quoted in Jane M. Dewey, "Biography of John Dewey," in *The Philosophy of John Dewey*, edited by Paul Arthur Schilpp (Evanston, Ill.: Northwestern University, 1939), 21.

7. Quoted in Coughlin, *Young John Dewey*, 92.

8. Quoted in ibid., 93.

9. Jane Dewey, "Biography of John Dewey," 21.

10. Quoted in Max Eastman, "The Hero as Teacher: The Life Story of John Dewey," in *Heroes I Have Known: Twelve Who Lived Great Lives* (New York: Simon & Schuster, 1942), 300.

11. Coughlin, *Young John Dewey*, 96.

12. Quoted in Willinda Hortense Savage, "The Evolution of John Dewey's Philosophy of Experimentalism as Developed at the University of Michigan" (Ed.D. diss., University of Michigan, 1950), 64–65.

13. Josiah Royce, "Present Ideals of American University Life," *Scribner's Magazine* 10 (September 1891): 383.

14. Quoted in Savage, "The Evolution of John Dewey's Philosophy," 153.

15. George Dykhuisen, "John Dewey and the University of Michigan," *Journal of the History of Ideas* 23 (October–December 1962): 522.

16. George Herbert Mead, "The Philosophy of John Dewey," *International Journal of Ethics* 46 (October 1935): 72.

17. Quoted in Darnell Rucker, *The Chicago Pragmatists* (Minneapolis: University of Minnesota Press, 1969), 27.

18. Steven J. Diner, *A City and Its Universities: Public Policy in Chicago, 1892–1919* (Chapel Hill: University of North Carolina Press, 1980), 17–18.

19. Memorandum, James H. Tufts to William Rainey Harper, n.d. (c. late 1893 or early 1894), Presidents' Papers, 1889–1925, Department of Special Collections, Joseph Regenstein Library, University of Chicago, Chicago (hereafter Presidents' Papers).

20. John Dewey to William Rainey Harper, 19 March 1894, Presidents' Papers.

21. John Dewey to Alice Chipman Dewey, 1 November 1894, Dewey Papers.

22. Daniel J. Wilson, *Science, Community, and the Transformation of American Philosophy, 1860–1930* (Chicago: University of Chicago Press, 1990).

23. John Dewey to Alice Chipman Dewey, 1 November 1894, Dewey Papers.

24. John Dewey, "A Pedagogical Experiment" (1896), in *John Dewey: The Early Works, 1882–1898*, edited by Jo Ann Boydston (Carbondale: Southern Illinois University Press, 1972), 5:245.

25. John Dewey, "The University School" (1896), in *Early Works*, 5:438.

26. This is especially well described in Andrew Feffer, *The Chicago Pragmatists and American Progressivism* (Ithaca, N.Y.: Cornell University Press, 1993), 98–103.

27. Quoted in John T. McManis, *Ella Flagg Young and a Half-Century of the Chicago Public Schools* (Chicago: A. C. McClurg, 1916), 120.

28. Ellen Condliffe Lagemann, "Experimenting with Education: John Dewey and Ella Flagg Young at the University of Chicago," *American Journal of Education* 104 (May 1996): 171–85.

29. Katherine Camp Mayhew and Anna Camp Edwards, *The Dewey School: The Laboratory School of the University of Chicago, 1896–1903* (New York: D. Appleton-Century, 1936), 7.

30. Dewey, "The University School" (1896), in *Early Works*, 5:436–37.

31. John Dewey, "The Need for a Laboratory School: Statement to President William Rainey Harper" (n.d. [1896?]), in *Early Works*, 5:434.

32. John Dewey, "Pedagogy as a University Discipline" (September 1896), in *Early Works*, 5:289. There is also an incisive discussion in Emily D. Cahan, "John Dewey and Human Development," *Developmental Psychology* 28 (March 1992): 205–14.

33. John Dewey, "Introduction," in Mayhew and Edwards, *The Dewey School*, xv.

34. John Dewey, "The School and Society" (1899), in *John Dewey: The Middle Works, 1899–1924*, edited by Jo Ann Boydston (Carbondale: Southern Illinois University, 1976), 1:44.

35. John Dewey, "Psychology and Social Practice" (1900), in *Middle Works*, 1:131.

36. Ibid., 1:134.

37. Ibid., 1:135.

38. John Dewey, "Democracy in Education" (1903), in *Middle Works*, 3:236.

39. Ibid., 3:232.

40. Lagemann, "Experimenting with Education," 171–85.

41. John Dewey, "From Absolutism to Experimentalism," in *Contemporary American Philosophy: Personal Statements*, edited by George P. Adams and William Pepperell Montague (New York: Macmillan, 1930).

42. James H. Tufts, "Autobiographical Notes," chap. 3, p. 2, James H. Tufts Papers, Department of Special Collections, Joseph Regenstein Library, University of Chicago, Chicago.

43. Ibid.

44. Ibid., chap. 3, pp. 1, 4.

45. George Herbert Mead, "The Philosophies of Royce, James, and Dewey in Their American Setting," *International Journal of Ethics* 40 (January 1930): 231; John Dewey, "George Herbert Mead," *Journal of Philosophy* 28 (4 June 1931): 310.

46. George Herbert Mead to Helen Castle Mead, 12 June 1901, George Herbert Mead Papers, Department of Special Collections, Joseph Regenstein Library, University of Chicago, Chicago.

47. Jane Dewey, "Biography of John Dewey," 26.

48. Martin Bulmer, *The Chicago School of Sociology: Institutionalization, Diversity, and the Rise of Sociological Research* (Chicago: University of Chicago Press, 1984); Roscoe C. Hinkle, *Founding Theory of American Sociology, 1881–1915* (Boston: Routledge & Kegan Paul, 1980).

49. Albion W. Small, "Some Demands of Sociology upon Pedagogy," *American Journal of Sociology* 2 (May 1897): 839–51 (pp. 842–43 for the quotes).

50. Philip J. Pauly, *Controlling Life: Jacques Loeb and the Engineering Ideal in Biology* (New York: Oxford University Press, 1987), 68.

51. Mayhew and Camp, *The Dewey School.*

52. Jane Dewey, "Biography of John Dewey," 30.

53. W. W. Charters letter, 10 April 1965, quoted in *Lectures in the Philosophy of Education: 1899 by John Dewey,* edited by Reginald D. Archambault (New York: Random House, 1966), xxxiv.

54. Quoted in Graham Taylor, *Pioneering on Social Frontiers* (Chicago: University of Chicago Press, 1930), 303–4.

55. John Dewey, "The Theory of the Chicago Experiment," in Mayhew and Edwards, *The Dewey School,* 476.

56. Peter L. Buttenwieser, "Unfulfilled Dreams: Thoughts on Progressive Education and the New York City Schools, 1900–1978," in *Educating an Urban People: The New York City Experience,* edited by Diane Ravitch and Ronald K. Goodenow (New York: Teachers College Press, 1981), 171–86. For a somewhat different argument, see Arthur Zilversmit, *Changing Schools: Progressive Education Theory and Practice, 1930–1960* (Chicago: University of Chicago Press, 1993).

57. Harold Rugg, *Foundations for American Education* (Yonkers-on-Hudson, N.Y.: World Book, 1947), 555.

58. Leonard P. Ayres, "History and Present Status of Educational Measurements," in National Society for the Study of Education, *Seventeenth Yearbook,* pt. 2, *The Measurement of Educational Products,* edited by Guy Montrose Whipple (Bloomington, Ind.: Public School Publishing, 1918), 9; Edward L. Thorndike, "The Nature, Purposes, and General Methods of Measurement of Educational Products," in ibid., 16.

59. Quoted in Geraldine Jonçich, *The Sane Positivist: A Biography of Edward L. Thorndike* (Middletown, Conn.: Wesleyan University Press, 1968), 3.

60. E. L. Thorndike to J. M. Cattell, 6 July 1904, quoted in Jonçich, *The Sane Positivist,* 244.

61. Edward L. Thorndike, "Quantitative Investigations in Education: With Special Reference to Co-operation within This Association," in *Research within the Field of Education, Its Organization and Encouragement,* edited by Ellwood P. Cubberley et al., School Review Monograph no. 1 (Chicago: University of Chicago Press, 1911), 35.

62. "Edward Lee Thorndike," in *A History of Psychology in Autobiography,* edited by Carl Murchison (Worcester, Mass.: Clark University Press, 1936), 3:263.

63. Ibid. At the time Thorndike was a graduate student, philosophy, psychology, anthropology, and education were all combined in one department at Columbia, but each of these fields was treated separately. See John Herman Randall Jr., "The Department of Philosophy," in *A History of the Faculty of Philosophy, Columbia University* (New York: Columbia University Press, 1957), 112–13.

64. "Edward Lee Thorndike," 268.

65. James McKeen Cattell, "Address of the President before the American Psychological Association, 1895," *Psychological Review* 3 (1896): 144.

66. Quoted in Jonçich, *The Sane Positivist,* 153.

67. Edward L. Thorndike, *The Principles of Teaching Based on Psychology* (1906; reprint, New York: A. G. Seiler, 1916), 34.

68. Edward L. Thorndike, *Educational Psychology* (New York: Teachers College, 1913), 2:1–5.

69. E. L. Thorndike and R. S. Woodworth, "The Influence of Improvement in One

Mental Function upon the Efficiency of Other Functions," *Psychological Review* 8 (1901): 247–61, 384–95, 553–64; Thorndike, *Educational Psychology*, vol. 2, chap. 12.

70. Leta S. Hollingworth, "[Edward L. Thorndike's] Contributions to Child Psychology," *Teachers College Record* 27 (February 1926): 531.

71. Jonçich, *The Sane Positivist*, 230–31.

72. Edward L. Thorndike, "The Quantitative Study of Education," *Forum* 36 (January 1905): 446.

73. Ibid., 443.

74. Thorndike, *Educational Psychology*, vol. 3, chap. 9.

75. Quoted in Maxine Seller, "G. Stanley Hall and Edward Thorndike on the Education of Women: Theory and Policy in the Progressive Era," *Educational Studies* 11 (winter 1981): 369.

76. Thorndike, *Principles of Teaching*, 6.

77. Ibid., 9.

78. Quoted in David E. Leary, "Telling Likely Stories: The Rhetoric of the New Psychology, 1880–1920," *Journal of the History of the Behavioral Sciences* 23 (October 1987): 323.

79. James E. Russell, "Recent Advances in the Professional Training of Teachers," *Teachers College Record* 26 (June 1925): 811.

80. John Dewey to Frank A. Manny, 26 July 1899, Dewey Papers.

81. James Earl Russell, *Founding Teachers College: Reminiscences of the Dean Emeritus* (New York: Bureau of Publications, Teachers College, 1937), 25.

82. For an account of antifeminism at Columbia, see Andrea Walton, "Women at Columbia: A Study of Power and Empowerment in the Lives of Six Scholars" (Ph.D. diss., Columbia University, 1995).

83. Quoted in Timothy F. O'Leary, *An Inquiry into the General Purposes, Functions, and Organization of Selected University Schools of Education* (Washington, D.C.: Catholic University of America Press, 1941), 12.

84. Ibid., 27.

85. James Earl Russell, "Standards of Scholarship and the Professional Spirit in Teachers College," *Columbia University Quarterly* 9 (June 1907): 277–84. For a general history of Teachers College, see Lawrence A. Cremin, David A. Shannon, and Mary Evelyn Townsend, *A History of Teachers College, Columbia University* (New York: Columbia University Press, 1954).

86. James Earl Russell, "An Appreciation of E. L. Thorndike 1926 and 1940," *Teachers College Record* 41 (May 1940): 696.

87. James Earl Russell, "The Function of the University in the Training of Teachers," *Teachers College Record* 1 (January 1900): 10; Jonçich, *The Sane Positivist*, 230–31.

88. "Tribute by Edward L. Thorndike: James Earl Russell, 1864–1945," *Teachers College Record* 47 (February 1946): 290.

89. Jonçich, *The Sane Positivist*, 216.

90. Ibid., 219.

91. Ibid., 234–35.

92. Robert S. Woodworth, "Edward Lee Thorndike, 1874–1949" in National Academy of Sciences, *Biographical Memoirs* (Washington, D.C.: National Academy of Sciences, 1952), 27:214.

93. Helen M. Walker, *Studies in the History of Statistical Method* (Baltimore: Williams & Wilkins, 1929).

94. Russell, "The Function of the University in the Training of Teachers," 8.

95. O'Leary, *An Inquiry into the General Purposes*, chap. 3.

96. G. H. Reavis, "The Development of Teacher Training as a Profession," *Teachers College Record* 24 (May 1923): 211–12.

97. Elmer Ellsworth Brown, "The Development of Education as a University Subject," *Teachers College Record* 24 (May 1923): 190–96.

98. Charles Hubbard Judd, "The Relation of Special Training to General Intelligence," *Educational Review* 36 (June 1908): 28–42.

99. Charles Hubbard Judd, *Education as Cultivation of the Higher Mental Processes* (New York: Macmillan, 1936); idem, *Psychological Analysis of the Fundamentals of Arithmetic* (Chicago: University of Chicago Press, 1927).

100. "Charles H. Judd," in *A History of Psychology in Autobiography,* edited by Carl Murchison (Worcester, Mass.: Clark University Press, 1932), 2:231.

101. Ralph W. Tyler, "Charles Hubbard Judd, 1873–1946," *School Review* 54 (September 1946): 376.

102. "Charles H. Judd," 221–22.

103. Charles H. Judd, "On Scientific Study of High-School Problems," *School Review* 18 (February 1910): 84–98; idem, in National Education Association, *Proceedings* (1912), 568–69; idem, "The Scientific Development and Evaluation of the Curriculum," in National Education Association, *Proceedings* (1933), 620–29.

104. "Charles H. Judd," 222–28.

105. Charles Hubbard Judd, "The Department of Education in American Universities," *School Review* 17 (November 1909): 593–608.

106. C. H. Judd to George S. Counts, 23 June 1930, Charles Hubbard Judd Papers, Department of Special Collections, Joseph Regenstein Library, University of Chicago, Chicago.

107. Robert L. McCaul, "Charles Hubbard Judd, February 1873–July 1946," *Education at Chicago* 3 (spring 1973): 16.

108. Quoted in Woodie Thomas White, "The Study of Education at the University of Chicago, 1892–1958," (Ph.D. diss., University of Chicago, 1977), 139.

109. Charles Hubbard Judd, *Introduction to the Scientific Study of Education* (Boston: Ginn, 1918), iii.

110. All of these changes are discussed in detail in White, "The Study of Education at the University of Chicago," and many are also reported in Harold S. Wechsler, "The Primary Journal for Secondary Education, 1893–1938: Part I of a History of *School Review,*" *American Journal of Education* 88 (November 1979): 83–106, and idem, "From Practice to Theory: A History of *School Review,* Part II," *American Journal of Education* 88 (February 1980): 216–44.

111. White, "The Study of Education."

112. Quoted in ibid., 160–61.

113. Harold Rugg, *That Men May Understand: An American in the Long Armistice* (New York: Doubleday, Doran, 1941), 306.

114. Samuel Chester Parker, *General Methods of Teaching in Elementary Schools* (Boston: Ginn, 1919), 265.

115. Quoted in McCaul, "Charles Hubbard Judd," 12.

Chapter Three

1. Paul H. Hanus, *School Administration and School Reports* (Boston: Houghton Mifflin, 1920), 13.

2. Arthur G. Powell, *The Uncertain Profession: Harvard University and the Search for Educational Authority* (Cambridge: Harvard University Press, 1980), 53.

3. Quoted in Eugene Charles Auerbach, "The Opposition to Schools of Education by Professors of the Liberal Arts: A Historical Analysis" (Ph.D. diss., University of Southern California, 1957), 43.

4. Quoted in Bruce Kuklick, *The Rise of American Philosophy, Cambridge, Massachusetts, 1860–1930* (New Haven, Conn.: Yale University Press, 1977), 247.

5. Powell, *The Uncertain Profession,* chaps. 3 and 4. See also Paul H. Hanus, *Adventuring in Education* (Cambridge: Harvard University Press, 1937).

6. Hugo Munsterberg, "School Reform," *Atlantic Monthly* 85 (May 1900): 666–67.

7. William H. Payne, *Contributions to the Science of Education* (New York: Harper & Brothers, 1887), 182.

8. Ibid., 131.

9. Natalie A. Naylor, "Paul Monroe: A Founding Father of the Professional Study of Education" (paper presented to the American Educational Research Association, New York, March 1982).

10. Paul Monroe, *A Text-Book in the History of Education* (New York: Macmillan, 1905), vii. Two years later he also published *A Brief Course in the History of Education* (New York: Macmillan, 1907).

11. "Register of Doctoral Dissertations, Vol. I (1899–1936)," *Teachers College Bulletin* 28, no. 4 (1937). See also Lawrence A. Cremin, *The Wonderful World of Ellwood Patterson Cubberley: An Essay on the Historiography of American Education* (New York: Bureau of Publications, Teachers College, Columbia University, 1965).

12. Peter Novick, *That Noble Dream: The "Objectivity Question" and the American Historical Profession* (Cambridge: Cambridge University Press, 1988).

13. Monroe, *Text-Book;* Ellwood P. Cubberley, *Public Education in the United States* (Boston: Houghton Mifflin, 1919).

14. Edgar B. Wesley, "Lo, the Poor History of Education," *School and Society* 37 (May 1933): 619–21.

15. Henry Johnson, *The Other Side of Main Street* (New York: Columbia University Press, 1943), 200.

16. Paul Monroe, "Opportunity and Need for Research Work in the History of Education," *Pedagogical Seminary* 17 (March 1910): 54.

17. Committee on Historical Foundations of the National Society of College Teachers of Education, "The Role of the History of Education in the Professional Preparation of Teachers," *History of Education Journal* 7 (fall 1955): esp. pt. 1 (Lawrence Cremin, "The Recent Development of the History of Education as a Field of Study in the United States," 1–35).

18. "Register of Doctoral Dissertations, Vol. I (1899–1936)."

19. Lawrence Augustus Averill, "A Plea for the Educational Survey," *School and Society* 7 (16 February 1918): 190.

20. Jesse Brundage Sears, *An Autobiography* (Palo Alto, Calif.: Privately Printed, 1959), 65.

21. Geraldine Jonçich Clifford and James W. Guthrie, *Ed School: A Brief for Professional Education* (Chicago: University of Chicago Press, 1988), 226–31.

22. Ellwood P. Cubberley to Edward Howard Griggs, 17 January 1898, quoted in Jesse B. Sears and Adin D. Henderson, *Cubberley of Stanford: And His Contribution to American Education* (Stanford, Calif.: Stanford University Press, 1957), 57.

23. Quoted in ibid.

24. Quoted in ibid., 63.

25. Ibid., 84.

26. Quoted in ibid., 70.

27. The group was part of what David Tyack and Elisabeth Hansot called "the educational trust" in *Managers of Virtue: Public School Leadership in America, 1820–1980* (New York: Basic Books, 1982).

28. Sears and Henderson, *Cubberley,* 57.

29. Ellwood P. Cubberley, *School Funds and Their Apportionment* (New York: Teachers College, Columbia University, 1905), 3.

30. Sears and Henderson, *Cubberley,* 88.

31. JoAnne Brown, in *The Definition of a Profession: The Authority of Metaphor in the History of Intelligence Testing, 1890–1930* (Princeton, N.J.: Princeton University Press, 1992), argues that the testers relied on both medical and engineering metaphors to win authority for their expertise.

32. Samuel Haber, *Efficiency and Uplift: Scientific Management in the Progressive Era, 1890–1920* (Chicago: University of Chicago Press, 1964); Judith A. Merkle, *Management and Ideology: The Legacy of the International Scientific Management Movement* (Berkeley: University of California Press, 1980).

33. David S. Snedden and William H. Allen, *School Reports and School Efficiency* (New York: Macmillan, 1908), 20.

34. Leonard P. Ayres, "History and Present Status of Educational Measurements," in National Society for the Study of Education, *Seventeenth Yearbook,* pt. 2, *The Measurement of Educational Products,* edited by Guy Montrose Whipple (Bloomington, Ind.: Public School Publishing, 1918), 11; J. M. Rice, "Educational Research," in *Scientific Management in Education* (New York: Hinds, Noble & Eldredge, 1914), 1–2. The last volume is a collection of some of Rice's *Forum* articles.

35. See also Raymond E. Callahan, *Education and the Cult of Efficiency: A Study of the Social Forces That Have Shaped the Administration of the Public Schools* (Chicago: University of Chicago Press, 1962), esp. 190–96. Although Spaulding spoke in the language of efficiency, I tend to agree with critics of Callahan who have argued that this was less a reflection of business values and of vulnerability than Callahan suggested. See Barbara Berman, "Business Efficiency, American Schooling and the Public School Superintendency: A Reconsideration of the Callahan Thesis," *History of Education Quarterly* 23 (fall 1983): 297–321; William Edward Eaton, ed., *Shaping the Superintendency: A Reexamination of Callahan and the Cult of Efficiency* (New York: Teachers College Press, 1990); William B. Thomas and Kevin J. Moran, "Reconsidering the Power of the Superintendent in the Progressive Period," *American Educational Research Journal* 29 (spring 1992): 22–50; Larry Cuban, *Urban School Chiefs under Fire* (Chicago: University of Chicago Press, 1976), 128–35.

36. J. M. Rice, "Educational Research," in *Scientific Management in Education,* 1–2.

37. Walter S. Monroe et al., *Ten Years of Educational Research, 1918–1927* (Urbana: University of Illinois Press, 1928), 38; Shelby M. Harrison, *The Social Survey: The Idea Defined and Its Development Traced* (New York: Russell Sage, 1931), 24–25.

38. Among the many contemporary writings that date the school survey movement from 1911 are Lawrence Augustus Averill, "A Plea for the Educational Survey," *School and Society* 7 (February 1918): 187–91, and Edward Franklin Buchner, *Educational Surveys,* Department of the Interior, Bureau of Education Bulletin no. 17 (Washington, D.C.: U.S. Government Printing Office, 1923).

39. Hollis Leland Caswell, *City School Surveys: An Interpretation and Analysis,* Contributions to Education no. 358 (New York: Bureau of Publications, Teachers College, Columbia University, 1929), 19–20.

40. Martin Bulmer, Kevin Bales, and Kathryn Kish Sklar, eds., *The Social Survey in Historical Perspective, 1880–1940* (Cambridge: Cambridge University Press, 1991); Jean M. Converse, *Survey Research in the United States: Roots and Emergence, 1890–1960* (Berkeley: University of California Press, 1987), chap. 1.

41. Maurine W. Greenwald and Margo Anderson, eds., *Pittsburgh Surveyed:*

Social Science and Social Reform in the Early Twentieth Century (Pittsburgh: University of Pittsburgh Press, 1996).

42. John M. Glenn, Lilian Brandt, and F. Emerson Andrews, *Russell Sage Foundation, 1907–1946* (New York: Russell Sage Foundation, 1947), 1:10–12.

43. Harrison, *Social Survey,* 21.

44. Ellen Condliffe Lagemann, *Private Power for the Public Good: A History of the Carnegie Foundation for the Advancement of Teaching* (Middletown, Conn.: Wesleyan University Press, 1983), chap. 4.

45. Harrison, *Social Survey,* 22.

46. Ellwood P. Cubberley, *Public School Administration,* rev. ed. (Boston: Houghton Mifflin, 1922), 325.

47. Quoted in Glenn, Brandt, and Andrews, *Russell Sage Foundation, 1907–1946,* 1:85. I am not aware of a full biography of Ayres. See "Neighbors," *Survey* 52 (1 July 1924): 417–18; Ralph Hayes, "Whole Flocks of Figures Eat Out of His Hand," *American Magazine* 110 (1924): 24–25, 185–90; W. Randolph Burgess, "Leonard P. Ayres: An Appreciation," *Journal of the American Statistical Association* 42 (March 1947): 128–33; *Dictionary of American Biography,* s.v. "Ayres, Leonard Porter."

48. Quoted in Edward Michael Miggins, "Businessmen, Pedagogues, and Progressive Reform: The Cleveland Foundation's 1915 School Survey" (Ph.D. diss., Case Western Reserve University, 1975), 158.

49. Leonard P. Ayres, "Measuring Educational Processes through Educational Results" (Address Delivered before the Harvard Teachers' Association, Cambridge, 9 March 1912), *School Review* 20 (May 1912): 301.

50. Leonard P. Ayres, *Laggards in Our Schools: A Study of Retardation and Elimination in City School Systems* (New York: Russell Sage, 1909), 5, 70, 217, 218; idem, "The Increasing Efficiency of Our City School Systems," lecture, n.d. (1908?), Leonard P. Ayres Papers, Library of Congress, Washington, D.C.; Edward L. Thorndike, *The Elimination of Pupils from School,* U.S. Office of Education, Bulletin no. 4, Whole Series no. 379 (Washington, D.C.: U.S. Government Printing Office, 1907). See also David B. Tyack, *The One Best System: A History of American Urban Education* (Cambridge: Harvard University Press, 1974), 200–202.

51. Report of the Division of Education, 2 December 1916, p. 1, Russell Sage Foundation Microfiche, Rockefeller Archive Center, Pocantico, New York (hereafter Russell Sage Microfiche).

52. Ibid., 1–2.

53. Press material on address by Dr. Ayres, Baltimore, 13 November 1914, p. 3, Russell Sage Microfiche.

54. Harold O. Rugg, *Statistical Methods Applied to Education* (Boston: Houghton Mifflin, 1917), x.

55. Harrison, *Social Survey,* 22.

56. Richard W. Pogue, *The Cleveland Foundation at Seventy-Five: An Evolving Community Resource* (New York: Newcomen Society of the United States, 1989), 10–13.

57. Leonard P. Ayres, *The Cleveland School Survey* (Summary Volume) (Cleveland, Ohio: Survey Committee of the Cleveland Foundation, 1917), 35.

58. Ibid., 37. Ayres also thought it was significant that the survey was published in twenty-five separate volumes, comparing it to "the sectional-unit idea in office furniture or modern bookcases." Leonard P. Ayres, "Significant Developments in Educational Surveying," in National Education Association, *Proceedings* (1916), 995.

59. Ayres, *Cleveland School Survey,* 63.

60. Ibid., 55, 63.

61. Quoted in Miggins, "Businessmen, Pedagogues, and Progressive Reform," 221.

62. Hanus, *School Administration and School Reports*, 13.

63. As defined by Paul F. Lazarsfeld and Samuel D. Sieber in *Organizing Educational Research: An Exploration* (Englewood Cliffs, N.J.: Prentice-Hall, 1964), "social book-keeping" differs from "applied research" in that it is less likely to yield "basic insight into social processes" (p. 5). For an earlier use of the term "social bookkeeping," see David S. Snedden, "Social Statistics as Presented in the Reports of State Boards of Charities," in National Conference of Charities and Corrections, *Proceedings* (1906), 424.

64. Ellwood P. Cubberley, *Public School Administration* (Boston: Houghton Mifflin, 1916), 328.

65. Ayres, "History and Present Status of Educational Measurements," 13.

66. Walter S. Monroe, *Encyclopedia of Educational Research*, rev. ed. (New York: Macmillan, 1950), 1461.

67. J. M. Cattell, "Mental Tests and Measurement," *Mind* 15 (1890): 374.

68. Michael M. Sokal, "James McKeen Cattell and Mental Anthropometry: Nineteenth-Century Science and Reform and the Origins of Psychological Testing," in *Psychological Testing and American Society, 1890–1930*, edited by Michael M. Sokal (New Brunswick, N.J.: Rutgers University Press, 1987).

69. Raymond E. Fancher, *The Intelligence Men: Makers of the IQ Controversy* (New York: W. W. Norton, 1985), 72.

70. Ibid., 38.

71. Quoted in Brown, *The Definition of a Profession*, 38–39.

72. W. Grant Dahlstrom, "The Development of Psychological Testing," in *Topics in the History of Psychology*, edited by Gregory A. Kimble and Kurt Schlesinger (Hillsdale, N.J.: Lawrence Erlbaum, 1985), 2:73–74.

73. Fancher, *The Intelligence Men*, 107.

74. Lewis M. Terman, "Trails to Psychology," in *A History of Psychology in Autobiography*, edited by Carl Murchison (Worcester, Mass.: Clark University Press, 1932), 2:308 (emphasis in original).

75. Ibid., 2:311.

76. Ibid., 2:318.

77. Lewis M. Terman, "Genius and Stupidity," *Pedagogical Seminary* 13 (September 1906): 351–52, 372 (emphasis in original).

78. Terman, "Trails to Psychology," 323.

79. Lewis M. Terman, "The Binet-Simon Scale for Measuring Intelligence," *Psychological Clinic* 5 (15 December 1911): 205.

80. Ibid., 204.

81. Terman, "Trails to Psychology," 324.

82. Ibid., 325–26.

83. Daniel J. Kevles, "Testing the Army's Intelligence: Psychologists and the Military in World War I," *Journal of American History* 55 (December 1968): 565–81; Thomas M. Camfield, "Psychologists at War: The History of American Psychology and the First World War" (Ph.D. diss., University of Texas, 1969); Franz Samuelson, "World War I Intelligence Testing and the Development of Psychology," *Journal of the History of the Behavioral Sciences* 13 (July 1977): 274–82; Richard T. von Mayrhauser, "The Triumph of Utility: The Forgotten Clash of American Psychologies in World War I" (Ph.D. diss., University of Chicago, 1986).

84. John Carson, "Army Alpha, Army Brass, and the Search for Army Intelligence," *Isis* 84 (June 1993): 279.

85. James Reed, "Robert M. Yerkes and the Mental Testing Movement," in Sokal, ed., *Psychological Testing and American Society*, 76.

86. National Center for Education Statistics, *120 Years of American Education: A Statistical Portrait* (Washington, D.C.: U.S. Department of Education, 1993), 36.

87. Paul Davis Chapman, *Schools as Sorters: Lewis M. Terman, Applied Psychology, and the Intelligence Testing Movement, 1890–1930* (New York: New York University Press, 1988), 99.

88. Ibid., 101.

89. Lewis M. Terman, "The Mental Test as a Psychological Method," *Psychological Review* 31 (March 1924): 100.

90. Elsie H. Martens, *Organization of Research Bureaus in City School Systems,* City School Leaflet no. 14 (Washington, D.C.: Department of the Interior, Bureau of Education, 1931), 8 (emphasis in original).

91. Douglas E. Scates makes a similar point in "Fifty Years of Objective Measurement and Research in Education," *Journal of Educational Research* 41 (December 1947): 255, when he argues: "Our understanding of educational measurement—perhaps our philosophy of measurement—is not well established and disseminated. Improvement in this area is difficult because technical workers have little regard for philosophy."

92. Charles H. Judd to D.C. Bliss, 26 January 1915, Papers of the Cleveland Conference, originally in the possession of H. Thomas James at the Spencer Foundation, but made available to the author by David Tyack.

93. B. R. Buckingham, "Our First Twenty-Five Years," in National Education Association, *Proceedings* (1941), 348.

94. Robert S. Woodworth, "Edward Lee Thorndike, 1874–1949," in National Academy of Sciences, *Biographical Memoirs* (Washington, D.C.: National Academy of Sciences, 1952), 27:214.

95. Monroe et al., *Ten Years of Educational Research,* 36.

96. William H. Maxwell, "Efficiency of Schools and School Systems," in National Education Association, *Proceedings* (1915), 401.

97. William H. Maxwell, "On a Certain Arrogance in Educational Theorists," *Educational Review* 47 (January–May 1914): 169, 168, 180.

98. *A History of the National Society of College Teachers of Education (1902–1950),* pamphlet, 1950, p. 7 for the quote, Special Collections, Milbank Memorial Library, Teachers College, Columbia University, New York.

99. Frank E. Spaulding, *School Superintendent in Action in Five Cities* (Rindge, N.H.: Richard R. Smith, 1935), 305.

100. Frank E. Spaulding, *The Aim, Scope, and Methods of a University Course in Public School Administration* (paper for the National Society of College Teachers of Education, Indianapolis, Indiana, 1 and 3 March 1910) (Iowa City, Iowa: National Society of College Teachers of Education, 1910), 3, 13, 26 (emphasis in original).

101. Ibid., 43.

102. P[aul] H. H[anus], "Editorial Notes," *School Review* 18 (January–December 1910): 427.

103. Ibid.

104. Henry W. Holmes, "The Professional Preparation of Superintendents of Schools," in *Educational Progress and School Administration: A Symposium by a Number of His Former Associates Written as a Tribute to Frank Ellsworth Spaulding,* edited by Clyde Milton Hill (New Haven, Conn.: Yale University Press, 1936), 57.

105. George Drayton Strayer and Edward L. Thorndike, *Educational Administration: Quantitative Studies* (New York: Macmillan, 1913), preface.

Part Two

1. Edward A. Purcell Jr., *The Crisis of Democratic Theory: Scientific Naturalism and the Problem of Value* (Lexington: University Press of Kentucky, 1973), pt. 3.

2. Stanley Cobden, *Rebellion against Victorianism: The Impetus for Cultural Change in 1920s America* (New York: Oxford University Press, 1991).

3. While Lawrence A. Cremin, *The Transformation of the School: Progressivism in American Education, 1876–1957* (New York: Alfred A. Knopf, 1961), remains the best overall description of "progressivism in education," the cautions concerning how generalized change was presented in Larry Cuban, *How Teachers Taught: Constancy and Change in American Classrooms, 1890–1990* (New York: Teachers College, Columbia University, 1993), are important.

4. Quoted in Edward A. Krug, *The Shaping of the American High School, 1920–1941* (Madison: University of Wisconsin Press, 1972), 9–10.

5. *Report of the Committee on Secondary School Studies* (Washington, D.C.: U.S. Government Printing Office, 1893); *Cardinal Principles of Secondary Education*, U.S. Bureau of Education Bulletin no. 35 (Washington, D.C.: U.S. Government Printing Office, 1918).

6. Krug, *The Shaping of the American High School, 1920–1941*, 27.

7. Edward A. Krug, *The Shaping of the American High School, 1880–1920* (Madison: University of Wisconsin Press, 1969), 398–99.

8. Commission on Life Adjustment Education for Youth, *Vitalizing Secondary Education: Report of the First Commission on Life Adjustment Education for Youth*, U.S. Office of Education Bulletin no. 3 (Washington, D.C.: U.S. Office of Education, 1951); Dorothy Elizabeth Broder, "Life Adjustment Education: An Historical Study of a Program of the United States Office of Education, 1945–1954" (Ed.D. diss., Teachers College, Columbia University, 1977), 191–92.

9. Quoted in Broder, "Life Adjustment Education," 109.

10. Geraldine Jonçich Clifford and James W. Guthrie, *Ed School: A Brief for Professional Education* (Chicago: University of Chicago Press, 1988), 74.

11. Ibid., 60.

Chapter Four

1. National Society for the Study of Education, *Twenty-Sixth Yearbook*, pt. 1, *The Foundations and Technique of Curriculum-Construction* (Bloomington, Ind.: Public School Publishing, 1926), ix.

2. Ibid., xiv (emphasis in original).

3. Ibid., 57.

4. Ibid., 63, xii.

5. Ibid., xii.

6. Ibid., 3.

7. John Franklin Bobbitt, "Practical Eugenics," *Pedagogical Seminary* 16 (September 1909): 385–94.

8. Bernard George DeWulf, "The Educational Ideas of John Franklin Bobbitt" (Ph.D. diss., Washington University, 1962), chap. 3.

9. J. Franklin Bobbitt, "Some General Principles of Management Applied to the Problems of City-School Systems," in National Society for the Study of Education, *Twelfth Yearbook* (Chicago: University of Chicago Press, 1913), 7–96.

10. J. Franklin Bobbitt, *The Curriculum* (Boston: Houghton Mifflin, 1918), 283, v (emphasis in original).

11. Ibid., iv, 42 (emphasis in original).

12. Mary Louise Seguel, *The Curriculum Field: Its Formative Years* (New York: Teachers College Press, 1966), 90–99.

13. W. W. Charters, *Curriculum Construction* (New York: Macmillan, 1923), 102.

14. W. W. Charters and Douglas Waples, *The Commonwealth Teacher-Training Study* (Chicago: University of Chicago Press, 1929), chap. 1.

15. Franklin Bobbitt, *How to Make a Curriculum* (Boston: Houghton Mifflin, 1924).

16. National Society for the Study of Education, *Twenty-Sixth Yearbook,* 43.

17. Quoted in Philip W. Jackson, "Shifting Visions of the Curriculum: Notes on the Aging of Franklin Bobbitt," *Elementary School Journal* 75 (Anniversary Issue 1975): 130.

18. DeWulf, "The Educational Ideas of John Franklin Bobbitt," 268.

19. Herbert M. Kliebard, *The Struggle for the American Curriculum, 1893–1958* (Boston: Routledge & Kegan Paul, 1986), 183.

20. John A. Beineke, "A Progressive at the Pinnacle: William Heard Kilpatrick's Final Years at Teachers College Columbia University," *Educational Theory* 39 (spring 1989): 139–49.

21. William H. Kilpatrick, "The Project Method," *Teachers College Record* 19 (September 1918): 319–35 (p. 320 for the quote).

22. Sara J. Van Ausdal, "William Heard Kilpatrick: Philosopher and Teacher," *Childhood Education* 64 (February 1988): 165.

23. Kilpatrick, "The Project Method," 334.

24. Kilpatrick Diary, 29 July 1918, Special Collections, Milbank Memorial Library, Teachers College, Columbia University, New York.

25. "As Reported," *Journal of Educational Method* 1 (September 1921): 37.

26. "Editorially Speaking," *Journal of Educational Method* 1 (September 1921): 1.

27. W. W. Charters, "The Limitations of the Project Method," *Journal of the NEA* 11 (January 1922): 17–19.

28. Ernest Horn, "Criteria for Judging the Project Method," 63 *Educational Review* (February 1922): 95.

29. [James Hosic], "Editorially Speaking: More Criteria for Judging the Project Method," *Journal of Educational Method* 1 (March 1922): 263–64.

30. Abraham Flexner, *A Modern College and a Modern School* (New York: Doubleday, Page, 1923), 100, 102, 131, 141, and 138–39 for the quotes.

31. James Earl Russell to Abraham Flexner, 23 September 1921, James Earl Russell Papers, Special Collections, Milbank Memorial Library, Teachers College, Columbia University, New York (hereafter Russell Papers).

32. Russell to Flexner, 11 November 1916, Russell Papers.

33. Ibid.

34. Samuel T. Dutton, "The New Horace Mann School," *Teachers College Record* 3 (January 1902): 28.

35. Lawrence A. Cremin, David A. Shannon, and Mary Evelyn Townsend, *A History of Teachers College, Columbia University* (New York: Columbia University, 1954), 101.

36. For another perspective on the early years of Teachers College, see James Earl Russell, *Founding Teachers College: Reminiscences of the Dean Emeritus* (New York: Bureau of Publications, Teachers College, Columbia University, 1937).

37. Quoted in Cremin, Shannon, and Townsend, *A History of Teachers College,* 86–87.

38. James Earl Russell, "The Purpose of the Speyer School," *Teachers College Record* 3 (November 1902): 3.

39. Speyer press release, n.d. (c. June 1901), Special Collections, Milbank Memorial Library, Teachers College, Columbia University, New York.

40. Jesse D. Burks, "History of the Speyer School," *Teachers College Record* 3 (November 1902): 9–10.

41. Speyer press release, n.d. (c. June 1901).

42. F. M. McM[urry], "The Speyer School," *Teachers College Record* 3 (January 1902): 40.

43. Speyer press release, n.d. (c. June 1901), p. 2.

44. William Van Til, "The Laboratory School: Its Rise and Fall?" (speech to the Laboratory Schools Administrators Association, Chicago, February 1969).

45. Cremin, Shannon, and Townsend, *A History of Teachers College,* 105–6.

46. Cremin, *The Transformation of the School,* 282–83.

47. Ibid., 286.

48. Ibid., 286–87.

49. James Earl Russell testimony to GEB, 21 December 1920, Russell Papers.

50. Peter L. Buttenwieser, "Unfulfilled Dreams: Thoughts on Progressive Education and the New York City Schools, 1900–1978," in *Educating an Urban People: The New York City Experience,* edited by Diane Ravitch and Ronald K. Goodenow (New York: Teachers College Press, 1981), 171–86.

51. Russell testimony to GEB, 21 December 1920, Russell Papers.

52. [Hollis Caswell], Memorandum to the staff of the Horace Mann–Lincoln School, February 1946, p. 2, William F. Russell Papers, Special Collections, Milbank Memorial Library, Teachers College, Columbia University, New York.

53. *The Denver Program of Curriculum Revision,* Denver Public Schools Monograph no. 12, 1927, pp. 11–12, Jesse H. Newlon Papers, Special Collections, Milbank Memorial Library, Teachers College, Columbia University, New York.

54. Jesse H. Newlon and A. L. Threlkeld, "The Denver Curriculum-Revision Program," in National Society for the Study of Education, *Twenty-Sixth Yearbook* (Chicago: University of Chicago Press, 1927), 229.

55. *The Denver Program of Curriculum Revision,* 12.

56. Gary L. Peltier, "Teacher Participation in Curriculum Revision: An Historical Case Study," *History of Education Quarterly* 7 (summer 1967): 209–19.

57. Jesse H. Newlon, "The Administration of the Curriculum," *Educational Method* 12 (May 1933): 479.

58. Quoted in Robert Lynd and Helen Merrell Lynd, *Middletown in Transition: A Study in Cultural Conflicts* (New York: Harcourt Brace, 1937), 241.

59. Charles H. Judd, "The Place of Research in a Program of Curriculum Development," *Journal of Educational Research* 17 (May 1928): 321, 322.

60. Charles H. Judd, "The High School Manager," *National Association of Secondary School Principals Yearbook* (1917), 30.

61. Interview no. 2 with Hollis L. Caswell by Thomas F. Hogan, 9 September 1967, p. 101, Oral History Project, Butler Library, Columbia University, New York.

62. Ibid. Regarding the GEB connection, see also Seguel, *The Curriculum Field,* 143.

63. "Study Course for Virginia State Curriculum Program," *Bulletin of the [Virginia] State Board of Education* 14 (January 1932), Hollis Caswell Papers, Special Collections, Milbank Memorial Library, Teachers College, Columbia University, New York.

64. Interview no. 2 with Caswell, 104.

65. Hollis L. Caswell and Doak S. Campbell, *Curriculum Development* (New York: American Book, 1935), 69, 80; William Featherstone, "Review of Curriculum Development," *Curriculum Journal* 6 (November 1935): 29–30.

66. Joint Committee on Curriculum, *The Changing Curriculum* (New York: D. Appleton-Century, 1937), 19.

67. Edgar B. Wesley, *NEA: The First Hundred Years: The Building of the Teaching Profession* (New York: Harper & Brothers, 1957), 115; "Hail and Farewell," *Curriculum Journal* 14 (May 1943): 193.

68. Hollis L. Caswell, "Emergence of the Curriculum as a Field of Professional Work and Study," in *Precedents and Promise in the Curriculum Field,* edited by Helen F. Robison (New York: Teachers College Press, 1966), 3.

69. Interview no. 2 with Hollis Caswell, 72.

70. Joint Committee on Curriculum, *The Changing Curriculum,* 1–2.

71. Harold Rugg, *Foundations for American Education* (Yonkers-on-Hudson, N.Y.: World Book, 1947), 578.

72. Joseph Edward Rowan, "'The Social Frontier' (1934–1943): Journal of Educational Criticism and Social Reconstructionism" (Ph.D. diss., Case Western Reserve University, 1969), 20.

73. Counts's biography is fully discussed in Ellen Condliffe Lagemann, "Prophecy or Profession? George S. Counts and the Social Study of Education," *American Journal of Education* 100 (February 1992): 137–65 (p. 141 for the quote).

74. The quotes are from George S. Counts, *The Social Composition of Boards of Education* (Chicago: University of Chicago Press, 1927), 81, and idem, *School and Society in Chicago* (New York: Harcourt Brace, 1928), vii.

75. George S. Counts, *Dare the School Build a New Social Order?* (New York: John Day, 1932), 7, 28–30.

76. *The Social Frontier* 1 (October 1934–35): 4–5.

77. Rowan, "'The Social Frontier.'"

78. Harold Rugg, *That Men May Understand: An American in the Long Armistice* (New York: Doubleday, Doran, 1941), 184.

79. Ibid., 188.

80. Harold Rugg and Ann Shumaker, *The Child-Centered School: An Appraisal of the New Education* (Yonkers-on-Hudson, N.Y.: World Book, 1928).

81. Rugg, *That Men May Understand,* 205–9.

82. Harold Rugg, *Changing Civilizations in the Modern World: A Textbook in World Geography with Historical Backgrounds* (Boston: Ginn, 1930), v, vii.

83. Elmer Winters, "Man and His Changing Society," *History of Education Quarterly* 7 (winter 1967): 510.

84. Quoted in Kliebard, *The Struggle for the American Curriculum,* 206. For another analysis of the Rugg textbooks, see Marian C. Schipper, "The Rugg Textbook Controversy: A Study in the Relationship between Popular Political Thinking and Educational Materials" (Ph.D. diss., New York University, 1979).

85. Martin Gill, "Paul R. Hanna: The Evolution of an Elementary Social Studies Textbook Series" (Ph.D. diss., Northwestern University, 1974), 80–86.

86. Ibid., 73–80.

87. Quoted in ibid., 85.

88. Ibid., 48–60.

89. Rugg, *That Men May Understand,* 206; Gill, "Paul R. Hanna," 34 et passim.

Chapter Five

1. Martin Bulmer and Joan Bulmer, "Philanthropy and Social Science in the 1920s: Beardsley Ruml and the Laura Spelman Rockefeller Memorial, 1922–1929," *Minerva* 19 (Autumn 1981): 347–407; Franz Samuelson, "Organizing for the Kingdom of Behavior: Academic Battles and Organizational Policies in the Twenties," *Journal of the History of the Behavioral Sciences* 21 (January 1985): 33–47.

2. Steven L. Schlossman, "Philanthropy and the Gospel of Child Development," in *Private Philanthropy and Public Elementary and Secondary Education, Proceedings of the Rockefeller Archive Center Conference Held on 8 June 1979,* edited by Gerald Benjamin (North Tarrytown, N.Y.: Rockefeller Archive Center, 1980), 16–19.

3. Dennis Raymond Bryson, "Lawrence K. Frank: Architect of Child Development, Prophet of Bio-Technocracy" (Ph.D. diss., University of California at Irvine, 1993), details this transformation.

4. Lawrence K. Frank, "Two Tasks for Education," *School and Society* 15 (17 June 1922): 656.

5. Ibid., 658.

6. Hamilton Cravens, *Before Head Start: The Iowa Station and America's Children* (Chapel Hill: University of North Carolina Press, 1993), 153.

7. Lawrence K. Frank, "The Problem of Child Development," *Child Development* 6 (March 1935): 7–18.

8. Lawrence K. Frank, "The Child," *American Journal of Sociology* 36 (May 1931): 1008.

9. Alice Boardman Smuts, "The National Research Council Committee on Child Development and the Founding of the Society for Research in Child Development, 1925–1933," in *History and Research in Child Development,* edited by Alice Boardman Smuts and John W. Hagen, Monographs of the Society for Research in Child Development, vol. 50, nos. 4–5 (Chicago: University of Chicago Press, 1985), 108–25.

10. Ibid., 62.

11. Stow Persons, *The University of Iowa in the Twentieth Century: An Institutional History* (Iowa City: University of Iowa Press, 1990).

12. George D. Stoddard, *The Pursuit of Education: An Autobiography* (New York: Vantage Press, 1981), 30–41; Cravens, *Before Head Start,* 106.

13. Cravens, *Before Head Start,* 109.

14. George D. Stoddard, *The Second Decade: A Review of the Activities of the Iowa Child Welfare Research Station, 1928–1938,* University of Iowa Studies, New Series no. 366 (Iowa City: University of Iowa Press, 1939), 6–7.

15. Julia Grant, "Constructing the Normal Child: The Rockefeller Philanthropies and the Science of Child Development, 1918–1940," in *Philanthropic Foundations: New Scholarship, New Possibilities,* edited by Ellen Condliffe Lagemann (Bloomington: Indiana University Press, 1999), chap. 6.

16. Mitchell G. Ash, "Cultural Contests and Scientific Change in Psychology: Kurt Lewin in Iowa," *American Psychologist* 47 (February 1992): 198–207.

17. George D. Stoddard, "The Long Step from Research to Practice," in *Iowa Child Welfare Research Station, State University of Iowa: The Fortieth Anniversary, 1917–1957,* Monographs of the Society for Research in Child Development, vol. 24, no. 5 (Iowa City: University of Iowa Press, 1959), 77.

18. "Nature and Nurture," in National Society for the Study of Education, *Twenty-Seventh Yearbook* (Bloomington, Ind.: Public School Publishing, 1928).

19. G. M. Whipple, editor's preface in "Intelligence: Its Nature and Nurture," in National Society for the Study of Education, *Thirty-Ninth Yearbook,* pt. 1, *Comparative and Critical Exposition* (Bloomington, Ind.: Public School Publishing, 1940), xvii.

20. Cravens, *Before Head Start,* 202–4.

21. Arnold Gesell to Florence L. Goodenough, 6 December 1938, Arnold Gesell Papers, Manuscript Division, Library of Congress, Washington, D.C. (hereafter Gesell Papers).

22. Lewis M. Terman to Arnold Gesell, 28 February 1939, Gesell Papers.

23. Quoted in Cravens, *Before Head Start,* 202.

24. Lewis M. Terman, "Personal Reactions of the Committee," in National Society for the Study of Education, *Thirty-Ninth Yearbook,* pt. 1, pp. 461, 464.

25. Quoted in Cravens, *Before Head Start*, 211.

26. Patricia Albjerg Graham, *Progressive Education: From Arcady to Academe, A History of the Progressive Education Association, 1919–1955* (New York: Teachers College Press, 1967), 89.

27. Wilford M. Aikin, "Report of the Commission on Relation of School and College," *Progressive Education* 9 (October 1932): 440–44.

28. Ibid., 442.

29. Ellen Condliffe Lagemann, *Private Power for the Public Good: A History of the Carnegie Foundation for the Advancement of Teaching* (Middletown, Conn.: Wesleyan University Press, 1983), 101–8.

30. Ibid.

31. James Phillip Echols, "The Rise of the Evaluation Movement: 1920–1942" (Ph.D. diss., Stanford University, 1973), 268.

32. Ralph W. Tyler, "Education: Curriculum Development and Evaluation," An Oral History Conducted 1985–1987 by Malca Chall, 1987, p. 31, Regional Oral History Office, Bancroft Library, University of California, Berkeley.

33. Quoted in Echols, "The Rise of the Evaluation Movement," 174.

34. Ralph W. Tyler, "Ability to Use Scientific Method," in *Constructing Achievement Tests* (Columbus: Bureau of Educational Research, Ohio State University, 1934), 24–25.

35. Ralph W. Tyler, "Formulating Objectives for Tests," in ibid., 14–15.

36. Quoted in Echols, "The Rise of the Evaluation Movement," 315.

37. Quoted in ibid.

38. Quoted in ibid., 305–6.

39. Graham, *Progressive Education*, 133.

40. Raymond B. Fosdick, *Adventure in Giving: The Story of the General Education Board* (New York: Harper & Row, 1962), chap. 17.

41. V. T. Thayer, "An Approach to the Reconstruction of the Secondary-School Curriculum," *Harvard Education Review* 7 (January 1937): 28.

42. Commission on Secondary School Curriculum of the Progressive Education Association Report, 23 November 1933, GEB Collection, Record Group 632.1, Series 1, Subseries 2, Box 279, Folder 2911, Rockefeller Archive Center, North Tarrytown, N.Y. (hereafter GEB Collection).

43. V. T. Thayer, Caroline B. Zachary, and Ruth Kotinsky, *Reorganizing Secondary Education* (New York: D. Appleton-Century, 1939), 17.

44. [Progressive Education Association's] Commission on Secondary School Curriculum, *The Social Studies in General Education* (New York: D. Appleton-Century, 1940), 14.

45. Thayer, Zachary, and Kotinsky, *Reorganizing Secondary Education*, 6.

46. V. T. Thayer, "A Basis for a New Secondary Curriculum," *Progressive Education* 12 (November 1935): 478.

47. Conference report [by L. K. Frank], 7 October 1933, GEB Collection, Record Group 632.1, Series 1, Subseries 2, Box 279, Folder 2911.

48. Margaret Mead to Helen [Lynd], 13 December 1938, Margaret Mead Papers, Manuscript Division, Library of Congress, Washington, D.C. (hereafter Mead Papers).

49. [Robert J. Havighurst] Conference with Prof. Bode, 23 October 1934, GEB Collection, Record Group 632.1, Series 1, Subseries 2, Box 279, Folder 2911.

50. This characterization of Zachary is derived from Robert J. Havighurst, "PEA: A Tentative Appraisal," 27 November 1940, GEB Collection, Record Group 632.1, Series 1, Subseries 2, Box 229, Folder 2914.

51. Caroline B. Zachary, "Personality Adjustment and Teacher Training," *Progressive Education* 8 (March 1931): 261–63; "Responsibility of Teacher-Training Institutions for the Mental Health of Prospective Teachers," in National Education Associa-

tion, *Proceedings* (1933), 409; idem, "Personality Adjustment of the School Teacher," in National Education Association, *Proceedings* (1934), 730–36.

52. Caroline B. Zachary, "A Progress Report on the Study of Adolescents," *Progressive Education* 12 (November 1935): 486.

53. Ibid.

54. Caroline B. Zachary, *Emotion and Conduct in Adolescence* (New York: D. Appleton-Century, 1940), 1.

55. Margaret Mead to Robert Redfield, 27 June 1935, Mead Papers.

56. PEA memo, December 1935, GEB Collection, Record Group 632.7, Series 1, Subseries 2, Box 283, Folder 2955.

57. Lawrence K. Frank to Alice Keliher, 15 May 1935, and Alice Keliher, draft memoir, chapter on Lawrence Kelso Frank, Alice Keliher Papers, Box 16, New York University Archive, Bobst Library, New York University, New York (hereafter Keliher Papers).

58. Alice Keliher to William H. Kilpatrick, 26 October 1931, Keliher Papers, Box 16.

59. Michael John Burlingham, *A Biography of Dorothy Tiffany Burlingham* (New York: Atheneum, 1989), 182–89.

60. Robert Coles, *Erik H. Erikson: The Growth of His Work* (Boston: Little, Brown, 1970), 18–19.

61. Quoted in *Notable American Women*, s.v. "Zachary, Caroline."

62. Peter Blos, *The Adolescent Personality: A Study of Individual Behavior* (New York: Appleton-Century-Crofts, 1941), 505.

63. "Peter Blos, a Psychoanalyst of Children, Is Dead at 93," *New York Times*, 19 June 1997, sec. D, p. 21.

64. Louise M. Rosenblatt, *Literature as Exploration* (New York: D. Appleton-Century, 1938), 5.

65. Ibid., 33–34.

66. Louise M. Rosenblatt, "Retrospect," in *Transactions with Literature: A Fifty Year Perspective*, edited by Edmund J. Farrell and James R. Squire (Urbana, Ill.: National Council of Teachers of English, 1990), 101.

67. Echols, "The Rise of the Evaluation Movement," 319–20.

68. Report of the Committee on Human Development to the Executive Committee of the Division of Social Sciences, October 1944, President's Papers, 1940–46, Special Collections, Joseph Regenstein Library, University of Chicago, Chicago.

69. Mildred Hall Warner, Burleigh Gardner, Robert J. Havighurst, and Associates, "W. Lloyd Warner: Social Anthropologist," chap. 4, p. 1 (unpublished typed ms.), W. Lloyd Warner Papers, Special Collections, Joseph Regenstein Library, University of Chicago, Chicago.

70. Quoted in Richard Gillespie, *Manufacturing Knowledge: A History of the Hawthorne Experiments* (Cambridge: Cambridge University Press, 1991), 157.

71. The Yankee City Studies included W. Lloyd Warner and Paul S. Lunt, *The Social Life of a Modern Community* (New Haven, Conn.: Yale University Press, 1941); W. Lloyd Warner and Paul S. Lunt, *The Status System of a Modern Community* (New Haven, Conn.: Yale University Press, 1942); W. Lloyd Warner and Leo Srole, *The Social Systems of American Ethnic Groups* (New Haven, Conn.: Yale University Press, 1945); W. Lloyd Warner and J. O. Low, *The Social System of a Modern Factory* (New Haven, Conn.: Yale University Press, 1947); and W. Lloyd Warner, *The Living and the Dead* (New Haven, Conn.: Yale University Press, 1959).

72. C. Wright Mills, review of *The Social Life of a Modern Community*, by W. Lloyd Warner and Paul S. Lunt, *American Sociological Review* 7 (April 1942): 263–71.

73. Allison Davis and John Dollard, *Children of Bondage: The Personality Development of Negro Youth in the Urban South* (Washington, D.C.: American Youth Commission, 1940); E. Franklin Frazier, *Negro Youth at the Crossways: Their Personality Development in the Middle States* (Washington, D.C.: American Youth Commission, 1940); Charles S. Johnson, *Growing Up in the Black Belt: Negro Youth in the Rural South* (Washington, D.C.: American Youth Commission, 1941); W. Lloyd Warner, Buford H. Junker, and Walter A. Adams, *Color and Human Nature: Negro Personality Development in a Northern City* (Washington, D.C.: American Youth Commission, 1941).

74. W. M. Brewer, review of *Children of Bondage,* by Allison Davis and John Dollard, *Journal of Negro History* 26 (January 1941): 113.

75. Donald C. Marsh, review of *Children of Bondage,* by Allison Davis and John Dollard, *American Sociological Review* 7 (August 1942): 575–76. Dollard's intellectual development is discussed in Ellen Condliffe Lagemann, *The Politics of Knowledge: The Carnegie Corporation, Philanthropy, and Public Policy* (1989; reprint, Chicago: University of Chicago Press, 1992), 154–58.

76. Catalog to the Allison Davis Papers, 1932–1984, p. 2, Special Collections, Joseph Regenstein Library, University of Chicago, Chicago.

77. "Remarks by Dr. John A. Davis, '33, upon the Occasion of the Issuance of a Commemorative Stamp in Honor of Dr. W. Allison Davis, '24, at Williams College, Williamstown, Mass., 1 February 1994," p. 4 (in the possession of Dr. John A. Davis).

78. Mildred Warner et al., "W. Lloyd Warner," chap. 8, p. 20.

79. W. Lloyd Warner, Robert J. Havighurst, and Martin B. Loeb, *Who Shall Be Educated? The Challenge of Unequal Opportunity* (New York: Harper & Brothers, 1944), 36, 120–23, 158.

80. Lagemann, *The Politics of Knowledge,* 180–204.

81. Robert Dreeban, "The Sociology of Education: Its Development in the United States," *Research in Sociology of Education and Socialization* 10 (1994): 52.

82. Allison Davis, *Social-Class Influences upon Learning* (Cambridge: Harvard University Press, 1951), 65.

83. Kenneth Eells, Allison Davis, Robert J. Havighurst, Virgil E. Herrick, and Ralph W. Tyler, in *Intelligence and Cultural Differences: A Study of Cultural Learning and Problem-Solving* (Chicago: University of Chicago Press, 1951), bring together the results of many of the empirical studies the group carried out.

84. "Remarks by Dr. John A. Davis," 5, re publication information.

85. Carl C. Brigham, "The Place of Research in a Testing Organization," *School and Society* 16 (December 1937): 756–59; Lagemann, *Private Power for the Public Good,* chap. 5 (pp. 117–18 for the quotes).

Part Three

1. Harlan P. Hanson, "Twenty-Five Years of the Advanced Placement Program: Encouraging Able Students," *College Board Review* 115 (spring 1980): 8–17.

2. Daniel J. Kevles, *The Physicists: The History of a Scientific Community in Modern America* (New York: Alfred A. Knopf, 1971), chap. 20.

3. *Science and Public Policy: A Report to the President by the President's Scientific Research Board,* vol. 1, *A Program for the Nation* (Washington, D.C.: U.S. Government Printing Office, 1947).

4. *A Decade of Comment on Education, 1956–1966,* edited by Mortimer Smith (Washington, D.C.: Council for Basic Education, 1966), 1 (first quote); "Where Stands Basic Education Now?" *Council for Basic Education Bulletin* 6 (September 1961): 1 (second quote).

5. Quoted in David M. Donahue, "Serving Students, Science, or Society? The Sec-

ondary School Physics Curriculum in the United States, 1930–65," *History of Education Quarterly* 33 (fall 1993): 329.

6. Arthur E. Bestor Jr., "Aimlessness in Education," *Scientific Monthly* 75 (August 1952): 114; *Educational Wastelands: The Retreat from Learning in Our Public Schools* (Urbana: University of Illinois Press, 1953).

7. Sidney Hook, "Modern Education and Its Critics," in American Association of Colleges for Teacher Education, *Seventh Yearbook* (Chicago: American Association of Colleges for Teacher Education, 1954), 157.

8. James D. Koerner, "How Not to Teach Teachers," *Atlantic Monthly* 211 (February 1963): 60.

9. H. G. Rickover, *Education and Freedom* (New York: E. P. Dutton, 1959), 221, 218.

10. Quoted in R. A. Dershimer, *The Federal Government and Educational R&D* (Lexington, Mass.: D.C. Heath, 1976), 50.

11. Harvey Kantor and Robert Lowe, "Class, Race, and the Emergence of Federal Education Policy: From the New Deal to the Great Society," *Educational Researcher* 24 (April 1994): 4.

12. Steve Fraser, "The Labor Question," in *The Rise and Fall of the New Deal Order,* edited by Steve Fraser and Gary Gerstle (Princeton, N.J.: Princeton University Press, 1989), 55–84.

13. Mark Tushnet, *The NAACP's Legal Strategy against Segregated Education, 1925–1950* (Chapel Hill: University of North Carolina Press, 1987).

14. Hugh Davis Graham, *The Uncertain Triumph: Federal Education Policy in the Kennedy and Johnson Years* (Chapel Hill: University of North Carolina Press, 1984).

15. The continuities between earlier state and subsequent federal policies are stressed in Carl F. Kaestle and Marshall S. Smith, "The Federal Role in Elementary and Secondary Education, 1940–1980," *Harvard Educational Review* 52 (November 1982): 384–417.

16. Edward Zigler, "Project Head Start: Success or Failure," in *Head Start: A Legacy of the War on Poverty,* edited by Edward Zigler and Jeannette Valentine (New York: Free Press, 1979), 496.

17. Robert H. Haveman, *Poverty Policy and Poverty Research: The Great Society and the Social Sciences* (Madison: University of Wisconsin Press, 1987), 4.

18. Egon G. Guba and Yvonna S. Lincoln, *Effective Evaluation* (San Francisco: Jossey-Bass, 1982), chap. 1; Egon G. Guba, "The Failure of Educational Evaluation," *Educational Technology* 9 (May 1969): 29–38.

19. Ernest R. House, "Trends in Evaluation," *Educational Researcher* 19 (April 1990): 24.

Chapter Six

1. William Betz, "Five Decades of Mathematical Reform—Evaluation and Challenge," *Mathematics Teacher* 43 (December 1950): 377–78, 383.

2. "Dr. Max Beberman Is Dead at 45; A Creator of New Mathematics," *New York Times,* 26 January 1971, 36.

3. Max Beberman, "Improving High School Mathematics Teaching," *Educational Leadership* 17 (December 1959): 164.

4. Ibid.

5. Howard F. Fehr, "Breakthroughs in Mathematical Thought," *Mathematics Teacher* 52 (January 1959): 15–19.

6. Max Beberman, "An Emerging Program of Secondary School Mathematics" (1958 Inglis Lecture), in *New Curricula,* edited by Robert W. Heath (New York: Harper & Row, 1964), chap. 2.

7. Ibid., 34.

8. Max Beberman to Frederick H. Jackson, 23 September 1960, Carnegie Corporation of New York, Rare Book and Manuscript Library, Columbia University, New York.

9. Quoted in Hillier Krieghbaum and Hugh Rawson, *An Investment in Knowledge: The First Dozen Years of the National Science Foundation's Summer Institutes Programs to Improve Secondary School Science and Mathematics Teaching, 1954–1965* (New York: New York University Press, 1969), 84.

10. Quoted in ibid., 6.

11. Francis A. J. Ianni and Lois S. Joseph, "The Curriculum Research and Development Program of the U.S. Office of Education: Project English, Project Social Studies and Beyond," in Heath, ed., *New Curricula*, 162.

12. Oral History of the Physical Sciences Study Committee, MIT Archives, quoted in Jack S. Goldstein, *A Different Sort of Time: The Life of Jerrold R. Zacharias; Scientist, Engineer, Educator* (Cambridge: MIT Press, 1992), 151 (emphasis in original).

13. Quoted in ibid., 154.

14. Jerome Bruner, *In Search of Mind: Essays in Autobiography* (New York: Harper & Row, 1983), 179.

15. Daniel J. Kevles, *The Physicists: The History of a Scientific Community in Modern America* (Cambridge: Harvard University Press, 1987), 200.

16. Goldstein, *A Different Sort of Time*, 172, 186; Paul E. Marsh and Ross A. Gortner, *Federal Aid to Science Education: Two Programs* (Syracuse, N.Y.: Syracuse University Press, 1963), xi.

17. Dorothy M. Fraser, *Current Curriculum Studies in Academic Subjects* (Washington, D.C.: National Education Association, 1962), 7–8.

18. Wayne W. Welch, "Twenty Years of Science Curriculum Development: A Look Back," in *Review of Research in Education*, edited by David C. Berliner (Washington, D.C.: American Educational Research Association, 1979), 7:288.

19. Goldstein, *A Different Sort of Time*, 186, 189.

20. Bruner, *In Search of Mind*, 182; Priscilla M. Chaffe-Stengel, "The Curriculum Reform Movement of the 1960s: Bruner's Impact" (Ph.D. diss., Stanford University, 1986).

21. Bruner, *In Search of Mind*, 183.

22. Andrew T. Weil, "Harvard's Bruner and His Yeasty Ideas," *Harper's Magazine* 229 (December 1964): 82.

23. Jerome S. Bruner, *The Process of Education* (Cambridge: Harvard University Press, 1960), 33.

24. Bruner, *In Search of Mind*, 191.

25. Peter B. Dow, *Schoolhouse Politics: Lessons from the Sputnik Era* (Cambridge: Harvard University Press, 1991), 139.

26. Ibid., 157–63.

27. Quoted in ibid., 179.

28. Quoted in ibid., 184. See also Dorothy Nelkin, *Science Textbook Controversies and the Politics of Equal Time* (Cambridge: MIT Press, 1977), chap. 7.

29. Quoted in Dow, *Schoolhouse Politics*, 197.

30. Steve Farkus and Jean Johnson with Anne Puffett, *Different Drummers: How Teachers View Public Education* (New York: Public Agenda Foundation, 1997).

31. Quoted in Dow, *Schoolhouse Politics*, 215.

32. Quoted in ibid.

33. Quoted in ibid., 229.

34. Ibid., 236–38.

35. Richard A. Dershimer, *The Federal Government and Educational R&D* (Lexington, Mass.: Lexington Books, 1976), 33.

36. Paul H. Buck, *The Role of Education in American History* (New York: Fund for the Advancement of Education, 1957), 1, 5, 6, 9.

37. Bernard Bailyn, *Education in the Forming of American Society* (Chapel Hill: University of North Carolina Press, 1960), 14.

38. Lawrence A. Cremin, *The Wonderful World of Ellwood Patterson Cubberley: An Essay on the Historiography of American Education* (New York: Bureau of Publications, Teachers College, Columbia University, 1965).

39. Lawrence A. Cremin, *American Education: The Metropolitan Experience, 1876–1980* (New York: Harper & Row, 1988), x.

40. Ralph W. Tyler, "Education: Curriculum Development and Evaluation," An Oral History Conducted 1985–1987 by Malca Chall, 1987, pp. 131–32 et passim, Regional Oral History Office, Bancroft Library, University of California, Berkeley.

41. Reports of the Cooperative Community Research Project, 1952 and 1953, Robert J. Havighurst Papers, Box 35, Special Collections, Joseph Regenstein Library, University of Chicago, Chicago.

42. Harold E. Moore, John H. Russell, and Donald G. Ferguson, *The Doctorate in Education*, vol. 2, *The Institutions* (Washington, D.C.: American Association of Colleges for Teacher Education, 1960), 71.

43. T. Fleming, "Management by Consensus Democratic Administration and Human Relations, 1929–1954" (Ph.D. diss., University of Oregon, 1982), 303–41.

44. Quoted in Jack A. Culbertson, "A Century's Quest for a Knowledge Base," in *Handbook of Research on Educational Administration: A Project of the American Educational Research Association*, edited by Norman J. Boyan (White Plains, N.Y.: Longman, 1988), 15.

45. Ibid.

46. J. W. Getzels, "A Psycho-Sociological Framework for the Study of Educational Administration," *Harvard Educational Review* 22 (fall 1952): 235–36; James M. Lipham, "Getzels's Models in Educational Administration," in Boyan, ed., *Handbook of Research on Educational Administration*, 171–73.

47. Daniel E. Griffiths, "Administrative Theory," in Boyan, ed., *Handbook of Research on Educational Administration*, 28.

48. Jack Culbertson, "Theory in Educational Administration: Echoes from Critical Thinkers," *Educational Researcher* 12 (December 1983): 15.

49. Griffiths, "Administrative Theory," 31.

50. Jacob W. Getzels, "Educational Administration Twenty Years Later, 1954–1974," in *Educational Administration: The Developing Decades*, edited by Luvern L. Cunningham, Walter G. Hack, and Raphael O. Nystrand (Berkeley, Calif.: McCutcheon, 1977), 9.

51. Andrew W. Halpin and Andrew E. Hayes, "The Broken Ikon, Or, What Ever Happened to Theory," in Cunningham, Hack, and Nystrand, eds., *Educational Administration: The Developing Decades*, 291, 266, 280, and 279.

52. Ibid., 277, 276.

53. Glenn L. Immegart, "The Study of Educational Administration, 1954–1974," in Cunningham, Hack, and Nystrand, eds., *Educational Administration: The Developing Decades*, 315, 304, and 312.

Chapter Seven

1. Donald R. Warren, *To Enforce Education: A History of the Founding Years of the United States Office of Education* (Detroit: Wayne State University Press, 1974), 204.

2. Ibid., 145.

3. Maris A. Vinovskis, *History and Educational Policymaking* (New Haven, Conn.: Yale University Press, 1999), 52–54.

4. Ibid., 63–64.

5. Richard A. Dershimer, *The Federal Government and Educational R & D* (Lexington, Mass.: D.C. Heath, 1976), 41.

6. Ibid., 42.

7. David L. Clark and William R. Carriker, "Educational Research and the Cooperative Research Program," *Phi Delta Kappan* 42 (March 1961): 226–30.

8. Quoted in ibid., 226.

9. Quoted in Lee Sproull, Stephen Weiner, and David Wolf, *Organizing an Anarchy: Belief, Bureaucracy, and Politics in the National Institute of Education* (Chicago: University of Chicago Press, 1978), 17.

10. U.S. Department of Health, Education, and Welfare, *Educational Research and Development in the United States* (Washington, D.C.: U.S. Government Printing Office, 1969), 104. Maris Vinovskis, "Analysis of Quality of Research and Development at OERI Research and Development Centers and at the OERI Regional Educational Laboratories," Final Report to OERI, June 1993, provides an incisive evaluation.

11. Quoted in Sproull, Weiner, and Wolf, *Organizing an Anarchy,* 18.

12. Ibid., 18–19.

13. Keith Melville, "Obstacles to Applied Social Research in Education: A Study of the National Institute of Education" (Ph.D. diss., Columbia University, 1984), 125–27.

14. Norman J. Boyan, "The Political Realities of Education R & D," *Journal of Research and Development in Education* 2 (summer 1969): 6.

15. Patricia Albjerg Graham, "Assimilation, Adjustment, and Access: An Antiquarian View of American Education," in *Learning from the Past: What History Teaches Us about School Reform,* edited by Diane Ravitch and Maris A. Vinovskis (Baltimore: Johns Hopkins University Press, 1985), 18.

16. Ellen Condliffe Lagemann, *The Politics of Knowledge: The Carnegie Corporation, Philanthropy, and Public Policy* (1989; reprint, Chicago: University of Chicago Press, 1992), 162.

17. Telephone interview with Patricia Albjerg Graham by the author, 28 January 1999.

18. James A. Hazlett, "A History of the National Assessment of Educational Progress, 1963–1973" (Ed.D. diss., University of Kentucky, 1974), 22.

19. Francis Keppel to John W. Gardner, 5 September 1963, Carnegie Corporation of New York, Grant Series, Box 516, Rare Book and Manuscript Library, Columbia University, New York.

20. Lagemann, *The Politics of Knowledge,* chaps. 8 and 9.

21. John W. Gardner to Ralph W. Tyler, 7 November 1963, Carnegie Corporation of New York, Grant Series, Box 516, Rare Book and Manuscript Library, Columbia University, New York.

22. William Greenbaum with Michael S. Garet and Ellen R. Soloman, *Measuring Educational Progress: A Study of the National Assessment* (New York: McGraw-Hill, 1977), 8.

23. Ibid., 12.

24. Ralph W. Tyler, "Education: Curriculum Development and Evaluation," An Oral History Conducted 1985–1987 by Malca Chall, 1987, p. 296, Regional Oral History Office, Bancroft Library, University of California, Berkeley.

25. Quoted in "The Battle over National Assessment," *Council for Basic Education Bulletin* 11 (February 1967): 2.

26. Ralph W. Tyler to Forrest Connor, 14 January 1967, Carnegie Corporation of New York, Grant Series 2, Box 518, Folder CAPE 1965–1969, Rare Book and Manuscript Library, Columbia University, New York.

27. This is evident from descriptions of meetings, notably that offered in A. M. Mood to Ralph W. Tyler, 25 January 1966, and Record of interview of M[argaret] E[.] M[ahoney] and William Miller, 8 and 11 February 1966, Carnegie Corporation of New York, Grant Series 2, Folder CAPE 1966, Rare Book and Manuscript Library, Columbia University, New York.

28. Quoted in Hazlett, "A History of the National Assessment of Educational Progress," 155.

29. James Bryant Conant, *Shaping Educational Policy* (New York: McGraw-Hill, 1964), 110, 124.

30. Greenbaum et al., *Measuring Educational Progress,* 18.

31. Martin T. Katzman and Ronald S. Rosen, "The Science and Politics of National Educational Assessment," *Teachers College Record* 71 (May 1970): 585.

32. National Academy of Education, *Assessment in Transition: Monitoring the Nation's Educational Progress* (Stanford, Calif.: National Academy of Education, 1997), XIII.

33. Greenbaum et al., *Measuring Educational Progress,* 107–8.

34. Quoted in ibid., 9.

35. Ibid., 185.

36. James S. Coleman, Ernest Q. Campbell, Carol J. Hobson, James McPartland, Alexander M. Mood, Frederic D. Weinfeld, and Robert L. York, *Equality of Educational Opportunity* (Washington, D.C.: U.S. Government Printing Office, 1966).

37. Quoted in ibid, iii.

38. Gerald Grant, "Shaping Social Policy: The Politics of the Coleman Report," *Teachers College Record* 75 (September 1973): 19.

39. Robert K. Merton, "Teaching James Coleman," in *James S. Coleman,* edited by Jon Clark (London: Falmer Press, 1996), 352.

40. Ibid., 352, 351.

41. James S. Coleman, "Reflections on Schools and Adolescents," in *James S. Coleman,* 18.

42. Ibid., 19.

43. Grant, "Shaping Social Policy," 20.

44. Coleman et al., *Equality of Educational Opportunity,* 549–54.

45. Quoted in Grant, "Shaping Social Policy," 22.

46. Coleman et al., *Equality of Educational Opportunity,* 21.

47. Quoted in Grant, "Shaping Social Policy," 29.

48. See, for example, Glen G. Cain and Harold W. Watts, "Problems in Making Policy Inferences from the Coleman Report," *American Sociological Review* 35 (April 1970): 228–42; Samuel Bowles and Henry M. Levin, "The Determinants of Scholastic Achievement—An Appraisal of Some Recent Evidence," *Journal of Human Resources* 3 (winter 1968): 3–24; "Review Symposium," *American Sociological Review* 32 (June 1967): 475–83.

49. Trudi C. Miller, "Political and Mathematical Perspectives on Educational Equity," *American Political Science Review* 75 (June 1981): 319–33.

50. "Professor's Work Was Misinterpreted," *Baltimore Sun,* 4 April 1995, p. 2B.

51. Daniel Patrick Moynihan, "The Lives They Lived: James S. Coleman," *New York Times,* 31 December 1995, sec. 6, p. 25.

52. Daniel Patrick Moynihan, *Family and Nation* (New York: Harcourt Brace Jovanovich, 1986), chap. 1.

53. Grant, "Shaping Social Policy," 33.

54. Frederick Mosteller and Daniel P. Moynihan, *On Equality of Educational Opportunity* (New York: Random House, 1972).

55. Ibid., 27.

56. Ibid.

57. Ibid., 13.

58. Quoted in Grant, "Shaping Social Policy," 36.

59. Ibid., 33–36.

60. David K. Cohen and Michael S. Garet, "Reforming Educational Policy with Applied Social Research," *Harvard Educational Review* 45 (February 1975): 17–43; Charles E. Lindblom and David K. Cohen, *Usable Knowledge: Social Science and Social Problem Solving* (New Haven, Conn.: Yale University Press, 1979).

61. M. T. Hallinan, "Equality of Educational Opportunity," *Annual Review of Sociology* 14 (1988): 255–58.

62. James S. Coleman, "Recent Trends in School Integration," *Educational Researcher* 4 (July–August 1975): 3–12.

63. Ibid., and quoted in "Coleman, Head of Equal Education Study, Says Judges Misuse His Report," *New York Times*, 9 April 1972, p. 55.

64. Mosteller and Moynihan, *On Equality of Educational Opportunity*, 63.

65. Eugene Eidenberg and Roy D. Morey, *An Act of Congress: The Legislative Process and the Making of Education Policy* (New York: W. W. Norton, 1969), 247–48.

66. Stephen K. Bailey and Edith K. Mosher, *ESEA: The Office of Education Administers a Law* (Syracuse, N.Y.: Syracuse University Press, 1968), 20.

67. Ibid., 21. Programmatically, but not politically, the Ford Foundation's Great Cities Schools program also helped "set the stage" for ESEA, as program officer Edward J. Meade Jr. suggested in "Recalling and Updating Philanthropy and Public Schools: One Foundation's Evolving Perspective," *Teachers College Record* 93 (spring 1992): 440–41.

68. Milbrey Wallin McLaughlin, *Evaluation and Reform: The Elementary and Secondary Education Act of 1965, Title I* (Cambridge, Mass.: Ballinger, 1975), 1–18 (p. 18 for the quote).

69. Bailey and Mosher, *ESEA*, 163.

70. Ibid., 179–80; Bruce L. R. Smith, *The Rand Corporation: Case Study of a Nonprofit Advisory Corporation* (Cambridge: Harvard University Press, 1966), 112–13.

71. McLaughlin, *Evaluation and Reform*, 7, 28.

72. Quoted in Bailey and Mosher, *ESEA*, 164–66.

73. Quoted in McLaughlin, *Evaluation and Reform*, 21.

74. Ibid., 28.

75. Joseph S. Wholey et al., *Title I: Evaluation and Technical Assistance* (Washington, D.C.: Urban Institute, 1971), app. B, p. 1.

76. McLaughlin, *Evaluation and Reform*, 24.

77. Ibid., 37.

78. Alice M. Rivlin, *Systematic Thinking for Social Action* (Washington, D.C.: Brookings Institution, 1971), 83.

79. McLaughlin, *Evaluation and Reform*, 59.

80. Quoted in ibid., 64.

81. American Educational Research Association, *A Proposal to Improve the Social and Communication Mechanism in Educational Research* (Office of Education Grant Number OEG-0-8-080751-4432) (Washington, D.C.: American Educational Research Association, 1967); R. Louis Bright and Hendrick D. Gideonese, *Education Research and Its Relation to Policy: An Analysis Based on the Experience of the United States* (Washington, D.C.: U.S. Department of Health, Education, and Welfare, 1967); Orville B. Brim, *Knowledge into Action: Improving the Nation's Use of the*

Social Sciences (Washington, D.C.: National Science Foundation, 1969); Francis S. Chase, *The National Program of Educational Laboratories: Report of a Study of Twenty Educational Laboratories and Nine University Research and Development Centers* (Washington, D.C.: U.S. Office of Education, Bureau of Research, 1969); Panel on Educational Research and Development of the President's Science Advisory Committee, *Innovation and Experiment in Education* (Washington, D.C.: U.S. Government Printing Office, March 1964); National Research Council, *The Behavioral Sciences and the Federal Government* (Washington, D.C.: National Academy of Sciences, 1968); Samuel D. Sieber and Paul F. Lazarsfeld, *The Organization of Educational Research in the United States* (New York: Bureau of Applied Social Research, 1966); Behavioral and Social Sciences Survey Committee, *The Behavioral and Social Sciences: Outlook and Needs* (Englewood Cliffs, N.J.: Prentice-Hall, 1969); U.S. Department of Health, Education, and Welfare, *Educational Research and Development in the United States* (Washington, D.C.: U.S. Government Printing Office, 1970); U.S. Department of Health, Education, and Welfare, *The Uses of Social Research in Federal Domestic Programs* (Washington, D.C.: U.S. Government Printing Office, 1967).

82. Quoted in Sproull, Weiner, and Wolf, *Organizing an Anarchy,* 29.

83. Wayne J. Urban, *More than the Facts: The Research Division of the National Education Association, 1922–1997* (Lanham, N.Y.: University Press of America, 1998).

84. Chester E. Finn Jr., "The National Institute of Education," *Yale Review* 64 (winter 1975): 235.

85. Daniel P. Moynihan, in *To Establish a National Institute of Education,* Hearings before the Select Subcommittee on Education of the Committee on Education and Labor, House of Representatives, 92nd Congress, 1st Session, 1971, p. 12.

86. Finn, "National Institute of Education," 234–43.

87. Roger E. Levien, *National Institute of Education: Preliminary Plan for the Proposed Institute,* A Report Prepared for the Department of HEW by the Rand Corp., February 1971, iii–xii.

88. Sproull, Weiner, and Wolf, *Organizing an Anarchy,* 45.

89. John Brademas with Lynne P. Brown, *The Politics of Education: Conflict and Consensus on Capital Hill* (Norman: University of Oklahoma Press, 1987).

90. Quoted in Sproull, Weiner, and Wolf, 70.

91. Ibid., 68–70.

92. Ibid., 65.

93. Richard E. Shutz, "The Politicization of American R&D in Education: A Progress Report," *Educational Researcher* 2 (December 1973): 1.

94. Melville, "Obstacles to Applied Social Research in Education," 56.

95. Quoted in ibid., 59.

96. Richard C. Atkinson and Gregg B. Jackson, eds., *Research and Education Reform: Roles for the Office of Educational Research and Improvement* (Washington, D.C.: National Academy Press, 1992), 58.

97. Ibid.

98. Philip Phaedon Zodhiates, "Bureaucrats and Politicians: The National Institute of Education and Educational Research under Reagan" (Ed.D. diss., Harvard Graduate School of Education, 1988), 21.

99. P. Michael Timpane, "Federal Progress in Educational Research," *Harvard Educational Review* 52 (November 1982): 543.

100. Telephone interview with Michael Timpane by the author, 3 March 1999.

101. Quoted in David L. Clark, "Federal Policy in Educational Research and Development," *Educational Researcher* 5 (January 1976): 5.

102. Quoted in Sproull, Weiner, and Wolf, *Organizing an Anarchy,* 98.

103. Quoted in Patricia E. Stivers, "NIE: Another Appropriations Crisis," *Educational Researcher* 3 (November 1974): 15.

104. Quoted in Sproull, Weiner, and Wolf, *Organizing an Anarchy,* 103.

105. Ibid., 94–95.

106. John Brademas, "A Congressional View of Education R&D and NIE," *Educational Researcher* 3 (March 1974): 15.

107. Ibid.

108. Zodhiates, "Bureaucrats and Politicians," 185.

109. Report to the Chairman, Select Subcommittee on Education, Committee on Education and Labor, House of Representatives, *Education Information: Changes in Funds and Priorities Have Affected Production and Quality* (Washington, D.C.: U.S. Government Printing Office, 1987).

110. Chester E. Finn Jr., "Lessons Learned: Federal Policy Making and the Education Research Community," *Phi Delta Kappan* 70 (October 1988): 130.

111. Atkinson and Jackson, eds., *Research and Education Reform,* 59.

Chapter Eight

1. Panel on Education Technology, President's Committee of Advisors on Science and Technology, *Report to the President on the Use of Technology to Strengthen K–12 Education in the United States,* March 1977, 96.

2. Howard E. Gruber and J. Jacques Voneche, *The Essential Piaget: An Interpretative Reference and Guide* (New York: Basic Books, 1977); Howard Gardner, *The Quest for Mind: Piaget, Levi-Strauss, and the Structuralist Movement* (Chicago: University of Chicago Press, 1972), chap. 3; Herbert P. Ginsburg and Sylvia Opper, *Piaget's Theory of Intellectual Development,* 3rd ed. (Englewood Cliffs, N.J.: Prentice-Hall, 1988).

3. Rochel Gelman and Ann L. Brown, "Changing Views of Cognitive Competence in the Young," in *Behavioral and Social Science: Fifty Years of Discovery,* edited by Neil J. Smelser and Dean R. Gerstein (Washington, D.C.: National Academy Press, 1986), 176.

4. Kerry W. Buckley, *Mechanical Man: John Broadus Watson and the Beginnings of Behaviorism* (New York: Guilford Press, 1989).

5. "Dr. Von Neumann, of A.E.C., 53, Dies," *New York Times* 9 February 1957, p. 19; *Current Biography, 1950,* s.v. "Wiener, Norbert"; *Current Biography, 1979,* s.v. "Simon, Herbert"; Ernest R. Hilgard, *Psychology in America: A Historical Survey* (New York: Harcourt Brace Jovanovich, 1987), 237–40.

6. Howard Gardner, *The Mind's New Science: A History of the Cognitive Revolution* (New York: Basic Books, 1985), 11.

7. K. S. Lashley, "The Problem of Serial Order in Behavior," in *Cerebral Mechanism in Behavior: The Hixon Symposium,* edited by Lloyd A. Jeffreys (New York: John Wiley & Son, 1951), 112.

8. Ibid., 113.

9. Quoted in Gardner, *The Mind's New Science,* 29.

10. William Hirst, ed., *The Making of Cognitive Science: Essays in Honor of George A. Miller* (Cambridge: Cambridge University Press, 1988), 89.

11. Jerome S. Bruner, "Founding the Center for Cognitive Studies," in ibid., 93.

12. Quoted in Hirst, *The Making of Cognitive Science,* 89.

13. Report of discussion among Jerome Bruner, George Miller, and John W. Gardner on 2/16/60, Carnegie Corporation of New York Papers, Grant Series 2, Box 66, Folder Harvard University 1959–1966, Rare Book and Manuscript Library, Columbia University, New York (hereafter Carnegie Corporation Papers).

14. Proposal with cover letter to Gardner from Bruner and Miller, 7 April 1960, Grant Series 2, Box 66, Folder Harvard University 1959–1966, Carnegie Corporation Papers.

15. Bruner, "Founding the Center for Cognitive Studies," in Hirst, ed., *The Making of Cognitive Science,* 95.

16. Donald A. Norman and Willem J. M. Levelt, "Life at the Center," in Hirst, ed., *The Making of Cognitive Science,* 101.

17. Ibid., 102.

18. Proposal letter to Gardner from Bruner and Miller, 21 January 1965, Grant Series 2, Box 66, Folder Harvard University 1959–1966, Carnegie Corporation Papers.

19. Gardner, *The Mind's New Science,* 32.

20. Jill H. Larkin, foreword, in *Classroom Lessons: Integrating Cognitive Theory,* edited by Kate McGilly (Cambridge: MIT Press, 1994), x.

21. Ibid., chap. 4.

22. Ibid., chap. 7.

23. Ibid., chap. 9.

24. Robert Glaser, "Cognitive Science and Education," *International Social Science Journal* 40 (February 1988): 21.

25. John Bruer, "Classroom Problems, School Culture, and Cognitive Research," in McGilly, ed., *Classroom Lessons,* 286.

26. Ray C. Rist, "Blitzkrieg Ethnography: On the Transformation of a Method into a Movement," *Educational Researcher* 9 (February 1980): 8–10. See also Shirley Brice Heath, "Discipline and Disciplines in Education Research—Elusive Goals?" in *Issues in Education Research,* edited by Ellen Condliffe Lagemann and Lee S. Shulman (San Francisco: Jossey-Bass, 1999), 203–23.

27. Frederick Erickson, "Qualitative Methods in Research on Teaching," in *Handbook of Research on Teaching,* edited by Merlin C. Wittrock, 3rd ed. (New York: Macmillan, 1986), 119. Unlike Erickson, some anthropologists draw a sharp distinction between ethnography and other interpretative approaches. For one discussion of this point of view, see Kathleen Wilcox, "Ethnography as a Methodology and Its Application to the Study of Schooling: A Review," in *Doing the Ethnography of Schooling: Educational Anthropology in Action,* edited by George Spindler (New York: Holt, Rinehart and Winston, 1982), 456–88.

28. Margaret Mead, *Coming of Age in Samoa* (New York: William Morrow, 1928).

29. George D. Spindler, "Roots Revisited: Three Decades of Perspective," *Anthropology & Education Quarterly* 15 (spring 1984): 3–10.

30. Elizabeth M. Eddy, "Theory, Research, and Application in Educational Anthropology," *Anthropology & Education Quarterly* 16 (summer 1985): 91–98 (p. 97 for the quote).

31. M. J. Dunkin and B. Biddle, *The Study of Teaching* (New York: Holt, Rinehart & Winston, 1974).

32. For a review of major criticisms by a leading proponent of process-product research, see Nathaniel L. Gage, "Process-Product Research on Teaching: A Review of Criticisms," *Elementary School Journal* 89 (January 1989): 254–300. For an overview of the debate, see Lee S. Shulman, "Paradigms and Research Programs in the Study of Teaching: A Contemporary Perspective," in Wittrock, ed., *Handbook of Research on Teaching,* 9–15.

33. Ray C. Rist, "On the Application of Ethnographic Inquiry to Education: Procedures and Possibilities," *Journal of Research in Science Teaching* 19 (September 1982): 439.

34. One important statement of disillusion with traditional methods was Lee J.

Cronbach, "Beyond the Two Disciplines of Scientific Psychology," *American Psychologist* 30 (February 1975): 116–27. On the importance of context, see Uri Bronfenbrenner, *The Ecology of Human Development: Experiments by Nature and Design* (Cambridge: Harvard University Press, 1979).

35. On NIE's role, see Courtney B. Cazden, "Classroom Discourse," in Wittrock, ed., *Handbook of Research on Teaching,* 433–32 (p. 432 for the quote).

36. Courtney B. Cazden, Vera P. John, and Dell Hymes, *Functions of Language in the Classroom* (New York: Teachers College Press, 1972).

37. William Labov, *Language in the Inner City* (Philadelphia: University of Pennsylvania Press, 1972); Sylvia Scribner and Michael Cole, *The Psychology of Literacy* (Cambridge: Harvard University Press, 1981); Shirley Brice Heath, *Ways with Words: Language, Life, and Work in Communities and Classrooms* (Cambridge: Cambridge University Press, 1983).

38. John Ogbu, *Minority Education and Caste: The American System in Cross-Cultural Perspective* (New York: Academic Press, 1978).

39. Erickson, "Qualitative Methods," in Wittrock, ed., *Handbook of Research on Teaching,* 121, 133.

40. Interestingly, the scholar who was arguably the most persistent and articulate in calling attention to the multiple settings in which education occurs had studied with Margaret Mead, although he was a historian rather than an anthropologist. See, as one example, Lawrence A. Cremin, *Public Education* (New York: Basic Books, 1976).

41. Henry A. Giroux, one of the most prolific scholars writing from a critical perspective, reviewed some of this literature in "Theories of Reproduction and Resistance in the New Sociology of Education: A Critical Analysis," *Harvard Educational Review* 53 (August 1983): 257–93. For a later statement of his position, see Stanley Aronowitz and Henry A. Giroux, *Postmodern Education: Politics, Culture, and Social Criticism* (Minneapolis: University of Minnesota Press, 1991).

42. For a review of a good deal of feminist literature, see Nell Noddings, "Feminist Critiques in the Professions," *Review of Research in Education* 16 (1990): 393–424.

43. Judith G. Touchton and Lynne Davis, *Fact Book in Higher Education* (New York: American Council on Education/Macmillan, 1991), 220. Even though higher education is awash with statistics, no readily available data exist concerning the demographic makeup of the education research community. I am grateful to Alex McCormick of the Carnegie Foundation for the Advancement of Teaching, Jack Schuster of the Claremont Graduate University, and Martin Finkelstein of Seton Hall University, who specialize on such matters, for this information.

44. Examples are R. R. Buckingham, "The Public-School Teacher as a Research Worker," *Journal of Educational Research* 11 (April 1925): 235–43; Bess Goodykoontz, "Opportunities for the Classroom Teacher as a Research Worker," *School Life* 15 (May 1930): 161–63; and Elizabeth Skelding Moore, "Can a Teacher of Young Children Carry on Research," *Childhood Education* 6 (January 1930): 197–200.

45. Marilyn Cochran-Smith and Susan L. Lytle, *Inside/Outside: Teacher Research and Knowledge* (New York: Teachers College Press, 1993), xi. For an explication of the ways teacher research differs from interpretative and process-product research, see Marilyn Cochran-Smith and Susan L. Lytle, "Research on Teaching and Teacher Research: The Issues That Divide," *Educational Research* 19 (March 1990): 2–11.

46. Cochran-Smith and Lytle, *Inside/Outside,* 7. See also Lawrence Stenhouse, *An Introduction to Curriculum Research and Development* (London: Heinman Educational Books, 1975), esp. 142–65; Jean Ruddick, ed., *An Education That Empowers: A Collection of Lectures in Memory of Lawrence Stenhouse* (Clevendon, Avon, U.K.: Multilingual Matters, 1995).

47. For the quote, see Cochran-Smith and Lytle, *Inside/Outside,* 5. See also Elea-

nor Duckworth, "Teaching as Research," *Harvard Educational Review* 56 (November 1986): 481–95; Dixie Goswami and Peter R. Stillman, eds., *Reclaiming the Classroom: Teacher Research as an Agency for Change* (Upper Montclair, N.J.: Boynton/Cook Publishers, 1987).

48. Lee S. Shulman was one scholar who saw value in teacher research. See his essays "Those Who Understand: Knowledge Growth in Teaching," *Educational Researcher* 15 (February 1986): 4–14, and "Knowledge and Teaching: Foundations of the New Reform," *Harvard Educational Review* 57 (February 1987): 1–22.

49. Magdalene Lampert, "How Do Teachers Manage to Teach? Perspectives on Problems in Practice," *Harvard Educational Review* 55 (May 1985): 178–94.

50. Magdalene Lampert, "When the Problem Is Not the Question and the Solution Is Not the Answer: Mathematical Knowing and Teaching, *American Educational Research Journal* 27 (spring 1990): 29–63.

51. James G. Greeno, Allan M. Collins, and Lauren B. Resnick, "Cognition and Learning," in *Handbook of Educational Psychology*, edited by David C. Berliner and Robert C. Calfee (New York: Macmillan, 1996), 41.

52. Ann L. Brown, "Design Experiments: Theoretical and Methodological Challenges in Creating Complex Interventions in Classroom Settings," *Journal of the Learning Sciences* 2 (1992): 141–43.

53. Ann L. Brown and Joseph C. Campione, "Guided Discovery in a Community of Learners," in McGilly, ed., *Classroom Lessons*, 229–70.

54. Eleanor Farrar, John E. Desanctis, and David K. Cohen, "Views from Below: Implementation Research in Education," *Teachers College Record* 82 (fall 1980–81): 77–100.

55. Henry W. Riecken and Robert F. Boruch, eds., *Social Experimentation: A Method for Planning and Evaluating Social Intervention* (New York: Academic Press, 1974).

56. P. Michael Timpane, "Educational Experimentation in National Social Policy," *Harvard Educational Review* 40 (November 1970): 557.

57. David K. Cohen, "The Value of Social Experiments," in *Planned Variation in Education: Should We Give Up or Try Harder?* edited by Alice M. Rivlin and P. Michael Timpane (Washington, D.C.: Brookings Institution, 1975), 150.

58. David K. Cohen, "Politics and Research: Evaluation of Social Action Programs in Education," *Review of Educational Research* 40 (April 1970): 231.

59. Paul Berman and Milbrey Wallin McLaughlin, *Federal Programs Supporting Educational Change*, vol. 1, *A Model of Educational Change* (Santa Monica, Calif.: Rand, 1975); Paul Berman and Edward W. Pauly, *Federal Programs Supporting Educational Change*, vol. 2, *Factors Affecting Change Agent Projects* (Santa Monica, Calif.: Rand, 1975); Peter W. Greenwood, Dale Mann, and Milbrey Wallin McLaughlin, *Federal Programs Supporting Educational Change*, vol. 3, *The Process of Change* (Santa Monica, Calif.: Rand, 1975); Paul Berman and Milbrey Wallin McLaughlin, *Federal Programs Supporting Educational Change*, vol. 4, *The Findings in Review* (Santa Monica, Calif.: Rand, 1975).

60. Milbrey Wallin McLaughlin, "Implementation as Mutual Adaptation: Change in Classroom Organization," *Teachers College Record* 77 (February 1976): 340.

61. Richard F. Elmore and Milbrey Wallin McLaughlin, *Steady Work: Policy, Practice and Reform of American Education* (Santa Monica, Calif.: Rand, 1988).

62. Milbrey W. McLaughlin, "The Rand Change Agent Study Revisited: Macro Perspectives and Micro Realities," *Educational Researcher* 19 (December 1990): 15.

63. National Commission on Excellence in Education, *A Nation at Risk: The Imperative for Educational Reform* (Washington, D.C.: U.S. Department of Education, April 1983), 5, 12.

64. Susan Fuhrman, William H. Clune, and Richard F. Elmore, "Research on Education Reform: Lessons on the Implementation of Policy," *Teachers College Record* 90 (winter 1988): 237–57; Allan R. Odden, *Education Policy Implementation* (Albany: SUNY Press, 1991), chap. 1.

65. Marshall S. Smith and Jennifer O'Day, "Systemic School Reform," in *The Politics of Curriculum and Testing: The 1990 Yearbook of the Politics of Education Association,* edited by Susan H. Fuhrman and Betty Malen (London: Falmer Press, 1991), 246.

66. Ibid., 247–62.

67. "New Eagleton Unit Will Study Schools," *New York Times,* 15 December 1985, 4.

68. Lorraine M. McDonnell, "Can Education Research Speak to State Policy?" *Theory into Practice* 27 (spring 1988): 93–95; Susan H. Fuhrman, "The Center for Policy Research in Education: An Overview," in *Organizations for Policy Analysis: Helping Government Think,* edited by Carol H. Weiss (Newbury Park, Calif.: Sage, 1992), 91.

69. Fuhrman, "The Center for Policy Research in Education," 93–96.

Conclusion

1. John Dewey, "The Sources of a Science of Education" (1929), in *John Dewey: The Later Works, 1925–1953,* edited by Jo Ann Boydston (Carbondale: Southern Illinois University, 1984), 5:4.

2. Ibid., 25.

3. Ibid., 9.

4. Carl Kaestle, "The Awful Reputation of Education Research," *Educational Researcher* 22 (January–February 1993): 23–31.

5. For an interesting discussion of this problem in social research, see Peter H. Rossi, "The Presidential Address: The Challenge and Opportunities of Applied Social Research," *American Sociological Review* 45 (December 1980): 889–904.

6. Joan Jacobs Brumberg and Nancy Tomes, "Women in the Professions: A Research Agenda for American Historians," *Reviews in American History* 10 (June 1982): 275–96. Relationships between doctors and nurses are also discussed in many of the essays in Ellen Condliffe Lagemann, ed., *Nursing History: New Perspectives, New Possibilities* (New York: Teachers College Press, 1983).

7. Edward L. Thorndike, "The Nature, Purposes, and General Methods of Measurements of Educational Products," in National Society for the Study of Education, *Seventeenth Yearbook,* pt. 2, *The Measurement of Educational Products,* edited by Guy Montrose Whipple (Bloomington, Ind.: Public School Publishing, 1918), 16.

8. Mary E. Richmond, *Social Diagnosis* (New York: Russell Sage Foundation, 1917).

9. George S. Counts, "Dare Progressive Education Be Progressive?" in *Dare the School Build a New Social Order* (1932; reprint, New York: Arno Press, 1969), 1–12.

10. Larry Cuban takes a rather different, more pessimistic view in *How Scholars Trumped Teachers: Change without Reform in University Curriculum, Teaching, and Research, 1890–1990* (New York: Teachers College Press, 1999).

11. Lee J. Cronbach and Patrick Suppes, eds., *Research for Tomorrow's Schools: Disciplined Inquiry for Education* (New York: Macmillan, 1969), 14–29.

INDEX

Page numbers in italics refer to tables.